THE SUBURBAN COMMUNITY

The
Suburban Community

Edited by

WILLIAM M. DOBRINER

Hofstra College

G. P. PUTNAM'S SONS

New York

Copyright © 1958 by G. P. Putnam's Sons

Library of Congress Catalog

Card Number: 58-8014

Manufactured in the United States of America

TO THE STUDENTS OF HOFSTRA COLLEGE

PREFACE

It is now a commonplace that the analysis of the suburban community has become a central, though recent, concern in the study of metropolitan areas and urban society. Yet, in spite of the burgeoning literature devoted to the suburbs there is nowhere a volume dedicated primarily to the analysis of the suburb as a functioning social system. A few books have emerged in the last year or two in which the suburbs constitute a locale or field site for empirical research. But the data that came from these studies were often concerned with other matters—child-rearing practices, socialization patterns, or the domestic folkways of "the organization man."

This present volume has as its principal focus the suburb itself, as a generic community type, in the forces of its creation, its manifest forms, and its internal processes. To suggest that it is encyclopedic or that it embraces the sociological totality of the suburban community would be an impertinence. The gathering of sound empirical data on suburbanization is a relatively recent development. Indeed, a systematic theory of community organization is first starting to appear; consequently, a comprehensive suburban "social theory" has not yet emerged.

Nevertheless, a truly impressive amount of data have already been gathered, and many sound conclusions have been drawn. Social scientists of stature have applied themselves to the study of suburbia, and their investigations have resulted in a wealth of pertinent information and valuable insights. Unfortunately, much of this material has appeared in periodicals of relatively small circulation or in publications that are otherwise not readily available. Indeed, much of it has not hitherto appeared at all, but has, rather, existed only in embryo—in the notebooks and in the minds of those scholars for whom the new suburbs has become a productive site for research.

Here, then, is the primary justification for this volume: analysis of the suburban community has now developed to a degree where especially significant contributions to that analysis can—and should—be made readily available to social scientists, to students, and to those interested members of the general public whose social, political, and economic fortunes are being shaped by suburbia.

Another justification for a volume of this sort at this particular time lies in the fact that there is currently an abundance of popular writings, speculations, musings, pseudo-scientific reports, and recriminations, all focused about the suburbs. The result has been a clouding and a serious distortion of the basic facts of suburbanization. It is hoped, therefore, that this collection of controlled material will effectively provide the base for a more realistic popular image of the suburban worlds. This would seem especially desirable now, for perhaps over forty million Americans live in areas or communities that may justifiably be called suburban.

This volume is perhaps as significant for what it does not say as for what it does say—and herein is a final justification for its appearance. The gaps in the materials available are considerable. There seems to be a particular need for suburban case studies dealing with many "types" of suburbs rising along the periphery of the great metropolitan centers. Then, too, the social-psychological implications of suburbanization have scarcely been investigated. There is a great need for reliable empirical data centering on suburban social relations and social organization. Before an entirely adequate theoretic schema for the analysis of suburbia can be erected, many more suburban "facts" need to be gathered. Perhaps this book will stimulate new and further investigations. It is especially hoped that it will arouse a lively interest in "suburban sociology" among the young men and women in our colleges and universities who are presently being trained to understand the society in which they live.

The book has been organized in six basic parts, in each of which information having a similar conceptual orientation is presented. The materials in Part I, *The Growth of the Suburbs,* are essentially demographic and ecological. The primary interest lies in the analysis of the forces which gave rise to suburbanization, the extent of its growth, its demographic character, and the implications of suburbanization for social theory. Part II, *The Sociology of the Suburbs,* is organized around questions relating to the fundamental, definitive social structure and processes of the suburban community. Part III, *The Social Organization of the Suburbs,* examines the character of formal and institutionalized organization in the suburbs. Here the impact of suburbanization on the structure and function of the family, the economy, and political organization are treated in detail. Part IV, *Suburban Life Styles,* is given over essentially to those aspects of the suburban community which are informal and unorganized. The nature of the suburban class system is discussed, along with an analysis of a dimension of suburban ideology in the form of familism. In addition, the implications of suburbanization to patterns of leisure are treated. Finally, there is a case history of Levittown, as one form of contemporary suburb. Part V, *Some Suburban Problems,* presents materials on a series of problems which have particular relevance to suburbia: the problems involved in education, race relations, planning, transportation, and communications. Part VI, *Suburban Perspectives,* is primarily concerned with efforts to evaluate the effects of suburbanization on American values and American society.

There are many who have figured importantly in the assembling of this volume to whom the editor would like to express his deep appreciation. First of all, of course, there are the many scholars, from all over the country, who gave of their time and skill to contribute to this volume or to offer valuable suggestions. Then there are the editor's colleagues at Hofstra, such as Professors Alan Campbell, Harold Yuker, and Herbert Rosenbaum, whose counsel and good advice are reflected throughout this publication. In addition, sincere thanks goes to Vice President Jack Johnson of Hofstra, whose good offices brought the editor and publisher together. Finally, the editor would like to thank Asa Elliott and James Roers of Putnam's, who made the publication of this volume possible.

Hempstead, New York   William M. Dobriner

Contents

Contents

Neighborhood Reactions to Isolated Negro Residents: An Alternative to Invasion and Succession   345
    By Arnold M. Rose, Frank J. Atelsek and
    Lawrence R. McDonald

Problems of Planning in the Suburbs   362
    By Henry Fagin

Part VI Suburban Perspectives

The Suburban Sadness   375
    By David Riesman

Index   409

Introduction

THEORY AND RESEARCH IN THE SOCIOLOGY OF THE SUBURBS

It is no longer necessary to justify the claim that the suburbs have become a major facet of the metropolitan area. The embryonic patterns of urban decentralization which were apparent to Adna F. Weber more than half a century ago, have developed into one of the most spectacular features of metropolitan areas today.[1] The loss of population from central London and sections of New York City which Weber noted in 1899, however, was merely a fragile demographic portent of urban social processes in the twentieth century. Thus, growth rates between central cities and their outlying suburban rings now dramatically vary. In the period from 1940 to 1950, for example, the population rings surrounding the central cities of the great metropolitan areas grew two and a half times as fast as did the central cities.[2]

The suburban boom of recent years is merely one indication of what is essentially the growing dominance of the metropolitan area. In 1900, metropolitan centers claimed less than a third of the total population; by 1950, more than half of the population lived in these areas; in addition, since 1900, the metropolitan centers have grown about 50 per cent faster than the non-metropolitan areas.[3]

The remarkable growth of the post World War II suburbs, however, pose a series of theoretic and empirical problems in the analysis of urban society. The traditional theory of community organization is built around a basic conceptual dichotomy, folk and urban, as the two contrasting modes of community organization. The term "theory" is perhaps too strong when applied to the kinds of orientations which social scientists currently employ in describing basic forms of community organization. There are a few summary statements of the salient features of "community," conceived as an inclusive form of social system: the works of MacIver and Davis are central in this regard.[4] However, the level of integrative concepts applied to rural and urban as contrasting forms of community social structure are little more than ideal-type generalizations. A few years ago these notions of "rural" and "urban" were adequate enough, in view of the prevailing level of sociological theory and the existing ecological conditions, to categorize the predominant modes of community organization in associational society. Today, however, the rise of the metropolis has shrunk the residential role of the central city and has spread vast populations beyond the city limits. In short, the sociologic image of *the city,* as the locus of urbanism, no longer pertains. Indeed, the shift toward metropolitanism has become so marked that the "metropolitan region" now threatens to supplant the "metropolitan area" as the basic unit of urban analysis.

Social scientists are apparently as susceptible to a conceptual "culture lag" as are the members of the functioning society in regard to their institutions. So recently have the suburbs burst upon the ecological and demographic scene that many sociologists are apparently still unaware of their implications in community analysis. The great majority of texts currently employed in courses in urban sociology scarcely refer to the suburbs and only a few have devoted as much as a chapter to them. However, in just the past few years a growing number of urban sociologists have begun to turn their attention to the metropolitan centers. Researches focusing on the suburban community or metropolitan area are fast becoming a part of the sociological tradition.

Generally speaking, there are four major analytic perspectives from which community organization can be sociologically defined: (1) the demographic, (2) the ecological, (3) the patterns of formal and informal social organization and (4) the normative and ideological ethos which largely defines the specific character of the demographic ecological, and organizational facets of the community. The empirical generalizations and summary concepts which define community are usually built upon these four analytic approaches. With the spectacular growth of the suburbs, the generic image of urban society and the metropolitan area is being reformulated along all four of these analytic dimensions. Since our concern is largely with the suburban community as a specialized sub system of the metropolitan area, we can proceed by examining the part each of these dimensions has played in delineating suburban social structures.

Demography

Interest in a sociology of the suburbs was an inevitable result of the demographic analysis of urban and metropolitan areas. The pioneering studies of McKenzie [5] and Thompson,[6] followed more recently by Bogue [7] and Hawley,[8] provided the quantitative evidence regarding the major shifts of population at the periphery. A recent study by Duncan and Reiss (pp. 45-66 *supra*) which compared demographic characteristics of central cities of urbanized areas with the suburban and urban fringe zones, brings to light some of the differences between these two units of metropolitan areas. Duncan and Reiss found that central cities, as a whole, have somewhat more females than do the suburbs, with sex ratios of 93.5 and 95.1 respectively. In addition, the suburban population is slightly younger than the central city population. The median age for the central city population was 32.7, while the suburban was 30.9, a difference of 1.8 years. The suburban population has a considerable excess of persons aged 0 to 4 and 5 to 13, and a slight preponderance of individuals in the age intervals 14 to 19, 25 to 34, and 35 to 44. Conversely, the central cities have a relatively larger number of persons aged 45 and older, than do the suburbs.

In general, the suburbs have higher fertility ratios than do central cities. In the sample of central cities studied by Duncan and Reiss there were 452 children under 5 years of age per 1,000 women in the age interval 20-44; on the other hand, there were 534 children per 1,000 women in the suburban population. In terms of marital status, for whites of both sexes, the percentage married is greater in the suburbs than is the case for central cities. Then, too, the suburbs have a deficiency of persons in the single, widowed and divorced categories.

In addition, the suburban family is somewhat larger (3.6) than those in the central cities (3.4).

In terms of racial composition, the suburbs seem to be predominantly white. Three times as many negroes reside in the central cities than in the suburbs. In educational achievement, white suburban residents seem to be a full year ahead of persons residing in central cities with educational levels of 11.3 and 10.3 respectively. On the other hand, for nonwhites, the central city median exceeded the suburban by 0.2 a year. In addition, the suburban labor force in general represents a higher occupational level when compared to the labor force of the central cities. The suburbs have somewhat larger proportions employed in white-collar occupations and smaller proportions in the clerical and blue-collar occupations. In addition, for all classes of income recipients, the suburban median is $250 greater than the central city median.

By way of summary, when compared with central cities, the suburbs have higher fertility ratios, higher percentages of married persons, lower percentages separated, higher percentages in primary families, higher socio-economic status in the labor forces, higher median income, lower median age, a higher percentage of mobile families and a higher level of educational achievement. When the suburbs are compared with independent cities, many of the same tendencies persist. Duncan and Reiss, in a study of suburbs and independent cities,[9] found the suburbs contained a smaller proportion of the nonwhite population, slightly larger households, higher proportions of married males, higher proportion of males in the labor force than independent cities, a higher socio-economic status, higher percentages in the white-collar occupations, craftsmen, foreman and similar occupations, a higher percentage of college-age persons enrolled in school, higher median family income and a higher percentage of home ownership.

Ecology

The formal analysis of urban ecology could probably be traced back to Burgess' ideal-type schema which posited the essentially concentric character of urban areas.[10] This orientation was generally supported for many years largely because there was no other set of hypotheses to challenge it. Later, there was Hoyt's reformulation, which argued that ecological areas rather than being concentric circles tended to be functional "sectors" which radiated out from the central city along the transportation routes of "least resistance." [11] In addition to Hoyt's macroscopic reconceptualization of the metropolis, there have appeared a series of papers addressed essentially to a critique of Burgess' view of the concentricity of the central city itself.[12]

In the past two decades, there have been attempts to conceptualize the emerging outer rings of the metropolitan area. Ecological theory, consequently, seems oriented toward the analysis of (1) the spatial patterning of central cities, and (2) the spatial patterning of the metropolitan center which includes both the central city and the surrounding tributary area. In this regard, the two concepts currently most employed are "suburbs" and "rural-urban fringe." The term "suburban" can easily be traced back to the works of Adna F. Weber and undoubtedly was used much earlier in the popular rubric of cities. However, the concept of the rural-urban fringe can be traced back scarcely twenty years in the sociological literature. Unfortunately, there have been few attempts to distinguish between these two terms.[13]

There is no official definition of a suburb provided by the Bureau of the Census, nor has the term received much systematic attention by sociologists. A rough "content analysis" of the relevant literature reveals that suburbs are (1) communities (2) outside the central city and politically independent of it (3) culturally and economically dependent upon the central city, and (4) in general, highly specialized communities particularly along familistic and residential lines.[14] Accordingly, a working definition of the suburb might be: *those urbanized, residential communities which are outside the corporate limits of a large central city, but which are culturally and economically dependent upon the central city.*

The rural-urban fringe is conceived in a somewhat different light. Some variety in language exists, but Blizzard and Anderson's definition is typical: "From an operational point of view in research, the rural-urban fringe has usually been designated at that area of mixed urban and rural land uses between the point where full city services cease to be available and the point where agricultural land uses predominate." [15] Thus, suburbs are conceived of as urbanized communities, while the rural-urban fringe is seen as a land belt surrounding the central city containing mixed urban and rural uses of land. It is that area where city and country come together.

As to relative location, the suburbs generally lie closer to the central city than does the urban fringe. They are characteristically urban, not only in their general demographic features, but in their uses of land as well. In plotting a model metropolitan area in terms of its characteristic ecology, three major specialized "zones" become apparent. In the very center is the built-up *central city* with its central business

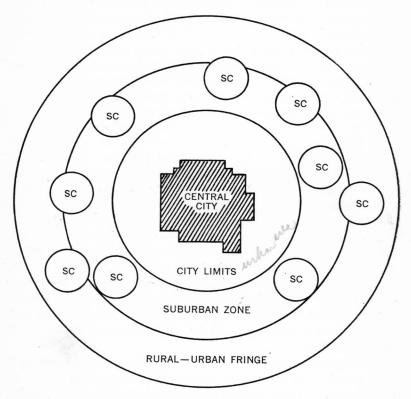

Fig. A.—A model metropolitan area showing the ecological relationship of a central city with the suburban zone, suburban community (SC), and rural-urban fringe.

district and sub areas. Outside of the corporate limits of the central city lies the second functional area, the *suburban zone*. This is a belt of suburban towns and villages lying relatively close to each other, with a population less dense than that of the central city but more dense than the outlying fringe area. Beyond the belt of suburban towns and villages with its typical web of busy communication lines leading to the central city, lies the third functional area of the metropolitan center, the *rural-urban fringe*.[16] Here the suburban communities thin out in an expanse of countryside. Only occasionally is there an urbanized settlement. This is the juncture where the suburbs, and urban industry and culture, collide with the rural village and the agricultural economy.

Thus have the ecologists been attempting to recast, with more adequate terms, the spatial patterning of metropolitan areas. Terms like "metropolitan ring," "suburban belt," and "rural-urban fringe" indicate that the ecological analysis of urbanism can no longer be treated within the framework of the central city itself.

Social Organization

With a comparatively formidable battery of demographic data and a growing body of ecological concepts, the analysis of the suburban community and suburban social organization has since World War II become increasingly more systematic. The 1930's and the early 40's saw a scattering of descriptive studies of the suburbs. In the main, however, these early researches focused on sheer description and case study of suburban settlement and on detailing of surface demographic variables.[17] There were comparisons between residential suburbs and "industrial suburbs," and attention was given to the sources of migration. In the main, however, the data from these reports were never applied to a set of theoretic propositions or systematic conceptual analysis.

In recent years, particularly as empirical data is increasingly brought to bear on theory, the implications of suburbanization are being incorporated into both community theory and the theory of social organization. Martin's discussion of the model forms of social relationships within the suburban community probably comes as close as any single effort toward the formal isolation of the distinctive sociological character of the suburbs.[18] This hypothesis states that there are essentially two "definitive characteristics" of suburban communities which shape a variety of "derivative" features which are "not essential to suburban status." The two definitive features of the suburban community are (1) the unique ecological relationship of the xx

suburb to the central city, and (2) the high rate of commuting to the central city. It is Martin's contention that these definitive variables structure the essential character of social relationships within the suburban community. Among the derivative features, he cites (1) the homogeneity of the suburbs (2) a high rate of informal interaction and formal participation, and (3) a set of suburban socio-psychological characteristics resulting from selective migration to the suburbs.

In addition to Martin's analysis, which is primarily addressed to generic characteristics of the suburban community, there are a growing number of researches oriented toward the distinctive pattern of suburban institutions and life styles. There is Bell's hypothesis that suburban migration constitutes the reinforcement of familistic themes in the life styles of the suburbanite.[19] There is Fava's contention that there is a socio-psychological selection of suburbanites in which the need for neighboring and informal interaction is a central criterion.[20] Mowrer has recently suggested that the suburban family is not as homogeneous as was previously supposed and that its particular form is quite dependent upon the *type* of suburb in which the family is located.[21] Form has indicated that in spite of the homogeneity of "planned communities," the "strain toward stratification" cannot be separated from those forces which shape the stratification system of the Great Society.[22] Thus, a series of studies, of more limited perspective, have begun to rough out empirically the distinctive pattern of suburban social organization.

In addition to the analysis of the unique organizational facets of the suburbs, there has been some attention given the analysis of functional types. In this regard, the early distinctions made by Douglas [23] between industrial, residential, and mixed suburbs as determined by percentage of the suburban labor force locally employed (later elaborated by Harris [24]) have been recently reformulated by Schnore.[25] Rather than continue Harris' complex, six-part typology, Schnore has combined centers of employment devoted to mining, education, manufacturing, etc., under the general heading "employing suburbs." In this manner, he has distinguished two basic types of suburbs, "residential suburbs" and "employing suburbs." The primary distinction between the two is ". . . whether or not the suburb tends to attract more workers to its confines every day than the number of working people who sleep there every night." [26]

Taylor's term of forty years ago, "satellite city," seems to apply directly to the concept of industrial or employing suburbs. As Schnore has indicated, there are some salient differences between the "satellite city" and the residential suburb.[27] In contrast to those of the model residential suburb, inhabitants of the satellite city have a lower average education, lower average rent levels, higher proportions of foreign-born whites, higher percentages of tenant-occupied dwellings, higher fertility rates, and a younger population of which two out of three workers are in "blue collar" occupations. In short, the employing satellites appear to be characterized by a young "working class" population, in contrast to the residential suburbs, whose residents seem distinctly "middle" and "upper-middle" class. What is perhaps even more important, as Schnore has demonstrated, the residential suburbs are growing almost twice as fast as satellite cities. In addition, they are becoming even more residential. On the other hand, the satellite cities, as are the central cities, are growing less rapidly and are characterized by a steady increase in industry and commerce. In short, two specialized "community" types seem to be appearing along the peripheral rings of the metropolitan centers—those given over to industry and commerce and those given over almost exclusively to residential functions.

Some Conceptual Problems

There are no studies addressed to the analysis of suburban culture *per se*. Yet, almost any report of the suburban community inadvertently takes into consideration suburban folkways, suburban norms, and suburban ideology. It is often at this particular juncture, the linkage of suburban organization to suburban culture, that some problems begin to appear. There seems to be a basic confusion between the concept of the suburbs as an ecological phenomenon and the suburbs as the burgeoning residences of the urban middle class. Many of the generalizations referring to the "suburban man" or "suburban society," or "suburban culture" are not manifestations of an ecological phenomenon, but, rather, a facet of the complex life styles of the middle class.

It is true, of course, that the term "middle class" has come to stand for many things. As a center of the class spectrum, it is relatively obscure in comparison with the "polar" classes. Consequently many attempts have been made to conceptualize the differences between those middle class elements which are closest to the polar classes. The result has been the emergence of such differentiating terms as "lower-middle class," "middle-middle," and "upper-middle."

Yet, in spite of the complexity of the middle class, suburban research often issues in a description of class behavior rather than ecological behavior. If the suburbanite is familistic, it is because he is responding to middle class definitions, not suburban definitions. If he is starting to vote Republican (an hypothesis often alleged but never confirmed), it is because his economic class and ideology have changed, not his location. If he participates in many voluntary associations, a class variable very probably underlies the community variable. The profile of the middle class—perhaps we should say the many middle classes—that has emerged from the literature since systematic class analysis began coincides with the "new" image of the suburbanite that has emerged from purely ecological research. Perhaps one of the central theoretic problems growing out of suburbanization *is the need to clarify to the relationship between the suburb as an ecological variable and the elements of suburban social organization and culture as class variables.*

There is an additional point that might be emphasized at this juncture. It is widely assumed that the suburbs are indeed "middle class" in character. Oftentimes this generalization is reflected in the delineation of suburbs as "homogeneous" communities. It is the notion of the "homogeneity" of the contemporary suburbs that needs clarification, for the middle classes are no longer homogeneous. As a consequence, neither are the suburbs. There was a time when residential suburbs were almost entirely "middle-middle" or "upper-middle." However, in the post World War II era, mass produced suburbs such as the Levittowns have been pulling the "working" or "blue collar" classes out of the central cities. The Drexelbrooks and Park Forests that Whyte reports on are quite different suburbs from the Levittowns.[28] A Drexelbrook, the dormitory of the "Organization Man," is clearly upper-middle class. It is characterized by "sophisticated" values, "very dry martini culture," and intellectual seminars of young matrons bored by the routines of child rearing and house work. The Levittowns, with their fusion of working class and middle class elements, do not fit the generalizations founded on research in the upper-middle class suburbs. Life styles on a single Levittown street may range from those of a second generation, working class, ex-Brooklynite of Italian "extraction" to those of a struggling young executive of "The Organization," to those of a medical intern from an "upper-upper" New England family who is completing his residence at a local hospital.[29] And, as the class factor varies, so does the character of the suburban community. The Drexelbrook suburbs tend toward class homogeneity and consequently reflect greater consistency in life styles. The Levittowns, on the other hand, are characterized by a considerably greater class spectrum and consequently its life styles almost defy generalization.

In addition to its social class, the particular point of time in its history affects the character of a suburb's social organization and ethos. The intensive fraternizations and the almost frenetic "organizing" into informal neighborhood cliques which Whyte reports of Park Forest and Drexelbrook simply do not apply to Levittown ten years after its "founding." The necessarily impressionistic observations of the author, as a resident of Levittown, Long Island, of informal clique behavior and of neighboring in general, suggest that it is generally unhurried and leisurely. Older residents recall more intensive neighboring in the first few years of the community's inception. At this time the "pioneer spirit" prevailed, and there existed a strong "consciousness of kind," based on the sharing of a novel and intimate experience— the founding of a neighborhood and community. As the years went by, however, and as families moved away and new ones took their place, the early solidarity and spontaneous cliquing gave way to greater formality and social insulation. Levittown today has been likened to a great "horizontalized" apartment house, in which urban anonymity and segmentalism prevails. The notion of the relatively intense neighboring in suburban communities, therefore, must be balanced against their particular level of "social maturity."

The social organization of the suburban community varies not only with the role of its social class and with its social maturity, but also with the conditions of its creation as a suburb. Some suburbs have been created by rational forces in the market economy. They are the calculated creations of builders and real estate speculators. Drexelbrook, Park Forest, and the two Levittowns are products of such forces. Some suburbs, however, are created by inadvertent invasion and urban decentralization—for example, the independent rural villages along the periphery of the rural-urban fringe which have been suddenly engulfed by the latest wave of suburbanites fleeing the city. The heterogeneity, therefore, of the "suburb-by-invasion" is likely to be considerably greater even than that of the mass produced suburb. Not only is the class structure more complex because of the super-imposing of the suburban population on the village population, but the structure of age and sex ratios is also rendered more complex. The suburb-by-invasion has an older population, a larger proportion of unmarried adults, and a smaller percentage of home ownership than does the mass produced suburb. Homogeneity decreases as one moves from the upper-middle class, mass produced suburb, to the middle class mass produced suburb, to the invaded village suburb.

This brief summary of theory and research in the sociology of the suburbs clearly indicates the need for more data and sharper and more revealing concepts. In 1951 Whetten called for research in seven basic areas: [30] (1) the classification of suburban populations into "meaningful groupings or community types" (2) more data on the "extent and selectivity" of suburban migration (3) studies of the "impact" of the suburban community on personality (4) research on the relationship of suburban migration to upward mobility (5) case studies focusing on the impact of suburbanization on existing villages and the resulting "conflict" between the two forms of community organization (6) the relationship of the suburb to the central city and (7) researches oriented around the problem of the extent to which the suburbanites have realized their dream of suburban living.

In the intervening six years, a good deal of work has been done along the lines Whetten proposed. The development of a more adequate typology, as already noted, has been a consistent concern. [31] Demographic analysis of urban, suburban, and rural populations has continued in greater detail. [32] A recent case study has been addressed to the problem of gauging the impact of a suburban invasion on a village social structure and to some of the problems resulting from the conflict between "villager" and "suburbanite." [33] In addition, there is currently some attention being given to the social-psychological problems of suburbanization. [34] Only the areas of the relationship between the central city and the suburb and the extent to which suburbanites have realized their expectations of suburban life remain relatively untouched. Even here, however, Martin's discussion of the relationship between commuting to the central city and suburban residence is a step in the direction Whetten suggested.[35]

Yet, in spite of what has been done in recent years, there is need for much more work. This, however, is the story of social science. The face of the future is in the suburbs, and there is no indication that urban decentralization is slowing up. The middle classes and the migrant rural population continue to feed the suburban maw. Apace with this growing importance of the suburbs in urban-associational society, there has been a marked increase in sociological interest in the suburban community. And when one considers the growth of scientific sophistication that has characterized sociology in the past fifty years and remembers that urban sociology as a formal field of community analysis scarcely goes back further than the 1920's, the prospects for a vigorous sociology of the suburbs are bright indeed.

FOOTNOTES

1. Adna F. Weber, *The Growth of Cities in the Nineteenth Century* (New York, Columbia University Press, 1899).
2. Donald J. Bogue, "Urbanism in the United States, 1950," *The American Journal of Sociology,* LX (March 1955), p. 481.
3. *Ibid.*
4. *Ibid.*
5. MacIver and Page have indicated that the essential characteristic of a community is "that one's life *may* be lived wholly within it." The sociological bases of the community, they point out, are "locality" and "community sentiment." See: Robert M. MacIver and Charles H. Page, *Society* (New York, Rinehart and Company, 1949) p. 9. Davis has linked a "physical criterion" (territorial proximity) to a "social criterion" (social completeness). Thus, Davis defines the community as, "the smallest territorial group that can embrace all aspects of social life." See: Kingsley Davis, *Human Society,* (New York, The Macmillan Company, 1948-49) p. 312.
6. R. D. McKenzie, *The Metropolitan Community* (New York, McGraw-Hill, 1933).
7. Warren S. Thompson, *The Growth of Metropolitan Districts in the United States, 1900-1940* (Washington, Government Printing Office, 1947).
8. Donald J. Bogue, *Metropolitan Decentralization: A Study of Differential Growth* (Oxford, Ohio, Scripps Foundation for Research in Population Problems, 1950); *Population Growth in Standard Metropolitan Areas, 1900-1950* (Washington, Government Printing Office, 1953).
9. Amos H. Hawley, *The Changing Shape of Metropolitan America* (Glencoe, Illinois, Free Press, 1956).

10. R. E. Park, E. W. Burgess, and R. D. McKenzie, *The City* (Chicago, The University of Chicago Press, 1925).

11. Homer Hoyt, "City Growth and Mortgage Risk," *Insured Mortgage Portfolio,* Vol. 1, Nos. 6-10 (Dec. 1936-April 1937), *passim;* U. S. Federal Housing Administration, *The Structure and Growth of Residential Neighborhoods in American Cities* (Washington, Government Printing Office, 1939), *passim;* "The Structure of American Cities in the Post War Era," *The American Journal of Sociology,* XLVIII (January 1943).

12. See Maurice R. Davie, "The Pattern of Urban Growth," in Paul K. Hatt and Albert J. Reiss (eds.) *Reader in Urban Sociology* (Glencoe, The Free Press, 1951) pp. 244-259 and Walter Firey, "Sentiment and Symbolism as Ecological Variables," *American Sociological Review,* Vol. 10 (April 1945), pp. 140-148.

13. Blizzard and Anderson have made a distinction between rural-urban fringe and the suburbs. They have defined the suburbs as those "political units which fall within the sphere or dominance of a metropolis..." On the other hand, they conceptualize the rural-urban fringe in terms of mixed urban and rural land use areas. See Samuel W. Blizzard and William F. Anderson, "Problems in Rural-Urban Fringe Research: Conceptualization and Delineation," The Pennsylvania State College Agricultural Experiment Station, Progress Report 89 (State College, Pennsylvania, November, 1952), mimeo.

14. There is an important question regarding the exclusively residential character of the suburbs, for some decentralized communities have an industrial rather than residential quality. The "employing" or "industrial" suburb has been recognized in the literature of suburban types. We are emphasizing the residential suburb in our discussion because its rate of growth is almost twice that of "employing suburbs," and there is some question if the industrial suburb or "satellite city" conforms to the definitive characteristics of suburban communities. For further discussion of this difficult question see Leo F. Schnore, "The Growth of Metropolitan Suburbs," pp. 26-44, in this volume; also, "Satellites and Suburbs," pp. 109-121, by the same author. For a penetrating analysis of the unique qualities of the suburban community see Walter T. Martin, "The Structuring of Social Relationships Engendered by Suburban Residence," pp. 95-108 in this volume.

15. Blizzard and Anderson, *op, cit.,* p. 11.

16. It is interesting to note that Duncan and Reiss conceptualized three functional demographic rings in their article "Suburbs and Urban Fringe," which appears on page 45 of this volume. For statistical purposes the suburbs and urban fringe were incorporated into a single category. Yet, the significant fact remains that demographers find the three ring concept of the urbanized area useful. As Duncan and Reiss put the matter, "Thus, the urbanized area is conceived as having three components, central city or cities, suburbs, and urban fringe." Original Source: Otis D. Duncan and Albert J. Reiss, Jr., *Social Characteristics of Urban and Rural Communities,* 1950 (New York, John Wiley & Sons, 1956), p. 118.

The present writer would like to emphasize the ideal-type character of the three functional rings of metropolitan areas. For diagrammatic and heuristic purposes I have plotted them as concentric circles around the central city. In "reality" they may not be concentric at all. Geographic factors such as rivers, mountains, oceans, lakes, deserts, *etc.*, may limit the manner in which decentralization may take place. In addition, ecological factors, such as a "satellite city" or concentrated area, may send decentralization off in another direction. What I am suggesting, in ideal-typical terms, is that the suburban belt lies closer to the central city than the rural-urban fringe. The fringe is that area which the suburbs are invading. There is a dynamic quality to the fringe. What is now the rural-urban fringe may be distinctly suburban five years from now.

17. Probably the best known studies from this period are N. L. Whetten, *Studies of Suburbanization in Connecticut:* I (with E. C. Devereux Jr.,) Windsor: *A Highly Developed Agricultural Area* (Storrs A.E.S. Bull. 212, Storrs, Conn., October 1936); II (with R. F. Field,) *Norwich; An Industrial Part-Time Farming Area* (Storrs, A.E.S. Bull. 26, Storrs, Conn., May, 1938); III Wilton: *A Rural Town Near Metropolitan New York* (Storrs, A.E.S. Bull. 230, Storrs, Conn., February, 1939. Also see G. A. Lundberg, M. Komarovsky and M. A. McInery, *Leisure—A Suburban Study* (New York, Columbia University Press, 1934); Earl L. Koos and Edmund deS. Brunner, *Suburbanization in Webster, New York* (University of Rochester, Department of Sociology, Rochester, New York, 1945).

18. Walter T. Martin, "The Structuring of Social Relationships Engendered by Suburban Residence," *American Sociological Review,* Vol. 21 (August 1956). Republished in this volume pp. 95-108.

19. Wendell Bell, "Social Choice, Life Styles, and Suburban Residence," pp. 225-247. This article is an elaborated version of a paper which first appeared in *Rural Sociology,* 21 (September-December, 1956) pp. 276-283, entitled, "Familism and Suburbanization: One Test of the Social Choice Hypothesis."

20. Sylvia Fleis Fava, "Suburbanism as a Way of Life," *American Sociological Review,* XXI (February 1956), also *Contrasts in Neighboring: New York City and a Suburban County,* a revised version of a paper read at the annual meetings of the American Sociological Society, Washington, D. C., August 1957, published in volume pp. 122-131.

21. Ernest R. Mowrer, "The Family in Suburbia," pp. 147-164 in this volume.

22. William H. Form, "Status Stratification in a Planned Community," *American Sociological Review,* Vol. X (October 1945). Republished in this volume pp. 209-224.

23. Harlan P. Douglass, *The Suburban Trend* (New York and London, The Century Company, 1925), pp. 74-92.

24. Chauncey D. Harris, "Suburbs," *The American Journal of Sociology,* XLIX (July 1943), pp. 1-13.

25. Leo F. Schnore, "The Growth of Metropolitan Suburbs," *American Sociological Review,* Vol. 22 (April 1957), pp. 165-173.

26. Leo F. Schnore, "The Growth of Metropolitan Suburbs," p. 30 in this volume.
27. Leo F. Schnore, "Satellites and Suburbs," pp. 109-121 in this volume.
28. William H. Whyte, *The Organization Man* (New York, Simon and Schuster, Inc., 1956).
29. For an interesting account of the diversity of occupations found on a typical Levittown street see Harold Wattel, "Levittown: A Suburban Community," p. 298 in this volume.
30. Nathan L. Whetten, "Suburbanization as a Field for Sociological Research," *Rural Sociology,* Vol. 16 (December 1951), pp. 319-330.
31. See: Leo F. Schnore, "Satellites and Suburbs," and "Metropolitan Growth and Decentralization," pp. 109-121 and 3-20 in this volume.
32. In this regard note the recent works of Bogue, Hawley, Duncan and Reiss already cited.
33. See: William M. Dobriner, *The Impact of Metropolitan Decentralization on a Village Social Structure: A Study in Suburbanization and Social Change,* unpublished Ph.D. dissertation, Columbia University, 1956.
34. See: Sylvia Fleis Fava, "Suburbanism as a Way of Life," *American Sociological Review,* XXI (February 1956) pp. 34-38 and also, William M. Dobriner, "Local and Cosmopolitan as Contemporary Suburban Character Types," pp. 132-143 in this volume.
35. Walter T. Martin, *op. cit.*

Part I

The Growth
of the Suburbs

---

*In four or five of the districts of the central area, the process
of depopulation began earlier than 1861. For our purpose it
will be sufficient to trace the process in the two oldest districts,
London City and Strand.... The Strand attained its maximum
population as far back as 1821, and since then it has regularly
lost.... London City reached its maximum population in 1851,
but this scarcely exceeded its population of 1801, so that we
can say that its population was stationary during the first half
of the century and has since declined....*

*The process thus sketched for New York, London, etc., is
known as "city-building." The original settlement becomes the
business center and for some time continues to grow rapidly.
But if the city prospers, the time will come when this old center
is more and more needed for strictly business purposes....
With continued growth, the business center extends itself and
steadily pushes the dwellings toward the circumference, until
at length the municipal limits are reached and passed.*

Adna Ferrin Weber, 1899

Leo F. Schnore

University of California

METROPOLITAN GROWTH
AND DECENTRALIZATION

A great deal of research effort has been devoted to metropolitan growth and decentralization in recent years. In particular, the detailed statistical studies by Thompson, Bogue, and Hawley have provided a clear image of the main demographic facts. However, a search of the literature on the subject reveals two important omissions. (1) Nowhere is there available a succinct *historical recapitulation* that provides a summary description of metropolitan development from its beginnings to the present time. (2) As a consequence of this lack of historical perspective, the literature contains very few explicitly *developmental hypotheses* regarding metropolitan growth and decentralization.

It is with these two broad problems that the present article is concerned. First, a brief narrative account of metropolitan growth and development is offered. Second, a number of implications derived from this historical review are set out in the form of concrete problems for research. In each of these problems, the focus is upon process, in a frank effort to offset the static orientation of the available literature. A number of the hypotheses refer specifically to the influence of transportation, a factor that is frequently mentioned but rarely studied in the metropolitan context. The historical treatment attempted here is

Reprinted from *The American Journal of Sociology*, LXIII (September 1957) pp. 171-172, by permission of the author and the University of Chicago Press. (Copyright 1957 by the University of Chicago.) Data assembled while writer held Research Training Fellowship from the Social Science Research Council.

deliberately phrased in very general terms. The demands of brevity, of course, mitigate against a fully documented account. Most of the statements are well established, although diverse in origin. Others rest upon more limited evidence, and a few are frankly speculative. The latter, however, are phrased as questions for empirical research, and not as final answers.[1]

A Half Century of Metropolitan Growth

Metropolitan development can best be conceived as a new form of urban growth especially characteristic of twentieth-century America.[2] It must be recognized, of course, that a large increase in urban population antedated this century. Urban places have grown faster than rural areas since 1820. The first decade of this century, however, marked the end of one important phase of urban development, for it was the last decade in which migration from other countries contributed large numbers to the growth of American cities. The decade from 1910 to 1920, including as it did the first World War, witnessed the stemming of the great streams of migrants from overseas, and over-all urban growth was slowed as a result.[3]

Restrictive legislation in the 1920's, including a rigid system of quotas, prevented the resumption of international migration on a pre-war scale, but the national population continued to increase, and urban places continued to grow rapidly. Their growth now, however, depended largely upon internal migration. The attenuated growth of cities in the 1930-1940 decade was also the result of a failure of migration, but in this instance it consisted of a lessened flow of internal rural-to-urban migrants. Job opportunities in urban areas, drastically reduced during the depression, multiplied during the early 1940's, largely due to the demands of war-time. Urban employment was maintained at fairly high levels in the years immediately following World War II as the nation returned to a peace-time economy, and it was further stimulated by the outbreak of hostilities in the Far East.

What have been the *metropolitan* concomitants of twentieth-century urban growth? Panel A of Table 1 shows interdecade rates of increase within the entire continental United States. In this table, the total land area of the nation is represented according to metropolitan status. The first distinction is that between metropolitan and non-metropolitan parts. The next sub-division in the table distinguishes between the metropolitan central cities and their surrounding "rings." Growth rates for urban and rural parts of the ring are then shown separately. Finally, within the "rural" portion of the ring, separate growth rates are given for incorporated and unincorporated areas. Panel B expresses all of these rates as ratios of the national increase; this introduces a control over variation in overall growth between decades.[4]

Table 1—Interdecade Rates of Increase in the Population of the United States, by Metropolitan Status, 1900-1950

Metropolitan status	1940-1950	1930-1940	1920-1930	1910-1920	1900-1910
A. INTERDECADE RATES OF POPULATION INCREASE					
Total United States	14.5	7.2	16.1	14.9	21.0
Non-metropolitan	6.1	5.5	6.0	6.7	13.6
Metropolitan	22.0	8.4	27.5	25.9	32.5
Central cities	13.8	5.5	24.2	27.9	37.1
Rings	34.2	13.4	33.2	22.4	25.6
Urban	26.0	8.0	42.6	35.9	49.2
Rural	45.2	21.3	22.0	9.4	8.4
Incorporated	34.1	13.2	28.6	24.1	45.0
Unincorporated	46.5	22.3	21.2	7.8	5.6
B. RATIOS OF TOTAL NATIONAL INCREASE					
Non-metropolitan	.43	.76	.37	.45	.65
Metropolitan	1.52	1.17	1.71	1.74	1.55
Central cities	.95	.76	1.50	1.87	1.77
Rings	2.36	1.86	2.06	1.50	1.22
Urban	1.79	1.11	2.65	2.41	2.34
Rural	3.12	2.96	1.37	.63	.40
Incorporated	2.35	1.83	1.78	1.62	2.14
Unincorporated	3.21	3.10	1.32	.52	.27

Source: See footnote 4.

Table 1 shows that the presently defined metropolitan areas have captured a disproportionately large share of the total national increase in population throughout the entire fifty-year period. Within metropolitan areas, however, central city growth has become progressively slower while the ring has tended to grow more and more rapidly. It is this over-all pattern of differential growth in favor of the peripheral area that is usually labelled "decentralization," although these rates reflect only net changes arising from a variety of sources.

A part of this slower rate of city growth is the result of their failure or inability to annex the surrounding densely-settled areas. Probably more significant, however, are two complementary trends in migration and residential mobility. The first of these is a tendency for residents of the central city to move in increasing numbers to various parts of the adjacent ring area. The other major trend is the tendency for migrants from outside the metropolitan area to move directly to the ring rather than to the city itself. The total effect of these two movements is a relative decentralization, or net peripheral growth in excess of that of the center. As far as migration and mobility are concerned, decentralization has two sources—outward *relocation* from the center and growth via *accretion* at the periphery. As yet, however, the relative contributions of these two distinct types of movement have not been firmly established.[5]

Despite inadequate answers to these basic questions, however, recent studies have established some important relationships between (a) the extent of decentralization and (b) certain structural and functional characteristics of metropolitan areas. One way to present these relationships is to take a deliberately over-simplified view of metropolitan development as a more or less continuous process, and to introduce the findings of recent research in historical sequence. Throughout this discussion, further reference will be made to the summary data presented in Table 1, while attention will be directed to the historical context of metropolitan growth and decentralization.

Toward Metropolitan Maturity

At the turn of the century, most urban centers were still rather compact and self-contained entities. Most of the larger cities were at deep-water sites, although a few had begun to develop inland at railway intersections. The residents of these large cities were concentrated near the principal workplaces, living in tenements and row houses. Most city-dwellers walked to work or rode on public transit systems. The horsecar was still very much in evidence on the city streets, although it was being replaced by the electric streetcar. However, the automobile was still a novelty and its price was beyond the range of all but a few of the more wealthy members of the community. Some of the latter, who could afford the time and the cost of the trip, had already begun to live outside the congested city and travel to their places of business by automobile or by inter-urban railway.[6]

These railways—powered by steam or electricity—spread out from the largest cities in radial strings, and along their lines began to appear clusters of dwellings. In the intersections lay wide areas of open country, much of it being devoted to farming. Small villages could be found scattered throughout this open country, serving the immediate needs of the farm population. These sub-centers were found at intersections of rural roads and near the railway lines, from which the larger cities distributed the processed goods required by the agricultural population. These small sub-centers also served as the primary collection points for the produce of the agricultural hinterland.

Larger urban sub-centers within the orbit of the central city provided the less frequently needed goods for the hinterland population. In addition to serving as collection and distribution points, these larger sub-centers were frequently engaged in the processing of goods, particularly if water power was immediately available. Most industry, however, was still concentrated in the large city, where the economies of steam power could be best realized.[7] Most of the larger sub-centers had direct railway service to the central city. Over these lines flowed the overwhelming bulk of inter-urban freight.

The whole spatial arrangement of these various urban and village agglomerations tended to resemble a planet and its satellites. The larger urban places in the area were still growing more rapidly than the smaller places, chiefly through migration, and the rural population was suffering a sustained outmigration as more and more efficient methods of farming were put into use, and as smaller subsistence farms were consolidated into larger holdings. The resulting low rates of rural growth can be clearly seen in Table 1. The surplus agricultural population flowed toward the city, probably in a series of intermediate moves, to be joined there by migrants from foreign countries.[8]

Metropolitan areas during the early years of the century were thus characterized by an axiate or star-shaped form of settlement. Most urban places beyond ten or fifteen miles remained largely independent of the center. Within that zone, however, inter-urban railways were gradually able to provide more regular service; as time passed, more and more people working in the city found it possible to live outside its formal boundaries. These early suburbanites lived in new residential developments that appeared within walking distance of the railway commuter stations. In Hoyt's words, ". . . as these communities gradually coalesced in solid bands, the settled area maps of the New York and Chicago metropolitan areas showed long finger-like appendages extending out, with large vacant areas lying in between. This was the result of the faster travel time on the suburban railroads than on other means of transportation." [9]

An appreciation of the importance of the railroad during the early part of this century can be gained from a review of historical statistics. Table 2 shows that there were more than four times as many railway locomotives than motor vehicles in operation at the turn of the century. As late as 1910, there were more miles of railroad track than miles of surface highways in use. After 1920, however, the number of motor vehicles increased significantly, while the number of locomotives began to decline. Similar trends can be discerned when the two types of route are compared.

Table 2—Comparison of Railroad and Motor Vehicle Routes and Carriers, 1900-1950

Year	Railroad trackage (in miles)	Surfaced highways (in miles)	Railroad locomotives (number)	Motor vehicles (number)
1950	223,779	1,714,000	42,951	48,566,984
1940	223,670	1,367,000	44,333	32,035,424
1930	249,052	694,000	60,189	26,531,999
1920	252,845	369,000	68,942	9,239,161
1910	240,293	204,000	60,019	468,500
1900	193,348	128,500	37,663	8,000

Source: U. S. Bureau of the Census, *Historical Statistics of the United States, 1789-1945*, Washington: Government Printing Office, 1949, Tables K-29, K-34, K-175, K-182, and K-229; and U. S. Bureau of the Census, *Continuation to 1952 of Historical Statistics of the United States, 1789-1945*, Washington: Government Printing Office, 1954, same tables.

The first World War brought two particularly significant developments. First, migration from abroad, which had provided a large share of the city's manpower needs, was practically cut off. The demands of war-time, however, meant that urban manufacturing centers had to increase their output. To staff the mills and plants, these cities had to depend on the population that could be attracted from other parts of the nation. As before, most of these people came from rural areas, but for the first time the migrant streams began to include large numbers of Negroes, particularly from the South. [10]

The second crucial development occasioned by the war was the rapid increase in the number of motor vehicles. Burdened to their capacity, the railroads were simply unable to carry all of the freight that had to be shipped. Motor trucks, which had been used primarily for local hauling within the city, were pressed into service in order to move less bulky goods between urban areas. An extensive program of highway improvement on all levels of government was put into effect, and hard-surfaced roads began to interlace the areas surrounding the largest centers. In addition, some of the methods learned under the pressure of the war-time demand for motor transport were applied to the production of private automobiles. Many of the techniques of modern mass production—later adopted in almost every sector of the economy—were first developed in the automobile industry. Truck transportation, moreover, was in effect subsidized by governmental funds, for highways were publicly financed.

The years immediately following World War I, although marked by a few minor fluctuations, ushered in a period of expansion. Enormous strides were made in industrial productivity, and as national production increased, significant advances were made in the level of real wages. The techniques of mass production and increased mechanization had the effect of reducing the manpower required in industry. Since a similar trend was continuing in agriculture as an effect of the introduction of power machinery, the surplus population from both agriculture and industry gradually shifted into occupations providing for the distribution of goods and services.[11]

Spatial changes also emanated from these technological innovations. At the very same time that these fundamental transitions were taking place in the national economy, the physical pattern of the large city and its surrounding area began to undergo crucial alterations. Decentralization, which had occurred first in only the largest centers, became a significant aspect of the growth of many smaller cities. It became evident in the 1920's that both industry and population were scattering as a response to the development of the motor vehicle. The hard-surfaced route, of course, was adaptable to the movement of people as well as to the carrying of goods. The elaborate networks of main arteries and feeder routes around large and middle-sized cities permitted a number of the functional components of the community to break away from the center. Most of these units were located at intersections in the highway network. Urban sub-centers appeared in increasing numbers and grew at rates in excess of that of the center. (See Table 1.) As residential population gathered in sufficient densities, many establishments arose to provide the suburbanites with urban conveniences. New construction was started in volume in the periphery of both large and middle-sized cities.

With the increased ease of travel, however, some of the larger sub-centers underwent a significant transition. They lost their high degree of independence, and fell under the dominating influence of the metropolis. For example, many establishments devoted to the provision of luxury goods abandoned these operations in the sub-centers, unable to compete with the metropolis, now within easy access of a wide market. At the same time, the principles of mass production were increasingly adapted to the function of distribution, and chains of retail outlets began to appear, particularly in the convenience goods lines. These units, under a single ownership and directed from a site in the central city, could take advantage of the economies of mass buying and standardization. During the same period, significant changes in communication came about with the development of the radio and the telephone. Instantaneous contact with a broad area became possible, and the independence of sub-centers was diminished accordingly.

At the same time, industry became increasingly free to locate away from the city itself. Cheap electrical power in place of steam was one important factor. Another was the telephone, which permitted peripheral location of production facilities while the functions of management and control could remain in the center. In addition, the widespread ownership of the automobile meant a more mobile labor force. Heavy industry, which tends to operate more efficiently in one-story buildings occupying large areas, apparently was particularly attracted by the lower costs of land in the ring, where the competition of alternative uses was less intense.

However, not all of the elements of the community were equally free to participate in the outward movement. During the early phases of decentralization, many activities were bound to the center as securely as in previous years. It appears that the retailing of luxury goods and the provision of services which are needed infrequently were particularly obliged to remain in central locations, in order to maintain maximum access to a large potential market. The management and direction functions also appeared to cling to central location, perhaps in order to facilitate contact with other units engaged in communication, finance, and marketing.

At any rate, the depression of the 1930's appears to have accentuated the trends of differential growth that were incipient in many areas in previous years. With decreased job opportunities to offer, central city growth dropped to a low level, with many cities sustaining net losses. The growth of the residential population of the metropolitan ring, although reduced from the levels of the previous decade in many instances, tended to remain above that of the center and of the nation as a whole. (See Table 1.) Although there is little evidence of a genuine "back-to-the-farm" movement during this decade, it appears that there was considerable "piling up" of potential migrants in the outlying areas.[12]

It is clear, however, that within metropolitan rings, "rural" growth exceeded urban growth during the depression decade, and the growth of unincorporated rural areas was in excess of that of small incorporated places.[13] (See Table 1.) The threat of war and the subsequent armament drive in the last years of the decade probably pushed the interdecade growth rates of many central cities to higher levels than would otherwise have been realized. In spite of the probable resumption of heavy city-ward migration toward the end of the 'thirties, ring growth tended to exceed the growth of even the smaller metropolitan cities. A distinct majority of the cities of 50,000 and over were now exhibiting the pattern of relative decentralization formerly seen around only the larger cities.[14]

Finally, the most recent intercensal decade (1940-1950) has witnessed a progressive diffusion of the patterns that began to emerge years earlier in the largest centers. Not only metropolitan centers, but the larger satellites within the metropolitan orbit are decentralizing. The growth of "rural" and unincorporated areas continues to outstrip that of the urban and incorporated places. (See Table 1.) The physical form of the metropolitan area, which had been axiate in pattern, has tended to fill in. The shape of the area resembles a great amorphous mass insofar as residential density is concerned, although the older star-shaped pattern can still be discerned in its outlines. More important, the functional boundaries of the metropolitan area, as they are indicated by the outward shift of high growth rates, appear to have shifted from a ring of approximately ten miles to one of 20 to 25 miles in diameter.[15]

Throughout these fifty years of transition, a number of structural and functional factors appear to have been related to the centrifugal growth tendency. The chief one of these is apparently the sheer population size of the area in question. In fact, most of the other factors found to be associated with centrifugal growth are themselves associated with metropolitan size. Regional location also appears to be a factor of real significance. Other variables associated with size and regional location, however, show associations with decentralization that remain when these two variables are controlled.

In addition to these primary factors, recent research has indicated that the areas in which decentralization occurred first and proceeded farthest tend to have densely populated central cities, in which growth has tended to be slow during the past fifty years. They are most frequently older cities found at coastal locations, and the distance to nearby metropolitan centers is relatively low. Manufacturing activity within the area has been decentralizing throughout most of the period.[16] All of these separate findings, when taken together, suggest the importance of what might be termed the "maturity" of metropolitan areas. *Those areas which have exhibited the earliest and most extreme evidence of decentralization appear to have reached an advanced stage of maturity that is merely reflected in the structural and functional characteristics enumerated here. In a rough sense, in fact, decentralization seems to serve as an index of the maturity of metropolitan areas.*

Some Research Implications

In addition to the research needs touched upon in the foregoing sections, a number of other problems present themselves for empirical scrutiny. One entire category of research problems can be subsumed under the rubric of the *sources* of differential growth within metropolitan areas. In addition to the relative contributions of natural increase and net migration, we need to know the origins of migrants in terms of areal and functional types. Another whole range of empirical questions emerges when we consider the demographic and functional *composition* of the various parts of the metropolitan area, and the migrant streams that flow between them. Imposing as these problems are, however, they relate only to the residential population of metropolitan areas.[17]

In addition to a concern with the re-distribution of residential population, of course, a full description of the changing organization of the metropolitan area must treat the other sociological units that constitute the total community. It appears that all of the typically urban activities—the so-called secondary and tertiary functions of fabrication, distribution, and control—have been subjected in some degree to the same forces of decentralization that have so dramatically altered the residential settlement pattern within local areas. The reduction of the friction imposed by distance has had noticeable effects in almost every sphere of life.

With respect to secondary activities, there is obviously increasing freedom of manufacturing to locate at the margins of the community. As Bogue has pointed out, "economists and industrialists have discovered that under modern conditions of transport it is no longer necessary for great industries to be located within the limits of the central city. There is a broad zone of indifference, probably several miles in diameter, which is locationally suitable." [18] Tertiary activities are probably undergoing similar changes in locational tolerance, but they have been less carefully studied. The decentralization of such functions as wholesaling, storage, and distribution deserves more research effort. These activities have been traditionally viewed as centrally oriented, but recent developments in metropolitan organization appear to warrant a reconsideration of the assumptions underlying these views. Faster and more frequent transportation, for example, may have decreased the need for central warehouse facilities. The handling of freight since the development of the motor truck has become a much more flexible operation, and a great deal of storage is apparently effected en route, without the necessity for large stockpiles and inventories immediately at hand.

Many administrative functions may also be increasingly free to leave the center and locate at the periphery of the metropolitan community. For example, the central offices of large insurance companies, whose chief contacts are with agents scattered throughout the nation, may represent one type of administration that can be efficiently managed in the ring as well as in the center. The control and direction of other industries, however, require frequent contact with lawyers, brokers, news media, advertising agencies, and out-of-town buyers, and they may continue to require central location. Further research should identify the other units with which a given function is in most frequent contact, in addition to its requirements for space, in both amount and kind. These facts would provide valuable clues to the amount of decentralization to be anticipated among various functions. Functional differences between suburban and satellite places still remain to be explored. Detailed knowledge of these differences is necessary to a full description of the social and economic organization of the expanded community.[19] In addition, more should be learned of the growth tendencies of different types of sub-nuclei in the metropolitan ring. Employing satellites, for example, show patterns of growth that are notably different from exclusively residential suburbs.[20] The growth of more specialized areas, including educational and recreational centers, may show divergent patterns in keeping with their narrowly specialized roles in the organization of the whole metropolitan area.

Trends in population growth within the central city itself are worthy of further exploration. Physical congestion in the center has been frequently advanced as one of the causes of decentralization. Most large cities, however, have high proportions of habitable land that remains vacant.[21] A substantial part of this total area is in small parcels held for speculation, forcing prices beyond the limits possible for residential development.

At the same time, a more accurate description of the role of congestion can probably be gained by turning attention to traffic congestion, itself a product of the separation of land uses seen in residential decentralization.[22] Traffic densities probably exert a greater influence than the more frequently measured densities of residential population. The daily massing of great volumes of people and vehicles in the central areas may inhibit movement to such an extent that the center loses its traditionally favored position as the point of maximum accessibility to the entire metropolitan area.

A closely related area of metropolitan research offers great promise for cross-cultural comparisons. A number of studies of the daily journey to work have been conducted in both Europe and the United States.[23] The studies in this country have been primarily based upon by-product data from traffic research, and they have been limited to those areas which are particularly subject to serious traffic problems. As a result, the areas covered in the American studies probably constitute a biased sample of all urban areas. Many of the European studies, however, have been based upon census materials, for the census schedules of most European nations include at least one question regarding the place of work of members of the employed labor force.[24] This is one of the rare instances in which the United States census has tended to lag behind the data collection systems of the other nations of the world. The inclusion of data on place of work in future censuses in this country would permit a much more complete description of the functional organization of the entire metropolitan area. The daily circulations and exchanges—centrifugal, centripetal, and lateral—between the various sub-parts of the area could be accurately determined.[25]

Previous remarks have tended to imply that long-distance commuting is restricted to the upper-income groups of the community. However, the rapid increase in automobile ownership in all social strata in our society has resulted in a modification of these limits. Suburbs and satellites, as well as the unincorporated places in the ring, are now accessible to those with moderate incomes, and even to some lower-income families. Wherever zoning regulations are not in effective force, cheap housing can be built on low-cost land. Scattered research has suggested that the European pattern of part-time farming by urban workers may have become established in the vicinity of many American industrial cities, particularly near those in which factory work is seasonal in character.[26] Ride-sharing arrangements between urban workers who live in the ring constitute still another device that permits a peripheral residential location of families which otherwise could not afford the high costs of transportation to the center.[27] More generally, trends in housing have had an important place in this entire development, but research in this problem area is seriously deficient. With the passage of the years, the techniques of mass production have been adapted to the construction of dwellings. We need to know the causal factors operating to bring about areal differentials in construction of various types within the metropolitan community. Such knowledge would throw light upon the problem of the redistribution of residential population, as well as other functional components such as industrial and commercial establishments.[28]

In this connection, some research attention should be directed toward the problem of delineating more carefully some of the differences in socio-economic level between suburban and satellite places within the metropolitan ring. Rental and income data are now available for at least the larger incorporated places in the ring, and these can be easily supplemented by statistics on education and the occupational and ethnic composition of these places. Many observers have pointed to the possibility of rigid segregation in the suburbs along social and economic lines. It is said that the mass production of suburban housing tends to attract persons of similar status.[29] This economic compulsion toward segregated living seems to be further implemented by zoning regulations. Whether these trends are any more coercive, however, than the forces that have long made for segregation within the city is a matter for future research.

This entire discussion has made use of the newly-developed census concept of the Standard Metropolitan Area. Every research use of such a statistical reporting unit, of course, constitutes something of a test of the validity of the unit. There is some evidence that the Standard Metropolitan Area encompasses only the zone of most rapid growth in recent years. Both Bogue and Hawley have shown that the influence of the metropolis is reflected in the growth rates of areas many miles beyond the commuting zone. Beyond this zone of primary interchange, of course, lies a much broader hinterland in which integration with the center is expressed through indirect contacts. Thus research cannot be confined to the Standard Metropolitan Area alone. The area of direct contact with the center, however, appears to be well delineated by the Standard Metropolitan Area definition. At any rate, the utility of these areas as reporting units is enhanced by the vast amount of data assembled on a county basis by other governmental and private agencies. Fuller use of these data will permit at least tentative answers to many of the research questions posed here.

Conclusions

Many problems of administration and planning arise out of our ignorance of the details of change in the form of the community. The provision of accurate descriptions of community structure is the responsibility of sociological research, but it is a task that is far from complete. If we are ever to solve the host of practical problems that are so rapidly developing in the wake of decentralization, we will have to assemble more and more facts. But even more important, we will have to provide conceptual schemes with which to interpret these facts.

The research problems raised in this paper point up the fact that we need a total theory, subsuming both structural and functional aspects of all the constituent units of the community. Moreover, such a theory should be capable of generating testable hypotheses referring to both static and dynamic relationships between variables. Our present fund of sociological theory is particularly deficient in the last-named respect. Technological innovation, land-use conversion, segregation, population growth and re-distribution—all of these are terms referring to *processes* taking place over time. Any sound conceptual approach must be phrased in dynamic terms such as these, if for no other reason than that the modern metropolitan community is constantly changing.

The construction of such a theory will be no mere intellectual exercise. As one demographer has recently asserted:

> One of the reasons for such strong disagreements and conflicting recommendations about so-called "decentralization" is that specialists in the field of urban population and human ecology have failed to produce a theory of urban growth that is valid for the mid-20th century. Perhaps we have been overly concerned with perfecting a static theory of city structure. ... Our study of structure needs to be accompanied by a rigorous program of research into growth and change. Research in urbanism and metropolitanism should have dynamic as well as static aspects.[30]

The writer can only agree with these ambitious goals, and hope that the discussion contained in this article will contribute to their ultimate achievement.

FOOTNOTES

1. Both of the major sections of this paper—the historical narrative and the derived outline of research problems—are based on the premise that the general pattern of metropolitan development should be established before individual variations are examined in detail. This is not to derogate case studies of individual areas, for they represent an extremely valuable source of hypotheses. However, an excessive concern with apparent exceptions appears to be premature at this point. A more fruitful approach would seem to involve the documentation of major trends. Once the broad set of relationships has been firmly established, the study of exceptions becomes the study of variations around these central tendencies, themselves subject to explanation. At any rate, highly generalized patterns are described here, in the hope that they will serve to indicate what remains to be learned.
2. See N. S. B. Gras, *An Introduction to Economic History* (New York: Har-

per and Brothers, 1922); and R. D. McKenzie, *The Metropolitan Community* (New York: McGraw-Hill Book Company, 1933).

3. Natural increase was apparently not a compensating factor of any consequence during this period, for city dwellers failed to reproduce at replacement levels. Donald J. Bogue has presented evidence, however, that this long-established fact did not hold during the most recent intercensal decade. See "Urbanism in the United States, 1950," *American Journal of Sociology*, 60 (March, 1955), pp. 471-486.

4. Source: Leo F. Schnore, *Patterns of Decentralization*, unpublished doctoral dissertation, University of Michigan, 1955, Table 101, p. 214. Official definitions of the 168 Standard Metropolitan Areas recognized by the Census Bureau have been retrojected to 1900 in this table, so that area is held constant. The "old" (1940) census definition of urban is used throughout. Due to differences in areal definition, these rates differ in minor detail from those given in Donald J. Bogue, *Population Growth in Standard Metropolitan Areas, 1900-1950* (Washington: Government Printing Office, 1953), Table 1. Bogue's data refer to 162 metropolitan areas with "county-equivalent" areas used in New England in place of the town-based areas defined by the Census Bureau. Because the official definitions of the Standard Metropolitan Areas are used here, the data are not comparable with those reported in Warren S. Thompson, *The Growth of Metropolitan Districts in the United States, 1900-1940* (Washington: Government Printing Office, 1947).

5. The relative importance of these two migrant streams are known for only a few areas, and for a limited (and probably atypical) time period. Migration data from the 1940 census can be examined in terms of the 1935 places of residence of migrants living in metropolitan central cities and rings in 1940. See Warren S. Thompson, *Migration Within Ohio, 1935-1940* (Oxford, Ohio: Scripps Foundation for Research in Population Problems, 1951); and Amos H. Hawley, *Intrastate Migration in Michigan, 1935-1940* (Ann Arbor: University of Michigan Institute of Public Administration, 1953). In addition, the demographic components of centrifugal growth are still unknown. An important research question is the relative contribution of net migration (including both relocation and accretion) as compared with natural increase in different time periods.

6. Adna F. Weber, *The Growth of Cities in the Nineteenth Century* (New York: Columbia University Press, 1899).

7. National Resources Committee, *Our Cities: Their Role in the National Economy* (Washington: Government Printing Office, 1937), pp. 29-30.

8. Early urban research, of course, concentrated on the clusters of ethnic settlements that developed within large cities. However, comparative data on segregation is notably deficient for more recent periods.

9. Homer Hoyt, "The Influence of Highways and Transportation in the Structure and Growth of Cities and Urban Land Values," in Jean Labatut and Wheaton J. Lane (editors), *Highways in Our National Life* (Princeton: Princeton University Press, 1950), p. 202.

10. Thus began a South-to-North movement that has yet to abate. Most of these Negro migrants continue to move directly to the central city, rather than to the metropolitan ring. Racial differentials in the various migrant streams involved in decentralization have yet to be fully explored. A number of empirical and practical questions inevitably arise as large cities undergo compositional changes resulting from selective in- and out-migration.

11. For the original distinction between primary, secondary, and tertiary industries and occupations, see Colin Clark, *The Conditions of Economic Progress* (London: The Macmillan Company, 1951, second edition).

12. *Our Cities, op. cit.*

13. The old (1940) definitions of urban and rural used here tend seriously to overstate the rural component. Many of the people classified as rural are actually urbanites by any reasonable functional definition.

14. Donald J. Bogue, *Metropolitan Decentralization: A Study of Differential Growth* (Oxford, Ohio: Scripps Foundation for Research in Population Problems, 1950).

15. Amos H. Hawley, *The Changing Shape of Metropolitan America: Deconcentration Since 1920* (Glencoe: The Free Press, 1956).

16. *Ibid.* In each instance, the direction of association between a given variable and centrifugal growth tends to be the same as that found between the variable in question and metropolitan size. The direction of these relationships remains the same, although reduced in extent, within size classes. Although no single area can be found to possess every one of these characteristics, they tend to be associated with each other.

17. Albert J. Reiss, Jr., has recently suggested a number of excellent topics for research in this area. See "Research Problems in Metropolitan Population Redistribution," *American Sociological Review,* 21 (October, 1956), pp. 571-577. A number of his topics, however, are static in orientation.

18. Donald J. Bogue (editor), *Needed Urban and Metropolitan Research,* (Oxford, Ohio: Scripps Foundation for Research in Population Problems, 1953), p. 40.

19. See Sanford M. Dornbusch, "A Typology of Suburban Communities: Chicago Metropolitan District, 1940," Urban Analysis Report No. 10, (Chicago: Chicago Community Inventory, May 1952); and Leo F. Schnore, "The Functions of Metropolitan Suburbs," *American Journal of Sociology,* 61 (March, 1956), pp. 453-458.

20. Leo F. Schnore, "The Growth of Metropolitan Suburbs," *American Sociological Review* (forthcoming).

21. Harland Bartholomew, *Land Uses in American Cities* (Cambridge: Harvard University Press, 1955).

22. Donald L. Foley, "Urban Day-time Population: A Field for Demographic-Ecological Analysis," *Social Forces,* 32 (May, 1954), pp. 323-330.

23. Foley, *ibid.;* and Kate K. Liepmann, *The Journey to Work* (New York: Oxford University Press, 1944).

24. Foley, *op. cit.*

25. Perhaps the rapid advances made in sampling techniques will permit this valuable addition to the 1960 census. Technical problems can be solved by experimentation with alternative methods in the Current Population Survey and in special state and local censuses prior to adoption in the federal decennial census.

26. Nathan L. Whetten and R. F. Field, *Studies of Suburbanization in Connecticut: 2. Norwich: An Industrial Part-time Farming Area* (Storrs: Connecticut State College Agricultural Experiment Station Bulletin 226, 1938); W. R. Gordon, *Satellite Acres* (Kingston: Rhode Island State College Agricultural Experiment Station Bulletin, 282, 1942); Walter Firey, *Social Aspects of Land Use Planning in the Country-City Fringe* (East Lansing: Michigan State College Agricultural Experiment Station Bulletin 339, 1946); Glenn H. Beyer, *Housing and Journey to Work* (Ithaca: Cornell University Agricultural Experiment Station Bulletin 877, 1951).

27. Leo F. Schnore, "The Separation of Home and Work: A Problem for Human Ecology," *Social Forces,* 32 (May, 1954), pp. 336-343. The so-called "marginal labor force" appears to be physically marginal to industrial cities. This suggests that the "rural-urban fringe" is amenable to identification in functional (occupational) as well as areal terms. The latter conception, in fact, may be misleading.

28. For important data on this question, see Dorothy K. Newman, "Metropolitan Area Structure and Growth as Shown by Building-Permit Statistics," *Business Topics,* 4 (November, 1956), pp. 1-7. Within metropolitan areas, new housing construction is especially rapid in the ring. Although Newman presents data for only a small number of areas, all but eight of the 168 currently-recognized Standard Metropolitan Areas have higher proportions of newly-constructed dwelling units in the ring than in the central city.

29. Leslie Kish, "Differentiation in Metropolitan Areas," *American Sociological Review,* 19 (August, 1954), pp. 388-398.

30. Bogue, *Needed Urban and Metropolitan Research, op. cit.,* p. 38.

Donald J. Bogue

Population Research and Training Center,
The University of Chicago

URBANISM AND METROPOLITANISM

The phenomenon of growth of cities to large size and the fact that large cities acquire unique attributes have given rise to a theory that major cities are focal points in the economic and social organization of modern industrial-commercial nations. From piecemeal evidence it appears that, as a nation becomes highly industrialized and committed to a system of interregional commerce and industry, its economic activities tend to be located with reference to large urban centers, or metropolises, as well as to natural resources and available raw materials. The specific forces and factors that produce a concentration of population and economic activities in metropolitan centers and distribute the remainder in a metropolitan hinterland have not been measured or studied in detail. Among its advantages are, one may say tentatively, low transportation costs, a concentrated market, a joint location for several industries, a large and varied labor supply, a large and varied supply of employment opportunities, and the opportunity for wholesalers and manfacturers to assemble a wide range of items. Also, business management tends to locate sales offices and its home office in large centers to have ready access to other business management, financial institutions, and good trans-

This article is an excerpt from "Urbanism in the United States, 1950," which originally appeared in *The American Journal of Sociology,* Vol. 60 (March, 1955), pp. 471-486. It is used with the permission of the author, *The American Journal of Sociology,* and the University of Chicago Press. (Copyright, 1955, by the University of Chicago.)

portation and communication facilities. The term "dominance" has been used as a class name to refer to the combined force of these factors in determining location. New economic units seeking to establish themselves, or old ones seeking to expand their activities, find that these forces are integral parts of the environment over which they have no control and to which they must adjust. Since they emanate from the metropolis and tend to locate activities with respect to the latter, large metropolitan centers are said to be dominant in determining the distribution of population and economic activities. Not an insignificant aspect of the dominant role of the metropolitan centers is the fact that medium-size and small cities, as well as dispersed rural populations, appear to perform their functions with reference to the metropolitan centers, while they themselves exert a more limited and integrative influence upon the territory about them. Thus metropolitan centers are dominant conditioners of the physical environment in the modern industrial-commercial society, while the smaller urban places are subdominant environmental conditioners.

A most familiar aspect of metropolitan dominance is the fact that a large territory outside of the metropolis is directly under the influence of the metropolitan center. This territory corresponds approximately to what one would regard as the combined labor market and retail trade area of the metropolis. Since transportation facilities now make it possible to live several miles distant from the place of work, a broad ring outside the urban fringe but adjacent to it is growing rapidly. A high proportion of the population in this ring is rural-nonfarm. Many new factories and other business establishments are locating themselves there. Even the rural-farm population in this zone differs from the farm population elsewhere, for there are numerous residential farms, part-time farms, and specialized farms. After all these aspects are considered, it is evident that the economic and social entity that may be termed "the metropolis and its immediate environs" or "metropolitan area" is much greater in scope than either the central city or even the urbanized area.

In order to provide separate statistics for these areas under direct and daily metropolitan influence, the Bureau of the Census recognized, at the 1950 census, 168 large population clusters that were termed "standard metropolitan areas." They consist of whole counties. In brief, a standard metropolitan area consists of the county containing a central city of 50,000 or more inhabitants plus any adjacent counties that also appear to be metropolitan in character and socially and economically integrated with the central city.[1] The delimitation of standard metropolitan areas was made with the co-operation of several agencies of the federal government. It is based upon a great amount of research, inquiry, and consultation with local authorities. Like the new urban and rural definitions, the use of standard metropolitan areas as statistical areas was an innovation of the 1950 census. However, by combining county statistics from each census since 1900, a recent monograph carries the standard metropolitan area definition back to cover the last half-century of population growth.[2] In order to accomplish this, 16 of the standard metropolitan areas of New England, which had been delimited along town lines by the Bureau of the Census, were redelimited along county lines. In some instances two or more New England standard metropolitan areas fall in the same county. For this reason it was necessary to combine some S.M.A.'s (the common abbreviation) while forming the county equivalent areas. This reduced the total number of S.M.A.'s to 162. The S.M.A. definition was extended to earlier censuses only for "principal S.M.A.'s," those with 100,000 or more total population at a given census. Tables 4 and 5 present data for the S.M.A.'s as thus modified for the half-century, 1900-1950.

Table 1—Growth Data for Standard Metropolitan Areas, Retrojected to Earlier Censuses, 1900-1950

Census Year	Number of S.M.A.'s	Population (millions)	Per Cent of U.S. Population	Rate of Growth During Preceding Decade			Per Cent of Total U.S. Population Growth Claimed by S.M.A.'s During Preceding Decade
				U.S. Total	Standard Metropolitan Areas	Nonmetropolitan Areas	
All S.M.A.'s, 1950	162	85.6	56.8	14.5	21.8	6.0	80.6
Principal S.M.A.'s:							
1950	147	84.3	56.0	14.5	21.8	6.3	79.3
1940	125	67.1	51.1	7.2	8.3	6.2	57.7
1930	115	61.0	49.8	16.1	27.0	7.1	76.2
1920	94	46.1	43.7	14.9	25.2	8.1	67.6
1910	71	34.5	37.6	21.0	32.6	15.0	53.1
1900	52	24.1	31.9	20.7	..	..	..

Source: Bogue, *Population Growth in Standard Metropolitan Areas, 1900-1950* (Washington, D.C., 1953).

In 1950, 56.8 per cent of the population of the United States lived in the 162 S.M.A.'s. These areas covered only 7.1 per cent of the total land area of the nation. Thus, considerably more than one-half of the total population was concentrated in one-fourteenth of the land area.

In the past half-century there has been a trend toward an increase in the number of S.M.A.'s and toward a rising proportion of the total population residing in the areas. The record of this trend is contained in Table 4. Had the S.M.A. delimitation been in effect in 1900, there would have been an estimated 52 areas. They would have contained less than one-third of the total population. At each succeeding census from 10 to 23 new S.M.A.'s would have been added. This, together

Table II—Growth Data for Central Cities and Rings of Standard Metropolitan Areas, Retrojected to Earlier Censuses, 1900-1950

Census Year	Number of S.M.A.'s	Per Cent of U.S. Population		Rate of Growth During Preceding Decade			Per Cent of Total U.S. Population Growth Claimed by S.M.A.'s During Preceding Decade	
		Central Cities	Rings	Metropolitan Areas, Total	Central Cities	Rings	Central Cities	Rings
All S.M.A.'s, 1950	162	32.8	24.0	21.8	13.9	34.7	31.6	49.0
Principal S.M.A.'s:								
1950	147	32.3	23.8	21.8	13.7	34.8	30.7	48.6
1940	125	31.6	19.5	8.3	5.1	13.8	22.8	34.9
1930	115	31.8	18.0	27.0	23.3	34.2	43.3	32.9
1920	94	28.9	14.8	25.2	26.7	22.4	46.8	20.8
1910	71	25.0	12.7	32.6	35.3	27.6	37.4	15.7
1900	52	21.2	10.7	. .	. .	. .	. .	. .

Source: Bogue, *Population Growth in Standard Metropolitan Areas, 1900-1950* (Washington, D.C., 1953).

with the better than average growth rate of S.M.A.'s already defined for earlier censuses, results in a steady rise in the proportion of the total United States population living in metropolitan areas. During every decade except one, the S.M.A.'s as defined for a particular time have grown 50 per cent faster than nonmetropolitan areas and have claimed a disproportionately large share of the total national growth. The band lying outside the central city but within the S.M.A. is generally termed the "metropolitan ring." During the 1900-1910 and the 1910-20 decades, central cities were growing faster than their rings. However, in each decade since 1920, rings have been growing faster than the central cities. Early in the present century, rings had only about one-ninth of the population of the nation; they now have about one-fourth of the national population. Between 1900 and 1910 the rings claimed only about one-sixth of the total national population growth; in 1940-50 they claimed almost one-half. The gap between the growth rate of central cities and the growth rate of rings has become very large; between 1940 and 1950 rings grew almost two and one-half times as fast as central cities. This rapid growth is not confined to the band lying immediately outside the central city (the urban fringe). It is characteristic of a much broader area, much of which has a fairly low population density at the present. (The new urban definition excludes much of the area of the periphery of the city where new growth will occur during succeeding decades.)

To summarize: The larger metropolitan centers are poles to which a very large share of the new population and economic growth are attracted. The sphere of this growth-stimulating influence is quite large. The number of metropolitan centers which exert such an influence is increasing. Meanwhile, except for a few isolated centers that will eventually become metropolitan centers, most of the non-metropolitan territory grows much more slowly. The progressive urbanization of the population has been, from one point of view, a progressive metropolitanization of the population.

FOOTNOTES

1. For the full definition, including rules for determining whether adjacent counties are integrated, see U.S. Bureau of the Census, *United States Census of Population: 1950,* Vol. I: *Number of Inhabitants, U.S. Summary,* pp. xxxi-xxxiii.
2. Donald J. Bogue, *Population Growth in Standard Metropolitan Areas, 1900-1950, with an Explanatory Analysis of Urbanized Areas* (Washington, D.C.: Housing and Home Finance Agency, 1953).

Leo F. Schnore

University of California

THE GROWTH OF
METROPOLITAN SUBURBS

Decentralization is clearly one of the most significant movements in the long history of urban communities. In the United States, the shift to the suburbs began around a few large cities toward the close of the nineteenth century, but it is no longer confined to a mere handful of super-cities.[1] As time has passed, the outward thrust of urban population has become increasingly characteristic of smaller and smaller places, and there is still no indication that the movement is abating.

Fortunately, social scientists have charted the major trends involved in this suburban revolution during recent decades. The careful historical studies by Thompson, Bogue, and Hawley have shown the outstanding shifts in population that have occurred from the turn of the century to the most recent census.[2] They show the principal patterns of growth in the major geographic components of the metropolitan areas as a whole, and though they concentrate on comparisons *between* the central city and its surrounding ring, they also show patterns of re-distribution *within* these broad areas. They report, for example, the growth differentials that have been developed between urban and rural parts of the ring, between outlying places of different size, and between various distance zones both inside and outside central cities.

Within the framework provided by these extensive studies of de-

Reprinted from *American Sociological Review,* Vol. 22 (April 1957) pp. 165-173, by permission of the author and *American Sociological Review.*

26

centralization, two principal tasks appear to remain: (1) intensive research filling in the *descriptive* details of the suburban movement, and (2) refinement of a general theory making greater *analytical* sense out of the facts assembled. This report is part of a larger study undertaken in accordance with these broad objectives.

On the *descriptive* side, this report has a narrow focus. Growth rates for a single decade (1940-1950) are shown for only the larger incorporated places (10,000 and over) lying within the rings of the Standard Metropolitan Areas of the United States.[3] On the *conceptual* side, however, this paper has a broader scope, for it explores the relationship between the growth and the functions of these larger suburbs. This effort requires a brief re-examination of existing urban theory, insofar as these two variables are discussed.

The Functions of Urban Areas

Theoretically, urban areas are usually conceived as large and dense concentrations of people engaged in certain non-agricultural functions, notably commerce, manufacturing, and transportation. Moreover, such areas are themselves considered as expressions of functional interdependence, for by their very nature they cannot be functionally self-sufficient. Every urban area must produce some goods and/or services for exchange, i.e., for consumption by another population. It is clearly recognized that urban areas differ widely in the major functions that they discharge, and the literature contains a large number of urban typologies, in which places are classified according to "economic base," "major industry," or "principal export." [4]

Internally, however, every urban area must maintain a substantial complement of persons employed in the ancillary activities that provide for the requirements of the inhabitants directly engaged in its major industries. Thus no matter what the principal export it produces, any urban area is also necessarily a center of consumption. Recognition of this fact has given rise to a further distinction between urban functions. As Mayer notes, "Studies of the urban economic base in recent years have established the principles that not all functions are equally significant, and that functions may be classified as *basic* and *non-basic*. Functions found to be basic to the economy of a city are functions performed for people outside that city. . . . Non-basic industries are industries whose entire product is consumed inside the city." [5]

However, a functional description in these terms provides only a *static* picture. The study of urban population growth clearly requires a more dynamic frame of reference.

Urban Population Growth

Population can grow by either natural increase or net migration, but the latter component has served as the major source of over-all urban growth in the past. As a result, the literature on urban growth has understandably stressed migration.

The usual treatment of free migration within a money economy hinges upon the presumed operation of *"the push and pull of economic opportunities."* Relative differences in the spatial distribution of these opportunities are thought to be the major influences operating to bring about changes in population distribution, by determining the size and the direction of migrant streams. The whole rural-to-urban movement of modern times is usually portrayed as the result of a relative shift of economic opportunities, with deficits in rural areas and expansion in urban areas. Statistical studies of whole regions and nations have been conducted within this conceptual framework. In addition, case studies of the growth or decline of individual places are commonly drawn along similar lines, with the upsurge of "boom towns" and the demise of "ghost towns" as contrasting cases in point.

Moreover, existing urban theory holds that population growth and the major functions of a given area are definitely related. Urban population is assumed to have a functional base, for the very support of the population of a particular place is thought to depend upon its participation in an extensive set of exchange relationships. Population growth requires an increase in this participation, with a corresponding expansion of economic opportunities.[6]

In this theoretical context, a number of writers have recently spoken of a so-called "multiplier principle" to describe the dynamics of urban population growth. Stated in simplified form, the principle is that (1) increasing economic opportunities in "basic" industries cause population growth; (2) population growth, in turn, causes further increases in employment opportunities—this time in the "nonbasic" industries—so that (3) still further increments are added to the total population of the area.[7]

On the whole, it appears that the available theory offers an unusually coherent set of hypotheses regarding urban population growth. Urban growth is related to urban functions in a remarkably clear-cut fashion. Moreover, empirical studies of large areal units have indicated a high degree of predictive power of this conceptual approach.[8]

Suburbs, however, pose a different problem when it comes to population growth. The relationships between growth and functions—as they are stated for urban areas in general—are not immediately evident when suburbs are examined. Let us briefly consider the functions of suburbs and then turn to the matter of their growth.

The Functions of Suburbs

Suburbs obviously differ widely in the functions that they discharge. It is true that the traditional popular image of the suburb tends to make it exclusively an area of residence. Lying within the commuting zone, the typical suburb is thought to be little more than the dwelling place of people who work in the central city. While it is correct to characterize many suburbs as literally "dormitory towns" and "bedroom cities" it is an error to conceive all suburbs in this way.

A true picture of metropolitan suburbs must not ignore the fact that many of them are far from exclusively residential areas. A number of them are primarily devoted to the fabrication of manufactured goods. At the present time, for example, both light and heavy industries are the dominant elements in the functioning of some suburbs in every part of the country. Industrial suburbs, in fact, have a long history.[9] Still other suburbs are basically given over to the provision of specialized services of one kind or another—notably education and recreation—and it is even possible to find suburbs which are primarily dependent upon extractive industries, such as mining and oil production. In an economic sense, then, it appears that the range of specialties found among suburbs approaches that discoverable in other cities.

Despite this wide variation in specific functions, however, a strong case has been made in the literature for the recognition of only two major types—*"industrial"* and *"residential."* Douglass, an observer of an earlier phase of suburban development, saw these as the two types most apparent in the 'twenties.[10] Moreover, this view was also adopted by Harris, despite the fact that he developed a detailed six-part suburban typology. "The commonest types of suburb," he wrote in 1943, "are *housing* or *dormitory* suburbs and *manufacturing* or *industrial* suburbs." [11]

More generally, suburbs can be identified as *"residential"* and *"employing,"* by combining centers of employment mainly devoted to education, mining, recreation, etc. with those concentrating in manufacturing as such. Such places can be called *"employing suburbs"* no matter what their specific product may be, and they can be clearly contrasted with *"residential suburbs,"* which employ relatively few people within their own boundaries. The basis of this distinction is exceedingly simple: whether or not the suburb tends to attract more workers to its confines every day than the number of working people who sleep there every night. These two types of suburb are "attracting" and "dispersing" areas, reflecting the shift between day-time and night-time population.[12]

Suburban Population Growth

With respect to population growth, existing theory would hold that both types of suburb—like other urban areas—grow primarily in response to an expansion of employment opportunities, particularly in the so-called "basic" industries. On theoretical grounds, however, they would not be expected to grow equally. Since the employing suburb has a net excess of jobs, it clearly offers more economic opportunities, and it should logically exhibit higher rates of growth than the residential suburb. Let us examine the available data regarding growth differentials between these two major types.

Findings. The only immediately relevant findings from prior research are to be found in a study by Harris, where growth rates between 1930 and 1940 were reported for the suburbs in eleven large Metropolitan Districts. "Among individual suburbs of more than 10,000 population," according to Harris, "those classified as residential average 11.7 per cent increase in population, compared to 1.7 per cent for those classified as industrial." [13]

In the present study, a similar differential was found for the 1940-1950 decade. The rate for all residential suburbs (31.9 per cent) was almost twice that for all employing suburbs (17.0 per cent). Although this differential is not as large as that reported by Harris, it is in the same direction, i.e., in favor of the residential suburb.

Moreover, this differential tends to persist when other relevant factors are held constant. The limited number of cases prohibits simultaneous control in a cross-tabular format, but successive controls can be applied.[14]

Horizontal examination of Table 1 shows that residential suburbs tended to grow faster than employing suburbs in all regions (Panel A), in all central city size classes (Panel B), in all suburban size classes (Panel C), in all concentric distance zones (Panel D), and in metropolitan areas of every major type of economic activity.

Moreover, only a slight exception appears in Panel F, where the prevailing differential is reversed in one of the three rental classes, i.e., among high-rent suburbs. The only major reversal is found in Panel G, where suburbs are classified according to their dates of incorporation. The differential in favor of residential suburbs is seen to characterize only the older suburbs, i.e., those incorporated before 1900.[15]

Interpretation

These data are very difficult to interpret in terms of economic opportunities. On first examination, the growth rates of *employing* suburbs in the past two decades might appear to support the theory. The very low average rate of growth between 1930 and 1940 can be viewed as nothing more than the result of the severe limitations on manufacturing activity that occurred during this depression decade. In turn, the resumption of substantial industrial activity between 1940 and 1950 might seem to account for the ten-fold increase in growth rates in this type of suburb.

By definition, the employing suburb does offer economic opportunities, since it provides jobs for more than the number of local residents who are employed. Still, the subordinate status of many employing suburbs prevents them from enjoying full autonomy with respect to growth. For example, employing suburbs which provide goods and services primarily for the central city are necessarily sensitive to events occurring there, such as changes in the number of inhabitants of the metropolis, or changes in its income level. At best, then, the theory appears to offer an incomplete explanation of growth in employing suburbs.

However, if the existing theory of urban growth meets resistance in the case of employing suburbs, *residential* suburbs are even less

Table 1—Growth Rates in Metropolitan Suburbs of 10,000 or More Inhabitants, by Functional Type and Other Characteristics

Selected characteristics of metropolitan suburbs	Per Cent Increase in Population, 1940-50			Number of Suburbs		
	Residential	Employing	All suburbs	Residential	Employing	All suburbs
A. REGIONAL LOCATION						
Northeast	13.3	6.1	8.1	65	110	175
North Central	30.0	17.1	22.8	65	57	122
West	63.6	47.1	53.1	37	43	80
South	77.4	47.4	60.4	20	19	39
B. CENTRAL CITY SIZE						
500,000 or more	27.8	12.4	18.2	136	142	278
100,000-500,000	36.1	13.8	21.6	32	40	72
Less than 100,000	79.5	36.9	42.9	19	47	66
C. SUBURBAN SIZE						
50,000 or more	15.1	10.0	11.5	17	31	48
25,000-50,000	18.8	14.9	15.8	18	55	73
10,000-25,000	30.9	19.1	24.4	90	102	192
Less than 10,000	104.1	92.6	99.3	62	41	103
D. DISTANCE FROM CENTRAL CITY						
0-10 miles	27.2	16.4	20.8	112	92	204
10-20 miles	40.8	18.2	25.3	61	84	145
20-/miles	29.4	15.9	18.1	14	53	67

E. METROPOLITAN AREA ECONOMIC BASE						
Manufacturing	23.6	12.2	16.1	79	105	184
Diversified	33.0	19.3	23.9	89	98	187
Retail	68.9	23.4	39.2	17	23	40
Other	412.7	64.8	103.4	2	3	5
F. SUBURBAN RENT LEVEL						
Low	31.7	12.8	15.9	7	26	33
Average	29.0	15.1	18.8	91	173	264
High	36.3	44.1	38.4	89	30	119
G. AGE OF SUBURB						
More than 50 years	21.8	12.2	15.0	102	178	280
40-50 years	33.1	36.2	34.6	35	31	66
30-40 years	51.8	66.2	57.5	25	12	37
Less than 30 years	116.6	168.5	126.6	25	8	33
ALL SUBURBS	31.9	17.0	22.1	187	229	416

amenable to it. The higher average rates of growth in these suburbs during both of the last two decades can hardly be attributed to an expansion of economic opportunities. It must be remembered that the residential suburb itself employs relatively few people within its own confines, and these chiefly in such "non-basic" activities as retail trade and services. As indicated above, increases in these "non-basic" employment opportunities are commonly treated, within the very framework of the theory, as *themselves* dependent upon local population growth.

More important, residential suburbs are intrinsically dependent upon other areas. With respect to population growth, almost nothing that can occur within the boundaries of such a suburb is potentially as significant as changes that may occur in the other areas that employ its residents. In the light of these considerations, existing theory obviously falls far short of explaining over-all suburban growth, and it fails entirely to account for growth differentials between types of suburbs.

Limitations of Existing Theory

Why should the available theory offer so much in explaining growth differentials between large areas (e.g., regions) and simultaneously fail to explain growth differentials between suburbs? The first major difficulty encountered by the theory in the case of suburbs stems from the fact that these places are only parts of a larger functional entity, the metropolitan community. The theory of economic opportunities appears to contain a hidden assumption with respect to functional self-containment. As a result, the theory can only be valid for areal units which possess a rather high degree of self-sufficiency. This is apparently the reason for the theory's great explanatory utility in the studies of whole regions and even nations.

Moreover, the theory does not take full account of the increasing flexibility of local transportation in recent decades. Innovations in transportation and communication have permitted community functions to be diffused over a wider territory, and this spatial spread involves an increasing flow of persons between the sites of their various activities. The significance of commuting for population growth is that it may supplant migration as an adjustment on the part of the local labor force to shifting or declining opportunities for employment. As a consequence, residential areas may continue to grow as long as employment opportunities continue to expand anywhere within an extremely broad commuting radius.[16]

It can hardly be said that transportation improvements have been ignored in urban theory. They have received some attention in most discussions of decentralization found in the literature. These innovations, however, have been conceived as little more than permissive factors. They are generally said to have set the conditions under which suburban growth could occur. Other factors are undoubtedly at work, but these other factors are increasingly sought in a rather narrow sphere.

Most analysts who have devoted attention to the subject of suburbanization have apparently assumed that the causes of the centrifugal shift are ultimately to be found in the motives of the individual involved in the movement. Even the human ecologists, who are often thought to be "anti-psychological," are prone to shift to motivational explanations when it comes to suburbanization. In keeping with a general tendency within our discipline, social psychology is coming to supplant the sociological approach in this problem area.

Thus while stressing the key role of economic opportunities for larger units, such as regions, most writers turn to an analysis of the motives of individual migrants in dealing with decentralization within local areas. Such a procedure rests upon the tacit assumption that explanations of growth in areas of different size must somehow require entirely different approaches, involving different units of analysis and a different range of variables.

It might appear that the evidence presented here offers additional support for such a procedure. After all, the theory—as it has been stated for urban areas in general—clearly fails to account for the observed growth differential in favor of residential suburbs. These results might seem to call for an immediate shift to a social-psychological approach. Indeed, the ultimate explanation may very well lie in the attitudes, motives, values, etc. of the individuals involved in this movement. However, there is a theoretical alternative at least worthy of exploration. The admitted weaknesses of the existing theory might better be resolved—not by its total rejection or abandonment—but by modification of certain concepts that are basic to the theory.

A Proposed Modification of the Theory

The first step in this direction is to state the conditions under which factors other than narrowly defined economic opportunities might be important in the determination of growth differentials. Rather than abandoning the concept of opportunities entirely, a logical alternative is to expand it to subsume more than merely employment. But what additional content is to be included?

One consideration so fundamental that it is easily overlooked is that the population of any area must have housing and the related amenities of life. Our attention is drawn to the housing factor for a very simple reason: dwelling units must exist in a given area before people can be enumerated there on a *de jure* basis, and before population growth can be registered in census statistics.

If the concept of opportunities is broadened to include opportunities for housing, we can propose the following general hypothesis: *within local areas of the metropolitan community, differential population growth is primarily determined by the distribution of differential housing opportunities, and especially by the different patterns of building activity evidenced in various sub-areas.*[17] Within this theoretical context, in which emphasis is placed upon *housing opportunities*, it is possible to develop specific sub-hypotheses regarding growth differentials between types of suburb. (1) *Residential suburbs are growing rapidly because they are becoming even more residential in character, by means of large increments in housing construction.* At the same time, (2) *employing suburbs are growing less rapidly because they are becoming more exclusively devoted to industry and other employment-providing activities.* In these employing places, the net effect of this increased specialization in production and employment is to (a) drive out pre-existent residential uses of land, and (b) to discourage new construction of housing.

Although still to be tested, some indirect evidence in support of these hypotheses can be adduced by considering central cities themselves. The typical central city is obviously undergoing a conversion to a different range of land uses. Formerly the principal place of residence of its own labor force, it is now being turned over to alternative uses—commerce, industry, and transportation. The concomitant of this trend in land-use conversion is the outward shift of population that is reflected in the growth differentials in favor of the metropolitan ring.

As to suburbs, the established employing suburbs appear to be undergoing the very same process of land-use conversion. Thus the oldest employing suburbs themselves are evidently decentralizing at a fairly rapid pace, with only their rates of natural increase preventing most of them from suffering absolute losses in population. In fact, the older employing suburbs are probably losing large numbers directly to the residential suburbs via migration.[18]

The Role of Housing

The hypotheses stated above assert that differential housing opportunities are the major determinants of growth differentials between sub-areas of the metropolitan community. In the interests of complete analysis, of course, we must go on to ask *why* new housing construction is occurring *where* it is, since we are dealing with growth in different types of area.

Here again a social-psychological approach might seem to be in order, since it is obviously individuals who occupy dwellings and who change residences. But it should be pointed out that relatively few people in any metropolitan area choose a site and then have a house "built to order." On the contrary, the typical purchase in this type of area is "ready-made" and it is found in a large development. Very few urbanites have any hand in the selection of sites where residential construction will take place, and control over location is even more limited in the case of renters.

In a complex economy, the function of construction is given over to specialists. The "choices" of building sites are made by contractors, real estate operators, and others, notably those involved in the initial capitalization of new developments. As Form has pointed out,

> "In general, resident groupings do not play dynamic roles in chang-
> ing urban land use ... Their position is tangential ... Most of their
> decisions on where to buy, when to buy, and what land to buy are
> fitted into an administered land market and are not, as many would
> assume, individual, discrete, free, and unrelated." [19]

Thus families and individuals are not decisive agents in the process of land-use conversion. When asked about their residential movements, the "reasons" they offer to an interviewer may be misleading in the extreme.

Individuals and families live where housing is available, and this is usually a matter that is beyond their immediate control. Like other "choices" the housing decisions of individuals are strictly limited by objective conditions. Among these objective conditions, which include the timing and the placing of available housing facilities, the *location* of dwelling units will continue to receive emphasis here, since we are dealing with growth differentials between types of area. Once again it will be instructive to consider the case of the metropolis itself.[20]

The existing literature contains a number of hypotheses that attempt to account for the rapid expansion of residential construction in the metropolitan ring as a whole, and the limited building activity within the central city. First of all, high rates of construction in the periphery may simply be a consequence of *the exhaustion of space for residential development* in the central city. There is undoubtedly some merit to this view, but sheer space alone is hardly decisive, since the percentage of vacant land in most large cities is strikingly high.[21] However, a large proportion of this area is unsuitable for residential development, for reasons of cost, location, or prohibitive zoning laws. Among these, it seems probable that *the high cost of land* in the central city is particularly significant, acting as a deterrent to residential use.

Less frequently mentioned, but a matter of increasing importance, is the fact that great economies are made possible by the *mass production of housing*. While vacant land within the city itself is considerable in the aggregate, it tends to be split into a multitude of small parcels. The increasing use of mass production methods in constructing dozens or even hundreds of dwelling units at the same time and in the same contiguous area permits large savings to be made by the builders, with mass buying of materials adding still further savings. The possible importance of large tracts of vacant and cheap land is itself suggested by the fact that the very highest rates of growth in the metropolitan area between 1940 and 1950 were registered in unincorporated rural territory.

However, purely "spatial" or "economic" considerations are not the only factors operating to determine the sites of housing. There is also an important *sociological* factor. It appears that the locations of the dominant units in the community set the broad pattern of land use for smaller and less powerful units, such as households.[22] In one sense, this is nothing more than another expression of the relationships we have already observed between (1) "basic" industries, (2) residential population, and (3) "non-basic" industries. Basic industries locate at particular sites, with the residential population taking up positions with reference to these centers of production and employment. The distribution of residential population, in turn, is the prime determinant of the location of such "non-basic" activities as retail trade and services.

At any rate, the re-distribution of residential population is a problem that must be viewed in a context that recognizes the vital influence of these other factors. The urban household operates within a spatial field that is narrowly limited, and within an economic sphere that is closely circumscribed, as far as housing opportunities are concerned. This is especially true in times and places in which there is high aggregate demand for housing, but some limitations are always present by virtue of the costs involved, and by virtue of the locational priorities exercised by the dominant units in the community.

Conclusions and Implications

If the hypotheses set forth here have any validity, one important theoretical conclusion is in order. The metropolitan community must be undergoing a process of increasingly specialized land use, in which sub-areas of the community are devoted more and more exclusively to a limited range of functions.[23] The result of this mounting "territorial differentiation" is an increasingly *segregated* pattern, in which similar units and similar functions cluster together. At the very least, there is a real bifurcation between the broad functions of consumption and production, i.e., between residence and employment, home and work. Thus the real significance of transportation improvements for local re-distribution of population is in creating a new scale of distance. *In this context, the growth differentials discussed here may be interpreted as mere reflections of a fundamental alteration of community organization in the direction of greater functional and territorial complexity.*

Technological and organizational changes are apparently crucial in determining both numerical and distributional changes in population. The outward shift of residential population measured in recent studies can be viewed as one aspect of an important modification in the internal organization of the modern urban community. Under the impetus of technological advances in transportation and communication, the compact city is a thing of the past. Increasing territorial differentiation has been made possible by the increased flexibility of movement within the total community. Urban functions and urban populations are now spread over a greatly expanded area. Such a radical change in the spatial distribution of urban functions—and urban people—apparently represents an adaptive response to the changing conditions of modern urban life. In long-range terms, decentralization can be conceived as a shift toward a new equilibrium that was initiated by the development of new facilities for the movement of persons, commodities, and information.

At any rate, it seems clear that these technological and organizational trends must be kept in the forefront of any analysis of growth differentials within the total community. The subordinate status of the modern suburb means that significant modifications must be made in the existing body of concepts relating to urban population growth and re-distribution if they are to be useful in the analysis of local areas. The growth of suburbs, which are merely parts of a larger functional entity, must be interpreted in the context of the whole metropolitan community.

The existing body of urban theory fails to explain growth differentials between sub-areas. Although admittedly a mundane consideration, the simple matter of housing availability appears to be a factor that is important enough to warrant theoretical attention. The role of differentially distributed housing opportunities appears to be crucial in bringing about differential growth patterns within the various parts of the metropolitan community. With this qualification, it appears that the general framework offered by existing theory need not be abandoned in its entirety, for it can be useful in explaining residential mobility and its contribution to population growth differentials within local areas.[24]

These considerations merely point up the fact that we need a *total* theory, subsuming all of the constituent functional units making up the modern urban community. Moreover, such a theory should be capable of generating testable hypotheses referring to dynamic as well as static relationships between variables. Population growth and re-distribution, land-use conversion, technological innovations, organizational changes in the direction of greater specialization, differentiation, and segregation—all of these are terms referring to *processes* taking place over time. Any sound conceptual approach must be phrased in dynamic terms such as these, if for no other reason than that the modern urban community is constantly changing.

This matter is of practical concern as well as theoretical interest. As Bogue has recently asserted, "One of the reasons for the existence of such strong disagreements and conflicting recommendations about so-called 'decentralization' is that specialists in the field of urban population and human ecology have failed to produce a theory of urban growth that is valid for the mid-20th century. Perhaps we have been overly concerned with perfecting a static theory of city structure... Our study of structure needs to be accompanied by a rigorous program of research into growth and change. Research in urbanism and metropolitanism should have dynamic as well as static aspects." [25]

The present writer can only agree with these ambitious goals, and hope that the discussion contained in this paper will contribute to their ultimate achievement.

FOOTNOTES

1. Adna F. Weber, *The Growth of Cities in the Nineteenth Century*, New York: Columbia University Press, 1899.
2. Warren S. Thompson, *The Growth of Metropolitan Districts in the United States, 1900-1940*, Washington: Government Printing Office, 1947; Donald J. Bogue, *Population Growth in Standard Metropolitan Areas, 1900-1950*, Washington: Government Printing Office, 1953; Amos H. Hawley, *The Changing Shape of Metropolitan America*, Glencoe: Free Press, 1956.
3. Among the 168 Standard Metropolitan Areas defined in the 1950 Census, only 66 contain incorporated suburbs of 10,000 or more inhabitants. Among those with more than one officially-designated central city, only the largest place is treated as the central city in this study, with all other places classified as suburbs. Exceptions to this procedure were made in the case of three areas (Allentown-Bethlehem, Pa., Minneapolis-St. Paul, Minn., and Springfield-Holyoke, Mass.) where twin central cities were recognized.
4. See the references cited in Leo F. Schnore, "The Functions of Metropolitan Suburbs," *American Journal of Sociology*, 61 (March, 1956), pp. 453-458.
5. Harold M. Mayer, "What We Need to Know About the Internal Structure of Cities and Metropolitan Areas," in Donald J. Bogue (editor), *Needed Urban and Metropolitan Research*, Oxford, Ohio: Scripps Foundation for Research in Population Problems, 1953, p. 12. See also Otis Dudley Duncan

and Albert J. Reiss, Jr., Part IV, "Functional Specialization of Communities," in their *Social Characteristics of Urban and Rural Communities, 1950*, New York: John Wiley, 1956; and John W. Alexander, "The Basic-Nonbasic Concept of Urban Economic Functions," *Economic Geography*, 30 (July, 1954), pp. 246-261.

6. Amos H. Hawley, *Human Ecology*, New York: Ronald Press, 1950.

7. For a detailed discussion and further references see John R. P. Friedmann, *The Spatial Structure of Economic Development in the Tennessee Valley*, Chicago: University of Chicago Program of Education and Research in Planning, Research Paper No. 1, 1955.

8. See Harry Jerome, *Migration and Business Cycles*, New York: National Bureau of Economic Research, 1926; and Dorothy S. Thomas, *Social and Economic Aspects of Swedish Population Movements, 1750-1933*, New York: Macmillan Company, 1941.

9. Graham R. Taylor, *Satellite Cities*, New York and London: D. Appleton and Company, 1915.

10. Harlan Paul Douglass, *The Suburban Trend*, New York and London: Century Company, 1925, and "Suburbs," in *The Encyclopaedia of the Social Sciences*, New York: Macmillan Company, 1934, 14, pp. 433-435.

11. Chauncy D. Harris, "Suburbs," *American Journal of Sociology*, 49 (May, 1943), p. 6; italics added.

12. This dichotomy is based upon the "employment-residence ratio" computed by Jones for all places of 10,000 or more inhabitants in 1950. It is simply the ratio of (1) *the number of people employed in the suburb in* (a) manufacturing, (b) retail trade, (c) wholesale trade, and (d) personal, business, and repair services to (2) *the number of employed residents of the suburb*, and it is computed by the formula: (1) ÷ (2) × 100. The suburbs identified as *employing* centers in this study have a ratio of 85 or above, with all suburbs having a lower ratio classified as *residential* centers. Source: Victor Jones, "Economic Classification of Cities and Metropolitan Areas," in *The Municipal Year Book, 1953*, Chicago: International City Managers' Association, 1953, pp. 49-57. These and the other data from the same source are used here with the kind permission of the publisher.

13. Harris, *op. cit.*, pp. 10-11.

14. The definitions of the control variables are as follows: (A) The *regional* delineation used here is the one developed by the U.S. Bureau of the Census. (B-C) *Size* classifications are according to the number of inhabitants in 1940, the beginning of the decade under study. (D) Each suburb's *distance* classification is based upon radial measurement between its approximate geographic center and the site of the city hall in the central city. (E) Each suburb is classified according to the *economic base* of the metropolitan area as a whole in 1950. The areas Jones has designated as "Mm" (manufacturing centers) are treated as *manufacturing* areas in this study. Areas classified by Jones as "M" (industrial centers) and "Mr" (diversified centers with manufacturing predominant) are here combined under the heading of *diversified* areas. Types "Rm" (diversified centers with retail trade pre-

dominant) and "Rr" (retail trade centers) are here labelled *retail* areas. All of the other types identified by Jones (mining, education, wholesale trade, government, transportation, and resort or retirement centers) are here combined in the residual *other* category. Space limitations preclude a listing of the detailed definitions of each type, which may be found in Jones, *op. cit.* (F) Median *rent levels* for the suburbs in 1950 are classified as follows: *Low*—five dollars or more below the median for the entire metropolitan area in which the suburb is located; *Average*—within a range of five dollars below to ten dollars above the median for the entire area; *High*—more than ten dollars above the median for the entire area. (Source: Jones, ibid.) (G) The *age* of the suburb is approximated by its date of incorporation.

15. A vertical examination of Table 1 suggests that growth rates are related to six out of the seven variables taken separately. These relationships merely serve here as *prima facie* evidence of the need for controlling these variables in the examination of growth differentials according to functional type.

16. See Kate K. Liepmann, *The Journey to Work,* New York: Oxford University Press, 1944.

17. Housing opportunities, of course, represented the operational definition used in Samuel Stouffer's well-known study, "Intervening Opportunities: A Theory Relating Mobility and Distance," *American Sociological Review,* 5 (December, 1940), pp. 845-857.

18. Space limitations preclude the discussion of fertility and mortality differentials between types of suburb that may contribute to the observed growth differentials.

19. William H. Form, "The Place of Social Structure in the Determination of Land Use," *Social Forces,* 32 (May, 1954), p. 319.

20. It may be objected that this presentation ignores the decision-making process among contractors and others who actually initiate housing construction. It is true that we are deliberately avoiding discussion of the social-psychological aspect of residential mobility and population redistribution in this paper. This procedure is used primarily in the interest of clarity of presentation, but there is also some justification for it on the grounds of theoretical parsimony. It seems preferable to hold the analysis to a single level of analysis. However, those who are interested in motivational aspects of decentralization might do well to begin exploring the motives of contractors, real estate operators and financiers, rather than concerning themselves exclusively with those of individual householders. All of the factors taken up below might be expected to receive careful consideration by those immediately involved in making decisions regarding the location of residential developments.

21. Harland Bartholomew, *Land Uses in American Cities,* Cambridge: Harvard University Press, 1955.

22. Hawley, *op. cit.,* pp. 276-286.

23. See Leslie Kish, "Differentiation in Metropolitan Areas," *American Sociological Review*, 19 (August, 1954), pp. 388-398.

24. An even more general modification requires the expansion of the concept to a broad notion of "opportunities for livelihood." Such a re-formulation is needed to make the theory—originally developed to describe the flow of migrants in a money economy—applicable to pre-industrial cultures lacking such an economic organization.

25. Bogue, *Needed Urban and Metropolitan Research, op. cit.*, p. 38.

Otis Dudley Duncan

Population Research and Training Center,
The University of Chicago

Albert J. Reiss, Jr.

Vanderbilt University

SUBURBS AND URBAN FRINGE

The concept of "suburb" has not been completely standardized in the research literature. Possibly one reason for this is that the Bureau of the Census has not provided an official definition of the concept, as it has for such concepts as "urban" and "rural." In the usage of most writers the term "suburb" appears to denote an urban place (usually an incorporated place) outside the corporate limits of a large city, but either adjacent thereto or near enough to be closely integrated into the economic life of the central city and within commuting distance of it. The criterion distinguishing a suburb from other territory on the city's periphery but within its corporate limits is, therefore, not economic or ecological, but political. There are even "suburbs," like Hamtramck and Highland Park in the Detroit (Mich.) Urbanized Area, which are completely enclosed by the central city.

In accordance with the conception of the suburb as a distinct political entity which is actually part of the economic city, many research workers have considered as suburbs those urban places which are within the limits of the metropolitan district but outside the central city or cities.[1] An analogous definition, more appropriate

Reprinted with permission from Otis D. Duncan and Albert J. Reiss, Jr., *Social Characteristics of Urban and Rural Communities, 1950* (New York, John Wiley & Sons, Inc., 1956) pp. 117-133, and the Social Science Research Council.

for use with the 1950 Census statistics, would classify as suburbs all places of 2,500 inhabitants or more within the urbanized area, but outside the central city or cities.

The 1950 Census uses the term "urban fringe" to denote all territory within urbanized areas but outside their central cities. This terminology is poorly chosen, because the term "fringe" has been applied heretofore to areas of mixed urban and rural types of settlement on the periphery of the well built-up urban area. But the "urban fringe" as defined in 1950 contains incorporated places as large as 250,000, and nearly half of the "urban-fringe" population (48.7 percent) resides in incorporated places of 10,000 or more, i.e., places generally designated as suburbs in previous research. Table 46 gives

Table 46—Distribution of the Population Inside Urbanized Areas Outside Central Cities, by Size of Place: 1950

Size of place	Number of places		Population (thousands)		Percent of total	
	Incorporated	Unincorporated [1]	Incorporated	Unincorporated [1]	Incorporated	Unincorporated [1]
Total	1,316	86	13,528	7,344	64.8	35.2
250,000 or more	1	. . .	251	. . .	1.2	. . .
100,000 to 250,000	10	1	1,234	135	5.9	0.6
50,000 to 100,000	37	2	2,562	142	12.3	0.7
25,000 to 50,000	71	21	2,495	718	11.9	3.4
10,000 to 25,000	231	36	3,629	577	17.4	2.8
5,000 to 10,000	268	13	1,893	89	9.1	0.4
2,500 to 5,000	241	13	886	57	4.2	0.3
Under 2,500	457	(2)	578	5,626	2.8	27.0

[1] Unincorporated places of 2,500 or more are those places designated as urban under special rules in 1940, and which remained unincorporated in 1950; the population given for these places is on the basis of the new urban definition.

[2] Places not separately identified.

Source: *1950 Census of Population*, Vol. II, *Characteristics of the Population*, Part 1, U. S. Summary, tables 3 and 5a.

a breakdown by size of place of the population inside urbanized areas but outside central cities, i.e., the "urban-fringe" category of the 1950 Census reports. Over three-fifths of this population (62.0 percent) is in incorporated places of 2,500 or more. An additional 8.2 percent is in unincorporated places of 2,500 or more which were designated as urban places under the special rules of the 1940 Census. Altogether at least seven-tenths of the census "urban-fringe" population lives in suburbs, rather than the "fringe," in any strict sense of the latter term. Actually, to include among "suburbs" the unincorporated places of 2,500 or more, which are not now separately identified, and incorporated places of 1,000 to 2,500 would raise the suburban proportion even higher. With some justification one might regard these places as small suburbs rather than as part of the fringe.

The term "urban fringe" will be used in this monograph to denote the nonsuburban population of the territory in urbanized areas outside central cities. Thus the urbanized area is conceived as having three components, central city or cities, suburbs, and urban fringe.[2] These three components account for 69.8, 21.2, and 9.0 percent respectively, of the total population in urbanized areas in 1950. Table 47 shows the composition of urbanized areas, by size of area. The central city component is substantially higher in the smaller than in the larger urbanized areas. Also, the relative magnitudes of the suburban and urban-fringe components vary by size of urbanized area. In the urbanized areas of 1 million or more about four-fifths of the non-central city population live in suburbs, compared with about three-fifths in the areas with under 250,000 inhabitants.

The analyses of this chapter compare population characteristics of central cities of urbanized areas with those of the portions of

Table 47—Central, Suburban, and Urban-Fringe Components of Urbanized Areas, by Size of Area: 1950

			Percent of total		
Size of area	Population	Total area	Central cities	Suburbs [1]	Urban fringe [2]
All urbanized areas	69,249,148	100.0	69.8	21.2	9.0
3,000,000 or more	21,213,879	100.0	67.1	26.1	6.8
1,000,000 to 3,000,000	16,603,189	100.0	60.7	31.9	7.4
250,000 to 1,000,000	17,427,511	100.0	74.8	15.4	9.8
Under 250,000	14,004,569	100.0	78.9	8.2	12.9

[1] Includes unincorporated places classified as urban under special rules in 1940 and all incorporated places of 2,500 inhabitants or more.

[2] Incorporated places of less than 2,500 and unincorporated territory except that classified as urban under special rules in 1940.

Source: Donald J. Bogue, *Population Growth in Standard Metropolitan Areas, 1900-1950, With an Explanatory Analysis of Urbanized Areas,* Government Printing Office, Washington, 1953, table 24.

urbanized areas outside central cities. The data are derived from the 3⅓-percent sample statistics of the "Characteristics by Size of Place" report used in Part I. Unfortunately, these statistics do not include a breakdown into suburban and urban-fringe components of the noncentral parts of urbanized areas. Hence these two categories are treated as a single group, referred to, for convenience, as "suburbs"; but it must be borne in mind that it includes a substantial population living outside suburbs, as that term is more conventionally used.

Age and Sex Composition

In all urbanized areas combined the sex ratio is 94.0, indicating a substantial excess of females in their population. As a whole, central cities have relatively more females than do suburbs; the respective sex ratios are 93.5 and 95.1. This difference reflects only slightly the disproportionate numbers of Armed Forces personnel in suburban areas. The sex ratios of the civilian population are 92.9 for all urbanized areas, 92.6 for central cities, and 93.8 for suburbs.

The sex ratio is lower in the central than in the suburban areas of each size group of urbanized areas, except the class of urbanized areas with more than 3 million inhabitants (table 48). The exception here is attributable entirely to the situation in the New York Urbanized Area, since both the Chicago and Los Angeles areas have slightly higher sex ratios in their suburbs than in the central cities.

On the average, the suburban population of urbanized areas is somewhat younger than the central city population. The median age in the central cities of all urbanized areas combined is 32.7 as compared with 30.9 for suburbs, a difference of 1.8 years. Such a difference appears for each of the size groups of urbanized areas (table 49). In fact, the smaller the urbanized area, the greater is the difference in median age between central city and suburbs.

Figure 15 shows population pyramids for the central city and suburban population of all urbanized areas combined. Although both graphs reveal the age-sex structure typical of the United States urban population in 1950, there are significant differences between them. As compared with the central city population, the suburban population has a substantial excess of persons aged 0 to 4 and 5 to 13, a slight excess of persons in the age intervals 14 to 19, 25 to 34, and

35 to 44, and relative deficiencies of persons in the interval 20 to 24, as well as in all age intervals above 45.

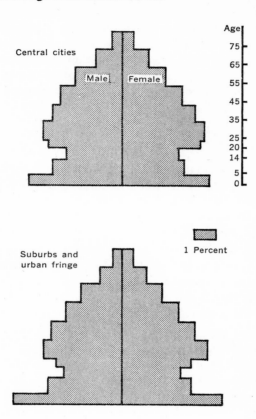

The age differences just noted are reflected as well in the higher fertility ratio of suburbs. In all central cities combined there are 452 children under 5 years of age per 1,000 women aged 20 to 44, as compared with 534 children per 1,000 women in the combined suburban population. The central and suburban parts of each of the four size groups of urbanized areas differ by about the same amount (table 50).

Dependency ratios are likewise higher in suburbs than in central cities. However, the differences are not great, since the suburban

excess of young persons is nearly balanced by the central city excess
of persons over 65. In the combined central cities there are 59 persons
under 20 and over 65 per 100 persons aged 20 to 64. The corresponding ratio for suburbs is 65, a difference of only 6 points. As

Table 48—Sex Ratio of the Population, for Central Cities and Suburbs of Urbanized Areas, by Size of Area: 1950

Size of area	Total area	Central cities	Suburbs and urban fringe
All urbanized areas	94.0	93.5	95.1
3,000,000 or more	94.0	94.2	93.5
1,000,000 to 3,000,000	94.3	93.8	95.0
250,000 to 1,000,000	94.0	93.3	96.0
Under 250,000	93.5	92.5	97.4

Source: 1950 Census of Population, Vol.
IV, Special Reports, Part 5, Chapter A,
Characteristics by Size of Place, table 1.

Table 49—Median Age of the Population, for Central Cities and Suburbs of Urbanized Areas, by Size of Area: 1950

Size of area	Total area	Central cities	Suburbs and urban fringe
All urbanized areas	32.2	32.7	30.9
3,000,000 or more	33.7	34.2	32.7
1,000,000 to 3,000,000	32.0	32.8	30.9
250,000 to 1,000,000	31.5	32.0	29.8
Under 250,000	30.9	31.5	28.9

Source: See table 48.

Table 50—Fertility Ratio of the Population, for Central Cities and Suburbs of Urbanized Areas, by Size of Area: 1950

Size of area	Total area	Central cities	Suburbs and urban fringe
All urbanized areas	476	452	534
3,000,000 or more	433	404	495
1,000,000 to 3,000,000	478	444	531
250,000 to 1,000,000	503	480	569
Under 250,000	510	490	586

Source: See table 48.

Table 51—Dependency Ratio of the Population, for Central Cities and Suburbs of Urbanized Areas, by Size of Area: 1950

Size of area	Total area	Central cities	Suburbs and urban fringe
All urbanized areas	61	59	65
3,000,000 or more	56	54	61
1,000,000 to 3,000,000	60	57	65
250,000 to 1,000,000	63	61	68
Under 250,000	66	65	72

Source: See table 48.

shown in table 51, there is a difference in the same direction of 7 or 8 points for each of the four size groups of urbanized areas.

Race and Nativity Composition

Table 52 shows the race-nativity distribution of the central city and suburban populations of all urbanized areas combined. The suburbs have a considerably higher proportion of native whites, and corresponding small proportions of the other three race-nativity groups than the central cities. It is especially striking that the proportion of Negroes in central cities is nearly 3 times that in the suburbs—12.6 as compared with 4.5 percent. This difference doubtlessly reflects a typical pattern of migration of nonwhites to the central portions of urbanized areas, the residential segregation of nonwhites, and socio-economic differences between central cities and suburbs.

Table 52—Percent Distribution of the Population by Race and Nativity, for Central Cities and Suburbs of Urbanized Areas: 1950

Race and Nativity	Total area	Central cities	Suburbs and urban fringe
All classes	100.0	100.0	100.0
Native white	78.9	75.9	86.2
Foreign-born white	10.5	11.1	9.1
Negro	10.2	12.6	4.5
Other races	0.4	0.4	0.2

Source: See table 48.

Table 53—Sex Ratio of the Population by Race and Nativity, for Central Cities and Suburbs of Urbanized Areas: 1950

Race and Nativity	Total area	Central cities	Suburbs and urban fringe
All classes	94.0	93.5	95.1
Native white	93.6	92.9	95.1
Foreign-born white	99.1	100.2	96.0
Negro	89.8	89.6	91.4
Other races	148.8	151.7	135.5

Source: See table 48.

The index of dissimilarity in race-nativity distribution of central cities *versus* suburbs is 10.3 percent. For the urbanized areas of 3 million or more, and those of 1 to 3 million, the indexes are 14.0 and 14.2, respectively, compared with only 8.0 and 6.9 for the two smaller size groups. This variation by size of community is due to the increasing predominance of native whites with decreasing size of place, which leaves little room for central-suburban variation in race-nativity composition.

Central-suburban differences in the sex ratio follow the pattern already noted for the total population, i.e., proportionately more females in the central cities, in the case of native whites and Negroes. However, for foreign-born whites and other nonwhites, the higher sex ratios are observed in the central cities (table 53). For all groups except foreign-born whites the sexes are more nearly equal in numbers in the suburbs than in the central cities.

Marital Status and Family Characteristics

Table 54 shows the distribution of the central city and suburban population aged 14 and over by marital status, for all urbanized areas combined. For whites of both sexes the percentage married is greater

Table 54—Percent Distribution of the Population by Marital Status, by Color and Sex, for Central Cities and Suburbs of Urbanized Areas: 1950

[Persons 14 years old and over]

Color and marital status	Total area		Central cities		Suburbs and urban fringe	
	Male	Female	Male	Female	Male	Female
White	100.0	100.0	100.0	100.0	100.0	100.0
Single	25.0	20.9	25.8	21.6	23.2	19.2
Married	68.7	63.9	67.4	62.3	71.6	67.8
Widowed	4.1	12.2	4.3	12.9	3.5	10.7
Divorced	2.2	3.0	2.5	3.2	1.7	2.3
Nonwhite	100.0	100.0	100.0	100.0	100.0	100.0
Single	25.2	18.9	25.0	18.8	26.4	20.0
Married	67.1	62.6	67.2	62.3	66.9	63.6
Widowed	5.3	14.8	5.3	15.1	4.7	13.2
Divorced	2.4	3.7	2.5	3.8	2.0	3.2

Source: 1950 Census of Population, Vol. IV, Special Reports, Part 5, Chapter A, Characteristics by Size of Place, tables 3 and 3a.

in the suburbs, and the percentage of each of the remaining marital status categories is smaller. In the case of nonwhites, central cities have somewhat higher percentages widowed and divorced, for both males and females. However, unlike whites, the percentage of males married is greater in central cities, while the percentage single for both males and females is greater in the suburbs.

When age is taken into account, central-suburban differences for white and nonwhites fall into the same pattern. Table 55 shows the deviation of the actual marital status distributions from those which would be observed if age-specific marital status distributions by sex

Table 55—Deviation of Actual Percent Distribution by Marital Status from the Distribution Expected on the Basis of Age, by Color and Sex, for Central Cities and Suburbs of Urbanized Areas: 1950

Color and marital status	Central cities		Suburbs and urban fringe	
	Male	Female	Male	Female
WHITE				
Single	1.8	3.5	—1.4	0.7
Married	—2.3	—4.7	1.9	0.2
Widowed	0.1	0.5	—0.2	—0.7
Divorced	0.4	0.7	—0.5	—0.2
NONWHITE				
Single	—0.6	—0.2	—1.4	—1.8
Married	—2.3	—6.9	—0.3	—4.0
Widowed	2.4	6.8	1.7	5.1
Divorced	0.5	1.3	...	0.7

Source: *1950 Census of Population, Vol. II, Characteristics of the Population, Part 1. U. S. Summary, table 104; Vol. IV, Special Reports, Part 5, Chapter A. Characteristics by Size of Place, tables 3 and 3a.*

were the same in central cities and suburbs as those of the total population of the United States. A comparison of these deviations for central cities and suburbs discloses that, relative to central cities, suburbs have an excess of married persons and a deficiency of single, widowed, and divorced persons, for each color and sex group. Thus a standardization for age composition enables one to show that suburbs are more selective of married persons than are central cities.

Table 56 shows the percentage of married persons reported as separated for central cities and suburbs of all urbanized areas combined. Although in the statistics on separated persons there is a discrepancy between the figures for males and those for females, the data are consistent in showing a substantially larger percentage

Table 56—Separated Persons as Percent of Married Persons by Color and Sex, for Central Cities and Suburbs of Urbanized Areas: 1950

Color and sex	Total area	Central cities	Suburbs and urban fringe
TOTAL			
Male	2.7	3.2	1.6
Female	4.0	4.7	2.3
WHITE			
Male	1.8	2.1	1.3
Female	2.5	2.8	1.8
NONWHITE			
Male	11.2	11.5	8.8
Female	16.9	17.5	13.4

Source: *1950 Census of Population*, Vol. IV, *Special Reports*, Part 5, Chapter A, Characteristics by Size of Place, tables 3 and 3a.

of separated persons in central cities than in suburbs. This holds for both whites and nonwhites, as well as for the total population.

Turning to an analysis of family and household characteristics, one sees first that there is little difference between central cities and suburbs of all urbanized areas combined in the percentage of the

Table 57—Percent Distribution of Population in Households by Family Status and Color, for Central Cities and Suburbs of Urbanized Areas: 1950

Color and family status	Total area	Central cities	Suburbs and urban fringe
Total	100.0	100.0	100.0
In primary families	92.6	91.5	95.0
Primary individuals	3.8	4.4	2.5
Nonrelative of head	3.6	4.1	2.5
White	100.0	100.0	100.0
In primary families	93.4	92.6	95.4
Primary individuals	3.7	4.2	2.4
Nonrelative of head	2.9	3.2	2.2
Nonwhite	100.0	100.0	100.0
In primary families	85.3	84.9	88.1
Primary individuals	4.9	5.1	3.5
Nonrelative of head	9.8	10.0	8.4

Source: See table 56.

population classified as inmates of institutions. Only 0.7 percent of the total central city population and 0.6 percent of the suburban population live in institutions. The same percentages are observed for whites, but the corresponding figures for nonwhites are 0.8 and 1.0 percent, respectively.

Residence in quasi-households other than institutions is somewhat more common in central cities than in suburbs. There are 4.3 persons in quasi-households per 100 persons residing in households in central cities, compared with a ratio of only 2.1 in suburbs. The corresponding ratios for the white population are 3.9 and 2.0, and for the nonwhite, 7.4 and 4.1.

The central city and suburban population residing in households is classified by family status in table 57. It is apparent that a somewhat larger percentage of suburban persons, in the case of both whites and nonwhites, lives in primary families, while there is a greater relative frequency of primary individuals and nonrelatives of the household head in central cities.

Table 58—Characteristics of Primary Families by Color, for Central Cities and Suburbs of Urbanized Areas: 1950

Area and color	Persons per family	Children of household head per family	Other relatives of household head per family	Female heads as percent of total heads
TOTAL				
Total area	3.5	1.3	0.32	10.4
Central cities	3.4	1.2	0.33	11.5
Suburbs and urban fringe	3.6	1.4	0.28	8.0
WHITE				
Total area	3.4	1.3	0.29	9.6
Central cities	3.4	1.2	0.30	10.5
Suburbs and urban fringe	3.5	1.3	0.27	7.7
NONWHITE				
Total area	3.8	1.4	0.62	19.4
Central cities	3.7	1.3	0.62	20.0
Suburbs and urban fringe	4.1	1.6	0.63	15.3

Source: See table 56.

Table 58 shows selected summary statistics characterizing primary families in central cities and suburbs. Although the difference is not great, suburban families are somewhat larger on the average (3.6 persons) than those in central cities (3.4). Suburban families have 1.4 children of the household head per family, as compared to 1.2 in central city primary families. Both these differences are somewhat more pronounced for nonwhite than for white families. On the other hand, there are slightly fewer "other relatives" of the household head in proportion to the number of families in suburbs than in central cities for the white population, though not for the nonwhite. A somewhat larger proportion of central city than of suburban primary families are headed by females.

Mobility

As table 59 indicates, the suburban population is somewhat more mobile than the central city population. Of the total population one year of age and over, 81.6 percent in the suburbs and 82.3 percent in

Table 59—Percent Distribution of the Population 1 Year Old and Over by Mobility Status and Color, for Central Cities and Suburbs of Urbanized Areas: 1950

Color and residence in 1949	Total area	Central cities	Suburbs and urban fringe
Total	100.0	100.0	100.0
Same house as 1950	82.0	82.3	81.6
Different house, same county	11.0	11.1	10.7
Different county, same State	2.1	1.7	2.8
Different State	2.7	2.4	3.2
Abroad and not reported	2.2	2.5	1.7
White	100.0	100.0	100.0
Same house as 1950	82.1	82.4	81.5
Different house, same county	10.8	10.8	10.7
Different county, same State	2.2	1.8	2.9
Different State	2.7	2.5	3.2
Abroad and not reported	2.2	2.5	1.7
Nonwhite	100.0	100.0	100.0
Same house as 1950	81.8	81.6	81.9
Different house, same county	12.6	12.8	11.7
Different county, same State	1.2	1.1	1.8
Different State	2.0	2.0	2.6
Abroad and not reported	2.4	2.5	2.0

Source: *1950 Census of Population*, Vol. IV, *Special Reports*, Part 5, Chapter A, Characteristics by Size of Place, tables 2 and 2a.

the central cities lived in the same house in 1950 as in 1949. The proportion of migrants from a different county is higher in the suburbs than in central cities; but the proportion of intracounty movers is slightly lower. The higher proportion of intracounty movers in central cities is largely accounted for by the difference in this direction for nonwhites, as there is scarcely any difference for whites.

Table 60 shows the rate of in-migration from other counties to central cities and suburbs. The suburbs have an in-migration rate nearly 50 percent higher than that of the central cities. Furthermore,

Table 60—In-Migrants per 1,000 Resident Population by Age, Color, and Sex, for Central Cities and Suburbs of Urbanized Areas: 1950

[Includes persons residing in different county, same State, and different county, different State, in 1950 as compared with 1949]

Age and color	Total area, both sexes	Central cities		Suburbs and urban fringe	
		Male	Female	Male	Female
Total population 1 year old and over	48	44	40	62	58
White	49	46	41	62	59
1 to 13 years	48	39	42	61	62
14 to 24 years	63	80	77	93	90
25 to 44 years	58	57	45	78	67
45 to 64 years	25	23	21	31	32
65 years and over	24	18	22	31	35
Nonwhite	32	31	30	46	42
1 to 13 years	20	24	11	34	30
14 to 24 years	60	58	59	75	62
25 to 44 years	33	35	28	55	46
45 to 64 years	18	16	17	29	30
65 years and over	17	15	18	12	30

Source: See table 59.

for each subgroup of the population, by age, color and sex (except for nonwhite males 65 and over), the suburban in-migration rate is higher than the corresponding rate for central cities. However, the central city and suburban migration rates have a similar pattern by age, with the highest rate observed for persons 14 to 24 years old. The in-migration rate for males, among both whites and nonwhites, is slightly higher than for females in both central cities and suburbs. The white in-migration rate exceeds the nonwhite rate for all age and sex groups in both central cities and suburbs. Hence, despite the higher in-migration rate to suburbs, there seems to be no outstanding pattern of selection of migrants—in terms of age, color, or sex—which distinguishes migration to suburbs from migration to central cities.

Persons whose 1949 residence was on a farm constitute a slightly larger percentage of all movers (intra- and intercounty combined) in central cities than in suburbs—the respective percentages being 3.3 and 3.0. When the numbers of movers from farms is related to the resident population, the in-migration rates for central cities and suburbs are practically identical: 5.0 and 4.9 per 1,000, respectively.

Education

Table 61 shows the median school years completed by the adult population in central cities and suburbs. For whites there is a difference of a full year in educational attainment, the median for central

Table 61—Median Years of School Completed by Persons 25 Years Old and Over by Color and Sex, for Central Cities and Suburbs of Urbanized Areas: 1950

Color and sex	Total area	Central cities	Suburbs and urban fringe
Total	10.3	9.9	11.1
Male	10.1	9.8	11.0
Female	10.4	10.0	11.2
White	10.6	10.3	11.3
Male	10.5	10.2	11.2
Female	10.7	10.4	11.4
Nonwhite	8.1	8.1	7.9
Male	7.9	7.9	7.6
Female	8.3	8.3	8.1

Source: See table 59.

cities being 10.3 years and for suburbs, 11.3 years. However, for non-whites the difference is in the opposite direction, the central city median exceeding that for the suburbs by 0.2 of a year. Differences between whites and nonwhites are, therefore, somewhat more pronounced in the suburbs than in the central cities. Central-suburban differences in educational attainment no doubt reflect differences in occupational composition.

When urbanized areas are classified by size, it is found that the greatest central-suburban differences in educational attainment occur for the larger areas. In the areas of 3 million or more and 1 to 3 million, the median for the total population in suburbs exceeds that of the central city population by 1.6 and 1.9 years, respectively; whereas in the smaller areas the differences, though in the same direction, amount to only 0.4 and 0.2 years. For nonwhites there is a slight difference in favor of central cities in each size category.

Labor Force and Occupation

Differences in labor force participation rates for males between central cities and suburbs are slight, as revealed by the data in table 62. In central cities 80.2 percent of white males are in the labor force,

Table 62—Percent of the Population in the Labor Force by Color and Sex, for Central Cities and Suburbs of Urbanized Areas: 1950

Color and sex	Total area	Central cities	Suburbs and urban fringe
Total	56.0	56.7	54.4
Male	80.4	79.9	81.5
Female	33.8	35.5	29.5
White	55.7	56.3	54.2
Male	80.7	80.2	81.6
Female	32.7	34.4	29.0
Nonwhite	59.1	59.3	58.0
Male	77.8	77.8	77.8
Female	42.5	42.9	40.0

Source: 1950 Census of Population, Vol. IV, Special Reports, Part 5, Chapter A, Characteristics by Size of Place, tables 4 and 4a.

compared with 81.6 percent in the suburbs. For nonwhite males there is no difference between central and suburban labor force rates. In the case of females, both white and nonwhite, the rate of labor force participation is somewhat higher in central cities than in suburbs.

The difference amounts to more than 5 percent for white females and nearly 3 percent for nonwhite females.

There is a somewhat higher proportion of unemployed persons in central cities than in suburbs for white persons in the civilian labor force, but there is scarcely any difference for nonwhites. In central cities 5.3 percent of whites are unemployed as compared to 4.2 percent in the suburbs. The corresponding figures for nonwhites are 9.9 and 10.1.

Table 63—Percent Distribution of Employed Persons by Major Occupation Group, by Color and Sex, for Central Cities and Suburbs of Urbanized Areas: 1950

Area, color, and sex	Total [1]	Profess'l, techn'l, and kindred workers	Managers, officials, & propr's, exc. farm	Clerical and kindred workers	Sales workers	Craftsmen, foremen, and kindred workers	Operatives and kindred workers	Private household workers	Service workers, exc. private hshld.	Laborers, except farm and mine	Farm occupations [2]
TOTAL											
Both sexes	100.0	10.5	10.0	16.9	8.2	15.0	20.8	2.6	9.1	5.5	0.4
Central cities	100.0	9.9	9.7	17.4	8.2	14.2	20.8	2.8	10.1	5.6	0.3
Suburbs and urban fringe	100.0	12.0	11.0	15.5	8.4	17.2	20.3	2.1	6.6	5.2	0.7
WHITE											
Male:											
Central cities	100.0	9.8	13.6	10.2	9.1	21.8	21.0	0.1	7.3	5.9	0.3
Suburbs and urban fringe	100.0	11.9	14.1	8.4	8.5	24.0	20.6	0.1	5.0	5.9	0.7
Female:											
Central cities	100.0	12.8	4.5	37.4	9.0	1.9	19.3	2.9	10.4	0.5	0.1
Suburbs and urban fringe	100.0	13.8	4.6	35.5	9.3	1.8	19.2	4.3	9.3	0.6	0.2
NONWHITE											
Male:											
Central cities	100.0	3.0	3.5	6.1	2.0	10.4	25.6	1.2	21.4	24.8	0.5
Suburbs and urban fringe	100.0	2.3	2.9	3.6	1.2	11.0	27.2	2.4	13.5	32.9	1.6
Female:											
Central cities	100.0	5.5	1.5	7.0	1.7	1.0	20.4	36.9	22.8	1.8	0.2
Suburbs and urban fringe	100.0	3.3	1.2	4.7	1.7	0.4	15.7	50.7	17.8	1.7	0.7

[1] Includes persons with occupation not reported.
[2] Includes "Farmers and farm managers" and "Farm laborers and foremen."

Source: 1950 Census of Population. Vol. IV, Special Reports, Part 5, Chapter A, Characteristics by Size of Place, tables 5 and 5a.

The distributions by major occupation groups of employed persons in central cities and suburbs are shown in table 63. For total employed persons the index of dissimilarity between the central city and suburban occupation distributions is 7.0 percent. By and large this difference represents the higher level of socio-economic status of the suburban as compared with the central city labor force. The suburbs have somewhat higher proportions employed in the white-collar occupations, except clerical and kindred, and in the craftsmen, foremen, and kindred group than do the central cities, and smaller proportions in the clerical and other manual occupations.

Both the pattern and the degree of central-suburban occupational differentiation vary by color and sex. The indexes of dissimilarity between suburbs and central cities are 5.2 and 3.2 white males and females, respectively, and 12.6 and 15.2 for nonwhite males and females. Thus, the least difference between suburbs and central cities occurs for white females, and the greatest difference for nonwhite females. Furthermore, while for whites, particularly males, the occupation groups of high socio-economic levels tend to be disproportionately represented in suburbs, the contrary is the case for nonwhites. As a consequence, the dissimilarity between the white and nonwhite occupation distributions is considerably greater in suburban areas than in central cities. The indexes of dissimilarity for whites *versus* nonwhites are 39.5 and 48.9 for males and females respectively, in central cities, and 45.9 and 57.2 for males and females in suburbs.

Income

The median incomes of central city and suburban residents of all urbanized areas combined are shown in table 64. For all classes of income recipients, the median in the suburbs is $250 greater than the median in central cities. However, central-suburban differences are more pronounced for whites than for nonwhites, and the difference for females is in the opposite direction from that for males. Thus, for white males, the suburban median exceeds the central city median by over $350, while for nonwhite males the difference is not quite $100. For white females the suburban median is $150 less than the central city median, and a difference in the same direction of $65 is observed for nonwhite females.

The index of income inequality for all income recipients is somewhat higher in the suburbs than in central cities, the respective index values being 0.423 and 0.408. The same qualifications must be placed on this computation as on those described in Chapter 9 of the original source of this article (*op. cit.*), owing to the crudeness of the estimates of aggregate income. In the central-suburban comparison the differ-

ence in inequality is in the same direction as the difference in median
income level, whereas in the size-of-place comparisons, the differences
are in opposite directions.

**Table 64—Median Income in 1949 of Persons 14 Years Old and Over
with Income by Color and Sex, for Central Cities and
Suburbs of Urbanized Areas: 1950**

[In dollars]

Color and sex	Total area	Central cities	Suburbs and urban fringe
Total	2,315	2,249	2,499
Male	2,912	2,808	3,166
Female	1,372	1,393	1,310
White	2,433	2,385	2,557
Male	3,053	2,970	3,227
Female	1,455	1,496	1,346
Nonwhite	1,470	1,467	1,499
Male	1,937	1,925	2,023
Female	889	896	831

Source: *1950 Census of Population*, Vol. IV, *Special Reports*, Part 5, Chapter A, Characteristics by Size of Place, tables 4 and 4a.

Summary and Conclusions

This study takes the point of view that the suburb is a specialized
area within the larger economic city. The implications of this position
sometimes have been overlooked in those urban research studies
which have compared suburbs and cities of similar size but of
independent status, without regard to the factors differentiating suburban and nonsuburban places. The implicit assumption of such
comparisons is that characteristcs distinguishing central cities and
suburbs are functions of the differences in size between them. A test
of this assumption can be made utilizing the materials presented in
this chapter and in the earlier chapters dealing with community size.[3]

If central-suburban differences are simply functions of differences
in size of place, then suburbs would be expected to differ systematically from central cities in the same way that small places differ
from large. Generally speaking, this expectation is confirmed with
regard to those characteristics related to family organization and

functions. It is not confirmed with regard to economic characteristics; and the picture is mixed for the remaining characteristics. Thus, as compared with central cities, suburbs have higher fertility ratios, higher percentages married, lower percentages separated, higher percentages in primary families, lower ratios of quasi-household residents to population in households, and lower percentages of women in the labor force. Essentially the same comparisons are obtained for urban places outside urbanized areas *versus* urbanized areas. With regard to economic characteristics, the suburban labor force has a higher socio-economic status, with a higher median income than that of central cities, whereas the smaller urban places differ from the urbanized areas in having lower median incomes and a labor force of a generally lower socio-economic level. Furthermore, no consistency exists between the central-suburban and size-of-place comparisons with respect to labor force participation of males or unemployment (when color is taken into account).

Suburbs have a lower median age than central cities, and small urban places a lower median than urbanized areas. However, this consistency reflects, at least in part, the fertility differentials already referred to. Whereas suburbs have a lower percentage of the population aged 65 and over than central cities, small urban places have a higher proportion than urbanized areas. The difference between suburbs and central cities in the sex ratio is not paralleled by a similar difference by size of place. Suburbs resemble small urban places in having a comparatively high proportion of their population classified as native white. There is also a resemblance in that both have a relatively low percentage classified as nonmovers; however, there is no counterpart in the central-suburban comparison to the marked difference between urbanized areas and small urban places in the rate of in-movement from farms. Finally, although the central-suburban and urbanized area-small city differences in educational attainment for nonwhites are somewhat similar, the same cannot be said for differences in median school years completed by the white population.

In sum, the type of intracommunity specialization and selection reflected in the differences between central cities and suburbs resemble only in part the differentiations associated with size of community. (It should be kept in mind that the data on "suburbs" in this article include with the suburbs the urban-fringe component of urbanized areas.)

Most of the foregoing analyses involve comparisons for all central cities of the United States with all suburbs, with little attention to the factors of size of urbanized area and regional location as possible influences on central-suburban differences. If the differences noted between central cities and suburban areas represent general tendencies of intracommunity specialization, then one may expect them to persist in comparisons within regions and size-of-place groups. To reach a summary judgment on the validity of this expectation, certain characteristics were selected for such a consistency check. Fifteen comparisons are involved—four size-of-place groups by four regions, with the South not being represented in the size group 3 million or more. (Limitations of space preclude the presentation of tables from which these comparisons are taken.)

The sex ratios of central cities are lower in 12 of the 15 comparisons, with all 3 of the exceptions being in the Northeast. The median age for central cities is higher than for suburbs in all 15 comparisons, as is the percentage of the population aged 65 and over. The suburbs have consistently higher fertility ratios. In each of the 15 comparisons the suburbs have a higher percentage classified as native white than the corresponding central cities.

A regional breakdown for marital status is lacking, but for both males and females in all four size-of-place groups the percentage married in the suburbs exceeds the percentage married in central cities. The percentage separated is consistently higher in central cities than in suburbs.

As regards mobility, suburbs have a higher percentage of movers than central cities in 10 of the 15 comparisons for males and 11 for females. The exceptions are in the smaller urbanized areas of the Northeast and North Central Regions. It was noted that central-suburban differences in educational attainment, in favor of the suburbs, are consistent as to direction by size of place; a regional breakdown is not available.

The pattern of differences in occupation composition between central cities and suburbs is not highly consistent under the test being used here. The percentage of all employed males in the two major occupation groups—professional, technical, and kindred workers, and managers, proprietors, and officials—is higher in suburbs in 10 of the 15 comparisons. The same is true for females. Four of the five exceptions for both sexes are accounted for by the urbanized areas of less than 250,000 in the North Central and the South and by those of less than 1 million in the West.

As noted above, the largest difference in median income between central cities and suburbs occurred for white males. In 14 of the 15 comparisons the median income for white males in the suburbs exceeds that in the central cities. The same is true in only 7 of the 15 comparisons for nonwhite males. The reverse difference—central city median income exceeding the suburban—is noted in all 15 comparisons for white females and in 14 of the 15 comparisons for nonwhite females.

In conclusion, it appears that rather persistent tendencies are involved in suburban-central city differentiation. This summary has, of course, neglected the magnitudes of the differences, which might well be a function of community size, type, and location. In any intensive research on the subject it would probably be necessary to subclassify suburbs according to their functional relationship to the central city, distinguishing, for instance, between industrial and dormitory suburbs.[4] Such distinctions would involve analysis of data for individual places, rather than the summary tabulations of the "Characteristics by Size of Place" report used here.

FOOTNOTES

1. Chauncy D. Harris, "Suburbs," *American Journal of Sociology 49,* July 1943, 1-13; Grace M. Kneedler, "Functional Types of Cities," *Public Management 27,* July 1945, 197-203; William F. Ogburn, *Social Characteristics of Cities,* International City Managers' Association, Chicago, 1937.
2. This is the only instance in this monograph in which a term is used deliberately with a different meaning from that given it in the census reports. The justifications for violating this rule are, first, that the Bureau of the Census terminology is inconsistent with an already established usage; second, that it was necessary to make a distinction (between suburbs and fringe) not explicitly recognized in census categories; and third that no suitable alternative term is available. Actually, the usage here is, in part, suggested by the Bureau's discussion of the components of urbanized areas on p. 4 of the "Characteristics by Size of Place" report: "The census definition of a place as a concentration of population, which may be independent of legal limits, implies the possibility that a place or city may be defined in terms of the entire area of continuous concentrated settlement rather than the area de-

fined by corporate limits. Under this definition a place or physical city includes not only the principal incorporated area or areas but also adjacent *suburban and satellite areas.* . . . To isolate the suburban and satellite areas, an urbanized area is divided into its central city or cities and urban fringe as indicated in the formal definitions" (italics added). The terminology used in this monograph involves substituting the term "suburbs and urban fringe" for the phrase "suburban and satellite areas," on the grounds already indicated. In this chapter, where the data do not permit a separation of suburbs and urban fringe, the combined category is referred to, for convenience, simply as "suburbs."

3. Additional materials relevant to this point are presented in Chapters 12 and 14 of the original source, *Social Characteristics of Urban and Rural Communities, 1950.*

4. Cf. Harris, "Suburbs," *op. cit.;* Kneedler, "Functional Types of Cities," *op. cit.* Data on manufacturing and nonmanufacturing suburbs are relevant to this point. Differences between central cities and suburbs may arise from residential specialization of the two parts of the extended urban area, without necessarily reflecting differences in economic function. This is because population data pertain to place of residence, rather than place of work.

Walter T. Martin

University of Oregon

ECOLOGICAL CHANGE IN
SATELLITE RURAL AREAS

The rapid changes taking place in the rural areas adjacent to cities are frequently objects of comment by observant citizens as well as social scientists. The relevant data available regarding these changes in the United States are limited in scope and widely known; local observations are frequently reported in the press. However, these reports, while interesting, are not concerned with the development of theory to account for the changes. The task of developing theory has not been ignored although such work has been overshadowed by the accumulation of a great deal of descriptive detail.[1] Indeed, the amount of research and theorizing which had been done in recent years makes it imperative that interested persons take time to summarize, evaluate, and synthesize accomplishments to date. This paper represents one such attempt. Attention has been deliberately restricted to ecological and demographic changes taking place in the *rural* sectors of *satellite areas*, a generic term used here to encompass all varieties of suburbs, satellite cities, fringe areas, commuters zones, and other areas under the immediate influence of the central city. This restriction results from space limitations rather than any idea that other types of change or other sectors of the satellite area are of lesser importance.

The first question to be considered is under what conditions does a heavily settled satellite area come to exist? The importance of industrialization to this development is discussed first.

Reprinted from *American Sociological Review*, Vol. 22, (April 1957), pp. 173-183, by permission of the author and *American Sociological Review*.

The Industrializing Society

In the discussion which follows it is postulated that both the urban and rural economies are functional parts of the larger economy, and, following Clark [2] and Fisher,[3] that industrialization involves a steady shift of employment and investment from the essential "primary" activities to "secondary" and "tertiary" activities. Indeed, it is possible to describe a model of a dynamic, industrializing society in which economic development occurs primarily in the urban type of locational matrix and in which the economic organization functions best in or near such locations.[4] In this model industry develops in and is concentrated in urban centers while agriculture is dispersed over the rural area. As industrialization progresses the urban-industrial sector steadily increases its share of the national labor force from possibly 25 per cent at one time to possibly 90 per cent at a later time. This shift in the allocation of the labor force is possible because of a continuously increasing agricultural productivity which permits an ever larger proportion of the total population to be engaged in nonagricultural activities. Obviously the changes occurring in the satellite areas of this model would be quite different from those taking place in a society with a stable allocation of the labor force or one with a steady shift from industrial to agricultural employment. It is also apparent that in an industrializing society it is the urban way of life which is dynamic and expanding and which has consequently the greatest impact upon the satellite areas. For this reason it is necessary to examine more closely the nature of the role played by the city in the industrializing society.

Cities are a type of organization with demonstrated ability to maintain large populations in small areas and at a relatively high level of living. Since the density of population in the city precludes the possibility that food stuffs for the population or raw materials for urban industry can be provided within the urban area it is impossible for the city to be self contained. With its specialization of function, its interdependency of differentiated parts, its emphasis on production, and its dependency upon other areas for materials, personnel, and markets for its products, the city resembles a single great factory in its operation. In a dynamic, industrializing society emphasizing the production and consumption of goods and services the city-factory grows through the development and extension of transportation and communication facilities which tap an ever larger area for raw materials and for potential customers.

One effect of the extension of transportation and communication facilities into rural areas is to orient farmers toward the urban market, and to speed up the impact of industrialization on farming methods. In contrast to the cities, industrialization on the farm leads to a declining need for workers, and the production of the nation's labor force employed in the agricultural sector declines toward a leveling off point of perhaps five or ten percent in spite of attempts to develop rural industries. Rural people migrate toward the employment opportunities of the city, a migration with important implications for the satellite rural areas.

Another effect of extending transportation and communication facilities out from the urban center is to make possible the deconcentration [5] of urban population and institutions. This takes place initially in the form of suburban towns strung out along the railroad lines, but with the coming of the automobile and electricity the pattern increasingly takes the form of a mass settlement of the immediate rural countryside with further settlement strung out for some distance along the highways. However, the total settlement is the result of movement of rural population toward the urban industrial location as well as urban population away from the city.[6]

In brief, the very factors which make possible the modern city and insure its continual growth also make possible the dispersion of population into the surrounding area. However, making an event possible does not insure that it will occur. As Schnore [7] has pointed out, the theories of differential economic opportunities which serve rather well in explaining the growth of independent cities are completely inadequate in explaining the growth of individual suburbs. It is quite clear that the suburbs with the fewest job opportunities are growing most rapidly.[8] In the face of this apparent lack of isomorphism between the economic opportunity theory and the empirical world, sociologists have tended to fall back on social psychological factors and explain deconcentration in terms of the attitudes and motivations of the individual involved. Schnore suggests as an alternative theory that in this period of rapid population growth the bulk of housing construction takes place where level and relatively unencumbered land suitable for mass production of homes is available. That is the suburban location of mass produced homes derives from the profit making aspects of the construction industry; the values and motivations of the families who occupy these homes are partly a carry over of rural and frontier traditions but are probably provided to a large extent by the sales programs of the promoters. This suggests, of course, that in a rapidly growing highly technological society oriented toward "new" and "modern" artifacts and suffering from a long inactive construction program, that almost any new residential neighborhoods will appear desirable. Where the society is also characterized by a shifting of a high proportion of its lower income families into middle class income brackets it can be expected that these neighborhoods of new, fully-equipped dwelling units would be quickly filled almost regardless of type of structure or location of the neighborhood. During recent years in the United States contractors have found it most convenient and profitable to locate such developments in the satellite areas. Wherever they have done so the satellite population has increased correspondingly.

It should be noted that the currently popular "rural" amenities offered by suburban or fringe residence frequently are illusory. For example, almost without exception the motivations most frequently offered for moving from the city to the satellite area pertain to a more enjoyable living situation, especially for the children. However, in a study of the fringe area of Flint, Michigan, dissatisfaction with recreation facilities for children (40.1 per cent of respondents) was surpassed only by dissatisfaction with street lighting (44.4 per cent) and public transportation (41.7 per cent). Dissatisfaction with recreation facilities for children was mentioned by 26.3 per cent of a comparable sample of Flint residents. The fringe residents were also more dissatisfied with recreational opportunities for teen-agers and adults.[9]

If it is advanced technology that provides the transportation and communication facilities and the level of living to make deconcentration of population possible, why are other industrializing countries not experiencing a deconcentration equal to that of the United States? In many of these countries land is not readily available in the satellite areas at a relatively inexpensive price. The limited amount of land must be conserved for essential agricultural uses through land use controls and building restrictions.[10] Few are the countries that are able to convert agricultural land to nonagricultural uses at the current rate of the United States.[11] Furthermore, these countries have not yet achieved a level of living which will support the development of a deconcentrated residential pattern such that homes in the satellite areas are provided with all the urban conveniences. Thus industrialization provides the technology for deconcentration but a high level of living and plentiful suitable land in the satellite areas are also necessary conditions. Any forecasts regarding the possible deconcentration of urban populations in countries now undergoing industrialization must take all such factors into consideration.

Two Principles of Urban Influenced Change

Given a nation which roughly approximates the model discussed above, what changes could be expected to take place in the ecological characteristics of the satellite rural area? Previous analysis regarding the extension of urban influenced changes in rural areas have emphasized variations of two broad principles of change—the gradient principle and the principle of differentiation. These same two principles will be utilized in the present discussion.

The gradient principle is based upon the work of those scholars who have emphasized the concentric zone and gradient effect of city influences on the rural areas. Outstanding among these is von Thünen who developed a theoretical model of the patterning of agricultural activity on a plain of uniform soil fertility surrounding a single city.[12] It will be recalled that he visualized a series of concentric zones of farming activities resulting from the differential requirements of various farm products for accessibility to the central market. The hypothesis is also related to the work of Steward,[13] Dodd,[14] and Zipf,[15] among others, on the influence of population at a distance. It is consistent with the ecological concept of urban dominance.

This principle holds that at any given moment of time urban characteristics would be distributed in the satellite rural area so as to form gradients of decreasing incidence with distance from the city. In a dynamic sense the influences of the expanding urban center can be thought of as extending into the rural area in a gradient which declines in accord with diminishing communication and transportation facilities. Stated in brief form the gradient principle reads: *the extent of urban-influenced changes in rural areas varies inversely with distance to the nearest city and directly with the size of that city.* It can be hypothesized that with increasing technological development the slope of the gradient would become less steep.

The second general principle is a statement of the known tendency for urbanization to transform previously undifferentiated territories by introducing complex specialization of function, differentiation of sub-areas, and functional interdependency of the differentiated parts.[16] This outstanding characteristic of urbanization is very inadequately measured by a scheme which merely considers differentiation by concentric zones. According to ecological theory areal differentiation within the city decreases with distance from the city center. Extension of this principle suggests that rural areas most under the influence of the city would show the greatest differentiation and rural areas most isolated from cities would show the least differentiation.[17] Or, stated formally, *the extent of specialization of function and differentiation of sub-areas in rural territory varies inversely with distance to the nearest city and directly with the size of that city.*

The two principles are considered complimentary rather than inherently contradictory. While both appear to be consistent with the model it remains to be seen whether only one or both are sustained by empirical evidence. The two are partially independent in the sense that demonstrated tenability of the gradient principle provides no basis for evaluating the differentiation principle; on the other hand, acceptance of the second indicates that the first holds true at least for this one characteristic.

These two principles are not proposed as hypotheses for rigorous empirical test in this paper; instead, they will serve as organizing devices for ordering and relating the relevant results of various studies which have been published in recent years. However, a number of specific propositions could be derived from these general principles.

It should be emphasized at the start that the data do not permit us to differentiate change occurring through the in-migration of outsiders from changes occurring in the resident population. Also, unfortunately, comparable data are not available for exactly the areas which should be examined so that approximate areas must be substituted. The best data are those pertaining to the parts of the standard metropolitan areas (S.M.A.'s) lying outside the central cities—the so-called metropolitan ring. Most of the data to be discussed pertain to the constituent parts of these S.M.A.'s. Such figures omit entirely the important suburban and fringe area developments around cities located outside the S.M.A.'s.

Consideration of the Evidence

The model described above postulates (1) that the over all trends in the economy of an industrializing society lead to increasing population concentration in great metropolitan regions, (2) that locations in or near the city are favorable to the working of the economic organization, and (3) that in the United States at the present time a number of factors including technological advancement, level of living, price, suitability and availability of land combine to bring about the location of new structures in a satellite area. Given this situation, what changes can be expected to occur in the satellite rural areas of the United States? To what extent do actual changes coincide with expectations?

The Gradient Hypothesis. Nearly a quarter of a century ago Mc-Kenzie wrote, "This gradient pattern of a city's influence may be illustrated by many different series of social statistics." [18] This statement has been re-affirmed repeatedly in more recent studies.

1. *Deconcentration of Industry.* The situation just described is clearly conducive to the location of industry in the metropolitan areas but suggests that increasingly such units would be located in the satellite areas rather than near the central area of the major city. That is, industrial units would be located in the satellite area for much the same reasons as those mentioned for residential construction. Any such redistribution of industrial plants would have many implications for change in the satellite areas. What are the findings?

a. *Industry is shifting from the central zone to the outer zone of the large city.* Reeder found that in Chicago during the 1940-50 decade the inner zone lost 112 industrial plants but the outer zone of the city gained plants.[19] Such shifts bring industrial jobs closer to the residents of satellite areas and affect their way of life correspondingly.

b. *Industry is locating in the metropolitan ring rather than the central city.* While some previous studies had found very little change in the distribution of industry since 1900, Kitagawa and Bogue conclude that "between 1929 and 1939 S.M.A.'s, on the average, underwent a sizable suburbanization of manufacturing." [20] They also demonstrate that the apparent lack of redistribution between 1939 and 1947 results from the fact that while 88 areas were deconcentrating, 44 areas were centralizing, thus producing an average rate around zero.[21] A recent study of building permits in 1955 shows that 64 per cent of the new industrial buildings in the S.M.A.'s and 65 per cent of the value of such buildings took place in the metropolitan rings.[22]

c. *The greatest concentration of manufacturing relative to population occurs in places of 10,000 population or more located in the metropolitan ring.* The central cities rank next and the ring rural area and places of less than 10,000 show the least concentration.[23] Other studies support this finding.[24]

d. *The amount of deconcentration of population is associated with the amount of deconcentration of industry.*[25] That is, areas favorable to deconcentration of industry also tend to be favorable to deconcentration of population.

Thus, many but not all, S.M.A.'s have been experiencing a continuing deconcentration of industry in line with the expectations based on the model. The National Industrial Dispersion Program with its quick tax write-off for properly located industries should to some extent help insure the continuation of this trend in the future.[26]

The data presented here do not explicitly demonstrate a gradient pattern in this distribution of industrial units but this is clearly the case with most new units being located in or near the city rather than at a considerable distance from it. While wide variation exists among the S.M.A.'s any one of the trends listed brings industrial employment closer to the door of the satellite rural resident.

2. *Deconcentration of Population.* Given the situation described in the earlier section, it would be expected that recent population growth would occur mainly in the standard metropolitan areas, and that within the S.M.A. the greatest growth would be in the satellite areas, especially the satellite rural areas where land suitable for mass produced housing is most readily available. This is definitely the case. Well known trends of the past are continuing with increasing intensity. According to the Bureau of Census [27] an estimated 11,827,000 people were added to the U.S. population between 1950 and 1955, an increase of 7.9 per cent. During this same period the S.M.A.'s increased 13.7 per cent, the central cities 3.8 per cent, the metropolitan ring urban 19.1 per cent, and the ring rural 46.5 per cent. The population residing outside the S.M.A.'s increased 0.5 per cent.

Of the total increase 97.4 per cent went to the S.M.A.'s: 16.0 per cent to the central cities, 38.3 per cent to the ring urban and 43.1 per cent to the ring rural. Further confirmation comes from an analysis of building permits in the S.M.A.'s in 1955. According to this report 69 per cent of the new dwelling units were located in the satellite areas. This comprised 72 per cent of the value of new dwelling units. In individual S.M.A.'s the percentages are much higher, of course.[28] Conformity to the gradient principle in this redistribution of population is confirmed by Bogue who found that the density of both the rural-farm and rural-nonfarm population decreased with distance from the nearest metropolis.[29]

Since we are primarily concerned with differential rates of growth within the metropolitan ring, details are presented in Table I. The ratios based on Hawley's [30] data show clearly that the rate of increase of the metropolitan ring in relation to the total S.M.A. rate has increased consistently each decade since 1900. The larger cities in the metropolitan ring had their most rapid relative growth in 1900-10, but since then the shift has been consistently toward rapid growth in the smaller places. This is the population of the areas of particular concern to this discussion. Unfortunately figures are not given separately for the farm and nonfarm components of this population.

Table 1—Relative Population Changes for S.M.A.'s and Component Parts, 1900-50

Type and Size of Place	Ratio of Sub-area Rate to Total S.M.A. Rate				
	1940-1950	1930-1940	1920-1930	1910-1920	1900-1910
S.M.A.	1.00	1.00	1.00	1.00	1.00
Metro ring	1.60*	1.58	1.24	.91	.88
50,000 and over	.55	.15	.53	.71	1.21*
25,000-50,000	.61	.34	1.25	.89	1.26*
10,000-25,000	.98	.99	1.20	1.39*	1.10
5,000-10,000	1.49	1.15	1.57*	1.10	1.47
2,500-5,000	1.82*	1.34	1.78	1.58	1.44
1,000-2,500	1.61	1.84	2.11*	1.27	1.28
Under 1,000	1.63	1.75*	1.46	.88	1.04
Unincorporated	2.42	2.72*	1.27	.71	.61

* Decade of most rapid rate of increase relative to the total S.M.A. for each size category.

3. *The Deconcentration of Business Activities.* The satellite rural areas are also changing through a deconcentration of business activi-

ties within the S.M.A.'s. While there is considerable variation among the individual S.M.A.'s, the general picture is one of rapid development in the metropolitan ring. Cuzzort [31] found for 147 S.M.A.'s in 1948 that the metropolitan ring, and especially the rural segment of the ring, did not have its proportionate share of service receipts, service establishments, or service employees. However, during the preceding decade the rate of redistribution of service activities had been so rapid as to indicate that eventually the distribution of these activities may approximate the distribution of population in the S.M.A.'s. [32] This deconcentration of service establishments is mainly explained by the deconcentration of population. [33] The B.L.S. survey of building permits for 1955 shows that 61 per cent of all stores and other mercantile buildings were built in the metropolitan ring. This comprises 65 per cent of the value of such new buildings. [34]

4. *Occupational Composition.* According to the model it would be expected that expanding urbanization would generate an urban type occupational composition in the rural areas as rural residents increasingly participate in the economic opportunities of the city. The evidence of recent studies supports the hypothesis that such specialization occurs and that it conforms to the gradient. Using a four way classification of counties in the United States, Duncan and Reiss found for employed males and females separately, in both the rural-nonfarm and rural-farm populations, that the per cent employed in white collar occupations ranged downward in a gradient from the "most urban" counties to the "least urban" counties. [35] For example, the proportion of employed males in the rural farm population that are engaged in white collar occupations is over two-and-one-half times as great in the most urban counties as in the least urban counties. [36] A similar downward gradient exists for the per cent of rural-farm females in the labor force [37] and for the per cent of employed farm males engaged in non-farm occupations. [38] For farm operators the per cent working 100 days or more off their farm is nearly twice as high in the most urban counties as in the least urban. [39]

5. *Rural Land Values.* Land value is another general measure of the adjustment made in rural area to location adjacent to the urban-industrial center.

As a general measure of urban influence, land values should be highest in areas nearest to urban centers and lowest in the most distant areas. Furthermore, this variation should be independent of soil fertility or other non-societal conditions. This hypothesis is substantiated by Hiller's study of tiers of townships in 53 areas in the Middle West. Both for the value of agricultural land per acre and the per acre value of buildings, it was found that the urban influence was to produce high values in the townships nearest the cities with a downward gradient to townships in the outer tier.[40] Similar support comes from a recent study of the influence of location on farmland prices in Oklahoma. This analysis showed that without exception the selling price per acre of farmland was higher on the average in locations with the greatest accessibility to urban markets and thus greater exposure to urban influences. These findings clearly held regardless of soil quality.[41] The high value of land is an important factor in the selective redistribution of population, farming, and commercial enterprises in the area.

6. *The Nature of the Farming Enterprise.* In relation to the high value of land in satellite areas it is generally recognized that farms are smaller and farming more intensive in areas near the city. The farming situation is undoubtedly affected by accessibility to the city: in this regard Losch has recently stated "... in a dynamic economy Thünen rings must be formed." [42] Duncan reported finding "significant urbanization gradients for the incidence of farm tenancy, the form of tenure, and farm characteristics related to tenure." [43]

7. *Income.* In accord with the model and the findings regarding occupational composition the satellite rural population should share the economic benefits of the urban-industrial situation.

Ruttan concludes on the basis of a painstaking analysis that "the (median) income level achieved by rural-farm families (from farm and non-farm sources) does bear a direct and positive relationship to the relative level of urban-industrial employment in the same area." [44] Furthermore, the total income of farm people in these areas has a moderately high positive correlation with the per cent of the total population which is nonfarm.[45] Indeed, the income of the farm population has almost as high a correlation with the level of urban-industrial employment in the area as does the income of the nonfarm population.[46] While the average income of farm worker from farming has a negative relationship with per cent of the farm population employed in nonfarm work, this probably results from the selection of nonfarm workers from the most productive age group of the rural population.[47] The per cent of farms with nonfarm family income exceeding farm income in 1949 shows a definite downward gradient from most urbanized to least urbanized counties.[48]

8. *Age and Sex Composition*. One effect of the characteristic just mentioned is on the age and sex composition in the satellite rural area. These areas have a spatial location which facilitates population exchange with both rural and urban areas. Rodehaver found a two directional influx with age and family cycle characteristics varying according to the origin of the in-migrants.[49] The rural-farm population of satellite areas is subjected to a greater than usual loss to the urban-industrial situation. In this regard Duncan reports, "rural farm population in most urbanized counties have high proportions of older adults and low proportions of children when compared with the rural farm populations of the least urbanized counties.[50] Hiller found that the attraction of cities for the mobile younger adult group varied considerably with the size of the city.[51] He also reported an upward gradient for the sex ratio of the total (rural and urban) population by tiers of townships around cities. [52] It is not clear in these studies just what influence is played by differential birth and death rates.

9. *Fertility*. The finding of a fertility gradient in previous studies [53] is further supported in the Duncan and Reiss analysis. Both rural-nonfarm and rural farm fertility ratios grade upward, moving from the most urban to the least urban counties but the effect is more pronounced for the rural-farm fertility ratio.[54]

10. *Educational Achievement*. Higher educational achievement is another urban characteristic. Duncan reports that the median number of school years completed is higher in the most urban counties than in the least urban counties: by 1.3 years for the rural nonfarm population and by about .5 for the rural farm population.[55] As he says, the differences may reflect both the superior educational opportunities of rural areas near cities and the stimulation to accept these opportunities provided by contact with the urban way of life. In addition, there is the unmeasured selective effect of the migration into the satellite rural areas.

11. *Participation in Urban Activities*. The gradient pattern almost certainly holds for the participation of rural residents in urban located activities.[56] Several investigators have found that former urbanites residing in the rural area participate more in urban affairs than other fringe residents.[57] In this instance, at least, the proportion of former urban dwellers in the population may be an important factor in the

observed variation between areas. It is not clear, however, whether these results obtain from the higher income which permits participation in urban activities, the experience gained by rural people from participation in urban occupations which might ease the way for social activities, or simply the greater accessibility to urban events.

Evidence from many different studies appears to consistently support the idea that ecological and demographic characteristics of satellite rural areas differ importantly from populations of more distant rural areas. Furthermore, continuing changes appear to be consistent with the expectations of the model and in conformity with the gradient principle.

The Differentiation Principle. The second principle, without denying the gradient effect of urban influences, holds that these influences are extended selectively rather than diffusing uniformly, and that the over all effect is to transform the homogeneity of the rural territory into an urban-like heterogeneity with specialization of labor, differentiation of subareas, and functional interdependency of parts. In spite of the almost complete lack of research concern with this principle, it would seem to have as much or greater implication for changes occurring in rural areas than does the gradient principle which has been dealt with so frequently. The differentiation principle concerns the dynamics of the relationship between the rural and urban sectors of the economy, and the increasing integration of rural areas into the great regional urban complexes. While this idea has been stressed by R. D. McKenzie and others,[58] there is a surprising lack of empirical research.

Bogue [59] has provided evidence on the selective extension of urban influences by showing that ecological and demographic characteristics of the satellite areas vary by type of sector as well as by distance to, and size of, the nearest metropolitan center. However, this selective extension of urban influences is only part of this hypothesis. The essence is the differentiating influence of the urban center—the transformation of rural homogeneity into heterogeneity. The writer is aware of only one study dealing with this problem and this concerns cities of the metropolitan ring rather than satellite rural areas. Kish [60] classified incorporated places by distance zones from the central city and demonstrated conclusively that for a variety of variables the cities of the distant zones made up a relatively homogenous universe while those in the inner zone were highly differentiated on the same counts.

On a logical *a priori* basis, it seems likely that the rural-farm and rural-nonfarm populations undergo a similar metamorphosis under the influence of urban centers. It was shown in connection with the first principle that a definite increase in the complexity of the division of labor does occur in such situations, and, as Lampard says, "specialization of functions makes inevitably for specialization of areas." [61] Similarly, differentiation of areas makes for functional interdependency of these specialized parts. Thus, the satellite rural areas change under the influence of the nearby city. Specialization increases and with it all the differentiation that goes with differences in occupation. The subareas of the satellite rural areas become intricately bound together, not only with one another, but even more so with the specialized areas of the adjacent city. All are part of the expending metropolitan economy.

Summary

The ecological and demographic changes taking place in the satellite rural areas of technological societies are directly related to changes in the dynamic relationship existing between the rural and urban sectors of the industrializing society. The changing allocation of the labor force in such societies insures urban growth at the very time that technological advances make possible the extensive separation of home and work. However, deconcentration can only take place to any sizeable extent when there is plentiful land available inexpensively in the satellite rural area and when the prevailing level of living is very high. In the United States where the necessary conditions prevail to an unequalled extent the heavy deconcentration of industry, population, and business, and the accompanying conversion of rural land to nonagricultural uses, is producing impressive changes in the rural sectors of the satellite areas.

The findings of a number of studies show that these changes in the satellite rural areas conform consistently with the gradient principle of urbanization. In contrast, the evidence that these changes are consistent with the differentiation principle tend to be impressionistic and unsystematic. In spite of the inadequacies of the data, however, it seems highly probable that the rural sectors of the satellite areas, like the urban sectors, more and more consist of well differentiated subareas as the influence of the central city is extended increasingly throughout the larger metropolitan area. The changing patterns in population density, age and sex composition, occupational composition, and land values, to name a few characteristics, are societal adjustments in the satellite areas to the evolving spatial organization of the metropolitan community. With this continuing "metropolitanization" selected parts of the satellite rural areas become incorporated legally as well as functionally into the city and their places are taken by other rural areas brought into the city's immediate sphere of influence. Thus, change is continuous in the satellite areas; a search for the characteristic sequential patterns of this change is the untouched task remaining to challenge the researcher.

FOOTNOTES

1. Actually, almost no attention has been paid to the effects of urban influences on the rural population as compared to studies of urban people migrating to the rural area. See Kingsley Davis, *Human Society,* New York: Macmillan Company, 1949, pp. 336-341; E. T. Hiller, "Extension of Urban Characteristics into Rural Areas," *Rural Sociology,* 6, 3 (September, 1941) 242-257; Vernon W. Ruttan, "The Impact of Urban-Industrial Development on Agriculture in the Tennessee Valley and the Southeast," *Journal of Farm Economics,* XXXVII, 1 (February, 1955) 38-56.

   In addition, there are a growing number of community case studies that suggest hypotheses: The Institute for Urban Studies, *Accelerated Urban Growth in a Metropolitan Area, A Study of Urbanization, Suburbanization and the Impact of the Fairless Works Steel Plant in Lower Bucks County,* Pennsylvania, Vols. I and II, Philadelphia: University of Pennsylvania, 1954; F. Stuart Chapin, Jr., *et. al., In the Shadow of a Defense Plant, A Study of Urbanization in Rural South Carolina,* Chapel Hill: Institute for Research in Social Science, University of North Carolina, 1954 (Mimeo.); Bureau of Population and Economic Research in cooperation with the Virginia Department of Highways and the U. S. Bureau of Public Roads, *The Impact of Industry in a Southern Rural County,* Charlottesville: University of Virginia, 1956.

2. Colin Clark, *The Conditions of Economic Progress,* London: Macmillan and Company, 1940, p. 7.

3. Allan G. B. Fisher, *Economic Progress and Social Security,* London: Macmillan and Company, 1945, p. 6.

4. T. W. Schultz, *The Economic Organization of Agriculture,* McGraw-Hill, New York, 1953, p. 147; Stephan L. McDonald, "Farm Outmigration as an Integrative Adjustment to Economic Growth," *Social Forces,* 34, 2 (December, 1955), 119-128.

5. The terms decentralization, suburbanization, dispersion, and deconcentration are used very loosely. By deconcentration the writer means an increase in the proportion of an area's activity which takes place outside of the central city. This corresponds to what Bogue calls suburbanization, a term the writer would prefer to give a more specialized meaning. For a discussion see Evelyn M. Kitagawa and Donald J. Bogue, *Suburbanization of Manufacturing Activity Within Standard Metropolitan Areas,* Oxford: Scripps Foundation for Research in Population Problems, and Chicago: Population Research and Training Center, University of Chicago, p. 18.

6. Rodehaver found that seven out of ten families in Madison's rural-urban fringe had moved there from urban places. Six out of ten family heads and their wives had been reared in non-urban places. Myles W. Rodehaver, "Fringe Settlement as a Two Directional Movement," *Rural Sociology,* 12, 1 (March, 1947) p. 50. Also see, Walter T. Martin, *The Rural-Urban Fringe,* Eugene: University of Oregon Press, 1953, pp. 60-63.

7. Leo F. Schnore, "The Growth of Metropolitan Suburbs," A revision of a paper read at the annual meeting of the American Sociological Society, September, 1956.

8. Ibid., pp. 10-11.

9. Thomas B. Brademas, "Fringe Living Attitudes," *Journal of the American Institute of Planners* (Spring 1956) p. 75.

10. Noel P. Gist and L. A. Halbert, *Urban Society* (Fourth edition), New York: Thomas Y. Crowell Company, 1956, p. 154.

11. Independent estimates agree that each year during the last decade about 1 million acres of rural land have been converted to urban and related non-agricultural uses. This includes some of the nation's flattest and most fertile farmland. Donald J. Bogue, *Metropolitan Growth and the Conversion of Land to Nonagricultural Uses,* published jointly by the Scripps Foundation for Research in Population Problems, Miami University and the Population Research and Training Center, University of Chicago, 1956, pp. 4-5.

12. J. H. von Thünen, *Der Isolierte Staat in Beziehung auf Landwirtschaft und National-ökonomie,* Jena, 1910.

13. John Q. Stewart, "Demographic Gravitation: Evidence and Applications," *Sociometry,* II, 1-2 (February-May, 1948) pp. 31-58. This author has numerous other relevant publications.

14. Stuart Carter Dodd, "The Interactance Hypothesis, A Gravity Model Fitting Physical Masses and Human Groups," *American Sociological Review,* 15, 2 (April, 1950) 245-256. This is one of several publications on this theme.

15. George Kingsley Zipf, *Human Behavior and the Principle of Least Effort,* Cambridge: Addison Wesley, 1949, especially Chapter 9.

16. Eric E. Lampard, "The History of Cities in the Economically Advanced Areas," *Economic Development and Cultural Change,* III, 2 (January 1955) pp. 86-92; R. D. McKenzie, *The Metropolitan Community,* New York: McGraw-Hill, 1933, Part IV; Amos H. Hawley, *Human Ecology,* New York: Ronald Press, 1950, Chs. 13-14.

17. This is recognized in Hawley's statement regarding the expanding metro‑ politan community: "The expanded community with its multi-nucleated pattern gains its unity, unlike its predecessor, through territorial differentiation of specialized functions rather than through mass participation in centrally located institutions," *Op. cit.,* p. 420.

18. McKenzie, *op. cit.,* p. 76.

19. Leo G. Reeder, "The Central Area of Chicago—A Re-examination of the Process of Decentralization," *Land Economics,* 28 (November, 1952) p. 373.

20. Kitagawa and Bogue, *op. cit.,* p. 120. Also, Leo G. Reeder, "Industrial Deconcentration as a Factor in Rural Urban Fringe Development," *Land Economics,* 31 (August 1955) 276-77.

21. Kitagawa and Bogue, *ibid.,* pp. 67-68.

22. Dorothy K. Newman and Arnold E. Chase, "Study of Metropolitan-Area Structure and Growth with Building-Permit Statistics," paper presented at the annual meeting of the American Sociological Society, September 9, 1956.

23. In 1947 the ring cities of 10,000 population or more had 21 per cent more than their share of value added by manufacturing, and 26 per cent more than their share of production workers, relative to their share of the S.M.A. population in 1948. Kitagawa and Bogue, *op. cit.,* p. 24.

24. Reeder, "Industrial Deconcentration as a Factor in Rural-Urban Fringe Development," *op. cit.,* p. 276.

25. Kitagawa and Bogue conclude that this relationship is "undoubtedly due primarily to accidental factors—the location of the boundaries of city limits being the principal one." *Op. cit.,* p. 120. Hawley reports a positive association between the proportion of the S.E.A. labor force engaged in manufacturing and the rate of population deconcentration. *Op. cit.,* p. 120. Also see Leo G. Reeder, "Industrial Location Trends in Chicago in Comparison to Population Growth," *Land Economics,* XXX, 2 (May, 1954) 177-182.

26. Peter Edson reported that during the preceding two year period "2,000 factories representing an investment of more than $2,000,000,000, have been quietly dispersed from congested urban and manufacturing areas" under this program. *Eugene Register-Guard,* (Eugene, Oregon), October 25, 1953.

27. U.S. Bureau of the Census, "Civilian Population of the United States by Type of Residence, April 1955 and 1950," *Current Population Reports, Population Characteristics,* Series p-20, No. 63, November 2, 1955.

28. Newman and Chase, *op. cit.*

29. Don J. Bogue, *The Structure of the Metropolitan Community,* Ann Arbor: Horace H. Rackham School of Graduate Studies, University of Michigan, 1949, p. 34.

30. Based on data from Amos H. Hawley, *The Changing Shape of Metropolitan America,* The Free Press, Glencoe, 1956, p. 25.

31. Raymond P. Cuzzort, *Suburbanization of Service Industries within Stand-*

ard *Metropolitan Areas,* Oxford: Scripps Foundation for Research in Population Problems, and Chicago: Population Research and Training Center, University of Chicago, 1955.

32. *Ibid.,* p. 50. For example, the number of service establishments had increased 18.9 per cent in the ring rural, decreased 5.4 per cent in the ring urban, and declined 13.7 per cent in the central cities. *Ibid.,* p. 14.

33. *Ibid.,* p. 51.

34. Newman and Chase, *op. cit.*

35. Otis Dudley Duncan and Albert J. Reiss, Jr., *Social Characteristics of Urban and Rural Communities, 1950,* New York: John Wiley and Sons, 1956, pp. 163-166. "Most urban" counties are metropolitan counties containing a city as large or larger than 250,000 population; "least urban" designates nonmetropolitan counties having no city as large as 25,000 population. The writer is indebted to Professor Duncan for the opportunity to review this and other manuscripts prior to publication.

36. *Ibid.,* p. 165.

37. *Ibid.,* p. 162.

38. *Ibid.,* p. 165.

39. *Ibid.,* p. 167.

40. Hiller, *op. cit.,* pp. 252-53.

41. L. A. Parcher, *The Influence of Location on Farmland Prices,* Oklahoma Agricultural Experiment Station, Oklahoma Agricultural and Mechanical College, Stillwater, March, 1954, pp. 5-6.

42. August Lösch, *The Economics of Location,* translated from the second revised edition by William H. Woglom with the assistance of Wolfgang F. Stolper, New Haven: Yale University Press, 1954, p. 57.

43. Otis Dudley Duncan, "Note on Farm Tenancy and Urbanization," a revision of a paper presented at a meeting of the North Central Land Tenure Research Committee in Chicago, April 19, 1956, p. 2.

44. Ruttan, *op. cit.,* pp. 40-42.

45. *Ibid.,* p. 46.

46. *Ibid.,* p. 42. This investigator also reports that between 1930 and 1950 most of the areas in the South which "caught up" with the national average on the Hagood level of living index for rural-farm families "either include, or are located in close proximity to, developing urban centers." Vernon W. Ruttan, "Economic Development and Adjustments of Southern Low-Income Agriculture: Discussion," *Journal of Farm Economics,* XXXVI, 5 (December, 1954), p. 1159.

47. *Ibid.,* p. 48.

48. Duncan and Reiss, *op. cit.,* pp. 167-68.

49. Rodehaver, *op. cit.,* pp. 53-55.

50. Otis Dudley Duncan, "Gradients of Urban Influence on the Rural Population," a paper read before the Midwest Sociological Society, Des Moines, April 21-23, 1955.

51. *Op. cit.,* pp. 251-54.

52. *Ibid.*

53. Stewart, *op. cit.*, p. 44; Warren S. Thompson and Nellie E. Jackson, "Fertility in Rural Areas in Relation to their Distance from Cities, 1930," *Rural Sociology*, V (June 1940), 143-162; Edmund de S. Brunner and J. H. Kolb, *Rural Social Trends*, McGraw-Hill, New York, 1933, pp. 114-116.

54. Duncan and Reiss, *op. cit.*, p. 157.

55. Duncan, "Gradients of Urban Influence on the Rural Population," *op. cit.*

56. N. L. Whetten and E. C. Devereux, Jr., *Studies of Suburbanization in Connecticut*, No. 1, "Windsor: A Highly Developed Agricultural Area," Bulletin 212, Storrs: Agricultural Experiment Station, Connecticut State College, October, 1936, p. 102; Harold C. Hoffsommer, *Relation of Cities and Larger Villages to Changes in Rural Trade and Social Areas in Wayne County, New York*, Bulletin 582, Ithaca: Cornell University Agricultural Experiment Station, February, 1934, p. 59.

57. Walter T. Martin, "A Consideration of Differences in the Extent and Location of the Formal Associational Activities of Rural-Urban Fringe Residents," *American Sociological Review*, XVII, 6 (December, 1952), p. 691; Rodehaver, *op. cit.*, p. 56.

58. McKenzie, *op. cit.*, Hiller, *op. cit.*; Hawley, *op. cit.*

59. Bogue, *The Structure of the Metropolitan Community, op. cit.*, p. 47.

60. Leslie Kish, "Differentiation in Metropolitan Areas," *American Sociological Review*, 19, 4 (August, 1954) 388-398.

61. Lampard, *op. cit.*, p. 92.

Part II

The Sociology of the Suburbs

Out toward the fringes and margins of cities comes a region where they begin to be less themselves than they are at the center, a place where the city looks countryward. No sharp boundary line defines it; there is rather a gradual tapering off from the urban type of civilization toward the rural type. It is the city thinned out. . . . It is the country thickened up. . . . It straddles the arbitrary line which statistics draw between the urban and rural spheres; but in reality it is the push of the city outward. It makes physical compromises with country ways but few compromises of spirit. It is the city trying to escape the consequences of being a city. . . .

Harlan Paul Douglass

Harlan Paul Douglass

THE SUBURBAN TREND

Merely articulating the skeleton of the suburbs fails to reveal their heart. They are far more than a certain physical dispersion of population in areas relatively near to city centers. Distance and spaciousness in contrast with nearness and congestion are only the conditions of suburbanization. The important fact is the increasing social separateness and the consciousness of independence which arise within the continued fact of dependence upon the city and the continued realization of it. That such an increasing separation, both in practical relations and in thought and feeling, accompanies every successive degree of departure from the city in distance and in difference of physical character, is the essence of the suburban trend. Within this trend a suburb may be defined as a community in which the social consequences of these separations from the city have become clear and demonstrable. It arises, in other words, only when these consequences have definably registered in such a way that they can be recorded. A suburb is more than a distant fringe of the city. It is a community developing according to a distinctive social pattern which it more or less distinctly realizes.

At what distance and in connection with what degree of spaciousness, in contrast with city congestion, such a pattern will arise, differs from suburb to suburb. . . . For the present it is important only to insist that in the suburbs one finds a social structure differing even from that of the outlying parts of the city, accompanied by a special type of community consciousness. Only when these things are encountered can one find a true suburb.

From: *The Suburban Trend* by Harlan Paul Douglass, pp. 33-36; 217-224. Reprinted by permission of the publishers Appleton-Century-Crofts, Inc.

... The soil and the pavements grow different crops, even though the soil is cut up into minute suburban plots. The actual explanation lies, ... however, in the difference between the total elements which make up the city and the part which gets transplanted to the suburbs. The things which are in the city, which go on in the city, which *are* the city, have a very unequal capacity for decentralization. Some can be suburbanized and others cannot. It is by studying these "cans" and "cannots" that one comes to understand the suburb as a social fact in the accompanying mind of its people.

The people of the residential suburbs, at least, live where they do by reason of natural selection based on a peculiar psychology and motivation. This is a second major clue to the heart of the suburban situation. As between families equally in position to exercise choice, some are naturally responsive to the suburban trend and others are not. The former desire to escape from the city or wish to preserve town forms in connection with urban opportunities; primarily, one assumes, for the sake of family privacy and independence. Again, they may have a sort of esthetic affinity for a suburban environment. In any case they are a chosen people separated from their fellow city-men by the strength of a particular group of inner attributes.

Both materially and humanly, then, the suburbs, all told, contain only part of the elements found in the city. They represent selection. Out of the particular elements which can be and actually are decentralized they build a peculiar community life. The stuff which they have to use is limited both in quantity and adaptability. Their materials are urban fragments rather than urban wholes. They must make what they can out of what they have, meanwhile remaining dependent upon the central city for what they have not.

The particular elements which are or are not available differ from suburb to suburb. Consequently the social results differ; the outcome is sometimes fortunate and at other times not. Hence no generalization is possible, as for example, that the suburbs are better or worse than the city. On the whole it is easier to build a true and self-conscious community out of the available materials than it is to do so out of the complex and conflicting materials of the city; but much harder than in the independent town of equal size. The sifting out for decentralization of a limited number of functions and of peculiar types of people does not often result in a good collection of elements for an all-round community life. On the other hand the suburb's materials are simpler than those of the city. In many respects it is fortunate not to have to deal with the whole mass of urban factors at once. As a community the suburb is more homogeneous. Furthermore it is newer than the city and hence more plastic, more likely to be tractable. It uses the old forms of village and town life to which human nature is accustomed because it was created in them. They are less of a strain upon it. Consequently in the suburbs it should show its better aspects.

Because they constitute an unscrambling of an over-complex situation, because they are largely composed of like-minded people to whom cooperation should not be difficult, and because of the environmental advantages of roominess, the suburbs, in spite of their limitations, are the most promising aspect of urban civilization. By the very experience of revulsion by which they have taken themselves out of the central congestion of city life they are committed to finding or creating a solution of the city's problems as well as of their own. Formed out of the dust of cities, they wait to have breathed into them the breath of community sentiment, of neighborly fraternity and peace. They reflect the unspoiled and youthful aspect of urban civilization, the adolescent and not yet disillusioned part of the city, where, if at all, happiness and worthy living may be achieved, as well as material well-being.

Suburban Social Deficiencies

The imperialism of the city over the minds and imaginations of its suburban population is a unique fact. It emancipates them from local ties and gives them an enlarged citizenship and sense of metropolitan relationship.

It is this imperious and disturbing quality of certain suburban characteristics which first suggests doubt as to whether they can be altogether normal. This doubt challenges the implicit assumption . . . that the suburban trend is advantageous and compels one to consider its grounds.

. . . In the cities and their suburbs we are dealing with an excessively bifocal type of civilization. Society has two centers of activity and interest so different in character and so far apart—in spite of all facilities for keeping them in touch—that it falls into very distinct halves. Social loyalties are divided, and run in opposite directions. Mankind is capable of about so much loyalty; dividing its strands makes them weaker in both directions. No such concentration and singleness of social purpose is possible as when they all ran in one direction and were combined into one strand. Man works in the city with half his will and loves it with half his heart. The other half he reserves for the suburbs: but he cannot focus both halves upon either.*

All this is not unlike the dissociation of personality and consequent moral dualism which the psychology of the individual finds so abnormal and injurious. The 300 communities, mostly of small population, which make up Greater New York are not so well integrated socially as an equal number of independent communities of the same size. They lack social development and community consciousness. They are not completely themselves.

. . . The residential suburbs are essentially the decentralization of a very limited selection of the activities and processes which make up a city, into social units of relatively small size but still within reach of the city. The sites of these activities are relatively spacious but the activities themselves are of narrow sorts. Even the industrial suburb, which decentralizes production as well as consumption, leaves behind in the central city many of the most important urban functions. Neither type is an all-sided social unit as the independent town is. Each is concerned with part—and the more characteristic residential suburb with not more than half of human interests.

. . . The half of life associated with the city is always relatively unsocialized. We know that man builds up a social and moral personality primarily with reference to a particular set of companionships and social demands. He is largely what his fellows expect him to be. The most effective social influences are those of fellows who stand nearest to him and his most vital interests; for example, his wife and children, neighbors and spontaneous friends, his spiritual advisers and teachers. But half of a suburbanite's mind is beyond the reach of these influences. His neighbors do not know how a man behaves in the city; his business associates do not know how he behaves at home. Neither aspect of his existence is normally controlled by his "other selves." This tends to make him two men, each with a distinct set of morals because each has a different set of fellows. The social peculiarity of suburban living thus has psychological and ethical consequences of graver seriousness.

---

* The industrial suburbs partly escape this disadvantage, but are likely to divide along lines of class suspicion and conflict.

In connection with the decentralization of consumption, as in the residential suburbs (production remaining in the city), suburban life exhibits two major interests, the home and recreation. To these it brings the man in his relaxed, non-achieving moods. It is true that play in the suburbs takes on a seriousness not elsewhere known, that . . . it erects a group of major institutions; and true also that youth for a brief period has surplus energy enough to play as hard as it works. Nevertheless, the play motive does not command the whole motivity of life. Some of the traits of suburban relaxation are very amiable. One has the gentle gardener, the vivacious bridge fan, the golf enthusiast; but none of these is of the stuff of which the builders of cities are made. Every seasoned suburbanite knows that very definite experience of "let down" between business and home. Undoubtedly this is an essential nervous safety-valve for him, a phase of inner rhythm which, as William James showed, changes the mental clothing and induces a fresh set of attitudes. Nevertheless, it is not the mood in which one heeds the clarion-calls of moral responsibility. When the suburbanite has once slumped down at home it is almost impossible to stir him. It is not good for a boy to know his father habitually in such moods. The town wife and children see their husband and father somewhat as his peers see him, because his work or business is within the practical range of their vision. What the suburban husband and father regards as most important is often but an echo to his family. The fields of his supreme triumphs and defeats are too remote for them, as they are also from the home circle of friends and neighbors. None of them ever knows the other as a complete man and in his greatest stature.

One thing alone partly saves the situation: the suburbanite has neighbors. In the city also work may be completely dissociated from whatever it offers of home and recreation. That it is not more generally so we owe to the fact that so much of city social life is along trade or craft lines. The fellowships of the job—organized into clubs, excursions, the social activities of trade-unions, as well as expressed through incidental groups and gangs based on industrial association—tend to keep work and play close together for the masses. But this is not the whole story. The tired man, especially of the more privileged classes, may easily slump down into anonymousness or take his pleasure without responsibility. No nearby person knows or cares; he has no real neighbors of what he calls his home.

In the suburbs, however, the individual is known. His neighbors demand something of him, and he dare not altogether refuse. Moreover, as a house-owner he faces increasing taxes which cry out to him not to forget his civic responsibility. This challenge of the suburbs to fulfil a minimum of social obligation is curiously demonstrated by religious surveys. City churches have very large fringes of remote and largely anonymous adherents, numbering, for example, 43 out of every 100 adult adherents to the St. Louis Protestant communions. The proportion of these non-member adherents declines with every added degree of suburbanization. It sinks to 29 per hundred adherents in the most residential district of the city, to 27 per hundred in the nearest suburbs, and to 23 per hundred in Webster Groves. In other words, the suburbs do not easily permit one to remain anonymous or irresponsible. There is something in them which says, "Be a full member or nothing." Part of the distinction is, of course, social in motive. The suburban "family" church carefully weighs who is socially acceptable and uses considerable urgence to get him into religious relations. It does not tolerate such marginal phases of attachment as the city does.

Compared with the little town, however, where everybody's status is sharply defined, the suburbs are a realm of incomplete social relationships and limited obligations—a refuge for many half-men, and they half-known men asleep most of the time they are there! Suburban society, therefore, is not the sphere of the human spirit at full play nor the habitat of the strongest social loyalties.

The results of dividing urban interests and locating the exercise of the two halves in separate places would be extreme even if the people involved represented a full cross-section of the city. But in the suburbs they do not do this. Suburbanites are a series of peculiar types. Not all kinds of productive activities, we found, nor all kinds of economic functions can be decentralized; no more can all kinds of people.

Walter T. Martin

University of Oregon

THE STRUCTURING OF SOCIAL RELATIONSHIPS ENGENDERED BY SUBURBAN RESIDENCE

I t is the major objective of this paper to examine the characteristics of suburban communities as they relate to the structuring of social relationships [1] of the resident populations. This presumes that the form taken by these phenomena in suburban communities somehow differs from the form to be observed in other types of communities, and, furthermore, that this difference is engendered by the suburban situation. The writer knows of no published research which provides substantial evidence to support either of these ideas. Numerous studies have been made of social participation and interaction on the neighborhood and community level, but they are concerned almost entirely with the description of these patterns as observed in individual, unrelated, and relatively unique residential areas. To the extent that all communities have a common core of characteristics it can be expected that this common influence is conducive to the development of similar patterns of interaction in all communities. [2] However, it can be hypothesized that the large urban center, the suburban community, and the rural village present such different social situations that importantly different patterns of interaction are generated. [3]

If it is accepted for purposes of discussion that the structuring of social relationships in suburbs does differ importantly from the

Reprinted from *American Sociological Review,* Vol. 21 (August, 1956) pp. 446-453, by permission of the author and *American Sociological Review.*

patterns found in nonsuburban communities, there still remains the basic question: To what extent is this structuring influenced by the *nature* of the suburban situation? A corollary question is: What aspects of the suburban situation exert an influence on social relationship patterns and in what way? These questions suggest that a classification of suburban characteristics will be required to deal with the general problem. These categories must make it possible to classify and examine independently the various aspects of the suburban situation as they relate to the structuring of social relationships which occur in such communities. Obviously other questions can be posed about the relationship between suburban status and social relationship patterns. The present analysis is restricted to social relationships as dependent variables, even though it is recognized that for many purposes it may be desirable to treat them as independent variables.

Suburban places make up an extremely heterogeneous universe of cities, even when marginal types are excluded. In general the term "suburb" refers to the relatively small but formally structured community adjacent to and dependent upon a larger central city. The referents of the term can be designated more precisely by establishing a distinction between the *definitive* characteristics of suburbs and those other features which may characterize suburbs but are not essential to suburban status. The latter will be called *derivative* characteristics. It is likely that valid generalizations about behavior patterns in suburbs can be made only in reference to specific types of suburbs. The categories to be described should prove useful in the development of such typologies.

The Definitive Characteristics

Certain features of suburban communities may be designated as definitive characteristics. These are the characteristics essential to suburban status. In combination they differentiate invariably between suburban and nonsuburban communities. The two definitive characteristics treated first are a unique ecological position in relation to a larger city and a high rate of commuting to that city. Two other traits—size and density of population—are dealt with less thoroughly since they are not unique to suburbs. The hypothesis being considered here is that the definitive characteristics of suburbs have an important influence on the structuring of social relationships in these communities.

Ecological Position. By definition suburban areas, however subcategorized, are primarily residential areas having a peculiar location; that is, they are farther away from the center of the major city than urban neighborhoods but closer than rural neighborhoods. They lie outside the limits of the central city but remain dependent upon the city as a source of necessary goods and services. The ecological position thus differs from both urban and rural positions. It is hypothesized that this positional relationship with the larger city has a definite influence on the social organization of the suburbs. A large number of empirical propositions need to be tested, but only a few can be considered here.

The downtown area of the central city plays an extremely important role for the entire metropolitan area. It is the focal point at which are located a great variety of agencies, associations, and interaction opportunities not available elsewhere. Lack of ready access to this area necessarily limits potential participants to interaction opportunities found in a different type of area. A testable hypothesis is that suburban residents are significantly less active than urban residents but significantly more active than rural farm residents in social events located at the city center. The importance of this point lies in the variety of interaction opportunities found in central cities but characteristically not available in outlying areas. While this proposition appears valid on a commonsense level, the writer knows of no systematic attempt to substantiate it empirically. An analysis now nearing completion throws some light on at least part of the hypothesis. The data pertain to the residents of a small community described elsewhere as Valley City II.[4] In this analysis the striking feature is the lack of significant differences between the city and the fringe populations for a large number and variety of social, economic, and demographic variables. On the other hand, for a number of questions concerning various aspects of involvement in the affairs of the community the fringe sample quite consistently shows less participation, e.g., a lack of awareness of the names of influential members of the community. In answering questions the fringe population was much more inclined to name organizations (e.g., school board), or positions (e.g., superintendent of schools), or to give a don't know response. It is possible that this limited involvement in the general community results from other factors than relative inaccessibility to the city center, but, at this point, the lack of ready accessibility to the central area of the community remains an important possibility. Unfortunately, comparable data for the population of the rural area adjacent to the fringe are not available, although it can be inferred that these individuals would be even less involved in social events occurring in the central city.

If the hypothesis is reworded to hold that the participation of suburban residents in the affairs of the central city varies inversely with their accessibility to the city, a little more evidence becomes available. Whetten found in his study of Windsor that for a number of services and activities the percentage of Windsor residents "obtaining the various services in Hartford (the central city) varies inversely with the distance from Hartford, and the percentage partronizing Windsor varies directly with the distance from Hartford." [5] In an earlier paper [6] the writer reported that Chapin Social Participation scores for fringe families were significantly associated with the availability during the daytime hours of an automobile, telephone, and bus service. Participation in voluntary associations located in the central city was significantly associated with daytime accessibility of the city center to the wife, and with the availability of transportation facilities.

Thus the suburban resident by the very nature of his residence location is restricted to some extent in his participation in social affairs taking place in the central city. At the same time he has greater accessibility than the central city dweller to the social interaction opportunities of the rural farm population. Most available of all are the interaction opportunities of his own relatively small, homogeneous, suburban community, which ordinarily has the characteristics usually associated with "neighboring" and other informal primary-type group contacts.[7] Accessibility to the central city varies widely, of course, from one suburb to another, but the influence of this factor on social relationships in the suburbs can be evaluated only when studies are made which measure the importance of accessibility at the same time that the influences of such factors as income, occupation, and age are taken into consideration.

Commuting. Commuting to work, the second definitive characteristic of suburbs, is a direct outgrowth of the ecological position. Thus communities located adjacent to larger urban centers but providing jobs for their own residents as well as others are classified as satellite cities rather than suburbs. Commuting, like ecological position, is hypothesized to have an important influence on the structuring of social relationships in the suburbs. For example, a number of investigators have produced findings that are in close agreement regarding the differences between the social relationships of commuters and noncommuters.

1. Commuters participate less than noncommuters in voluntary associations and informal groupings in the residence community. This finding was advanced by Lundberg,[8] Whetten,[9] and Scaff,[10] among others. Further evidence to support this position is provided by the preliminary analysis of data compiled by the writer in Coburg, a village of 600 population about eight miles from Eugene, Oregon.[11] More than half of the labor force of Coburg is employed in Eugene. When these commuters were compared with persons employed in Coburg on the General Community Participation Scale, an instrument measuring a variety of types of community involvement other than membership in voluntary associations,[12] the noncommuters were significantly more likely to get high scores than the commuters. Similarly, noncommuters (27.6 per cent) were much more likely to have been actively interested in working for the recently completed city hall than were commuters (6.9 per cent).

2. Commuters participate more than noncommuters in the affairs of some community other than the residence community. Again this position has been supported consistently by the findings of investigators.[13] In the writer's study of the fringe area around Eugene and Springfield, Oregon, working in one of these cities was significantly associated with membership in voluntary associations located in the city. Commuting was also associated with city location of the family most frequently visited. There seems to be little doubt that commuters tend to be involved socially as well as economically in the work community.[14]

3. As a result of the daily commuting of males, women play an unusually important role in voluntary association and other inter-action situations in the suburbs.[15] As Henderson says, women "are the telephoners, organizers, and arrangers of community organizational life." [16] For many women the suburban situation opens new vistas and provides real avenues for expression and meaningful activity. This is in contrast to the rural-urban fringe situation which frequently leaves a city-reared woman in semi-isolation during the

day while the family automobile is parked near her husband's place of work in the city. This restriction on social relationships can be a source of frustration for the woman and a point of contention within the family.[17]

While there is almost complete agreement on the differences between commuter and noncommuter social relationship patterns, there is no conclusive evidence that these differences necessarily result from the commuting experience itself. That is, the studies just referred to agree that commuters tend to be more recent arrivals,[18] younger,[19] have a higher income [20] and more education [21] than non-noncommuters. In addition to these differences, in the writer's fringe study commuting was associated with residence near the city and with previous urban residence. These significant differences, singly or in combination, may well account for the variations in social relations now usually explained as resulting from the commuting experience.[22] On a common sense level, however, it is to be expected that when variations in age, income, and occupation are taken into account, the daily economic participation of the bread-winner in another community will still be found to deeply influence his family's relationships in the community of residence. Preliminary analysis of the Coburg data suggests that this is the case.[23]

Size and Density. The range in size and density of places meeting the criteria of suburbs discussed to this point is so great that these two variables may not seem to be definitive characteristics. Actually, however, in common practice settled areas at either extreme of size or density are not called suburbs, for example, Oakland in relation to San Francisco, and the unincorporated areas more appropriately labelled fringe areas rather than suburbs. Thus these characteristics, while not unique to suburbs, are two criteria used in designating suburbs.

Both size and density are undoubtedly delated to the form and content of social relationships, although very little has been done in specifying the nature of this relationship.[24] At this point, only this can be said: that the relatively small size and low density of most suburban populations would provide a social situation conducive to certain types of relationships (e.g., neighboring, visiting, and primary type relations in general) [25] and disadvantageous to others, (e.g., gatherings of individuals with extremely rare interests ordinarily occur only in urban centers large enough to include several such persons) even though the suburban status did not exist. We need to know how much of the suburban pattern of relationships actually is accounted for by factors such as size and density rather than ecological position and commuting.

The Derivative Characteristics

Certain characteristics of suburbs appear to result from the differential reaction of the larger society to the definitive characteristics of the suburban situation. These derivative features—demographic, socio-economic, and cultural—are brought about by selective migration to and from the suburban area. Actually, as the derivative characteristics become well established, the flow of migration is also a response to the derivative characteristics as well as the definitive characteristics. Since these derivative characteristics are shared by all communities, they are less useful than the definitive characteristics in predicting form of interaction. On the other hand, to the extent these derivative characteristics appear in suburbs in a form or to a degree not found in other types of communities, they become suburban characteristics and must be considered as part of the suburban influence on behavior patterns.

Demographic Characteristics. The hypothesis is that the selective nature of net migration results in a suburban population with demographic characteristics conducive to distinctive patterns of interpersonal relationships. These characteristics are usually described as a low proportion of unrelated individuals, a predominance of young married adults, and an abundance of young children. Such characteristics of course have significance for the structuring of social relationships.[26] Again the lack of a suitable typology plagues the investigator. To what extent are suburbs characterized by a uniformity of demographic composition? Bergel reports, for example, that upper class suburbs "have fewer children, more older people, and more women than the national average."[27] Thus, in spite of the Park Forests it may be dangerous to conclude that the rearing of children is the pivot around which suburban life revolves.

It is not the presence of young married adults and their children in the suburbs which is so important, since such individuals are found in all communities. It is the allegedly greater homogeneity of suburban communities in such demographic characteristics that has important implications for the patterning of social relationships. Such characteristics need to be controlled in the analysis of community differences in interaction patterns. Would suburbs and independent communities of identical size and demographic characteristics still differ in the structure of social relationships? According to the reasoning in the discussion on definitive characteristics, they definitely would.

Socio-economic Characteristics. Selective migration also accounts for the socio-economic characteristics of suburban populations. Suburbs are usually described as middle-class, middle-income communities. Consequently middle-class patterns of interaction and participation can be expected to predominate. These are said to be more "neighboring," greater participation in voluntary associations, and greater activity in leadership roles in the local community.[28] Actually, however, there is a wide variation in income, mean rental, and similar socio-economic variables among suburbs. Consequently it is likely that the important consideration is not the average rent of suburban places as much as the unusual homogeneity of individual suburbs in this regard that is of the most importance to the structuring of social relationships. Again the question must be asked, if suburban and independent communities were identical in all socio-economic characteristics, would they no longer differ in patterns of social relationships? An affirmative response appears to be impossible in view of the definitive characteristics of suburbs.

Socio-psychological Characteristics. It is likely that selective migration operates to produce suburban residents with characteristic attitudes and values regarding residential situations. The relative homogeneity of suburban dwellers in background experiences, stage in the family cycle, and occupational roles, among other things, is reflected in their agreement on the desirability of a residential location which is supposed to combine the assets of both urban and country living.[29] This agreement on the residential situation presumably includes a sharing of other values including regard for the type of neighboring activities which are likely to be limited in urban situations.

It would be a mistake, however, to overemphasize the homogeneity of suburbs in regard to the values of the residents. For example, suburban migration draws upon the rural area—farm and village—as well as the large city. In addition to newcomers directly from rural areas an important part of migrants from the city are farm reared.[30] On the other hand, a certain proportion of the residents have always lived in large urban places or in suburbs. Thus it can be expected that in spite of agreement regarding residential location suburbanites will find many of their values on conflict.

In the writer's study of the Eugene-Springfield fringe area, the urban-reared residents as compared to the rural-reared persons were significantly more likely to participate in associations located in town, to work in town, to want to move to town rather than farther away from town, and to feel that their friends would visit them more frequently if they lived in town. They were less likely to have a large amount of land and less likely to maintain a family garden. If such findings also hold for the suburbs, the urban-reared person brings to the suburbs an urban value system which differentiates his behavior from that of his farm-reared neighbor and probably leads to different structuring of interaction patterns. This conclusion is borne out by the Coburg study where the urban-reared respondents were much more likely to have specific complaints about the community. They were more inclined to complain about the lack of transportation service, high bus fares, and distance to work. They were also more vocal about the lack of civic maintenance, the inadequate police protection, inadequate sidewalks, inadequate sanitation facilities, and the poor condition of the streets. This attachment to urban standards is likely to bring the former city resident into sharp conflict with his neighbors.[31] In many small towns being transformed into suburbs by the expansion of a nearby city, this conflict takes the form of antagonisms between the older residents of the area and the newcomers, and in addition it may influence informal relations and lead to differential formal organization.

Homogeneity. As suggested by the discussion to this point on the derivative characteristics of suburbs, homogeneity is probably the most important outcome of the selective migration to and from the suburbs. Kish has demonstrated for a number of variables that communities located immediately adjacent to large metropolitan cities are highly differentiated among themselves but highly homogeneous internally.[32] These characteristics decrease with distance from the central city. This internal homogeneity of suburbs is heightened in the recent mass-produced communities where all houses are similar in size and design and nearly identical in price. In addition, in some new suburban developments there is careful screening of applicants. While some emphasis has been placed on possible value conflicts among suburban residents, it seems clear that the more homogeneous the population becomes the less likely it is that value conflicts become the source of major community cleavages.

In such highly selective residential situations the homogeneity of neighborhood groupings probably tends to maximize interaction on a neighborhood basis.[33] In these suburbs neighbors are almost sure to be of similar age, in the same stage of the family cycle, and to have common occupational interests. The lack of common interests and other differences which so frequently limit interaction between urban neighbors is thus likely to be missing in the suburb. The "neighboring" activities, "kaffeeklatsches," and almost frantic "socializing" of the residents of the newer suburban areas have been graphically described.[34]

While the homogeneity of suburbs is conducive to interaction, it can hardly be called a sufficient cause for interaction. Some of the populations frequently referred to because of their *lack* of neighboring activities live in equally homogeneous, middle-class districts—the sub-areas of large cities. It appears that the difference between the interaction patterns observed in middle-class apartment house areas and in the suburbs must be related to differences in interests, attitudes, and values. Nothing about the physical arrangement of units in apartment houses appears to be incompatible with neighboring activities. People are attracted or repelled by suburban locations to the extent they are perceived as places where certain goals can be achieved. Thus, the demographic and socio-economic features of suburbs may be important mainly because they ensure the youth, energy, and financial ability to carry on the interaction which develops in a homogeneous population having the interests and attitudes attributed to suburban residents.

Conclusion

In evaluating the relative influence of the various components of suburban status emphasis has been placed on the important influence of the definitive features on the structuring of social relationships. As unique characteristics of suburbs the positional relationship to a larger city and the daily commuting pattern of suburbanites would appear to have an important influence on the patterns of social interaction and participation regardless of the nature of the derivative characteristics.

However, it was recognized that the derivative characteristics of suburbs have an important influence primarily through their homogeneity but also because they provide the demographic and socioeconomic traits which facilitate certain types of relationships. An important derivative characteristic of suburban populations is the configuration of attitudes, interests, and values which favors a high rate of both informal interaction and formal participation. This social psychological aspect of the suburban population appears to be an important factor in developing patterns of social relationships in suburbs which differ from those found in the equally homogeneous, middle-class populations of some urban subareas. However, regardless of variations in age, income, family status, or attitudes, the structuring of social relationships in suburbs is always influenced by the definitive characteristics—the size and density of population, the accessibility of the large city, and the daily commuting pattern. Thus it can be anticipated that when the suburban pattern of social relationships has been more fully documented it will be found to be an outgrowth of the definitive ecological characteristics on one hand and such derivative characteristics as homogeneity and a particular socio-psychological milieu on the other. At that time, also, it should be possible to weigh the influences of the respective factors more precisely than has been done to date.

FOOTNOTES

1. In this paper "social relationships" refers both to patterns of interaction between two or more individuals in informal situations and to participation in more formally organized associations. Since much of so called informal interaction takes place before, during, and after formally organized meetings, it is difficult to isolate the two types. Separation was not essential to the purpose of this discussion.

2. There is evidence that in the United States variations in social interaction and participation are rather uniformly associated with variations in socioeconomic status, length of residence, and accessibility to social interaction opportunities regardless of the type of community. See Walter T. Martin, "A Consideration of Differences in the Extent and Location of the Formal Associational Activities of Rural-Urban Fringe Residents," *American Sociological Review,* 17 (December, 1952), *passim.*

3. In spite of considerable literature regarding the differences found between cities, suburbs, and rural villages in their relative emphasis on neighboring, visiting, and participation in secondary groups, to the writer's knowledge

only Key has made a systematic comparison. Key used six scales to compare various patterns of social relationships for rural areas, villages, small urban places, and two large cities. His findings support some but not all of the usual claims made about differences in social relationships found among these types of communities. Unfortunately his analysis did not include suburbs. [William H. Key, "Rural-Urban Differences in Social Participation," unpublished doctoral dissertation, Washington University, 1953.] Sylvia Fleis Fava is presently comparing neighboring patterns among suburbanites and central city residents. ["Suburbanism as a Way of Life," *American Sociological Review,* 21 (February, 1956), p. 37.]

4. This is a rapidly growing community located about three miles from a western university city. Population is now 16,000, an increase of 250 per cent since 1940. The sample population consists of 752 randomly selected adults of both sexes. See John M. Foskett, "Social Structure and Social Participation," *American Sociological Review,* 20 (August, 1955), p. 432. Since the outlying area is more aptly described as a fringe area rather than a structured suburban community, considerable caution must be used in relating the results to the general problem being considered.

5. N. L. Whetten and E. C. Devereaux, Jr., *Studies of Suburbanization in Connecticut,* 1. "Windsor: A Highly Developed Agricultural Area," Bulletin 212, Agricultural Experiment Station, Connecticut State College, Storrs, October, 1936, p. 102.

6. Martin, *op. cit.,* pp. 687-694. Also see N. L. Whetten and R. F. Field, *Studies of Suburbanization in Connecticut,* 2. "Norwich: An Industrialized Part-time Farming Area," Bulletin 226, Agricultural Experiment Station, Connecticut State College, Storrs, May, 1938, p. 107.

7. For a cogent discussion of the characteristics of suburbs which are conducive to high rates of informal social participation see Fava, *op. cit.,* pp. 34-37.

8. Lundberg, *et al., Leisure: A Suburban Study,* New York: Columbia University Press, 1934, p. 132.

9. Whetten and Field, *op. cit.,* p. 110.

10. Alvin H. Scaff, "The Effect of Commuting on Participation in Community Organization," *American Sociological Review,* 17 (April, 1952), p. 217.

11. Figures presented for Coburg are provisional and may differ slightly in future reports.

12. Foskett, *op. cit.,* p. 432.

13. Whetten and Devereaux, *op. cit.,* p. 127; Whetten and Field, *op. cit.,* p. 110.

14. "Thus it would seem that the city has a much stronger pull on the family of the householder who works in the city than it does on families in which the householder works in the local area." [Whetten and Devereaux, *op. cit.,* p. 102.]

15. Lundberg, *et al., op. cit.,* p. 129.

16. H. Henderson, "The Mass Produced Suburbs," Part II, *Harper's,* 207 (December, 1953), p. 83; also see Lundberg, *et al., op. cit., passim;* William

H. Whyte, Jr., "The Transients," (in four parts) *Fortune,* 49 (May, June, July and August, 1953), *passim.*

17. Walter T. Martin, *The Rural Urban Fringe,* Eugene: University of Oregon Press, 1953, pp. 39-41.

18. Whetten and Devereaux, *op. cit.,* pp. 58-59; Scaff, *op. cit.,* p. 217.

19. Whetten and Devereaux, *op. cit.,* p. 60; Scaff, *ibid.;* Glenn H. Byer, *Housing and the Journey to Work,* Bulletin 877, Agricultural Experiment Station, Cornell University, August, 1951, p. 5.

20. Byer, *op. cit.,* p. 6.

21. Whetten and Devereaux, *ibid.;* Byer, *ibid.*

22. The proportion of the labor force that commutes, the proportion of the commuters that have their work located in the major central city, and the proportion of commuters that are workers are important variables themselves. Lundberg and his associates report that in the communities in Westchester County in 1930 there was a range from about 10 per cent to 30 per cent of the adult population involved in daily commuting. [*Op. cit.,* p. 48.] In the writer's study of Coburg over 50 per cent of the labor force commuted to one larger city, whereas Scaff reports that of the 46 per cent of the Claremont labor force commuting only 4 per cent work in Los Angeles. These variations hold important implications for formal and informal relationships in these communities. [Alvin H. Scaff, "The Effect of Commuting on Participation in Community Organizations," *American Sociological Review,* 17 (April, 1952), p. 219.]

23. Differences in participation rates are even incorporated into the social expectancies of the community. In Coburg the question was asked of Coburg residents, "Which do you think should be more active in community affairs, a man that works in Eugene or Springfield, or a man that works in Coburg?" Of 161 respondents, 34.2 per cent said the Coburg worker, 4.3 per cent said the Eugene-Springfield worker, and 54.0 per cent said both the same. Interestingly, respondents from Coburg-worker families were inclined to say Coburg workers should be more active while respondents from Eugene-Springfield-worker families tended to say both the same. The expressed expectancies of the Coburg workers appear to be closer to reality than those of the commuters. Cf., Emory J. Brown, "The Self as Related to Formal Participation in Three Pennsylvania Rural Communities," *Rural Sociology,* 18 (December, 1953), pp. 318-319.

24. A review of available estimates of the number of voluntary associations for given cities suggests a consistent inverse relationship with city size. For 5 cities the reported number of associations per 1,000 population ranged from 4 per 1,000 for the largest city (736,000 population) to 27 per 1,000 for the smallest city (7,500 population). Granting variations in the completeness of count and the mean size of associations, these figures suggest that suburbs fall in a size group offering a large number of associations per 1,000 population. Also see George A. Lundberg, *et al., Leisure: A Suburban Study,* New York: Columbia University Press, 1934, p. 135.

25. Jessie Bernard, "An Instrument for the Measurement of Neighborhood with

Experimental Application," *Southwestern Political Science Quarterly,* 18 (September, 1937), p. 156; Theodore Caplow and Robert Forman, "Neighborhood Interaction in a Homogeneous Community," *American Sociological Review,* 15 (June, 1950), p. 360.

26. Fava, *op. cit.,* arrives at this conclusion after careful consideration of available information. For an impressionistic but stimulating account see Whyte, *op. cit.,* Part IV, *passim.*

27. Egon E. Bergel, *Urban Sociology,* New York: McGraw-Hill, 1955, pp. 161-162.

28. Leonard Reissman, "Class, Leisure, and Social Participation," *American Sociological Review,* 19 (February, 1954), pp. 76-84.

29. For an analysis of the attitudes of rural-urban fringe residents regarding the desirability of fringe residence see Martin, *The Rural-Urban Fringe, op. cit.*

30. Miles Rodehaver, "Fringe Settlement as a Two Directional Movement," *Rural Sociology,* 12 (March, 1947), pp. 49-50.

31. Whetten and Field, *op. cit.,* p. 114.

32. Leslie Kish, "Differentiation in Metropolitan Areas," *American Sociological Review,* 19 (August, 1954), pp. 388-398.

33. Caplow and Forman, *op. cit.,* p. 366; Leon Festinger, *et al., Social Influences in Informal Groups,* New York: Harper's, 1950; Whyte, *op. cit.,* Part IV.

34. Whyte, *ibid.*

Leo F. Schnore

University of California

SATELLITES AND SUBURBS

My purpose here is three-fold: (1) to set forth an explicit distinction between two types of metropolitan sub-center—suburbs and satellites; (2) to summarize presently available information on these two basic types; and (3) to suggest some important and immediate implications for research that seem to follow from these considerations.

Suburbs Versus Satellites

The distinction made here cannot be claimed as original. In a book published over forty years ago, Taylor discussed the unique functional position of "satellite cities." Such places were recognized by Taylor as basically subordinate to larger centers, yet retaining a high degree of independence stemming from their importance as production and employment centers.[1] It was Douglass, however, who first made this distinction in clear-cut terms when he discussed two broad types labelled "suburbs of production" and "suburbs of consumption." [2]

By "suburbs of production," Douglass referred to the type of sub-center discussed by Taylor—the satellite offering employment for at least its own residents, and frequently for other commuting workers as well. By "suburbs of consumption," Douglass referred to the suburb as it is described in its popular connotation, i.e., as a "dormitory town" or "bedroom city." The key functions of such sub-centers are

Reprinted from *Social Forces*, Volume 36 (December, 1957), pp. 121-129. By permission of the author and *Social Forces*.

not production or employment, but rather the provision of residential amenities. They serve, in a sense, as reservoirs of the manpower required to staff the productive enterprises in the central city, in satellite employing places, and elsewhere.

In one form or another, this distinction has gained some currency. In a 1943 article on "Suburbs," Chauncy Harris claimed that "the commonest types of suburb are housing or dormitory suburbs and manufacturing or industrial suburbs." [3] More recently, Reiss has noted that "suburbs often are polarized as 'residential' and 'industrial suburbs,' the residential suburb being considered the modal type." [4] Despite this seeming agreement, a careful and systematic definition has yet to become established among sociologists. As Shryock has indicated, "in the literature, *suburb* is used almost as loosely by the social scientist as by the layman. . . . We badly need some basic concepts here to guide our operational definitions." [5]

The most logically conceived set of definitions appears to be the one recently outlined by Walter T. Martin:

> In general, the term "suburb" refers to the relatively small but formally structured community adjacent to and dependent upon a large central city. . . . Certain features of suburban communities may be designated as definitive characteristics. These are the characteristics essential to suburban status. In combination they differentiate invariably between suburban and non-suburban communities. The two definitive characteristics treated first are a unique ecological position in relation to a larger city and a high rate of commuting to that city. . . .
>
> *Ecological position.* By definition *suburban areas,* however sub-categorized, are *primarily residential areas* having a peculiar location; that is, they are farther away from the center of the major city than urban neighborhoods but closer than rural neighborhoods. They lie outside the limits of the central city but remain dependent upon the city as a source of necessary goods and services. The ecological position thus differs from both urban and rural positions. . . .
>
> *Commuting.* Commuting to work, the second definitive characteristic of suburbs, is a direct outgrowth of the ecological position. Thus communities located adjacent to larger urban centers but *providing jobs for their own residents as well as others* are classified as *satellite cities* rather than suburbs. . . . [6]

Taking Martin's core definitions as a basis, it seems desirable to make explicit some of the outstanding structural and functional differences between the two types.

Structure. In *spatial* terms, both suburbs and satellites are often physically indistinguishable from adjacent areas, hemmed in on all sides by other municipalities. Many of these sub-centers, of course, were originally independent and self-contained cities in their own right; now engulfed by the expanding metropolis, they have somehow resisted annexation and have retained at least political autonomy. Other suburbs and satellites apparently had their origin in the exhaustion of space in the nearby central city, developing as the metropolis spilled over its former boundaries. Yet they are treated as separate legal entities.[7] Whatever their past history, however, *all* suburbs and satellites have one structural feature in common. Although they are treated as separate units for a limited range of purposes, including the reporting of data, *they are themselves merely constituent parts of a larger urban complex*—the metropolitan structure as a whole.

The structure of suburbs and satellites can also be treated in *temporal* terms.[8] Like other parts of the entire metropolitan area, they represent *sources* and *destinations* of the internal circulation of commodities and people that makes up the daily rhythm of community activity. It is at this point, however, that the two types can be distinguished most clearly. We can say that *goods and services* tend to flow out of the *employing satellites* to other areas (both local and non-local), while *persons* are attracted into these areas for employment. On the other hand, *residential suburbs* send out *workers*, and tend to receive an influx of *goods and services* for consumption by their inhabitants. These are the major components of the daily ebb and flow of movement that gives the whole metropolitan community its temporal organization.

Functions. The general functions of the two types of sub-center can thus be conceived as polar in nature. Stated in most succinct terms, (1) *residential suburbs are suppliers of labor and consumers of commodities.* Conversely, (2) *employing satellites are consumers of labor and suppliers of commodities.* This conception is in accord with Douglass' original idea that manufacturing sub-centers represent the decentralization of production, while residential suburbs manifest the decentralization of consumption.

Characteristics of Suburbs and Satellites

Assuming the validity of this simple dichotomy, the first question that occurs is the sheer number of sub-centers of each type that may be found within metropolitan areas. Here we are able to draw upon two studies using essentially similar methodology. Kneedler presented an "economic base" classification of all of the incorporated places of 10,000 or more inhabitants lying within the Metropolitan Districts defined in the 1940 census.[9] In this study, 160 "dormitory" suburbs were identified, together with 173 satellite sub-centers, with the latter classified according to their major economic functions (manufacturing, retail trade, wholesale trade, mining, education, and government). The same general economic types were recognized in a follow-up study by Jones, who classified 183 suburbs and 180 satellites lying within the Standard Metropolitan Areas identified in the 1950 census.[10]

Despite minor differences in the operational definitions used by Kneedler and Jones, the two studies yield the same general picture. First of all, the relative balance between the two types appears to have been similar at both dates, with satellites slightly out-numbering suburbs in both census years. However, it must be remembered that these data refer only to incorporated places of 10,000 and over; other data (to be presented below) suggest that satellites tend to be larger in size than suburbs. Thus if data were available for the full size range of sub-centers, it is probable that residential suburbs would predominate numerically.

Secondly, with respect to the *economic bases* of satellites, both studies reveal that the overwhelming majority (81 per cent in 1940 and 77 per cent in 1950) are manufacturing sub-centers. The next most frequent major activity is retail trade (12 per cent in 1940 and 18 per cent in 1950). Mining is the major function of only a few metropolitan satellites, while areas in which wholesale trade, education, and government predominate are even more infrequent.[11]

In general, then, employing satellites are typically industrial sub-centers, so that their characterization as producing places seems most appropriate. Unfortunately, these studies give us no detailed information on the economic activities predominating in residential suburbs. However, it can be generally stated that the bulk of employment that does occur in this type of sub-center lies in the general categories of retail trade and services—particularly in the lines that are relatively inexpensive and frequently needed by a residential population.

The economic characteristics of these sub-centers serve to document the basic distinction under discussion. But what of the other characteristics of the two major types? Are there any other general features that serve to distinguish between them? Fortunately, the use of Jones' classification of 1950 metropolitan sub-centers allowed the present writer to make a summary comparison of the two basic types. At the risk of oversimplification, the results of that study can be summarized very briefly.[12]

In general, *employing satellites* tend to be concentrated in the heavily industrialized areas of the Northeastern and North Central regions. They appear relatively more frequently in the metropolitan areas with smaller central cities, but they tend themselves to be larger than residential suburbs. Satellites also tend to be older than suburbs. Although satellites appear throughout the metropolitan area, they are more frequently found beyond the limits of the densely settled urban core. As distance from the central city increases, in fact, satellites are found with relatively greater frequency. Finally, these employing satellites are typically characterized by low rent levels.

In contrast, *residential suburbs* are distinctly different, although they are found in the metropolitan areas of all the major regions. They tend to appear with increasing relative frequency near larger central cities, but they are themselves smaller than satellites. Residential suburbs predominate among the more recently incorporated sub-centers. Very few of them lie either outside the densely occupied urbanized area or farther than 30 miles from the central city. Finally, rents are higher than average in these residential suburbs.

These data throw further light on the nature of satellites and suburbs, and they also serve to underscore the utility of the distinction. Still further insights can be gained, however, by a closer look at more detailed data on *the characteristics of the population* occupying these two types of place. At this point we can draw upon a case study of the Chicago Metropolitan District (1940) by Dornbusch.[13] Dornbusch used the basic dichotomy discussed here, further sub-dividing residential suburbs according to rent level. However, rather than to discuss the detailed comparisons between the three resulting types, we will continue to confine our attention to the major differences between satellites and suburbs in general.

Dornbusch's research shows that residents of Chicago satellites tend to have lower average education, and they contain higher proportions of foreign-born whites. In the matter of housing, these employing satellites exhibit lower average rent levels, they have higher proportions of tenant-occupied dwellings, and they have higher proportions of crowded dwellings. The satellites appear to have slightly higher fertility than residential suburbs. In fact, the satellites contain somewhat younger populations. In terms of occupational make-up, roughly two out of three of the employed residents of satellites are found in the "blue-collar" categories, as contrasted with one out of three in the suburban population. At the same time, a somewhat smaller percentage of persons is found to be employed in satellites.

In general, the images that emerge from Dornbusch's results are those of two rather clearly contrasting types: (1) *Employing satellites containing younger populations of lower than average socio-economic status*—as measured by educational, ethnic, residential, and occupational variables; and (2) *residential suburbs containing slightly older populations of higher than average socio-economic status.* Suggestive as these data may be, it must be remembered that they refer to the suburbs and satellites of only one Metropolitan District in 1940. However, the conceptual significance of the results—together with the relative simplicity of the methodology employed—would seem to recommend replication for other areas and more recent periods.

Satellite and Suburban Growth

Having reviewed the relative numbers of satellites and suburbs, as well as some of their more distinctive characteristics, we may now turn to the matter of their relative rates of growth in recent years.

A study by Harris provides information for the 1930-1940 decade. On the basis of an examination of growth rates in all places of 10,000 and over in 11 Metropolitan Districts, Harris reported that the growth rates of residential suburbs (average 11.7 per cent) were well in excess of the rates found in industrial satellites (average 1.7 per cent).[14]

A more recent study by the present writer revealed that the same general tendency persisted in the 1940-1950 decade. Suburban growth (average 31.9 per cent) was well in excess of that of satellites (average 17.0 per cent). This study covered all of the suburbs and satellites of 10,000 and over in all of the Standard Metropolitan Areas of the United States, and the relatively large number of cases (416) permitted the successive control of a number of relevant variables.

On the average, suburbs grew faster than satellites in all regions, in all central city size classes, in all satellite and suburban size classes, in all concentric distance zones, and in metropolitan areas of every major type of economic activity. One minor exception appeared when rent level was controlled, for the prevailing differential was reversed in the high-rent category. The only major reversal was found when suburbs were classified according to their dates of incorporation; the differential in favor of residential suburbs was found to characterize only the older places, i.e., those incorporated before 1900. Thus the control of six out of seven relevant factors dit not alter the over-all pattern of growth differentials in any significant respect. Suburban growth appears to have continued well in excess of that of satellites in the most recent inter-censal decade.

These findings may be viewed as reflections of a fundamental alteration of metropolitan organization in the direction of greater functional and territorial complexity. In many respects, it can be argued that these growth differentials simply mirror the changing distribution of housing opportunities emerging as a result of new patterns of building activity in these areas.

Residential suburbs appear to be growing more rapidly because they are becoming even more residential in character, by means of large increments in housing construction. At the same time, employing satellites appear to be growing less rapidly because they—like the central cities themselves—are becoming more *exclusively* devoted to industry and other employment-producing activities. In these employing satellites, the process of land-use conversion—from residential to industrial, commercial, and transportation uses—is apparently (a) driving out pre-existent residential uses of land and (b) discouraging new construction of housing.[15]

Research Implications

The first research question that presents itself concerns the *source* of these growth differentials. However, "source" can be taken to mean either of two things. First of all, we can pose the question in broad demographic terms, by asking "what are the relative contributions of (a) natural increase and (b) net migration to these observed differentials?" In addition, we can ask about the areal or geographic sources of the migrants contributing to the growth of suburbs and satellites. The question then becomes "what are the relative sizes of migrant streams from (a) the central city, (b) other suburbs, satellites, and nearby fringe areas, and (c) areas outside the metropolitan community in question?" Both of these detailed questions are in need of answers. Moreover, the basic distinction between suburbs and satellites should be kept in the forefront of the analysis, for these two types appear to differ with respect to the relative importance of natural increase and net migration, and they may also differ with respect to the geographic sources of persons migrating to them.

Demographic sources of growth. The data from Dornbusch's study of Chicago suburbs and satellites might suggest that natural increase contributes more importantly to the growth of satellites than to suburbs. After all, his data indicate that satellites have higher fertility ratios. In addition, satellites tend to have lower proportions of persons over 65 years of age, so that it might be expected that they have lower death rates.

However, the apparent trends in population growth and residential construction in metropolitan areas suggest that this hypothesis be given more elaboration. On the basis of a preliminary analysis of the growth of satellites and suburbs between 1940 and 1950, it appears that natural increase may indeed be especially important to the typical satellite because it offsets net losses of migrants. In other words, satellites may be able to exhibit growth only because of recent high rates of natural increase. Suburbs, on the other hand, appear to be growing more rapidly from *both* demographic sources—natural increase and net in-migration. Thus it appears that employing satellites—which are *functionally* similar to the central city, in that they draw workers from other areas—are also highly similar to the metropolis in their sources of growth.[16]

Geographic sources of growth. Unfortunately, available census data do not permit investigation of the detailed geographic sources of recent migrants to satellites and suburbs. The 1950 census data on migrants are coded in categories (based on county units) that are inappropriate to the type of study needed here. For the moment, we will have to be content with inferences drawn from scattered case studies and older census data.

Case studies of outlying areas indicate that the popular notion of "decentralization" as simply a "flight from the city" is a gross oversimplification.[17] In addition, studies by Thompson and Hawley, based upon 1935-1940 migration data, show that a substantial component of metropolitan ring growth comes from other areas.[18] Much of this growth—which may be labelled "accretion at the periphery" in contrast to outward re-location from the city—must have taken place in satellites and suburbs, as well as in the "fringe" and open country.

It seems feasible to use the sample survey technique in studies focussed *specifically* upon the geographic sources of migrants to suburbs and satellites. In view of the lack of appropriate census data on this question, such case studies will probably remain the major source of our information for some time.

The question of classification. We need more data on daily commuting (recurrent movements) as well as migration (non-recurrent movements). In fact, a major research question concerns the very basis of the distinction between these two functional types of area. Up to this time, we have had to depend upon manipulation of census data in order to classify sub-centers in these terms. The work of Harris, Kneedler, and Jones has been particularly ingenious, but deficiencies in the basic data reduce the potential value of their contributions.

In *theory*, the types developed by these writers depend essentially upon a comparison of (a) the number of employed people *living* in a given area with (b) the number of people *working* in that area. This is basically a question of "day-time" versus "night-time" population, for suburbs and satellites are dispersing and attracting areas in the daily ebb and flow of movement. Subordinate centers that attract more workers every day than the number of employed people who sleep there every night are labelled satellites, while those having substantially more residents than jobs are classified as suburbs.

In *practice,* however, many difficulties are encountered in the use of census data in classifying particular areas in these terms. For one thing, the requisite data on employment (the number of jobs in a given area) are not generally available for smaller places—those under 10,000 inhabitants. Moreover, the data for larger places are inadequate in many respects. The employment data have been derived from the Censuses of Business and Manufacturing, while the numbers of employed residents have been drawn from the Population Census. The discrepancy in the very dates of these censuses (e.g., 1947, 1948, and 1950) means that inaccuracies enter the final results. Annexations comprise a major source of difficulties. In addition, any substantial change in employment opportunities or in available housing between these dates can seriously distort the basic "employment-residence ratio." The statistics for the numerator and the denominator of this ratio refer to different time periods, and changes in either element can artificially raise or lower the true value of the ratio. Still another weakness is the fact that all job categories have not been included in the computation of the ratio.

Many of these difficulties may be surmounted in the forthcoming population census. It seems almost a certainty that the 1960 Census will contain a question on the individual's place of work. It remains to be seen, however, whether the Census Bureau will be able to present tabulations in sufficient detail to permit the accurate classification of individual suburbs and satellites in these terms. Considerations of cost will undoubtedly prohibit full detail for smaller places, and other priorities will inevitably compete for the funds available. In view of these considerations—and mindful of the additional fact that published census data are at least five years away—we might do better to consider alternative sources of data.

Because the fundamental distinction between satellites and suburbs is essentially a question of commuting flows, our attention is immediately drawn to traffic data as a possible source of information. "Origin-and-destination" data available from sample studies permit the identification of satellites and suburbs in a number of metropolitan areas. Punchcards for individual workers contain information on place of employment and place of residence, together with other characteristics. All work-trips to a given satellite or suburb can simply be tabulated by the place of residence of the workers. The simple balance between residents and job opportunities yields an identification of the two main types of sub-center discussed here. In addition, detailed information can be gained on main streams of commuters, and the direction of these streams throughout the entire area—centripetal, centrifugal, and lateral. Furthermore, the characteristics of the workers in these various commuting streams can be compared.

In summary, these detailed commuting data can be used to identify individual suburbs and satellites according to their basic type in many metropolitan areas. Comparison of such results with those derived from analysis of census data should be particularly interesting. In addition, these commuting data will yield information that is not presently available from census sources.

Conclusion

As Woodbury has observed, "dormitory towns are only one species of suburbs." [19] This paper calls attention to the available evidence supporting a fundamental distinction between satellites (employing sub-centers) and suburbs (residential sub-centers). However, it may well be that these two types are too broadly defined for many research purposes. Dornbusch's study indicates that rent level is another variable of real significance, while Martin suggests population size and density as additional criteria. The demographic source of growth may even be an important distinguishing characteristic. On the face of it, it seems that a place growing or maintaining its size by natural increase might be significantly different from one expanding mainly via net migration.

Whetten has argued that "there is need for further identification and classification of suburban populations into meaningful groupings or community types." [20] The present writer can only agree—and hope that this paper will help to fill this gap in our knowledge of metropolitan areas. But there are other gaps to be closed. A single example will suffice. One closely related concept that has been ignored in this presentation is that of the "fringe." Although it is used with increasing frequency, there is still little agreement on the fundamental meaning that should be assigned to the term. However, if we are careful to build upon the theoretical and research foundations already established, it should not be too long before we have a much more complete understanding of the structure and functions of the metropolitan area and *all* of its constituent parts.

FOOTNOTES

1. Graham R. Taylor, *Satellite Cities,* New York and London: D. Appleton and Co., 1915.
2. Harlan Paul Douglass, *The Suburban Trend,* New York and London: The Century Co., 1925, pp. 74-92. See also his article, "Suburbs," in *The Encyclopedia of the Social Sciences,* New York: The Macmillan Co., 1934, XIV, pp. 433-435.
3. C. D. Harris, "Suburbs," *American Journal of Sociology,* 49 (May, 1943), p. 6.
4. Albert J. Reiss, Jr., "Research Problems in Metropolitan Population Redistribution," *American Sociological Review,* 21 (October, 1956), p. 575.
5. Henry S. Shryock, Jr., "Population Redistribution within Metropolitan Areas: Evaluation of Research," *Social Forces,* 35 (December, 1956), pp. 155-156.
6. Walter T. Martin, "The Structuring of Social Relationships Engendered by Suburban Residence," *American Sociological Review,* 21 (August, 1956) pp. 447-448; italics added.
7. These diverse historical origins comprise a key dimension in an interesting typology of suburbs developed by Stuart A. Queen and David B. Carpenter. See *The American City,* New York: McGraw-Hill Book Co., 1953, pp. 116-131.
8. For a complete discussion of the temporal aspect of community structure, see Amos H. Hawley, *Human Ecology,* New York: The Ronald Press, 1950, pp. 288-316.
9. Grace M. Kneedler, "Functional Types of Cities," *Public Management,* 27 (July, 1945), pp. 197-203; reprinted in Paul K. Hatt and Albert J. Reiss, Jr. (editors), *Reader in Urban Sociology,* Glencoe: The Free Press, 1951, pp. 49-57.
10. Victor Jones, "Economic Classification of Cities and Metropolitan Areas," in *The Municipal Year Book 1953,* Chicago: The International City Managers' Association, 1953, pp. 49-57.
11. It is rather interesting to note the specialties in which *no* satellites are represented—transportation, and resort, retirement, and recreational services. These functions are more likely to be found in independent cities, far from metropolitan centers.
12. Leo F. Schnore, "The Functions of Metropolitan Suburbs," *American Journal of Sociology,* 61 (March, 1956), pp. 453-458.
13. Sanford M. Dornbusch, "A Typology of Suburban Communities: Chicago Metropolitan District, 1940," Urban Analysis Report No. 10, University of Chicago: Chicago Community Inventory, May 1952.
14. C. D. Harris, *op. cit.*
15. See Leo F. Schnore, "The Growth of Metropolitan Suburbs," *American Sociological Review,* 22 (April, 1957), pp. 165-173. It might also be noted here that this general process of land-use conversion has yet to run its

course. See Dorothy K. Newman, "Metropolitan Area Structure and Growth as Shown by Building-Permit Statistics," *Business Topics,* 4 (November, 1956), pp. 1-7.

16. This analysis was confined to the suburbs and satellites of 10,000 and over in the five largest Standard Metropolitan Areas (New York, Chicago, Los Angeles, Philadelphia, and Detroit), and utilized the general method described in detail in Donald J. Bogue and Emerson Seim, "Components of Population Change in Suburban and Central City Populations of Standard Metropolitan Areas: 1940 to 1950," *Rural Sociology,* 21 (September-December, 1956), pp. 267-275. In this study, Bogue and Seim present compelling evidence to the effect that recent central city growth was largely a function of natural increase, high enough to offset migration losses. This reverses the long-term situation, in which net in-migration offset extremely low rates of natural increase or even natural decrease. Ideally, of course, suburbs and satellites should be compared with *parts* of the central city, rather than with the central city as a whole. (See Reiss, *op. cit.*) It should also be noted that *individual* suburbs and satellites exhibit considerable variation within each of these types. Much of this variation may be due to variations in size, age, location and other characteristics that were not controlled here. One major difficulty that has yet to be surmounted in studies of suburban growth stems from a lack of appropriate data; there are no reliable statistics on the amount of vacant land available for residential development in sub-centers throughout the nation.

17. See Myles W. Rodehaver, "Fringe Settlement as a Two-Directional Movement," *Rural Sociology,* 12 (March, 1947), pp. 49-57; Walter T. Martin, *The Rural-Urban Fringe,* Eugene: University of Oregon Press, 1953, pp. 60-63; Wendell Bell, "Familism and Suburbanization," *Rural Sociology,* 21 (September-December 1956), pp. 276-283.

18. Warren S. Thompson, *Migration Within Ohio, 1935-40,* Oxford, Ohio: Scripps Foundation for Research in Population Problems, 1951; Amos H. Hawley, *Intrastate Migration in Michigan, 1935-40,* Ann Arbor: Institute of Public Administration, University of Michigan, 1953.

19. Coleman Woodbury, "Suburbanization and Suburbia," *American Journal of Public Health,* 45 (January, 1955), p. 2.

20. Nathan L. Whetten, "Suburbanization as a Field of Sociological Research," *Rural Sociology,* 16 (December, 1951), p. 325.

Sylvia Fleis Fava

Brooklyn College

CONTRASTS IN NEIGHBORING: NEW YORK CITY AND A SUBURBAN COUNTY

The whole rationale for the study of communities by sociologists rests on the assumption that living arrangements and social organization are interrelated. Otherwise communities could be described entirely by architects, lawyers, engineers, economists, and censustakers. Sociologists have long been concerned with determining what social traits differentiate rural and urban communities and with searching for the causes of these differences. The most well-known attempt in the urban field is Wirth's analysis of the social effects of size, density and heterogeneity of population.[1] Others have pointed to non-agricultural employment, to producing for a market rather than for self-sufficiency, or to the specialization of the division of labor as the socially relevant community characteristics, and to a whole network of effects on the family, leisure, education, stratification, etc. One of the most recent attempts relies on the idea that urbanism is a matter of increased "scale" (the degree of interaction and interdependency), and is accompanied by many changes in institutional structure and social control.[2] Rural sociologists from Sorokin and Zimmerman [3] to Loomis and Beegle [4] have similarly tried to define— and to explain—the essential differences in social organization be-

Revised version of a paper read at the annual meeting of the American Sociological Society, Washington, D. C., August 1957; published for the first time in this volume.

tween rural and urban areas. There is considerable variation among both urban and rural sociologists as to the traits which they consider crucial,[5] but the important thing is that there is a continuing search both for the social characteristics which are generic to a given community type and for the dynamics which produce these characteristics.

The task of the sociologist, *as sociologist,* in studying suburbs [6] would therefore also seem to fall into two parts: first, determining the social attributes of suburbia, and second, explaining what elements of suburban community structure are socially relevant. The answers to these questions are being sought by sociologists but are still far from adequate.

Thus in their attempts to discover whether suburbanism is a way of life, *i.e.,* a distinctive social organization, virtually all sociological studies have been of suburbs *alone.* The distinctiveness of those aspects of the suburban social structure examined is therefore more apparent than real, since the suburban data are presented without comparable urban or rural norms. Thus the many studies of suburban leisure, family life, formal and informal participation, and so on, are isolated descriptive studies whose usefulness is limited. It is revealing of the state of suburban research that many of the most frequently cited studies in this regard are not by sociologists.[7] The authors, mainly journalists, have described easy sociability, conformity, child-centeredness, and a subtle but pervasive concern with social status as characteristic of suburbia. These studies, too, are inadequate because, although they combine close observation and intelligent insight, they lack an explicit form of procedure. One is at a loss in judging how far the conclusions are generalizable.

Sociologists' efforts to deal with the second part of suburban study, that is, to ascertain the causes of the special social structure of suburbs, have been few and are handicapped by the fact that the formulations are untested except by such fragments of relevant data which happen to be available. Thus, two of the most recent attempts have been in the nature of research proposals. For example, in a recent article the author hypothesized that several of the physical and demographic traits of suburbs have predictable social effects.[8] In a similar way, Martin has contended that certain basic characteristics of suburbs —ecological position in relation to a larger city and high commuting rate to that city—have important results in structuring social relationships.[9]

In summary, both the "what" and the "why" of suburban social structure are largely unanswered. This paper reports a study, conducted in New York City and the adjacent suburban area of Nassau County, of one aspect of suburban social organization—neighboring —which demonstrates through comparative urban-suburban data what some of the differences are.[10] On this basis some answers to why urban and suburban communities differ in social organization will be offered.

Our study contrasted three groups: 208 residents of a central city area (the borough of Manhattan in New York City); 239 residents of an outer city area (the borough of Queens in New York City); and 170 residents of a suburban area (Nassau County, a residential district adjacent to Queens borough but not a legal part of New York City), making a total sample of 617. Respondents' names had been randomly selected from the telephone directories of these areas, except that substitutions were made for addresses in predominantly non-white census tracts. Thus almost all our respondents are assumed to be white and our conclusions are restricted to this group. Comparison of the distribution of our respondents' characteristics with the distribution of these characteristics in the universe [11] indicates that each of the three areal sub-samples underrepresents unmarried individuals, those with low socio-economic status, and renters.

The 617 respondents returned a neighboring scale developed by Paul Wallin, which was designed to measure informal association and contacts with geographic neighbors.[12] Thus, neighboring was defined operationally as the practice of certain folkways. Chi-square analysis of the distribution of neighboring scores by place of residence indicated that residents of the suburban area, Nassau County, have significantly higher neighboring scores.[13]

Although this shows that with respect to this trait suburban social organization differs from urban, two further steps were taken to ascertain whether it was a "real" difference. First, various factors relating to status and role differentials, the residential site, and the previous rural or urban experience of the individual were tested by chi-square in order to determine whether they were associated with neighboring scores. It was found that neighboring was associated with various factors indicative of a "settling down" process; being or having been married, home-ownership, stability of residence, ages between 30 and 65, etc.

Second, since neighboring was thus found to be affected by factors other than place of residence, these factors were held constant by matching sub-samples of the Manhattan, Queens and Nassau County populations on seven factors: sex, age, marital status, education, length of residence, nativity, and size of community of childhood residence.[14] The matched sub-samples were tested by chi-square and neighboring scores were still found to be very significantly related to place of residence. The data are presented in Table I. This means, for example, that since we know that married people in general are more

Table I—Cross-Tabulation of Neighboring Scores in Quartiles * with Place of Residence in a Matched Sample

| | Neighboring | | | | |
	First Quartile (Low)	Second Quartile	Third Quartile	Fourth Quartile (High)	Sample Totals
Manhattan	25	21	14	10	70
Queens	10	22	25	13	70
Nassau	7	16	28	19	70
Totals	42	59	67	42	210

The sum of Chi-square is 22.22, which is significant at the .001 level. The coefficient of contingency is .31.

* The quartiles are: (1) neighboring scores 0, 1, 2; (2) scores 3, 4, 5; (3) scores 6, 7; (4) score 8.

neighborly than the single we have controlled this factor through matching; nevertheless married suburbanites are more neighborly than married urbanites, and single suburbanites are more neighborly than single urbanites. Thus the procedure demonstrates, more conclusively, that there are basic differences between the urban and suburban ways of life, with respect to neighboring.

However, our procedure also has important implications for the generalizability of our results. The conditions associated with high neighboring scores, such as marriage, home-ownership, ages between 30 and 65, are more characteristic of the Nassau County universe and other residential suburbs than of the Manhattan and Queens universes or other city areas.[15] On the basis of the distribution of these traits in the universe we should therefore, have added reasons to expect to find universe differences in the related neighboring behavior.

By way of summary we may ask what light this research sheds on the two questions raised at the beginning of this presentation. First, are suburbs a social reality as a community form, with certain distinguishing features from urbanism as a form of social organization? Second, what factors are relevant in explaining these urban-suburban differences in social structure? In response to the first question our study shows that, insofar as neighboring practices are concerned, New York City and one of its suburban counties differ very significantly. There are indications that these results are generalizable. In response to the second question, our study indicates that the differences in neighboring cannot be entirely due to demographic, economic or similar factors, since when these factors are held constant, the suburban residents still have significantly higher neighboring scores than the urban residents.

These findings on urban-suburban contrasts in neighboring are relevant to community theory at a number of points. An obvious comparison is that of the distribution we obtained with that expected under ecological theory. Examination of Table I makes it clear that the outer city (Queens) not only lies geographically between the central city (Manhattan) and the suburbs (Nassau County), but that the neighboring pattern of the outer city falls between those of the central city and the suburban area. This suggests that neighboring gradually increases with distance from the city center and may be distributed in the gradient or zonal fashion made so familiar by the ecologists' work.

Ecological theory therefore seems equal to account for the urban-suburban contrasts as a static phenomenon. However, when we turn to ecological theory to explain the dynamics of the situation we find it inadequate. Thus we would assume on the basis of ecological theory that the demographic and economic characteristics of communities, which are indicative of the selective ecological processes at work, would explain many if not all the community differences in social organization. However, our data show that even when such factors are held constant, the social organizations of an urban and a suburban area—as measured by neighboring scores—remain significantly different. It has been suggested in a previous article by the author that selectivity on the basis of non-rational elements of habit, belief, feelings, and experience, which may be called social-psychological, should be added to standard ecological factors in explaining suburban social characteristics.[16] There is obviously a large reservoir of urban dwellers who have both the financial means to move to suburbs and the "need" in terms of inadequate play space for children, lack of outdoor activity, and so on. Yet only a portion of families with these objectively similar characteristics, do move to suburbs. Do the migrants have a particular value system which makes the suburban environment acceptable or inviting to them? Our data on the persistent differences in neighboring patterns between city and suburban dwellers whose overt character-istics of sex, age, marital status, education, etc., were similar conform to such an explanation and further research has also given it some support.[17] The possibility that the suburban migration differentially attracts those who are willing to neighbor is strengthened by the finding that about three quarters of those interviewed in a recent study of two Chicago suburbs, included, "more friendly neighbors, greater com-munity participation, and a sense of belonging to the community," among their reasons for moving to the suburbs.[18]

The need for examining the part played by social-psychological selectivity is heightened by the fact that the majority of our sample of suburbanites grew up in New York City. This raises the question of how community experience affects the individual and, particularly, how neighboring may be produced by the largest and most urban of environments. Urban living provides several sources for high neigh-boring.

First, several authors have pointed to "rural survivals," practices and beliefs developed in and suited to rural life, which have been carried over into urban living.[19] "Rural survivals" are not surprising in view of the fact that even statistically the United States became predominantly urban, by a bare majority, as late as 1920, and had only about two-thirds of its population classified as urban in 1950. Neighboring and intensive participation on a territorial basis have generally been regarded as typical of rural areas. It is therefore relevant that in 1950 one of every three adults living in a nonfarm place in the United States was reared on a farm, and even in the twelve largest metropolitan areas fifteen percent of the population was farm-reared.[20] It would be surprising if the stream of peasant and rural migrants did not reestablish the familiar associational form in cities.

The second set of factors fostering neighboring are those associated with urban heterogeneity. The differentiation among the urban popu-lation results in the formation of relatively homogeneous sub-areas in the city. These sub-areas have been recognized by human ecologists in their description of the "natural area," and by the Bureau of the Census in setting up the census tract system. These "villages in metropolis" tend to foster neighboring and other social contacts. The many studies of geographic propinquity in mate selection in American cities are an interesting confirmation of this. Many city sub-areas are also "ghettos" for foreign-born groups who have traditional peasant values of land ownership and local orientation, and who pass such values on to their children.

The third set of factors fostering neighboring in the city are those associated with the size of the city. Until recently, urban sociologists have generally assumed, uncritically, that city size exerts a cumulative effect, i.e., the larger the city the less primary group association because the numbers engender anonymity and mobility. The notion of such a rural-urban continuum may be an oversimplification, however. It is possible that at a certain point increased size functions to increase some types of informal contacts rather than to decrease them. There are some data to support such an interpretation. Key's study of several types of social participation in rural and urban communities of various sizes found that the traditional point of view with regard to the influence of size was not always supported. Certain types of informal association tended to fall into "U-shaped" distributions with the low point of the "U" at the small urban size.[21] So-called "rural" patterns of association may, in other words, be produced not only by rural conditions but also by the extremes of urban conditions. Keyes, another investigator of the rural-urban distribution of social phenomena, also found that the distribution was not a smooth one. He concluded that there were major changes at the 25,000, the 100,000 and the 500,000 points.[22]

We have indicated that "rural survivals," heterogeneity, and the very size of the city set up conditions which may be conducive to neighboring. Many recent studies have already begun to show that neighboring is more common in cities than had been expected.[23] It appears that the seeds of local intimacy have already been planted in much of the urban population. A complex set of factors selects a segment of the urban population for the suburban migration. It is well-documented that the suburban population is typically composed of white married couples who are in the child-rearing phase of the family cycle and who are of the middle-class status which enables them to afford suburban living.[24] These characteristics are in themselves conducive to neighboring relations and may be accentuated, as this paper has suggested, by the possibility that people are also drawn to suburbs because of their "quest for community." Given a population with these particular characteristics living in the home-centered, out-of-doors suburban setting, the seeds of neighboring, which survive even in the city, grow and flourish.

FOOTNOTES

1. L. Wirth, "Urbanism as a Way of Life," *American Journal of Sociology,* 44 (July 1938), pp. 1-24.
2. E. Shevky and W. Bell, *Social Area Analysis,* Stanford, California: Stanford University Press, 1955, pp. 3-19.
3. P. Sorokin and C. Zimmerman, *Principles of Rural-Urban Sociology,* New York, Henry Holt, 1929.
4. C. Loomis and J. A. Beegle, *Rural Sociology: The Strategy of Change,* New York: Prentice-Hall, 1957.
5. For example, see the review and critique by Albert Reiss, Jr., "An Analysis of Urban Phenomena," in *The Metropolis in Modern Life* (ed. by R. M. Fisher), Garden City, New York: Doubleday, 1956, pp. 41-49.
6. "Suburbs," as the term is used in this paper, refers particularly to the residential or dormitory variety, characterized by dependence on the city occupationally and for various specialized types of goods and services, shopping, recreation, etc. A working definition would comprise the area outside the legal city limits but within commuting distance.
7. For example, F. L. Allen, "The Big Change in Suburbia" (in two parts), *Harper's Magazine* (June 1954), pp. 21-28 and (July 1954), pp. 47-53; H. Henderson, "The Mass-Produced Suburbs," (in two parts), *Harper's Magazine* (November 1953), pp. 25-32 and (December 1953), pp. 80-86; John Keats, *The Crack in the Picture Window,* Boston: Houghton Mifflin, 1956; William H. Whyte, Jr., "The Transients," (in four parts), *Fortune* (May, June, July, August, 1953); A. C. Spectorsky, *The Exurbanites,* New York and Philadelphia: J. B. Lippincott, 1955.
8. S. F. Fava, "Suburbanism as a Way of Life," *American Sociological Review,* 21 (February 1956), pp. 34-38.
9. W. T. Martin, "The Structuring of Social Relationships Engendered by Suburban Residence," *American Sociological Review,* 21 (August 1956), pp. 446-453.
10. Details of the study and the procedures used are in S. F. Fava, "Urban-Suburban Contrasts in Social Participation: A Study of Neighboring in New York City and Nassau County," Unpublished Ph.D. dissertation, Northwestern University, 1956.
11. Census data for the three areas were used as universe data.
12. P. Wallin, "A Guttman Scale for Measuring Women's Neighborliness," *American Journal of Sociology,* 59 (November 1953), pp. 243-246. Analysis by Cornell technique indicated that only eight of Wallin's twelve questions formed a scale with our Manhattan, Queens and Nassau samples.

Coefficients of reproducibility were .89 and .93 for men and women, respectively. On this basis nine neighboring score types were derived.

13. A 4 x 3 table cross-tabulating neighboring scores in quartiles by place of residence (Manhattan, Queens, Nassau) had a sum of chi-square of 44.89 which is significant beyond the .001 level. The coefficient of contingency was .27.

14. Matching was done by frequency distribution on each of the seven factors. This reduced the sample from 617 to 210.

15. For example, 1950 census data show the following percentages of male population married: 59, 71, 74 for Manhattan, Queens, and Nassau County, respectively. For the female population the corresponding percentages are: 54, 66, 70. The general contrasts in economic, demographic, and social traits between cities and suburbs in the United States are well-summarized in L. F. Schnore and D. W. Varley, "Some Concomitants of Metropolitan Size," *American Sociological Review,* 20 (August 1955), pp. 408-414; Otis D. Duncan and Albert J. Reiss, Jr., *Social Characteristics of Urban and Rural Communities, 1950,* New York: J. Wiley and Sons, 1956, pp. 117-133.

16. Fava, "Suburbanism as a Way of Life," *op. cit.*

17. Data relevant to social-psychological selectivity were collected in the course of the present study and the results will be presented in future publications.

18. Wendell Bell, "Familism and Suburbanization: One Test of the Social Choice Hypothesis," *Rural Sociology,* 21 (September-December 1956), p. 282.

19. A. Tomars, "Rural Survivals in American Urban Life," in *Sociological Analysis* (ed. by L. Wilson and C. Kolb), New York: Harcourt, Brace, 1949; E. Harms, "Rural Attitudes in Modern American Life," *Social Forces,* 17 (1939).

20. Ronald and Deborah Freedman, "Farm-Reared Elements in the Nonfarm Population," *Rural Sociology,* 21 (March 1956), pp. 50-61.

21. W. Key, "Rural-urban Differences in Social Participation," Unpublished Ph.D. dissertation, Washington University, St. Louis, 1953, p. 89 ff.

22. F. Keyes, "The Correlation of Social Phenomena with Community Size," Unpublished Ph.D. dissertation, Yale University, 1942.

23. Morris Axelrod, "Urban Structure and Social Participation," *American Sociological Review,* 21 (February 1956), pp. 13-18; Wendell Bell and Marion D. Boat, "Urban Neighborhoods and Informal Social Relations," *American Journal of Sociology,* 62 (January 1957), pp. 391-398; Donald Foley, *Neighbors or Urbanites?* New York: Department of Sociology, University of Rochester, 1952; W. H. Form, J. Smith, G. P. Stone, and J. Cowhig, "The Compatibility of Alternative Approaches to the Delimitation of Urban Sub-areas," *American Sociological Review,* 19 (August 1954), pp. 434-440; Scott Greer, "Urbanism Reconsidered: A Comparative Study of Local Areas in a Metropolis," *American Sociological Review,* 21 (February 1956), pp. 19-25; Key, *op. cit.;* Report of the Detroit Area

Study, *A Social Profile of Detroit: 1952,* Ann Arbor, Michigan: University of Michigan, 1952, pp. 24-26; J. Smith, W. H. Form and G. P. Stone, "Local Intimacy in a Middle-sized City," *American Journal of Sociology,* 60 (November 1954), pp. 276-284.

24. The evidence on this point, using 1950 U.S. census data, is summarized in Schnore and Varley, *op. cit.;* Duncan and Reiss, *op. cit.*

William M. Dobriner

Hofstra College

LOCAL AND COSMOPOLITAN AS CONTEMPORARY SUBURBAN CHARACTER TYPES

Currently, the theory of community organization is built around a fundamental conceptual dichotomy, rural and urban, as two basic and contrasting types of social organization. In recent years, however, as the deconcentration of urban populations and the decentralization of functions have become such major demographic and ecological variables, many students of social organization have turned their attention to the suburban community. These new forms of community organization, though essentially urban, now characterize a sociologically important segment of the contemporary metropolitan community. Martin's recent discussion of the characteristic forms of social relationships within the suburbs,[1] Fava's description of "Suburbanism as a Way of Life," [2] Bell's hypothesis regarding familism and suburbanization [3] and Schnore's study of the growth of metropolitan suburbs,[4] all demonstrate the current swing of sociological interest toward these rapidly emerging communities of urban-associational society.

While a sizable body of ecological and demographic data has been amassed, coupled to a few modest conceptualizations and theoretic propositions, there has been virtually no effort to treat the social-psychological phenomena arising from suburbanization. This paper, therefore, is an effort in that general direction. Basically, we shall be

This is an original article, prepared for this publication.

reporting an exploratory empirical study which focused on certain characterological variables between a sample of suburbanites and "small-town" villagers.

There are a few scattered references in the literature relating to the "suburban type." In 1925, Douglas indicated that there was a "psychological selection of suburbanites." [5] He contended that the suburbanite was essentially an expatriate city dweller in escape from the congestion, noise and pace of urban life. Later, Lundberg and his associates also argued that "certain selective influences are at work in determining the inhabitants of a suburb." [6] The two basic psychological traits which differentiate the suburbanite from the unreconstructed city dweller, they pointed out, are (1) ". . . a greater sensitivity to nature and the outdoor life . . ." and (2) "the suburbanite's comparatively deep attachment to neighborhood and domestic life and the traditional family pattern. . . ." [7] Recently, Fava has also suggested that there is a social-psychological selectivity in suburban migration.[8] Somewhat similar to the Lundberg position, this hypothesis suggests that the suburbanite as a "type" is differentially attracted to rural patterns of interaction in which the "high" amount of suburban neighboring becomes a significant indicator of rurality.

In the study to be reported, we were not so much interested in the problem of unique social type, if such a type exists at all, but rather to demonstrate the existence of some general patterns of character that suburbanites would tend to share. It was our basic hypothesis that the "suburban man" would be characterized by certain broad yet salient personality configurations more typical of urban social systems than rural. While previous attempts to treat suburban character have emphasized the rural leanings of the suburbanite, it was our belief that this position had distorted the essentially urban social processes of the suburban community and certain urban personality characteristics of the suburbanite. In short, we concluded that suburban character structure was far more urban than rural, inasmuch as the suburbanite has lengthy and continuous experience in the metropolitan complex and is constantly exposed to the patterned and institutionalized relationships within the urban social system.

The first problem was to isolate that dimension of character which at least partially reflected the urban ethos and then to construct a device to measure the quality. In spite of the lack of measuring instrument, there is a long tradition of conceptual-qualitative propositions concerning the social-psychological nature of urban man. Simmel, noting the sheer quantity of relationships within the city, argued that the result in urban character was a sort of blase sophistication in which the value of "efficiency" replaces "personal feelings." [9] Thus, Simmel's notion of urban rationality coincides with Tonnies classic distinction of rural, Gemeinschaft solidarity relationships versus urban, Gesellschaft, associational-contractural relationships. More recently, the terms "localistic" and "cosmopolitan" have been employed to refer to the characteristics of individuals who are responding to Gemeinschaft (localistic) or Gesellschaft (cosmopolitan) as a fundamental orientation to social relationships. Indeed, Zimmerman, in his translation of Tonnies, used the terms local-cosmopolitan synonymously with Gemeinschaft-Gesellschaft. All of these materials tend to suggest, therefore, that there is a well-established set of concepts which critically differentiate elements of character and social relations between rural and urban social systems.

In his Rovere study of opinion leadership, Merton employed local and cosmopolitan as concepts differentiating types of opinion leaders.[10] Thus locals and cosmopolitans were regarded as types of persons with contrasting interests and identifications (reference groups) to local or national social structures. Merton describes the typical local in this way:

> "The localite largely confines his interests to this community. Rovere is essentially his world. Devoting little thought or energy to the Great Society, he is preoccupied with local problems, to the virtual exclusion of the national and international scene. He is, strictly speaking, a parochial." [11]

On the other side of the continuum is the cosmopolitan, an individual who identifies and relates himself to issues, events and organizations *outside* of the local community. Describing the cosmopolitan opinion leader, Merton says:

> "He has some interest in Rovere and must, of course, maintain a minimum of relations within the community since he, too, exerts influence there. But he is also oriented significantly to the world outside Rovere, and regards himself as an integral part of that world. He resides in Rovere but lives in the Great Society." [12]

The usefulness of local-cosmopolitan character types as a conceptual tool has been reinforced by Foley in his study of a Rochester urban area in which he classifies community residents as "urbanites" or "neighbors." [13] According to Foley, "the urbanite" has "emancipated himself from any marked dependence on or identification with a local neighborhood." [14] Yet, "the neighbor" organizes "his living much more completely around the facilities and the friendships of his own residential neighborhood." [15] It seems quite clear that Merton with the local-cosmopolitan distinction, and Foley with the urbanite-neighbor dichotomy are referring to types of persons who have internalized two highly divergent modes of social relationships—those oriented toward Gemeinschaft-localistic-solidarity relationships and those oriented toward Gesellschaft-cosmopolitan-associational relationships. The sociological significance of the two dichotomies lies in the assumption that the syndromes result from experience in the basic and essential mode of social relations which are characteristic of rural or urban social systems. This is not to suggest, of course, that all metropolitan communities produce cosmopolitans and all rural hamlets socialize their inhabitants into locals. However, if the generalizations concerning rural and urban social structures and processes which social scientists have evolved over the past one hundred years have any validity, then these unique rural and urban social systems must have a characterological counterpart. Thus, the city man almost has to have an awareness of the metropolitan society and his dependence on it. The ruralite, particularly in the 19th century, alone with his farm, family and small community could easily become a local. For the urbanite, on the other hand, a strike of subway workers, or a failure in the power supply, acutely makes him aware of the functional social system of which he is a part.

We can carry the cosmopolitan dimension of the city man too far. Many fairly recent studies of the city have shown that the metropolis on the "neighborhood" level is a vast complex of small and surprisingly cohesive communities. Here, Foley has demonstrated the existence of the "neighbor." Here, too, there is face to face interaction, primary relations and a sense of the Gemeinschaft. However, it is the broad social-psychological consequences of urban society that concerns us here. And on this basis we may conclude that cosmopolitan orientations are distinctly more urban and rural.

That element of character, then, which closely coincides with

urbanism we have identified as cosmopolitanism. Thus, if we are to
demonstrate the pervasiveness of urban orientations in the character
of suburban man, we need a device to measure the cosmopolitan
syndrome. However, the great majority of attitude scales and personality inventories currently available are addressed primarily to
psychological categories. There are relatively few devices which
measure characterological variables directly or indirectly related to
the actor's internalization of the modal pattern of social relationships
within a social system. In short, while there are instruments which
measure segments or facets of the actor's total experience (political,
economic, psychological or social) there are none which attempt to
distinguish the impact of the principal pattern of social relationships
characteristic of a given community *on* the actor.

Although they principally relate to the local-cosmopolitan dimension
in terms of the communications behavior of informal opinion leaders,
Merton's findings are of particular value for they emerged from a field
research and are readily adaptable to a series of items scaling the
syndrome. Consequently, a scale built up from Merton's substantive
findings might prove to be the quantitative instrument needed to
measure the local-cosmopolitan tendencies of suburban character.
Accordingly, the qualitative distinctions noted by Merton were
incorporated in a ten item Likert-type scale. Normally, ten items are
hardly sufficient to produce a valid and reliable scale. However, the
purposes of the study were purely exploratory and one of the research
goals, indeed, was to explore the usefulness of the LC dimension
among a sample of suburbanites. The validity of the scale was
checked primarily by a "logical validation" of the continuum largely
as indicated by Merton's findings. The reliability of the scale was
checked primitively by administering the scale to selected groups
of college students and comparing similar groups for consistency in
score. The scale items were as follows:

1. National and International happenings rarely seem as interesting and important as events that occur right in the local
   community in which one lives.
2. Generally speaking, news commentators on radio or TV who
   give personal interpretations of the news and human interest
   stories are more worth listening to than commentators who
   just give the news straight.

3. National and international events are important largely because of the way they effect Huntington as a community.
4. Many personal relationships and contacts with other people in the local community are essential in life today.
5. The most rewarding organizations a person can belong to are local organizations serving local needs.
6. Huntington is one of the finest communities in the United States.
7. Meeting and knowing many people is extremely important in establishing oneself in the community.
8. Big cities may have their place, but when you get right down to it, the local community is the backbone of America.
9. Huntington's weekly newspapers are extremely important in order to know what is going on.
10. News about Huntington is generally more interesting than national and international news.

The scale was exposed to a sample of 275 residents in Huntington Village, Long Island, New York. Huntington Village is currently on the periphery of the New York metropolitan area; in the past ten years the village population has about doubled under the impact of an intense suburban migration. Up to this time, the village was a relatively isolated, homogeneous semi-rural community whose history goes back before the American Revolution. The village was selected as the research site because it contained two populations that were regarded as essential for the study—an "oldtimer" group in which localism was expected to prevail, and the new suburbanites who we felt would share the characteristic cosmopolitan orientations of the city. The following table records the "LC" scores of the two resident groups. The scale was scored so that the higher scores indicate "high" localism: [16]

Table 1—Median Scores in the Local-Cosmopolitan Scale

Group	Number	Score
Oldtimers who were born in Huntington	41	10.0
Oldtimers of ten years or more residence in Huntington	87	8.5
Total Oldtimers (villagers)	128	9.7
Total Newcomers (suburbanites)	147	5.0
Newcomers of one to nine years residence	105	5.9
Newcomers of less than one year residence	42	3.6

The median scores indicated that the total suburban group scored 4.7 lower in the scale than did the villagers. Since high on the plus side of the scale indicates high localism, it appears that the suburbanites are indeed considerably more cosmopolitan than the villagers. Thus, the hypothesis on the basis of these scores seems borne out. The spread between oldtimers and newcomers is even more apparent when comparing the median scores of the oldtimers who were born in Huntington with the recent arrivals of less than a year. Here the differential in score is 6.4, which even more clearly indicates the high degree of cosmopolitanism of the suburbanites.

Correlates of Localism and Cosmopolitanism

It may be legitimately inferred that the differences in LC score between the villagers and suburbanites may actually be due to more basic differences in personality or in status characteristics other than length of residence in Huntington Village. Or, it may be that the syndrome is only a surface expression of a more fundamental variable which underlies the differences in local or cosmopolitan orientations. For example, it might be argued that localism is merely one of many possible expressions of a basic conservative predisposition on the part of the respondent. Consequently, in order to more accurately determine the relationship between the LC syndrome and a liberal-conservative orientation, a political-economic conservatism (PEC) scale was also included on the questionnaire administered to the sample of village residents.[17]

Table 2—Median Scores in the Political-Economic Conservatism Scale

Group	Number	Score
Oldtimers who were born in Huntington	41	8.6
Oldtimers of ten years or more residence	87	7.5
Total Oldtimers (villagers)	128	7.8
Total Newcomers (suburbanites)	147	7.0
Newcomers of one to nine years residence	105	6.7
Newcomers of less than one year residence	42	7.5

Where the LC scale revealed considerable differences between suburbanite and villager, the PEC scale indicated little change in the political-economic liberalism or conservatism between the two groups.

Consequently, the similarity of scores from the PEC scale, in contrast to the considerable dispersion of scores in the LC scale, indicates that the local-cosmopolitan syndrome constitutes quite a different dimension of the person than liberal-conservative predispositions.

The problem still persists, however, regarding the role of other status characteristics in contributing to local or cosmopolitan orientations. For example, from an analysis of the questionnaire data it was found that the suburbanites had considerably higher incomes, greater education and more prestige occupations than did the villagers. The possibility remains, therefore, that occupation or education may be a greater determinant of localism or cosmopolitanism than mere involvement in urban social relations. Merton, however, discounts the determining role of educational or occupational status.

> "...These differences in occupational or educational status do not appear to determine the diverse types.... When we compare the behavior and orientations of professionals among the locals or cosmopolitans, their characteristic differences persist, even though they have the same types of occupation and have received the same type of education. Education and occupational differences may *contribute* to the differences between the two types ... but they are not the *source* of these differences." [18]

Because of the small sample, it was not possible to meaningfully compare the LC scores of all suburbanites and villagers with the same educational and occupational status. However, some comparison of status sets was possible, although the small number of respondents in some categories indicates the data must be interpreted as indicators of only the broadest trends. For example, the twenty oldtimer Protestants who were professionally employed had an LC score of 11.0, on the other hand, the fifty-two suburbanite Protestant professionals had an LC score of 3.5. In this case, it seems clear that occupation and education do not play a significant role in shaping the LC syndrome.

However, the case for the Jewish professionals is not quite so clear. The eight oldtimer Jewish professionals had an LC score of 3.0 while a score of 3.6 was obtained by the twelve newcomer Jewish professionals. It would appear that Jews are cosmopolitan regardless of length of residence in Huntington Village. It is possible that the minority group position accorded the Jews, in the dominant Protestant culture of Huntington, prevents the adaptation of a localistic frame of reference. Their world is still outside of the local community for their ethnic status prevents complete identification with the village and the consequent emergence of the localistic syndrome. This hypothesis is further supported by noting that both the Protestant and Jewish professionals, among the suburbanites, begin with the same LC score (3.5), but over the years the Protestant professionals apparently become increasingly localistic while the Jews continue to maintain a high cosmopolitan orientation. One interesting note, however, which suggests some degree of Jewish assimilation into village society, is in the differences in PEC scores between the oldtimer and newcomer Jewish professionals. The oldtimer Jewish professionals had a PEC score of 6.5 which was not significantly below the median score of all the oldtimers. On the other hand, the newcomer Jewish professionals scored −1.3 which was significantly more liberal than any other group in the occupational-religious status set. These data suggest that the oldtimer Jews, all of whom are locally employed, have adopted a political-economic ideology characteristic of the local community (an indication of assimilation) while the twelve newcomer Jews, eight of whom are employed outside of the community and who are still comparatively "uninvolved" in the local social system, maintain a distinctly liberal political-economic ideology.

In general, Catholics, both among the newcomers and oldtimers, tended to be more localistic than were Jews or Protestants; although, in the main, Catholic oldtimers were more localistic than were Catholic suburbanites. For example, the eighteen Catholic suburbanites who were *not* in the upper white-collar occupations had an LC score of 8.2 while a score of 11.0 was obtained by the twenty-nine oldtimer Catholics in the same occupational category. On the other hand, the twelve oldtimer Catholic professionals scored slightly more localistic than did the twenty-seven newcomers in the same category. This again may be due to the dominant position of Protestants in the village social structure. The "upper class" Catholic oldtimers may perceive the nature of Protestant dominance and find it difficult to adopt a localistic frame of reference. The case of the Catholic and Jewish oldtimers suggests that religious affiliation, or any other status that is marginal or regarded negatively in the dominant norm system, may consequently prevent the occupant of the status in identifying with the dominant social structure.

A cross tabulation of age, sex and income statuses failed to reveal that any of these variables are highly associated with localism or cosmopolitanism. Only education seems to have a relationship; as educational achievement increases, generally cosmopolitanism also increases. This would seem logical in view of the characteristics of cosmopolitanism. Generally speaking, higher education can be expected to move an individual outside of the social and intellectual confines of the local community and give him a sense for and interest in the events which shape the "Great Society." In short, the individual's "world view," through education, is considerably widened. Thus the process of involvement in the scope and complexity of things, which theoretically is one of the goals of higher education, seems to be actually borne out in the high cosmopolitan orientations of respondents with the most education.

Conclusion

The literature concerning the modal character of the suburban man has tended to emphasize the "rural values" of the suburbanite which supposedly send him fleeing from the anonymity and density of the city, to the comparative "rurality" of the suburbs. This position, it was felt, sorely distorted the essential urban aspects of suburban character in which a cosmopolitan frame of reference was one significant criterion. Through the development of an exploratory LC scale, which attempted to secure a partial measure of the actor's internalization of the modal pattern of social relationships with the social system (rural or urban), we hoped to note the relative degree of cosmopolitan or localistic orientations among a sample of residents from a New York suburban community. The data indicated that cosmopolitanism is a significant characteristic of the newcomer-suburbanites and that localism is concentrated among the oldtimer-villagers. Additional variables, however, occasionally intervened other than merely the newcomer-oldtimer distinction, to effect changes in the syndrome. Villagers occupying ethnic or religious statuses of the out-group, for example, may not be able to develop localistic orientations because of their inability to completely identify with the local community.

The data from this exploratory study has indicated that the LC dimension is an extremely important conceptual tool, for its deriva-

142   The Sociology of the Suburbs

tives lie in purely sociological variables—modal themes in the pattern of relations within the community. The extent and pervasiveness of local and cosmopolitan as contemporary character types, however, must wait upon many additional researches utilizing larger samples, a more valid and reliable scale and more sensitive statistical procedures.

FOOTNOTES

1. Walter T. Martin, "The Structuring of Social Relationships Engendered by Suburban Residence," *American Sociological Review,* 21, August 1956.
2. Sylvia Fleis Fava, "Suburbanism as a Way of Life," *American Sociological Review,* 21, February 1956.
3. Wendell Bell, "Familism and Suburbanization: One Test of the Social Choice Hypothesis," *Rural Sociology,* 21, September-December 1956.
4. Leo Schnore, "The Growth of Metropolitan Suburbs," *American Sociological Review,* 22, April 1957.
5. H. P. Douglas, *The Suburban Trend,* p. 34. New York: The Century Co., 1925.
6. George A. Lundberg, Mirra Komarovsky and Mary Alice McInerny, *Leisure: A Suburban Study,* p. 42. New York: Columbia Univ. Press, 1934.
7. *Ibid.,* p. 60.
8. Sylvia Fleis Fava, *op. cit.*
9. Georg Simmel, "The Metropolis and Mental Life," from *The Sociology of Georg Simmel,* translated by Kurt Wolff. Glencoe, Ill.: The Free Press, 1950.
10. Robert K. Merton, "Patterns of Influence: A Study of Interpersonal Influence and of Communications Behavior in a Local Community," in Paul F. Lazarsfeld and Frank N. Stanton (eds.) *Communications Research 1948-1949.* New York: Harper and Brothers, 1948-1949.
11. *Ibid.,* p. 189.
12. *Ibid.,* pp. 189-190.
13. Donald Foley, *Neighbors or Urbanites?,* p. 56. Rochester: Univ. of Rochester, Dept. of Sociology, 1952.
14. *Ibid.*
15. *Ibid.*
16. The respondent was instructed to indicate the degree of his agreement or disagreement with each scale item by placing +3 to +1 next to those statements he agreed with, and −3 to −1 next to those statements he disagreed with. Minus 3 to +3 indicated the greatest amount of disagreement or agreement, −1 and +1 the least amount. The respondent's final score was computed by subtracting the total minus score from the total plus score.
17. The PEC scale materials were taken almost directly from the scale discussed in T. W. Adorno, et al., *The Authoritarian Personality* (New York,

Harper and Brothers, 1950), pp. 153-207. The only change in the scale was the introduction of item 3 which deals with attitudes toward national health insurance. The original scale item related to attitudes concerning O.P.A. (the government agency that regulated consumer prices during World War II) which, we felt, was no longer a meaningful question in 1955. The scale items are as follows: (1) Labor unions should become stronger and have more influence generally. (2) America may not be perfect, but the American Way has brought us as close as human beings can get to a perfect society. (3) In order to protect the health of the nation the Congress should pass a law in which the Federal Government would contribute to our medical bills. (4) Men like Henry Ford or J. P. Morgan, who overcame all competition on the road to success are models for all young people to admire and imitate. (5) In general, full economic security is bad; most men wouldn't work if they didn't need the money for eating and living.

18. Robert K. Merton, *op. cit.*, p. 200.

Part III

The Social Organization of the Suburbs

I am going to call it a Social Ethic. With reason it could be called an organization ethic, or a bureaucratic ethic; more than anything else it rationalizes the organization's demands for fealty and gives those who offer it wholeheartedly a sense of dedication in doing so—in extremis, *you might say, it converts what would seem in other times a bill of no rights into a statement of individualism.*

William H. Whyte, Jr.

Ernest R. Mowrer

Northwestern University

THE FAMILY IN SUBURBIA

O ne of the most apparent changes in the development of social organization in the United States in the post World-War II period has been the rapid migration of people to the areas surrounding and contiguous to large cities. This is the flight to the suburbs with its rapid development of new neighborhoods and the expansion of old ones. Not only has this movement spawned large numbers of residential areas where few persons lived before, but it has also been marked with the development of shopping centers as well as the building of factories with little regard for rail transportation which historically has played such a dominant role in the location of commercial and industrial enterprises. The explanation of this decentralization process in residence, in commerce, and industry is largely in terms of the automobile and the truck, which have freed the movement of expansion from the confining influences of railway networks so dominant in the first quarter of the twentieth century.

While suburbs have always grown up around urban centers, the beginnings of the present movement are to be found chiefly in the period of the Roaring Twenties. At this time there was a mushrooming of suburban areas, but much of this movement went relatively unnoticed since it involved the building up of vacant areas within the confines of the limits of large cities which had incorporated large areas of unoccupied land. Expansion beyond these limits developed

This is part of a chapter to appear shortly in a book on The Family and Marriage, with the collaboration of Harriet R. Mowrer, and to be published by Rinehart and Company, New York.

in spoke-like projections along rail lines at a furious pace until by the end of the decade enough land had been platted in subdivisions to accommodate the needs for normal growth for a period of perhaps a quarter of a century.[1]

Residential real estate developments in suburban areas during the Twenties differed from today's practice in that emphasis was primarily upon the selling of residential sites rather than of houses. The result was that to a large extent the real estate promoter liquidated his interest in the subdivision once he had sold all the lots which he had platted. And while he often paved streets and put in sewers, the task of building the house was left to the individual purchaser. Many of the purchasers did not have the capital required to build homes and the result was that there was only limited activity in home building in many of the elaborately promoted subdivisions. The stock market crash quickly brought to an end whatever building was in progress, leaving in some instances structures only partially completed, eventually to be demolished as storm and wind took their toll. In other places, temporary structures were erected which it was planned would eventually become garages, many of these providing homes for the owners for the period of the depression. In still other areas, completed residential structures particularly two-flat apartments, were soon to be left vacant and unkept as the depression deepened. The blight was on the suburbs to remain until prosperity should once more return.

The return of economic prosperity revived the suburban movement; slowly at first, but inevitably growing in volume. The establishment of the Federal Housing Administration by the Roosevelt administration provided an instrumentality which was to act increasingly to encourage home ownership by providing for the guaranteeing of home mortgages and for a monthly system of collection of costs including insurance, taxes, interest, and amortization of mortgage. Down payments required by the F.H.A. were low in comparison to the previous practice of private loaning agencies, and the period of amortization somewhat longer than had been generally permitted. The results of this new formula of home ownership was to encourage real estate organizations to undertake the construction and sale of houses ready for occupancy rather than only the lots upon which the buyer might build to his own plans. The new formula also produced another significant result in that it brought into the market for homes a group of people who before this time would have had some difficulty in providing the necessary down payments customarily required and in establishing credit within the limits generally prevailing at the time the new formula was adopted.

The revival of home construction in the suburbs was well under way at the outbreak of World War II, only to languish during the war period. During the war period, however, the potentials of expansion were in the making. The marriage rate increased and with it the birth rate. The declining rate of growth of population was reversed, which with the obsolescence of the established housing facilities built up an enormous potential ready to find realization once hostilities were over. Special encouragement to veterans to become home owners through even lower requirements of down payments (or none at all) and longer periods of mortgage at lower interest rates provided the necessary conditions for even a broader segment of the population to become home owners. The result was an increase in demand for homes unprecedented in recent times.

Forces in Suburban Expansion

In the development of suburbia and the resulting changes in the family under conditions of suburban living, three sets of factors (two economic and one social psychological) need to be taken into account. These factors are: (1) prosperity, (2) government encouragement of home ownership, and (3) the suburban vision. The first, prosperity, is an integral part of the post-war period, whereas the other two have somewhat longer histories. Even prosperity itself must be regarded as in the making prior to World War II, but there may be some question whether the continuous expansion of our economy from the end of the war to the present could have shown comparable growth without World War II and its deployment of industrial production from peace-time needs to the demands of warfare. Nevertheless this shift from a peace to a war economy was instrumental in building up an enormous potential reservoir of demand for consumers goods which was to provide incentive for industrial expansion far beyond the dreams of the most optimistic, while at the same time curtailing current expenditures and resulting in the accumulation of savings by large segments of the population not in the military forces to be used eventually in providing a base for an expanding economy.

Prosperity has contributed to the suburban expansion in many ways, particularly in providing the incentives to home ownership in the expansion of investment capital and the reduction in interest rates. While many families accumulated the savings necessary for down-payments on homes during the war period with its restricted consumer economy and price controls, increased demands for labor after the war with rising wage-rates contributed greatly to the further accumulation of investment capital in the hands of large numbers of persons, making home ownership possible on a larger scale than had been previously experienced. Prosperity also provided an enormous expansion of credit with its normal accompaniment of reduction in interest rates. And not to be overlooked, were the products of inflation which calmed the apprehensions of many a potential home owner. If he already owned a home he could sell his older house at a price well-above what he had paid some years previously, and if he hesitated to buy because he found the price too high, he would come back "tomorrow" and find that the price had advanced.

Intertwined with increasing prosperity as an incentive to home ownership is, of course, the encouragement on the part of the federal government through the facilities of the Federal Housing Administration and the Veterans Administration. The guaranteeing of mortgages by these administrative agencies and the establishment of interest rates, size of down payment, and the period of amortization as a basis for guaranteeing mortgages, has encouraged lending organizations to assume the risks themselves in many instances and thus to offer funds at even lower rates of interest than provided in the government arrangement.

Home ownership in the post-war period has also been facilitated by another set of circumstances. The combination of low interest rates and small down payments has placed the home purchaser at an advantage as compared to the person who rents, since although his actual monthly outlay to cover interest, retirement of mortgage, taxes, and fire insurance, might be greater than he would normally pay in rent, exemption from federal income taxes of payments made in interest and real estate taxes often offset the higher costs of home ownership. Furthermore, the availability of housing facilities for rent was decreased by federal rent control for a time following the end of the war which also discouraged investors from building further facilities for rental purposes. Likewise the increased technical improvement of single houses (attached garages, automatic heating, storm windows and screens which are self-storing, power lawn mowers, etc.) made the individual house virtually as convenient a place in which to live as a city apartment. Furthermore, with the decrease in the availability of apartment facilities, landlords widely adopted the "no young children" rule, thus forcing families with young children into home ownership.

Prosperity has also resulted in lowering the age at marriage. In part this is the consequence of the increased ability of young persons entering upon vocational apprenticeship to afford the higher costs of family life because of higher wages, and in part an increased capacity of parents of young people to subsidize their children's marriages for at least the first few years. The result of lowering the age at marriage has been to accelerate the rate of family formation as is indicated by the fact that wives, ages 15-44, increased by one-seventh in the nine years following 1945, and more than one-third since 1933.[2]

Another consequence of prosperity has been the increase in the birth rate. In 1954 one child was born to each ten families in the United States, an astounding record particularly in view of the fact that at least four of the wives in each of the ten families had passed the normal child-bearing age. This would mean, therefore, an additional child added during the year to every sixth family in which there was a wife of child-bearing age in contrast to one in eight in the middle 1930's.[3]

Prosperity, however, has been more than a thrusting force, pushing people into the suburbs to escape the restraints of landlords, to circumvent the pressures of more families and of larger families with the inevitable shortages of homes. Prosperity provides the means for the realization of the suburban vision, the country estate with its flowers and elbow room where one can live like a king and achieve the good life. All of this made possible by modern technological developments in the form of television, the deep freeze, automatic washing machines and clothes dryers, automatic house heating, air-conditioning, electric dishwashers, and the supermarket. These contrivances of modern ingenuity take the place of servants and make the realization of the suburban vision a reality for great masses of people.

The Suburban Vision

Central to the suburban vision is the struggle for status in American society. The upper class has long since established the custom of "country" living as a symbol of affluence; a symbol made more glamorous by movie and television stars. Prosperity makes possible widespread imitation of the elite, even if on a restricted scale, upon the part of the upwardly mobile population to whom there is no more culturally accepted symbol of superior status than living in the suburbs.

The widespread belief that the central city teems with wickedness and moral degradation has also contributed to the suburban vision. The simple virtues of the countryside have long been a part of the American stereotype, but for many persons these attractions paled in the sparkling glitter of neon lights which symbolize the technological advantages of urban life responsible for the urban migration. The suburb offers a compromise in which all the conveniences of the city may be achieved while retaining the simple virtues of the country-side without its inconveniences.

The suburban vision is nourished by the current vogue for pets, made more attractive through the motion pictures of Walt Disney. "Every child wants a pet," is almost the universal conviction of parents in and out of suburbs. One is sometimes tempted to speculate that a more realistic statement may be: "Every parent wants a child who wants a pet," the parent having the deeper need for the pet than the child, much as the proverbial father who buys his son an electric train for Christmas and then monopolizes its use and thus acquired under the guise of his son's interest his own satisfactions. But whether the parent or the child is the prime source of desire for pets, the city is hardly a place for the achievement of this satisfaction, whereas the suburb favors pet ownership and enjoyment.

How often the imputed interests of the child are projections of those of the parents, does not becloud the fact that contemporary American culture is child-centered. Parents in contemporary America indulge and pamper their children as never before and the open spaces of the suburbs seems to promise greater opportunities than elsewhere. In part this indulgence is a reflection of the uncertainty about the future where the specter of nuclear destruction is always on the horizon. In part it is an expression of escapism in which the parent identifies himself with the simpler pleasures of childhood and thus recaptures the simpler life of the past.

Then there is the increased emphasis upon "living it up" in its mechanical, psychological, and social aspects. All of this is a continuation of a wartime philosophy in which the future was so uncertain as to be hardly worthy of consideration. Nuclear threat and peacetime uncertainty abetted by prosperity have perpetuated this philosophy into the neurosis of our times. This philosophy finds expression in the constant demand for the new in mechanical contrivances in the home (automatic dishwashers, electric stoves which turn on and off automatically once the dinner is cooked, vacuum cleaners which do everything from cleaning the house to spraying insecticides), speedier automobiles, power tools for the home workshop, etc., many of which scarcely fit into apartment living as readily as into single homes.

Likewise the wearing of casual clothes for which comfort is the basic criterion of worth rather than style; outdoor dining whether on porch or patio; the cultivation of flowers; the manicuring of lawns and shrubs; the breeding of pets; all of these and many more pay psychological dividends, in the form of indvidual achievement, pride in ownership and workmanship, and community approval and admiration. Added to these are the social assets of more intimate associations with neighbors; the pleasures of gossip, and of neighborhood visiting. The net result is to glamorize life in the suburbs as a place of retreat from the threats and frustrations of urban living, and where the Hollywood picture of family life in a hacienda can be realized.

Retreat from the frustrations of urban life is, in fact, a basic virtue of the suburbs. Public transportation has generally deteriorated in urban centers and with this has come increased dependence upon the automobile. Much of the past advantage of living in the central city was the accessibility of public transportation which brought all of the varied institutions of the city within easy reach. With the deterioration of public transportation the city no longer presents this advantage; automobile ownership provides greater freedom in the choice of place of residence without sacrificing the advantages which the city provides. Suburban residence provides a compromise between the accessibility to urban institutions and the pleasures of a more leisurely pace of life.[4]

Likewise the five-day week with its forty or less hours of work has contributed to the suburban vision. The shorter week and day means more time for sports, for visiting with friends and neighbors, for play with the children, for puttering around the house and yard, for developing hobbies in varied forms, and all of the other things which serve as escapes from the routine and regimentation of work, including the wider participation in community organizations and activities. What the urbanite achieves vicariously in the intimacy of the night-club, the suburbanite achieves more directly in his participation in the local organizations of his community.

The forces (economic, technological, and social psychological) which make the suburb what it has become upon the contemporary scene have also had their impact upon the suburban family. Im-pressionistically new paterns of family relationship would seem to be evolving and in the process many of the older forms are seemingly being obliterated. It is not surprising, therefore, that the consequences of these changes upon the suburban family has become the subject of current sociological speculation and research.[5]

The Suburban Family

Jaco and Belknap, drawing upon a variety of sources, have suggested that a new type of family is developing the suburbs.[6] Among hypothe-ses suggested for the study of this new type of family, these writers have proposed the following: (1) social stratification is becoming more rigid and disparate in the suburbs, (2) sibling and parental roles are being defined more along kinship lines than of voluntary associa-tion, (3) famliy unity is increased, (4) there is greater participation of the family in local social institutions, (5) the family performs enlarged functions in the suburbs, (6) role differentiations are be-coming less rigid, and (7) parental controls are making for greater conventionalization of marital choice and courtship patterns.[7]

Jaco and Belknap's hypotheses, however, are based upon a synthesis and re-evaluation of extant data upon urban population and economic trends rather than upon the first-hand collection of data. What the present writer proposes to do in the following pages is to draw upon data secured through interviews of suburban families as a part of a research project now in progress under his direction in the Chicago suburban area.[8] This project has as its goal the scientific analysis of some of the basic features of the suburban family of the newer neighborhoods established since World War II and the ultimate comparison of these families with those in the older neighborhoods of the same suburban communities. For present purposes, generalizations will be confined to data obtained from families living in neighborhoods established since World War II in 19 North and Northwest communities, constituting a contiguous segment of the suburban area beginning with the city limits of Chicago and extending outward from the city for approximately twenty-five to thirty miles. The new homes in these communities vary in value from about fifteen to sixty-five thousand dollars. Generalizations will be restricted to North and Northwest segment of the suburban area of Chicago because of the present availability of a more representative sample than for the South, Southwest and West suburbs. As for the older neighborhoods, no data are available as yet for any of the suburban communities, North, Northwest, South Southwest, or West.

Suburban families even in the newest suburbs may be, however, essentially like families everywhere so far as the age of their members are concerned if one considers age in terms of the arithmetic mean. Newcomers to suburban neighborhoods north and northwest of Chicago show a mean age of the husbands at about forty years, which is five years younger than the mean age of all husbands in the United States in 1952.[9] If, however, comparison is made between husbands having children both in these suburban neighborhoods and the United States, the mean ages of both groups is essentially alike at between thirty-eight and thirty-nine years. But whereas about one-third of the husbands in the United States in 1952 had no children, the proportion among the newcomers in the suburban neighborhoods studied is about half that for the United States, viz., fifteen percent. This would suggest that the typical family unit in the new suburban areas consists of husband and wife with one or more children, with a tendency for those married couples who do not as yet have any children to live elsewhere than in the suburbs, and for those couples whose children have grown up to move either out of the suburbs or to remain in the older sections.

Where the family comes from as it moves into the newer suburban areas throws some light upon its characteristics. In the first place, the newly married couple seldom establishes its first residence in the new suburban areas. More often than not, the move is made after the birth of the first child and often in anticipation of a second child. About an equal proportion of newcomers have previously lived either in another suburb within the metropolitan area or in the central city and these constitute about four-fifths of all those who move in. The remainder are from outside the metropolitan area.[10] As for family size, the mean is about 3.8 persons which is somewhat above that for the United States as a whole in 1951, although upon moving to its suburban home the mean size of the family was 3.5 persons, slightly below the United States mean of 3.6 persons.[11] Thus there seems to be some basis for the wide-spread belief that fertility is higher in suburbs, but if so the greater prolificness is not very marked.[12] It must be remembered, however that the bulk of these families are still well within the expanding phase of the family cycle, the "average" mother having completed but two-thirds of her potential thirty years of child-bearing.

From the standpoint of activities, the two roles which most eloquently characterize suburban life of adults is the role of the wife as a chauffeur and the role of the husband as a handyman. The suburban wife finds herself constantly occupied with furnishing transportation for other members of the family; to the railway station to take and meet her husband before and after work, to school and other places of activity to take and bring home the children. In addition there are trips to the neighborhood stores to do the family shopping. Her husband find himself not only called upon to mow and care for the lawn, but also to become an amateur plumber, house painter, repairer of children's toys and the various gadgets about the household, landscaper, and even construction engineer. In this role of handyman he is aided by a whole host of tools designed to make it possible to do an expert job without training and what is more important, to make his tasks more socially acceptable as a hobby, and this is for the suburban husband his most common hobby. When the suburban husband turns indoors, he is often joined by his wife and together they become interior craftsmen, painting walls and ceilings, hanging paper, and refinishing furniture.

Flexibility of role is, in fact, characteristic of suburban family life, the husband often performing characteristically feminine functions and the wife masculine functions. There is probably no place in contemporary life where the equalitarian pattern of the family is more prevalent than in the newer suburbs. When the children are young, husbands help with the household tasks, sharing in feeding and sometimes diapering the infants; wives shovel snow from walks and help in caring for the yard and garden. In fact care of the house, yard, and garden is second only to cooking, sewing and knitting as the most common hobby of suburban wives. The children as they become older sometimes under pressure share in the tasks of the household within the limits made possible by the priority demands of school and social activities. Nevertheless, the father continues to be the authority figure, with his wife as the conciliator as conflicts arise between father and child. The role of the mother tends to become that of the instrument through which all the wishes of the child may be satisfied while at the same time preserving the fiction of the father as the source of authority.

Fundamentally the suburban family in the newer suburbs is child-centered to a greater degree than elsewhere in contemporary America. How much of this child-centeredness is a mirage is difficult to say for undoubtedly the adult often finds much of his greatest enjoyment in those features of suburban life which he attributes as contributing to the welfare of his children. Thus the most common reason given by interviewees for moving to the suburban homes is that here is a better place in which to rear children. But when he is asked to explain why suburbia is a better place in which to rear children, the reasons he gives apply equally as well to himself as to his child. Fresh air and sunshine, cultural opportunities, absence of disturbing noises, more spacious homes, more friendly contacts, place for pets, etc., are attributes which recognize no age differentials. Likewise less crowded conditions with more space for play are less restrictive of adult as well as of child behavior.

But the suburban family is not only child-centered, it is also home centered. Much more of the time of both husband and wife tend to be spent in the home. Participation in recreational activities outside the home, if there are small children, necessitates the employment of a sitter to look after the children. Families in the interviewed group having children under ten years of age employ a sitter on an average of 4 hours a week. This means that the parents can go out one evening a week together, otherwise one parent must stay at home and care for the children or take them along as mothers do when they go grocery shopping. If there is an older daughter, she may be left in charge of the younger siblings on her parents' evening out even though she herself is as young as ten years, while sons of comparable age seldom if ever are given this task.

Wives in the new suburban areas studied are less gainfully employed than are married women in general. Employment of married women is about 9 percent as compared to 27 percent in 1953 for the United States.[13] Only two-fifths of this nine percent are employed full time. Thus the typical role of the suburban wife is that of a homemaker and deviation from this role is rare./

While the reasons for living in suburbia apply equally to adults and children (at least to children as seen through the eyes of their parents), the disliked features reported are those of the adult. The most common complaint is about transportation; the time expended by the husband, the inadequacy of public transportation and dependence upon the automobile. This complaint is closely followed by that of the lack of adequate shopping facilities conveniently located.

The Suburban Cycle

Perhaps the most characteristic feature of life in the newer suburban areas is the loss of class distinctions which function so compellingly in the city. In part this is the consequence of the homogeneity of suburbia and in part a reflection of the "pioneering" spirit; a pioneering spirit which is the initial stage of the suburban cycle. In fact undue emphasis upon the character of the suburban family as observed in this initial stage can easily be misleading, for the family of the pioneering stage is not the family of the stage of division nor of the stage of the limited dream. Each stage produces its own distinctive family patterns.

Seventy-three percent of suburban husbands in the Chicago sample are engaged in business, predominantly managerial and executive in functions. The professions make up 18 percent and craftsmen in the upper wage brackets constitute the remainder of those employed. About 2 per cent of all husbands are retired. There is also a fair degree of homogeneity in educational background. The mean years of schooling of husbands is almost 15 years and of wives slightly under 14. Nevertheless the modal husband has had a college education and the modal wife has completed high school, although the proportion of wives who have completed four years or more of college is greater than the number who have completed high school only.

The "pioneering" spirit is reflected in the fact that everybody knows everybody else and the discussion of personal affairs becomes a common interest. But it is not the "gossip" heard on the "party line" of rural life; it is the reports of children on the "school bus" passed on to parents and by them to their neighbors. And it has to do exclusively with the present, as do all intimate relations, without any illuminating context of the past, for suburbanites know no more about each other's past than do their urban counterparts whose relations are much more casual. Thus in the initial stage of suburban development there is intimacy of association within the context of the impersonal which differentiates this experience from the rural on the one hand and the urban on the other.

There is evidence that every suburban neighborhood begins with a period of high esprit de corps in which the symbols of division are lost for the time being much as happens in crises. Each individual enters vicariously into the enterprises of the other with pride and admiration. Every one finds ways of being helpful in solving the problems of suburban living, sharing knowledge about horticulture and the know-how of household chores. Informal neighborhood get-to-gethers and visiting become the chief recreational outlets for everyone. Even participation in activities outside the neighborhood tend to become common to all. Children go to the same Sunday School and adults subscribe to the same concert series. Premium is placed upon neighborhood identity and the individual or family who does not participate in the common pattern is a lost soul.[14]

This initial stage, however, is but a part of the cycle of suburban life and not the whole of it. The initial stage passes shortly as the individuals become identified with the specialized activities of the larger community. The symbols of status of the community reassert themselves and class distinctions again appear. The use of diaper service, the employment of maids, the make of automobile, the winter vacation in the Southland, emphasis upon the acquisition of the newest models of material things, all become symbols of status and mark the individual family as higher or lower in the prestige scale. Intimacy of association slowly dissipates except for small clusters, each individual becoming absorbed into multi-differentiated groups of the larger community. Eventually there is developed in the suburban neighborhood a condition of secondary relations not unlike that in apartment-house areas of the city, except for the vestiges of more intimate association built up in the initial stage which re-assert themselves on occasion among the "pioneers."

It is at this stage of development that the vision of the suburb begins to fade for some and they move back to the city. Commuting schedules become burdensome for the husband and the chores of house and yard maintenance lose their glamor. No less galling for the wife is the incessant chauffering of the family automobile. All of this may be symbolized in the explanation of a returnee to Manhattan:

> Maybe it's me, but I couldn't understand the good life. I lived there for eight months and it didn't suit any member of the family. On the railroad, everyone schemed to get a seat and a carpool arrangement didn't appeal to me. The house had plaster walls and was very bad acoustically—impossible to get away from the noise of my children and my neighbor's television set. Then there was the business of the garden. Week-ends I spent cutting grass. This community was so damn civic-minded that one man down the street who let his lawn go to crabgrass was shunned.[15]

Another returnee complained about the rigidity of commuting schedules timed for Wall Street brokers and railroad executives. And as for his wife:

> My wife couldn't stand the conversations she heard in the suburbs. They were always on two subjects; obstetrics and houses. The talk, too, was all materialistic—how to import maids and keep them in peonage, and so on. Everyone's life ambition was to have a bigger house a little farther out in Westchester in an excellent school community where the people were "their kind"—not too snobbishly poor or ostentatiously rich.[16]

The features of the suburban family which stand out and command attention are, it would seem, the consequence of the homogeneity of the initial stage of suburban life found only in the newly developing suburban areas. The intimacy and cohesiveness of the family is the direct counterpart of the intimacy and cohesiveness of neighborhood social life in its intial stages of suburban development. Much of this intimacy and cohesiveness is lost both in the family and in the neighborhood as the cycle of social life moves in the direction of urban pattern. Interest in common enterprises becomes the binding element in associations and not the individual as a functioning unit. His relationship to local groups is upon a segmental basis rather than upon the functioning of the personality as a whole. The suburban becomes urban both with respect to the family and the community although the single dwelling remains as a symbol of the suburban vision. /

The suburbanite is seeking no bucolic retreat from the technological revolution of the Twentieth Century. Instead he is searching for a "cleaner, less congested community in which he can live an urban way of life."[17] If, in the process he loses what may seem to be the characteristic features of urbanism with its emphasis upon the impersonal, relative scale of values, individual anonymity, formal symbols of class and status, specialized contacts in which individuals are identified with a single common interest, formal controls, and the like, it is only because the needs for co-operation and mutual dependence are the inevitable counterparts of the initial stage of development. Having passed this initial stage with its pioneering outlook acting as a temporary mask to the basic urban pattern, the suburbanite once again turns to the urban way of life both in his individual and family relations.[18]

The Suburban Family Pattern

Whereas the family in the newer areas of suburbia tend toward a homogeneity of patterning, as a whole the suburbs present a variety of family patterns. In general the differentiating element seems to evolve out of the employment status of the husband and father, the nominal head of the family. The families of commuting husbands differ from those of non-commuting husbands, and the retired form a third group.

Crucial to the differentiation of family patterns in terms of the employment status of the head of the family are the variations in participation in the activities of organized groups within the community. The highest participation score found by Scaff in Claremont, California, was for the retired non-commuters. The families whose heads are employed within the community were intermediate in participation score with the commuter families lowest in participation.[19] The rank of the three groups is not changed when consideration is given to the participation of the breadwinner without regard to the rest of the family except that the participation score is the same for both the family and the breadwinner in the retired non-commuting group, whereas for the other two groups the participation score of the breadwinner is always smaller than for the family as a whole, suggesting that the differentials in participation may be largely due to differences in the activities of the heads of families rather than the other members.[20]

The retired and the employed non-commuter families are essentially alike in mean length of residence (13.1 vs. 13.0 years), mean years of school completed (13.8 vs. 13.7), but as would be anticipated the mean age of the breadwinner in the retired families is higher than those in which the breadwinner is employed (72.1 vs. 55.5), and the mean family size differs (1.5 vs. 2.8). The commuters have lived in the community about half as long (7.6 years), have larger families (3.4), the breadwinner is younger (38.4), although in years of schooling completed they are substantially like the other families (14.0).[21]

The findings of Scaff support the hypothesis of the tendency for the families of commuters to become maternal in organization, the wife and mother performing the roles of homemaker and community representative of the family. Her world is the local community and the household her central fortress, with occasional sallies into the central city. In contrast, the central city is the world of her husband with the household as a retreat and an occasional sally into the local community. What the commuting husband lacks in community participation he makes up for in his activities in organizations in the central city.

The maternal character of the families of non-commuters is less apparent, if not non-existent. The worlds of husband and wife converge upon each other, even though division of labor makes in part for differential contacts. Mrs. B. does not know her husband's business associates as well as he does, but she knows their wives better than he! Mr. B's children find him a much warmer and understanding person than do the children of his counterpart, the commuting father.

In turn the equalitarian character of the family unit of the retired non-commuter is more pronounced. As has already been pointed out with reference to Claremont, the participation score of this group is the same for both the family and the breadwinner and since these families are seldom if ever made up of more than one other person, this would seem to be the only group in which both husband and wife achieve a common participation level and the organizations are likely to be confined to the local community for the most part. This would suggest a third family pattern as compared with those of the employed non-commuter and the commuter.

All of this is tantamount to the conclusion that the suburban family pattern is multiple, just as the style of life of the suburbanite is plural in patterning. But unlike the heterogeneity of many an urban neighborhood, the suburban neighborhood tends to be characterized by the particular stage of development of the suburban cycle, each neighborhood tending to reflect the particular stage in which one finds it at a particular moment of examination. And all this because the cycle of suburban life is in microcosm the cycle from the rural to the urban both with respect to the family relationship and community organization.

The consequence is a fluidity of stratification in the new areas, rigidity in the older areas; emphasis upon kinship associations in the new areas, voluntary associations in the old: family unity is higher in the new areas, lower in the old; the functions of the family are enlarged in the new areas, contracted in the old; intimacy of association in the new areas, impersonal and segmental association in the old.

All of this suggests that the suburban family is scarcely as homogeneous as is often assumed and that in its complexity it manifests all of the significant features of the modern family with its close intimate features of identification and interdependence while at the same time developing the diversification and independence of its members and a high degree of individualization of behavior. Thus in the suburban cycle the suburban becomes urban both with respect to the family and the community although the single dwelling still remains as the symbol of the suburban vision as a limited dream.

FOOTNOTES

1. See Allen, Frederick Lewis, *Only Yesterday,* pp. 317-318.
2. Metropolitan Life Insurance Co., *Statistical Bulletin,* 36, April 1955, p. 3.
3. See *Ibid.,* p. 3 and *op. cit.,* 36, October 1955, pp. 1-2.
4. *Cf.,* Dewey, Richard, "Peripheral Expansion in Milwaukee County," *American Journal of Sociology,* 54 (September, 1948), p. 125.
5. See for example, Seeley, John R., Simm, R. Alexander, and Loosley, Elizabeth, *Crestwood Heights;* Spectorsky, A. C., *The Exurbanite;* Palmer, C. B., *Slightly Cooler in the Suburbs.*
6. Jaco, E. Gartly and Belknap, Ivan, "Is a New Family Form Emerging in the Urban Fringe?" *American Sociological Review,* 18 (October, 1953), pp. 551-557.

7. *Ibid.,* p. 557.

8. This project is being carried out with financial support from the Center for Metropolitan Studies of Northwestern University.

9. See Metropolitan Life Insurance Co., *Statistical Bulletin,* 34, December 1953, p. 9.

10. Dewey found that of the families who moved to the suburbs of Milwaukee, 60 per cent came from the city of Milwaukee, 20 per cent from the six largest suburbs, 12 per cent from the rural area of Milwaukee County, and 8 per cent from outside the county.—Dewey, Richard, "Peripheral Expansion in Milwaukee County," *Amer. Journ. Sociol.,* 54 (September, 1948), p. 119.

11. Metropolitan Life Insurance Co., *Statistical Bulletin,* 35, November 1954, p. 5.

12. *Cf.,* Jaco, E. Gartly and Belknap, Ivan, "Is a New Family Form Emerging in the Urban Fringe?" *Amer. Sociol. Rev.,* 18 (October, 1953), pp. 556-557.

13. Metropolitan Life Insurance Co., *Statistical Bulletin,* 36, October, 1955, pp. 2-3.

14. Cf. Spectorsky, A. C., *Op. cit.,* pp. 264 ff.

15. Mitgang, Herbert, "From the Suburbs Back to the City," *The New York Times Magazine,* May 15, 1955, p. 17.

16. *Ibid.,* pp. 17 and 37.

17. Dewey, Richard, *op. cit.,* p. 124.

18. *Cf.,* Spectorsky, A. C., *op. cit.,* chapter 10.

19. See Scaff, Alvin H., "The Effect of Commuting on Participation in Community Organizations," *Amer. Socio. Rev.,* 17 (April 1952), pp. 215-220.

20. The participation scores for retired non-commuters: breadwinner, 2.4, family 2.4; non-commuters: breadwinner 1.9, family 2.2; commuters: breadwinner 1.2, family 1.7.—Scaff, Alvin H., *op. cit.,* p. 217.

21. *Ibid.,* p. 217.

Robert C. Wood

Massachusetts Institute of Technology

THE GOVERNING OF SUBURBIA

To political science, suburban government, strictly speaking, is neither different from other governments in the United States nor new at all. Governments in suburbia have the same names, the same powers, the same political and administrative processes as do local governments in urban and rural areas. These are counties, cities, towns, townships, boroughs, special districts, and authorities, creatures of the state, operating by law or under charters authorized by the state. These names, these powers, these authorizations are traditional: they were established long before suburbia, as we know it today, ever existed. There is no political map on which suburban boundaries appear and across which the name SUBURBIA in bold black letters is inscribed.

If the public services suburban governments supply are poor in quality and inadequate in scope, so are the services of many urban and rural governments. If the suburban tax system is archaic and unbalanced, so is the revenue structure of almost every local government in the country. If suburban citizens are apathetic, local voters everywhere stay away from the polls in droves. If the administrative organization of suburban government is poorly manned and poorly led, few municipal governments in other places offer an attractive contrast.

Yet if there are no differences in kind between suburban and other local governments, either in legal form or in their generally mediocre records of performance, there are important differences in degree. The metropolitan environment wraps suburban government in an

This is an original article, prepared for this volume

ethos of localism peculiar to the area and produces problems other governments do not face. Further, amid the ceaseless changes in metropolitan life—the steady growth and restless migration of population, the new demands for public service in transportation and education, the development of a distinctly regional economic structure—suburbia has emerged as the modern champion of an ancient American political belief and has advanced this belief against practical odds no other local government faces.

All local governments in the United States owe their existence to a special tenet in the American political creed: a conviction that the best government is the one closest to home. In our folklore, we turn back to the archtype of the colonial New England town when we seek an ideal for democracy. This commitment to grassroots democracy is of long standing: Jefferson heralded its benefits in his disquisition on Virginia wards; De Tocqueville highlighted its virtues in his classic distinction between centralized government and decentralized administration. Our shoddy subsequent history of municipal affairs has not shaken our belief that liberty is best protected, the general welfare most assured, in our lowest echelons of government.

It is suburbia's role today to proclaim, with the memories of the big city fresh in mind, that even in a modern habitat, grassroots government can continue. In the twentieth century, when truly small governments seem to be disappearing everywhere, suburbia provides the means for a renaissance of the miniature republic. While reformers have struggled to purify and redeem the great city, to overthrow the bosses, to invent new mechanisms for popular participation, and to strengthen urban administration, the suburbs have appeared to offer at least a facsimile of the genuine article. Through the miracle of the automobile and the commuter train, the city dweller can escape the urban machine, the corrupt politics and partisan controversy of the metropolis. While economically he retains his association with the central city, politically he can re-enter the civic life of a small community where a man is no longer a faceless member of a mass rally, but a citizen whose vote counts and whose political participation makes a difference.

In his small suburban governments, the suburbanite de-emphasizes partisanship, develops a politics of personality in place of issues, joins the Parent-Teachers Association, speaks highly of the League of Women Voters, works to advance the good of the community as a whole.[1] In all these ways he seems to be on the verge of recapturing the special flavor of consensus, the tone of personalized government and active interest which characterized earlier small towns on the Eastern Seaboard and, on the frontier of the Old Northwest.[2]

This conviction that good governments come invariably in small packages is an important element in the entire suburban movement. When the urban exodus was only incipient, Patrick Geddes and Ebenezer Howard, advocates of a planned suburbia, counted grass-roots politics as one of the benefits their garden cities would inevitably offer and spoke of a "burgher people governing themselves from their own town hall."[3] As the public problems in the congested cities of the nineteenth century mounted, more and more observers became convinced that suburbia promised political as well as social solutions to the baffling disharmonies of urban life. And down through the years, those who bless the suburbs as a means for making modern civilization more palatable have clung to the conviction that their small governments might again be the foundations of the Republic.[4]

The modern suburbs have not fulfilled the aesthetic and social vision of the early planners, but to most of us their politics still seem preferable to those of the central city. Scholars continue to speak of the small community as a prerequisite for traditional democratic government and to emphasize the qualities of neighborliness, participation, and "a widespread sense of personal competence to make a difference" which suburban living seems to engender. Although no suburb duplicates the New England town of old, they are clearly closer approximations of that life than the great city, viable alternatives to urban loneliness, suspicion, and misunderstanding. They stand against the trend of metropolitan dominance, and by self-consciously retaining their local autonomy and prerogatives, thwart the partisan controversy of big government.[5]

In this respect, most laymen agree with scholars. Survey after survey reports a sturdy disinclination of suburbanites to consolidate their governments with the central city. They document a popular conviction that suburban governments are "better, more honest, and more efficient." Along with "green grass, new brass door knobs, washing machines, a car, commuter trains, fresh air and new social status," comes, in Louis Harris' words, a desire to escape Tammany Hall and the "thousand images of an indecent uncivilized past." Over the years, proposals for consolidation in metropolitan government flounder on the rocks of suburban memories of city politics and suburban insistence that their politics, nonpartisan, small in scope, close to home, is best.[6]

The constant reminder of the perils of big city politics is one way the metropolitan environment influences suburban politics and government, but it is not the only way. At the same time that suburbanites are stimulated to a grassroots renaissance, they are beset by awesome problems. Capriciously, the metropolitan environment makes possible the creation of hundreds of small governments, then robs them of the physical isolation and resources which are necessary for their proper functioning.

The basic dilemma, suburban governments have discovered, is that while legally they are autonomous, financially and administratively they are not. Because they are only segments of the metropolitan area, jostling one another in the metropolitan backyard, unequipped with a hinterland to provide financial resources for their town centers, and faced with the burgeoning costs of a welfare state, they lack the capacity to carry the service loads demanded of them. Because each suburb, to be faithful to the grassroots ideal, must retain its own independence, it cannot take advantage of administrative and organizational economies of size and scale.[7]

Current statistics on the proliferation and total number of local governments in metropolitan areas show how far the process of dividing up resources and duplicating services has gone. As the quiet, half-deserted villages and towns on the fringes of the cities have filled up and new developments have been incorporated, the number of suburban governments has steadily increased. In 1900, the New York Region had 127; by 1920, 204, today over 1000 exist in metropolitan New York. In St. Louis County, there were 8 incorporated municipalities in 1911, 39 in 1940, 94 by 1952. This pattern is duplicated across the country. Today, none of the 173 metropolitan areas has less than a dozen separate governments, most have over 100. In 1950, 3000 governments in metropolitan areas could be said to possess more or less general powers of government and there were 16,210 legally distinguishable local units.[8]

The most obvious financial effect of this "scatteration" of governments is the inequitable distribution of tax resources among jurisdictions within the region. When 16,000 odd governments exist in less than 7% of the country's area, political boundary lines dissect the resources of the entire metropolitan area into unequal shares. In the general exodus from the central cities, people and industry have not moved out together: In 1948, the suburban share of the total metropolitan value added by manufacturing was 40%, but of the 29 million suburban inhabitants in the 7 largest metropolitan areas, less than 500,000 live in areas where industrial growth has been faster than population increases.[9] Neither has commercial or high-value residential construction spread out equally throughout suburbia; instead land use for these purposes has tended to concentrate in particular locations.[10] Thus some suburban governments receive windfalls in tax revenues as exclusive residential sections, shopping centers, and industrial plants locate within their jurisdictions. Others are left to provide the services for mass developments composed of houses of such low value that only a very high tax rate balances the local budget. The game of musical chairs which suburban governments play in their scramble for resources began early. By 1930, tax rates among metropolitan suburbs in New York varied from $2.21 to $4.73 per $100 valuation; in Detroit, from $1.89 to $2.54; in Cleveland from $.93 to $2.19; and in Boston from $1.92 to $4.88.[11] They have continued to this day, so that as differences in land values increase among suburbs, the rich get richer, the poor poorer, and "them that has gets." [12]

Not only are resources inequitably divided. A blanket of municipal poverty covers almost all of a typical metropolitan region. This second problem is intensified by the haphazard division of the resource base, but even if suburbs possessed the reasonably balanced economic foundations typical of an isolated town, they would face an uphill budgetary battle today. Since suburbs constitute the growing edge of our metropolitan areas, absorbing 97% of our population increase, demands for public services have skyrocketed. Suburban governments must carry out those functions most affected by population increases: schools, waterworks, sewerage systems, streets, fire and police protection. Simultaneously, with an increase in quantitative demand has come a public insistence on improving quality standards. The burdens of the welfare state do not fall on the national government alone. Suburbanites expect better schools, better health departments, libraries, parking lots—a higher standard of service and more services than local governments traditionally provide. As the rush to the suburbs goes on, a prosperous, expanding, white collar people demand more public programs of better quality than before and tax rates climb inexorably.

Reliable expenditure figures for suburban governments alone are not available, but the general trend of local expenditures in the United States gives some indication of the problem. In 1927, all local governments combined spent a little over 700 million dollars for all purposes; in 1952, they were spending 14 billion dollars from their own resources alone, and a total of about 22 billion dollars. Even after correcting for inflation and population increase, total local revenue collections are seen to have tripled in the last twenty-five years, and total local debt has passed the 25 billion dollar mark. Since the end of World War II, the rate of local expenditures has risen faster than that of the Federal government, and it shows no sign of leveling off.[13]

Although these are figures for all local government, we can be fairly certain that the suburban experience at least approaches the national average. Suburbs do not bear the welfare, urban development, and public transportation costs typical of larger cities; but their school expenditures are proportionately higher, and the education function is generally between 40% to 50% of local budgets in any area. Moreover, most suburbs, emerging from a state of rural somnolence, experience heavy "get going" costs, expensive initial outlays for water systems, sewage disposal plants, schools, roads, fire stations, and police headquarters, most of which never existed before. Starting from scratch, their facilities are often overtaxed almost as fast as they are completed and suburban capital improvement programs go on endlessly in an era of the highest building costs in the nation's history. Most probably, suburban costs per capita are sizeably above —not below—the nation's average, and most probably they are rising faster than other units. Charles Adrian summarizes the current expectation of authorities in the field of local finances: "taxes may start at what appears to be a much lower level than those of the core city, but the suburban buyer can be assured that they will increase at a rapid rate."[14]

Special financial problems are not the only difficulties which set suburban government apart. Organizationally and administratively, they have unique problems. Because the maintenance of legal autonomy is essential to preserving the grassroots tradition, suburban governments cannot easily cooperate to solve obviously common problems. Independence demands separate police and fire departments, individual public works programs, separate city halls, refuse collection systems—in short, duplication of services which can only be accomplished efficiently in a much larger territory than a single suburb can possibly encompass. This maintenance of separate suburban bureaucracies is not only costly, it is also an affront to common sense. A crazy-quilt hodge-podge of local agencies appears, criminals escape because no police jurisdiction can mount an effective pursuit, fires rage while equipment lies idle in the next town, and sewage is dumped into the river by one government to contaminate the waters of the neighboring jurisdiction.[15]

The inevitable result of squeezing too many local governments into too small a space is controversy and confusion, and squabbling among officials and citizens. A more basic result is administrative amateurism. Plagued by inadequate resources, forced to maintain a complete bureaucratic superstructure and to duplicate the services of its neighbors, a suburban government usually foregoes the professional personnel standards on which a larger city insists. It relies upon a volunteer fire department; it does not adequately train or equip its policemen; it uses part-time health officers and building inspectors. It may omit many services entirely: storm sewers, playgrounds, trash collections, libraries, street lights. Even in the most treasured of suburban public functions, the school, compromises are made in the form of double sessions, inexperienced teachers, overcrowding—all, of course in the name of "local control." In short, suburban governments tend to be incomplete governments, and though their officials may be honest and hardworking, their end-products rarely exceed the minimum standards of professional public administration.

Beside the renaissance of the grassroots image inflicting penalties on suburban governments themselves, it also injures the entire metropolitan area. Three basic regional consequences flow from the decision of each suburb to go it alone: the central city is often left neglected, politically and financially; public problems of the entire area are ignored or treated on an *ad hoc* basis; and little or no provision is made for anticipating the future direction of metropolitan change.

The plight of the core city is the regional problem arising from "fractured" metropolitan government most usually emphasized. The reasoning runs that the metropolis suffers politically from the exodus of the middle class, which leaves only the very rich and very poor to guide urban destinies. Lacking the sturdy burgher to provide a solid base for citizenship, urban politics degenerate into a struggle between the elite and the mob, the one cautiously pulling strings behind the scenes, the other rampaging through the electoral process in search of spoils. Concurrently the metropolis is callously used by suburbanites for their economic gain; they work in the city, have their public and cultural centers there, partake of its amenities, but they do not pay their way. The commuter trains symbolize a two-way squeeze: on the one hand, the city is required to provide services in transport, water, police, and fire protection for a daytime population which is thirty to fifty percent above the number of permanent residents. On the other hand, taxable resources decline after the exodus to suburbia. Tax-exempt civic centers, public buildings, and educational centers take up more and more space. In the end, industry and trade follow the market, and the city is left as a receptacle of necessary functions the suburbs do not care to support.[16]

This picture can be overdrawn. Big city politics have shown healthy signs of rejuvenation in recent years; strong, responsible executive leadership has appeared, and dramatic new programs have begun to effect some progress in urban redevelopment. As some types of economic activities leave the city, others appear to be taking their place. And commuters are not getting off scot-free. Earnings taxes, as in St. Louis, state aid programs in which the suburbanites pay their share, state assumption of metropolitan responsibilities, spread the cost of daytime metropolitan services. Nonetheless, it is still true that the suburban encirclement of the metropolis deprives the city of a potential richness in variety of inhabitants and tax resources which would make its rejuvenation easier and the development of an orderly financial structure more likely.

The second region-wide consequence of suburban independence is perhaps more serious. The lack of genuine metropolitan institutions to make regional decisions precludes the establishment of a decision-making process for the region as a whole. In the typical urban area of today, there is no central authority responsible for the development and execution of a comprehensive transportation system which can balance the related needs for rapid transit lines, highways, and terminals and can view the metropolitan circulatory system from an over-all perspective. There are rarely common means to attack the obviously common problems of preventing harbor and stream pollution, of assuring adequate water supply, and controlling contagious diseases. These problems do not respect political boundaries, and no suburban government can solve them on its own.

Under present circumstances, these regional matters, if they are handled at all, are dealt with on an *ad hoc* basis. Contractual agreements among governments, by which one unit undertakes to supply common services for all, procedures for the joint use of equipment, and unwritten understandings are sometimes worked out. More frequently, special districts and government authorities are established, directed by appointed officials and responsible for the money-making public works activities—the construction of bridges, tunnels, terminals, and airports. These districts and authorities are popular with suburbanites, for sometimes they relieve financial burdens or allow assessments to be levied above constitutional limits. They do not seem to threaten suburban independence, for, by a curious *non sequitor* kind of reasoning, the suburbanite has convinced himself that authorities take government "out of politics." Because their commissioners are aloof from the undignified ordeal of vote getting, they are not to be feared as the big city is. But, by no stretch of the imagination can the districts and authorities be classified as genuine governments, democratically responsible and sensitive to popular expressions of needs. Nor do they provide adequate vehicles for the determination of regional priorities. Piecemeal, a bridge here, a park there, they offer the essential facilities for orderly community existence, but seldom in logical sequence or with direct regard to public demands.

Finally, the present pattern of suburban governments offers few means by which the typical region can plan sensibly and logically for the future. Some metropolitan areas have established official regional planning agencies; in others, private organizations struggle to alert the public of things to come. But generally, these agencies do not have the authority to guide the region's development; frequently they are not sufficiently staffed even to study it adequately. Always the suburbs can ignore a master plan and by their own zoning ordinances flaunt with impunity the obvious best interests of the region.[17]

This absence of arrangements for providing for the future is probably the most unhappy consequence of suburban independence.

Metropolitan resources are not always ample, already a shortage of water threatens entire urban areas, pollution makes "open sewers" of rivers, and transportation facilities each year are becoming increasingly outmoded. More important, change is the trademark of a metropolitan region and there is an urgent need to anticipate its direction. Linear cities, vast urban strips from Boston to Richmond, from San Francisco to Los Angeles, in which one metropolitan area merges into another are appearing, and black top culture is extending continuously along our seaboards. Under these circumstances, no unit of government, established or proposed, may be adequate to the task of providing local services efficiently and economically. Entirely new political inventions may well be necessary, and such inventions require advance and official planning.

The special problems which suburban governments face and which they engender are not new, and political science has not been oblivious to them. But political science has been extraordinarily unsuccessful in providing for their solution. At least for thirty years, reformers have sought to reorganize the structure of metropolitan government, to provide some means for reconciling the American commitment to the Republic in miniature with the obvious demands of modernity, to balance the divergent forces of autonomy and interdependence at work in the metropolitan environment. The results of their efforts were compassionately summarized by Thomas Reed, "Many better and wiser city planners and political scientists than myself have poured out millions of words, by tongue, pen and typewriter, on the same theme, but frankness requires one to say that so far we have accomplished little more than the world's record for words used in proportion to cures affected."

The first attack launched against suburbia was reform by annexation. This simplest and most direct approach called for the progressive extension of central city boundaries as population moved outward. At first this formula worked well. Until 1918, the ten largest cities at least doubled their areas and some increased ten fold. In Virginia and Texas the legislatures established "automatic" annexation procedures, and even now, each year some portions of the urban fringe are absorbed. Yet annexation has not kept pace with metropolitan growth, and as time passed, it grew less and less effective. Today, problems of balancing service costs and revenue potential expected from areas for which annexation is proposed deter many plans. More frequently, stubborn suburban resistance to the idea of returning to the metropolis defeats the proposals, and suburban enclaves in Los Angeles, Boston, Cincinnati, Detroit, and Pittsburgh, completely surrounded by central city territory, attest to the unpopularity of the scheme. As a general practical reform, annexation was abandoned by the 1930s; and except in selected parts of the country, most notably the southwest, the prospects for its revival have not improved in the intervening years.

Its obvious answer rejected, political science has experimented with a host of less ambitious schemes. Plans for intermunicipal cooperation, for exchanges of services, consolidation of city and country, separation of city and country, special authorities, federations, mergers, solutions with "no structural changes" and solutions with "structural changes," have flowed from scholars' studies and administrators' desks. From the welter of studies, reports, recommendations, and suggestions, three reasonably comprehensive major proposals have emerged: the creation of an urban county encompassing the important regional functions of the area, the establishment of a multi-purpose special district with roughly the same powers; or the adoption of a federal government uniting central cities and suburbs in a new superstructure.[18]

The urban county solution envisions the retooling of that ancient unit of local government to the point where it is equipped to assume almost all the municipal functions of the area. A consolidation of existing units would take place, and the county would emerge as the dominant, if not single jurisdiction. In contrast to previous reorganizations which involved central city-county consolidation (with the city usually emerging on top) or city-county separation (with each unit going its own way), a genuine metropolitan unit would result. The urban county plan is obviously limited for maximum effectiveness to one county metropolitan region, but it avoids the establishment of a new government and makes maximum use of a going concern.

The multi-purpose special district plan aims ultimately at transforming present pseudo-governments of this type into a genuine set of political institutions. It foresees a gradual addition to the duties of existing districts and authorities, a series of mergers, and new provision for the democratic selection and control of district officials—until a full-grown metropolitan butterfly emerges from the cocoon of a bridge or highway authority. Legally by far the easiest type of government to establish, the multi-purpose district approach has subtle pitfalls, for arrangements must be made to relieve existing local units of their responsibilites or prevent them from assuming new ones. Inter-governmental coordination is likely to remain a problem as the district asserts its growing authority. Federation plans differ from the other proposals in the degree of emphasis they give to maintaining existing local governments. They call for the creation of a new metropolitan unit, but usually they represent a studied effort to preserve loal autonomy. Frequently, there is difficulty in deciding which functions should be transferred to the new governments and which retained by the old, as well as trouble in deciding the basis of representation in the new government; but the federation approach grows increasingly popular because it both offers a genuine solution to public problems and pays proper respect to the prerogatives of existing units.

Theoretically there is little reason for preferring one of the three solutions to the other two. All establish a metropolitan government with a range of functions wide enough to deal with the most serious regional problems. All provide broad, independenct financial bases, and all include arrangements to ensure democratic accountability to the people. In a negative sense, none adequately solves the problems which arise in metropolitan areas covering two or more states, and probably none could be effective when several counties are involved. Certainly, however, any of these alternatives would provide a substantial step toward eliminating the administrative and financial deficiencies which now exist among suburban governments and providing a democratically responsible instrument for tackling regional problems.

The bald fact remains that, as a general rule, suburbanites have not welcomed these plans with open arms. Breakthroughs occur here and there, as in Toronto, Miami, and Atlanta, but in the first case the Canadian political process made suburban veto impossible, and in the latter cases only partial advances seem to have been made. Generally, suburban governments suspect—and suspect correctly—that the creation of any metropolitan governing institution threatens their authority, removes significant functions from their control, jeopardizes their status as legally autonomous entities, and imperils the continuation of the small government they have worked so hard to preserve. Suburbanites prefer to shoulder the financial and administrative burdens fractured government entails, tolerate traffic jams, highway bottlenecks, contaminated rivers, water shortages, anything rather than run the risk of mammoth government again. The reformers may have demonstrated conclusively that the cost of maintaining a suburb as a separate political jurisdiction is needlessly expensive, but to most suburbanites their figures merely prove that the price of liberty is always high. They stand pat—the modern defenders of grassroots in an urban context.

Suburbia, it should be emphasized, can probably continue to stand pat, so far as metropolitan reform is concerned, without risking catastrophe. At least so long as national prosperity continues, it can afford its increasing taxes, tolerate its administrative absurdities, ignore the plight of its neighbors, the big city and the poor suburb. It can even fail to look ahead—and survive, for the *ad hoc* agreements, the special district, the business-like authority, and federal and state grants in aid, will doubtless pull it through.

The basic question, therefore, is not the necessity of reform in suburban governments—but its desirability. Traditionally, political science, with some strong assists from sociology, has carried water on both shoulders. It has accepted uncritically the American legacy that truly effective, democratic local government must be small in size. It has placed high value on the moral integration, the sense of communion, the participation, and the social interdependence which small town life encourages. At the same time, professional doctrine has insisted that local affairs should be financially self-supporting and make administrative and organizational sense.

Metropolitan ecology has set contradictory forces at work and destroyed the coincidence between political communities and economic communities. The twin principles of autonomy and democracy which formerly went hand-in-hand as the obvious benefits of the grassroots faith have been turned against each other. The renaissance of small town democracy and close communion in the suburb has almost guaranteed financial poverty for the suburb itself and ineffective government for the region as a whole. Sometimes, reformers have sought to answer the problem by denouncing the suburb as artifact—sham small towns, phony communities—pointing to the breakdown of social isolation and the economic interdependence of the area as a whole. But they have not been able to convince the suburbanite of that fact, and modern sociology, by documenting the suburban penchant for participation, neighborliness, adjustment, and conformity, supports the latter in his instinctive feelings.[19] The horns of the dilemma are quite real: democracy and ineffective organization both exist in suburbia.

The traditional reform answer, then, not only fails to secure suburban support, it fails to face the dilemma honestly. It proposes an apparently compromise solution, purports to give priority to neither value, claims to preserve local units and to secure efficiency. It is unwilling to admit what suburbanites know intuitively, that all metropolitan reforms push power upstairs and decrease the authority of suburban governments, that in short, it covertly favors the value of efficiency over "democracy."

One way out, of course, is to look more closely at the legacy of grassroots democracy. It may be that governments nearest to home govern best; it may be that close communion is a political necessity—but again it may not. American tradition has been suspicious of theories which place the group above the individual, which rely on personalized associations rather than contractual relations to secure justice and liberty. It is possible to argue, for example, that the great city offers the freedom of choice, economic, political, and social, which liberates the individual. It is possible to argue that variety in outlook, occupation, prejudice and belief rather than homogeneity best fulfills the democratic promise. A case can be made that party government, the presentation of two more or less opposing alternatives, is superior to the town meeting, where the unarticulate are penalized, the unorganized ignored, and where government by wisecrack frequently prevails. Heretical as the statement appears, grassroots democracy may not be the ideal form of popular government; a single metropolitan government may not only be more efficient, it may also be more democratic.

However a debate between advocates of small town and big city democracy may end, it seems increasingly clear that such a debate strikes at the heart of the matter. Serious as the public problems of suburbia may be, they are not of such crisis proportions as to force a fundamental reorganization of the government of metropolitan areas. While they rob the central city and the suburbs alike of the chance to realize their potential as places to live and work, the problems do not make consolidation inevitable. Only a conscious public decision that large local governments are better—more democratic as well as more efficient—will secure the objective of metropolitan reform. The popular support for this choice depends on a hard, honest look at the representative qualities of most suburban governments. It is this inquiry with which students of local government are now concerning themselves, and though the conclusion of such inquiries may not preserve suburbia, it may provide better metropolitan government for us all.

FOOTNOTES

1. Cf., for example, discussions of suburban political activity in Louis Harris, *Is There a Republican Majority?* Samuel Lubell, *The Revolt of the Moderates;* William Whyte, *The Organization Man;* and John Seeley and others, *Crestwood Heights;* as well as recent articles in *Harpers'* and *Fortune* magazines.

2. For a direct comparison between modern suburbs and early American communities, see Stuart and Elkins, "A Meaning for Turner's Frontier," *The Annals of the American Political Science Society,* September and December, 1954.

3. Patrick Geddes, *Cities in Evolution;* Ebenezer Howard, *Garden Cities of Tomorrow;* and more recently, in the literature of planning, Wright and Mumford.

4. The general references are Harlan Douglass, *The Suburban Trend;* and Arthur E. Morgan, *The Small Community.*

5. Cf., Scott Greer, "Individual Participation in a Mass Society," *Conference Study of the Community,* 1956; Stuart and Elkins, *op. cit.,* and Conrad Arnesberg, "American Communities," *The American Anthropologist,* December 1955.

6. Cf., proceedings of the National Conference on Metropolitan Affairs, as to the actual reforms resulting from metropolitan surveys, May, 1956, as well as the reports on suburban attitudes toward government reorganization conducted in St. Louis and in Flint, Michigan, and reported in *Public Administration Review, Journal of Land Economics* and elsewhere.

7. The basic work describing the "metropolitan dilemma" is Victor Jones' *Metropolitan Government.* There are, however, over 100 surveys of individual metropolitan areas which document the financial and administrative problems both of suburbs and central cities, and a sizable literature is devoted to this topic.

8. Jones, *op. cit.;* Bureau of the Census, *Census of Governments,* 1946, and various later special releases.

9. Caves, Richard, *Memorandum prepared for Bureau for Research in Municipal Government,* Harvard University, Summer, 1946, based on censuses of population and manufacturing.

10. Duggar, George, "The Tax System and a Responsible Housing Program," Unpublished Ph.D. Dissertation, Harvard University, April 1955.
11. National Municipal League, *The Metropolitan Area,* 1933.
12. Duggar, *op. cit.*
13. Charles Adrian, *Governing Urban America,* 1954, Chapter 11; Association of City Managers *Municipal Yearbook,* Annual Editions.
14. Charles Adrian, *op. cit.,* p. 46.
15. Tableman, Betty, *Government Organization in Metropolitan Areas,* 1951.
16. Jones and Tableman provide particularly effective summaries of this regional consequence. Cf., especially chapter by Jones in *The Future of Cities,* Part II, Coleman Woodbury, editor.
17. The literature in the field of urban planning is now sizable, standard texts outline more fully the problems summarized above. See particularly Robert A. Walker's *The Planning Function in Urban Government* and the publications of the Regional Plan Association of New York.
18. For a more comprehensive discussion, cf. John C. Bollens, *The States and the Metropolitan Problem,* published by the Council of State Governments, 1956.
19. The similarities in political and possibly social behavior between the new American character Riesman and Whyte describe, for example, and the image of the colonial citizen whom Stuart and Elkins reconstruct are intriguing. Historically, it appears that the strand of the conformist, group-oriented individual goes a long way back in the United States.

William N. Leonard

Hofstra College

ECONOMIC ASPECTS
OF SUBURBANIZATION

With the spilling over of the American city into adjacent land areas, large urban conglomerates have developed in which one populated place shades into the next, making it difficult to distinguish the city, the suburb, and sometimes the metropolitan area itself. In six East Coast states—Massachusetts, Rhode Island, Connecticut, New York, New Jersey and Pennsylvania—eighty-two per cent of the population live in thirty-nine metropolitan areas, eight of which overlap state lines.[1] Many of these thirty-nine areas grow right into each other—for example, New York, Trenton, and Philadelphia—and in twenty-five years there will probably be continuous settlement of the Atlantic Coast from Boston, Massachusetts, to Washington, D.C. Once referred to as "six suburbs in search of a city," Los Angeles now has fifty-two incorporated cities in its metropolitan area, which covers nearly 5,000 square miles in Southern California.

In the larger metropolitan areas there are normally three essential orbits of economic activity: (1) a Core, or central business district, comprising office buildings, stores, hotels and places of entertainment; (2) an Inner Ring of industry, small stores, and tightly packed dwelling units, mostly apartments; and (3) an Outer Ring, consisting of scattered industries, small and large stores, and above all, single family dwellings. It is mainly the Outer Ring which fits the term "suburb," located as it is on the periphery of the metropolis, composed of

This is an original article, prepared for this volume.

individual homes, with the head of the household often a managerial or professional person commuting into the Core for his livelihood, and is "middle class" in its economic origins and orientation.[2]

The Suburban Explosion

In America the Industrial Revolution and the rise of cities transformed the nation over in one hundred and fifty years from a rural to an urban society. In recent decades, however, the spectacular growth of suburbs has shifted the character of American life from an urban to a metropolitan basis. In 1900 metropolitan areas had 32 per cent of the nation's population; by 1950 they had 57 per cent, and reported 80 per cent of the population growth occurring between 1940 and 1950.[3] Most of this growth took place outside city limits. Between 1910 and 1950, while the nation grew by 64 per cent (from 92 million to 151 million), suburban communities more than doubled (from an estimated 18 million to 38 million), and the available evidence indicates that in the period since 1950 the trek to the suburbs has continued. In the New York area, 85 per cent of the population growth since 1950 has occurred in counties lying outside the five boroughs of New York City. One of these counties, Nassau, grew by 71 per cent between 1950 and 1957. In the same period, around Washington, D.C., Montgomery and Prince George Counties in Maryland, and Arlington County, Virginia, experienced an estimated 52 per cent growth in population. Spectacular gains have been registered in the Los Angeles and San Francisco areas in California, and around Houston, Texas. Presently it is estimated that 47 million Americans have their homes in the suburbs.[4]

Though some have called the development of suburbs a revolution in the American way of life, in economic perspective the suburb represents the outcome of a series of profound forces which consistently for several decades have influenced the growth of the economy in population and material welfare. Among them has been rapid industrialization, rising productivity, higher incomes and a redistribution of income in favor of upper middle class families. Accompanying this has been the concentration of a growing population into limited land areas fostered by the factory system and the higher costs of providing services over more extended geographic areas.

Fundamental to the post-war mushrooming of suburbs is the spectacular growth in real disposable income which rose from $576 per person in 1940 to $1708 in 1956. In the latter year family income stood at $4250 in the country as a whole, but was estimated at $4900 in the suburbs, fully 15 per cent above the national average. American families, earning more money and working fewer hours than in previous decades, had been able to afford more homes, more cars, and more children than any one had thought possible. And the suburb had been chosen as the place to enjoy these perquisites of living.

Besides the secular growth in family income in the United States, there has occurred over the past several decades a redistribution of earnings in favor of the middle income brackets, particularly those just below the wealthiest group of American families. Between 1929 and 1956 the proportion of total money income received by the highest tenth of income recipients dropped from 39 per cent to 31 per cent; but the share accruing to the second and third tenths rose from a combined total of 22 per cent to 27 per cent. Many suburbanites come from these upper middle income groups.

Table I—Distribution of Total Money Income before Taxes by Income Tenths, 1929 and 1956. Mean Income within Tenth, 1956

Income Tenth	Per cent of total money income		Mean Income within Tenth	Lowest Income within Tenth
	1929	1956	1956	1956
Highest tenth	39	31	$15,760	$9,050
Second "	12	15	7,850	7,000
Third "	10	12	6,330	5,850
Fourth "	9	10	5,370	5,000
Fifth "	8	9	4,660	4,270
Sixth "	7	8	3,920	3,520
Seventh "	6	6	3,130	2,740
Eighth "	5	5	2,310	1,900
Ninth "	4	3	1,450	1,050
Lowest "	2	1	660	. .

Source: Statistical Abstract of the U.S. (Supplement), 1956 Federal Reserve Bulletin, August 1957, p. 893.

Most notable in the pattern of living made possible by the rise in incomes is the preference for single family dwellings which dot the outer rings of metropolitan areas. Between 1945 and 1956 inclusive, some 12,070,000 non-farm dwelling units were started in the United States, of which 10,280,000, or 85.2 per cent, were single family units. New apartments accounted for 11.3 per cent of dwelling unit construction, while two-family units made up the remaining 3.5 per cent.[5] In 1940 only four out of ten families owned their own homes, but with the rise of home ownership it was predicted by one expert that by 1960 seven out of ten would likely be owners of homes, many of them located in the suburbs.[6]

Migration to the suburb has been made possible by the mobility given the American worker by the private automobile. For the city dweller the ownership of a car was unnecessary because of the availability of public transportation, or if he succumbed to the temptation to buy a large, powerful and thirsty American automobile, he found its operation cumbersome and expensive. If he moved to the suburb, however, he found car ownership not only possible, and sometimes pleasant, but a distinct necessity. A car was often used for commuting, generally for shopping, and regularly for recreation and amusement. It is not surprising to find that more than 90 per cent of suburban families own cars, compared to an average of 68 per cent for all American families.[7]

High land costs in the central city combined with the availability of less expensive land in outlying areas have furnished compelling reasons for suburban growth, once incomes sufficed to satisfy the appetite for private homes and cars. In addition to savings in land costs, builders have frequently acquired large farms and estates in fringe areas on which hundreds of homes could be simultaneously erected, thus achieving economies of construction through more efficient use of labor and equipment, and through mass purchasing of materials and furnishings. Such economies, though not always large, have permitted some shaving of the spiraling costs of building. The zeal to cut costs often led to hasty and sub-standard construction, and sometimes to traumatic housing experiences,[8] but in the main suburban homes have given the expanding American family, more space and greater efficiency in the home, more adequate play and recreation areas for children, and more streets and parkways suited to the operation of private automobiles.

A silent partner of suburban development has been the tax system of the United States. The more progressive rates of federal income, have worked in favor of upper middle income groups who have swarmed into the suburbs. At the same time the tax system has caught the wealthy landowning suburbanite in a scissors: even as the federal income tax sheared away much of his income, rising local property taxes increased costs of land ownership, so that finally the estate owner was compelled to sell and subdivide his property. In the City the boosting of taxes to meet the expenses of local services induced many families (and some firms) to seek the milder tax climate of the outlying areas, though this climate on occasion proved to be quite variable. Lastly, the extension of Social Security and of pension plans, made possible the financial independence of the fast-rising percentage of older persons retired from the work force, many of whom migrated to homes in suburban areas, particularly in California and Florida.

In all likelihood these forces will continue to operate in favor of the suburb. Although a recession or depression may slow family formation and retard migration, population experts have predicted that the inhabitants of Suburbia will grow in numbers from 47 million in 1957 to 85.2 million in 1975, at which time they will represent 41 per cent of the nation's people. While all the principal metropolitan areas are expected to increase and to obtain a greater share of total population,[9] Los Angeles and San Francisco, California and Miami, Florida were forecast to be the fastest growing areas in the nation.

Economic Change in the Suburb

Although suburbanization permits metropolitan areas to continue to increase and to concentrate population and industry in key geographic areas, the extension of suburbs effects a redistribution of people and economic activity within the metropolitan area itself. First, the sparsely settled fringe areas evidence the greatest growth in population. Secondly, while industry may be forced out of the Core because of costs, if not by zoning, the Inner Ring can usually maintain its industrial belts, while the Outer Ring becomes the chief beneficiary of new industrial location. Commerce also will extend with the new homes and factories towards the periphery of the area, though it remains concentrated in the Core. The chief victim of suburban encroachment is agriculture which is forced farther and farther away from the city. Because of the mounting cost of land, only high value crops can stay in the area. Dairying, poultry and crop farming, will be compelled to move, but horticulture and some truck gardening may be able to remain in the metropolitan area.

When population first begins flowing into the suburb land values are chiefly based upon chance location, with scenic qualities serving to enhance the price of residential property. As a suburban area becomes built up, however, access to arterial highways becomes the factor which increasingly determines land values. This holds true not only for homes located near highways which are regarded as convenient for commuting, shopping and other family business, but also for stores and industrial plants dependent upon the passenger car for customers or employees, and upon trucks for deliveries or outbound shipments. The presence of shopping centers usually serves as a factor to boost land values in residential areas, while location of industry close to homes may depress land values, depending upon the character of industry, its screening from residential zones, and the manner, in which its operations are handled, for example, noise, traffic, parking, fumes, and other problems. Well-managed suburbs usually have strict zoning requirements for the various classes of land use, the main object being to preserve residential values, and secondly, to locate stores, plants, schools, parks, hospitals and other service facilities in the places most advantageous to effective operation, with minimum impact upon the privacy of homes or the level of public services.

One of the immediate effects is to change the economic character of the Core itself. With the middle income classes moving out, the Central City becomes the home either of the well-to-do or the poor. As the middle class moves out, a vacuum is created into which low income families tend to move, families from rural areas, from the South, or from abroad. Population data of cities for 1950 indicate that the number of non-whites living in cities has increased at a rate twice as high as that of whites.[10] This poses problems of education, welfare and other public services for the City which tend to augment costs (for example, in New York City, special language classes are offered Puerto Ricans who have flocked into Manhattan apartments). At the same time, the Core's sprouting office buildings, shopping and entertainment facilities, bring a steadily increasing stream of commuters and patrons from the burgeoning suburbs adding to the strain on highways, streets and transit generally. The handling of riders, the management of traffic, the accommodation and parking of private cars become problems of immense magnitude and soaring cost which beset city administrators, and lead to boosts in taxes which increase the restlessness of remaining residents and businessmen. However, the need of large national and international companies to have access to banks and brokerage houses, to advertising, accounting, engineering, legal and other professional firms, as well as to other members of the business community, tends to hold and even increase the number of company offices in the downtown area.

Migration of Manufacturing

Although the Inner Ring continues to hold a great deal of industry, the outlying suburbs become the favorite points of location for new manufacturing plants. Apart from the practical matter of site availability, a number of forces operate to bring industry to the suburbs, forces deriving from the changing character of industry and of markets.

The scattering of industry over the satellite area has been facilitated by the electrification of power, the mobility of labor provided by the automobile, the building of highways, and the separation of production from central office functions which are carried on in the downtown area.[11]

Among the internal factors pulling business to the suburbs is the need for space and modern plant layout on the part of an industry which has been producing within the Inner Ring of the area. Industries which have for short periods or for decades operated in a multi-story building, or a loft, find that the needs for new equipment, for mass producing, or for efficient flow of materials, require a single-story operation, and that the space needed for building can be supplied only in the fringe areas. By reducing the labor component of production in favor of small mechanized and electronically controlled plants, automation tends to accentuate the shift to the suburbs.

Considerations relating to the supply of labor may also induce migration to outlying areas. This is not so much a matter of the availability of labor, nor of wage levels, nor of union organization within the city, as compared with the suburb, though these matters may be involved, as it is a question of the quality of labor. Studies have shown that many employers prefer to hire labor which resides near its place of work,[12] believing that such employees are happier and better workers. Furthermore, as the commuting radius lengthens with the growth of the metropolitan area, the time, energy and cost associated with commutation increase to the point of worker dissatisfaction and demand for wages higher than those prevailing in the general area or justified on the basis of productivity. This pertains, of course, only to those employees who reside in the suburbs, but these are apt to be among the more highly skilled and hence valuable members of the work force. Once a labor supply has been developed in the suburbs, particularly a skilled occupational group, a strong magnet exists for the location of industry requiring this type of employee.

Industry has a self-generating quality which is most evident in the suburb. This refers to the fact that the presence of a prime producer, e.g., of steel, will encourage the location of fabricators and steel users in the area, as has occurred about Pittsburgh, Pennsylvania or Cleveland, Ohio. Or a cluster of automotive plants, e.g., at Detroit, may produce within the area a secondary cluster of suppliers of parts or accessories to the major industry. The development of the instruments and electronics industries about major aircraft producers in the New York (Long Island) area and about Los Angeles is another instance of the self-generative aspect of industry which has had a marked influence on suburban growth.

Finally, the suburb represents an attractive market to manufacturers in residentiary industries. The latter include bakeries and canneries, manufacturers of printing and publishing, building materials, home furnishings and appliances, and builders all of whom find their sales chiefly local in character. As population concentrates increasingly in metropolitan areas, industries are drawn into the outskirts to develop the mass market at their doorstep.

However, the bulk of industries located in the suburb are concerned with national and international markets rather than the immediate metropolitan market. On a national level the decentralization of manufacturing in the United States has favored the location of branch plants, processing plants, packaging plants, or plants for the final assembly of parts, in the major urban areas of the nation. Because sites could be had only in fringe areas, the latter have been the beneficiaries.

Strict zoning requirements and the insistent opposition of suburbanites to the location of industry in their neighborhoods have compelled suburban developers and government officials to review carefully both the kind of industry to be admitted to a community and the plant site. One device for satisfying the needs of industry and preserving the character of the community is the evolution of "industrial parks," large blocs of land with sites for a number of industrial plants, close to arterial highways and other needed utilities, and separated by a landscaped border or "screen" from neighboring residential areas.

Despite occasional local opposition, government officials in the suburbs have favored the location of industry both to provide local jobs and to broaden the tax base. It is generally felt, though not always statistically established, that industry more than pays the costs of governmental services afforded it.[13] As the result of the scattering of plants over the outskirts of the metropolis, and the employment by industry of persons already living in the suburbs or induced to migrate thereto, the character of many suburban areas has changed from a series of "Bedrooms" for managerial and professional persons commuting to the city's core with scattered stores and services to a chain of communities evidencing a more diversified distribution of skills among its resident population. Although individual suburbs may differ considerably in the proportion of business and professional workers, skilled workers and other occupational groups, as well as in personal income, the entire suburban configuration now reveals a much greater balance of skills and a clustering of incomes than existed prior to its post-war upbuilding.

The deconcentration of American cities has resulted in the spreading of services within metropolitan areas. With its base of manufacturing activity and personal income higher than for rural areas, cities have always enjoyed a high level of services, and the transfer of population to the suburb, particularly the upper middle income groups, has meant a sharp outward shift of the pattern of demand for services in the metropolitan areas. Further, as industry has begun to dot the Outer Ring of metropolitan areas, and skilled workers have located in the fringes, additional force has been given to the outward pull for services.[14]

This does not mean that all city services have sought the lush suburban market in equal proportions. To some extent the expanding suburban need for services has been met by local services operating before the population bulge began, and by additional stores, shops and firms established in the post-war small business boom. But national food stores, drug, jewelry, five-and-ten and other chains have hastened to build outlets in the suburbs, alongside branches of department stores, specialty shops, brokerage houses, insurance companies, banks and savings and loan associations with headquarters in the central business district.[15] To a considerable extent, however, financial and business services have remained concentrated in the Core, and while retailing has sought the suburb, wholesaling has tended to stay in the city. Hotels and entertainment have also continued to operate in the Core area of the metropolis.

The special character of suburbs has called forth certain distinct qualities of services. High incomes have meant more doctors, dentists and professional workers per capita than in the cities, and the widespread use of private cars has multiplied car salesmen, garages and service stations. The amount of home construction and renovation going on in the suburbs has called forth a host of building material, home furnishings and appliance outlets, as well as landscaping, insect-killing, lawn-mowing and other home services. Sellers of household tools and hardware have profited from the "Do-it-yourself" fad, while sporting goods stores have done a lush business with the recreation-minded suburbanite.

With the widespread use of cars in the suburbs, stores instead of stringing out in a "ribbon" type of development along highways and streets have tended to bunch in certain areas of the suburbs. In some cases advance zoning set aside certain areas for commercial use, in other cases the development of shopping centers has brought together in one spot a department store and a variety of other stores whose products and services complemented each other, with adequate off-street parking for customers. The insistence upon "one-stop" stores has favored the location of large self-service super-markets selling everything from food and drugs to kitchenware and sporting equipment, each owning its own parking field. The super-market, shopping center and the discount house [16] have created a revolution in retailing design and techniques and have put many small retailers out of business or forced them to adopt new merchandising methods. This has been particularly true of stores in suburban municipal commercial districts which have lacked access highways or off-street parking to accommodate their customers.

Studies of consumption patterns reveal that an increase in personal income is accompanied by a correspondingly greater increase in spending for medical care, education and recreation. The suburb evidences an appetite for all these services which is great but not always satisfied. While doctors and dentists abound, costs are high and there are frequently insufficient hospitals or hospital beds to meet local needs. The style in schools and hospitals, as in homes and plants, is for low buildings and off-street parking, requiring extensive use of land, and this cannot always be made available. As younger families move into the suburbs and send their children to the schools, the revenue needs of building and staffing schools sends taxes soaring, leading to unhappy protests from property owners. With increased population density and taxes, private golf clubs and recreational areas often give way and public parks become overcrowded, making it imperative to clear other acreages for park development.

Suburban consumption standards reveal a high individuality of taste for what is normally thought to be an area eminently conformist in character. First, the styling of homes evidences considerable difference and an aversion to the sameness of apartments or of row houses. Even homes in large-scale developments using a few basic models have been individualized by their owners through additional building, painting, landscaping and furnishing. Suburban families furnish a ready market for a variety of car models, including station wagons, sports cars, convertibles, small American cars and foreign makes, and as many tastes are shown for reading, sports and entertainment as are found in the city.

In one important aspect, however, there exists considerable conformity among suburbanites, namely in the use made of credit. The building and remodeling of homes, the purchase of cars, home furnishings and appliances, have been accompanied by extensive borrowing. Many suburban home-buyers, especially veterans, paid little or nothing to acquire their property apart from the initial purchase fees. For years many will be paying more in interest rates than on principal, and not a few homes will depreciate more in value in ten or twenty years than their buyer will have reduced the principal, thus postponing the real cost to the buyer. With the family under a load of debt, with living costs and local taxes rising, suburban families have become very price conscious, patronizing stores with discounts and sales, even at the sacrifice of the personalized service often more available in other stores. In addition, once her children have entered school, the housewife has increasingly sought work, either full or part-time, in the local area in order to supplement her husband's income. In view of the thin financial ice on which many suburban families are now skating, it appears certain that a serious recession or depression would strike hard at these newer areas of population.

Economic Problems of the Suburb

Many economic difficulties found in the suburb are not peculiar to its way of life but cut across the entire American economy. The maintenance of employment and income, the payment of debts by consumers and businessmen depend upon the continued vigor of the American economy. Other problems are basically those of the general metropolitan area in which the suburb finds itself, for example, problems of water supply, air pollution, water pollution, sewage and waste disposal.

Critical to suburban living and to the pattern of metropolitan development is transportation. As the use of automobiles has increased, public transit systems have lost money while government at every level has had to strain to provide streets, highways, and parkways. The improvement of transportation routes, the handling of traffic, the provision of adequate parking, continue to be the most serious problems facing government in metropolitan areas.

Associated with the responsibility for transportation and traffic is the need to develop better land use analysis and planning. The high level of services demanded by suburbanites, particularly in the areas of health, education, recreation and welfare, augment the importance of anticipating the needs of a growing population for these services, and setting aside land required for roads and parking, and also for schools, hospitals and parks.

In many suburban areas the provision of water or other municipal services is on a small scale and uneconomic basis. Different zoning requirements create wide variations in land use patterns and in the tax burden, as for example between districts with considerable industry in the tax base but few residences and districts with large populations of families with young children but little industry.

Such inequity of tax burden and the general rise of local property taxes have led to demands for relief (and also to cutbacks in school budgets) on the part of taxpayers. In some cases resort has been made to other local sources of revenue, for example, sales and business taxes; in most cases, local governments have sought increased aid from state and federal treasuries. In all probability, the fiscal problems of suburbs will spur significant changes in public finance and administration in the next several decades.

FOOTNOTES

1. Reported by Conference on Metropolitan Area Problems, *New York Times,* September 24, 1957.
2. Settlement of the suburb, while largely caused by families escaping the congestion of the Inner Ring, may also come from persons moving from a rural environment to a fringe metropolitan area in search of economic and educational opportunities. Again, the orientation is largely middle class. M. W. Rodehaver, "Fringe Settlement as a Two-Directional Movement," *Rural Sociology,* March 1947.
3. D. J. Bogue, "Urbanization in the United States, 1950," *American Journal of Sociology,* January, 1955.
4. *Newsweek,* April 1, 1957.
5. Statistical Bulletin, U.S. Bureau of Labor Statistics, Washington, D.C., December, 1956.
6. G. H. Kleisner, "Marketing Implications of Population Growth," *Industrial Development,* July-August, 1956.
7. A study by the Hofstra College Bureau of Business Research in 1955 revealed that 94 per cent of families in Nassau and Suffolk counties owned cars, while 18 per cent owned two or more cars. Corresponding figures for the entire country at that time were: 68 per cent of families had cars, and 8 per cent had two or more cars. *Survey of Consumer Finances, 1956,* Federal Reserve Board, Washington, D.C.
8. See House Report No. 2501 (82nd Congress, 2nd Sess.) Sept. 11, 1952.
9. The ten largest metropolitan areas which in 1957 had a combined population of 45.4 million persons, 22.1 per cent of the national total, were predicted to have 63 million persons in 1975, or 33 per cent of the nation's population. *U.S. News & World Report,* August 7, 1957.
10. Bogue, *op. cit.,* p. 474.
11. A. H. Hawley, *The Changing Shape of Metropolitan America,* Free Press, Glencoe, Illinois, 1955, p. 114.
12. William Leonard and Charles Stonier, "Industry Looks at Long Island," Hofstra College Bureau of Business Research, Hempstead, N.Y., 1956.
13. One study found that industry paid in taxes 2.75 times as much as the cost of services furnished it by government. "Does Industry Pay Its Way?" Hofstra College, Hempstead, N.Y., 1956.
14. It is a well known economic fact that because of respending, every job in manufacturing and construction (secondary area) generates jobs in the tertiary area, that is, in transportation and utilities, in distribution, in household, business and financial services, in entertainment, education, medicine and other professional services, and in government. For the 12 largest metropolitan areas in 1950 the ratio of workers in the tertiary occupations to workers in secondary occupations was 1.65 to 1. See G.

Alexandersson, "The Industrial Structure of Cities," Univ. of Nebraska Press, 1955, Appendix 2.

15. Branch banking has in some areas of the country been restricted by state law, and local suburban banks have spread out to satisfy the need for new services.

16. A large department store with low prices, high volume and a great deal of self-service, which pioneered in violating state resale price maintenance laws.

James D. Tarver

Oklahoma A. and M. College

SUBURBANIZATION OF RETAIL TRADE IN THE STANDARD METROPOLITAN AREAS OF THE UNITED STATES, 1948–54

One of the most momentous population trends in this country is the increasing concentration of people in the standard metropolitan areas (S.M.A.'s). Not only do nearly 60 per cent of our people live in the 168 S.M.A.'s, but the population of these areas is increasing at a much more rapid rate than the rest of the United States. Between April, 1950 and April, 1955, the population in the 168 S.M.A.'s increased 13.7 per cent, whereas the nonmetropolitan areas gained only 0.5 per cent.[1]

Significantly, the greatest population shifts into the metropolitan areas are to the suburbs rather than to the central cities. This suburban sprawl, or "scatteration," has accelerated since World War II and is expanding the huge metropolitan areas, or "conurbations," farther and farther out into the rural hinterlands. Constellations of satellite communities encircle the large core cities. During 1950-55, the suburban populations increased more than seven times as fast, proportionately, as the central cities. In fact, over 80 per cent of the population growth for the entire nation during this five-year period occurred in the metropolitan areas outside the central cities. Of the 84.5 million

Reprinted from *American Sociological Review,* Vol. 22 (August 1957) pp. 429-433, by permission of the author and *American Sociological Review.* Approved by the Oklahoma Agricultural Experiment Station.

people living in the 168 S.M.A.'s in 1950, 35 million, or 42 per cent, resided in the peripheral areas of the central cities; and, in 1955, 46 per cent of all residents of the metropolitan areas lived in the surrounding suburban areas of the central cities.

The three objectives of this study are: *First,* to measure the differential changes in retail trade between the S.M.A.'s and the nonmetropolitan areas in the United States during 1948-54; *second,* to determine the relative changes in retail trade separately for the central cities and for the outlying areas of the S.M.A.'s; and *third,* to ascertain the relationship between central city-size and regional location and changes in retail trade in the S.M.A.'s.

Table 1—Retail Trade by Metropolitan and Nonmetropolitan Areas, 1948-54 *

Area	Total Establishments			Total Sales, All Establishments, Adjusted for Change in Price Level †		
	Number (Thousands)		Per Cent Change,	Retail Sales (Billions of Dollars)		Per Cent Change,
	1948	1954	1948-54	1948	1954	1948-54
United States	1,668.5	1,721.7	3.2	128.8	157.1	21.9
S.M.A.'s	906.9	948.8	4.6	81.5	100.9	23.8
Central cities	583.5	606.7	4.0	58.7	67.9	15.8
Balance of area	323.5	342.1	5.8	22.9	32.9	44.1
Cities—50,000 or more pop.‡	50.9	51.5	1.2	4.5	5.7	25.2
Remainder of Area	272.5	290.6	6.6	18.3	27.3	48.7
Outside S.M.A.'s §	761.6	772.9	1.5	47.3	56.2	18.7

* The number of establishments and sales do not necessarily add to totals because of rounding.

† The indexes of retail prices of all commodities, with the 1935-39 base = 100, were 192.7 in 1948 and 208.5 in 1954. By multiplying the 1954 retail sales data by .924, the 1954 figures were adjusted to reflect the 1948 price level as = 100. Source: *The Economic Almanac, 1956,* Frederick W. Jones, Editor, New York: Thomas Y. Crowell Co., 1956, p. 75.

‡ These cities of 50,000 or more population are the 53 noncentral cities located in 15 of the S.M.A.'s.

§ Nonmetropolitan area data obtained by subtracting standard metropolitan figures from the United States total.

Source: *Retail Trade, United States Summary—Advance Report,* Bulletin R-1-1 Advance, 1954 *Census of Business,* U. S. Dept. of Commerce, Bureau of the Census, Washington, 1956, p. 5; and *Retail Trade State Bulletins R-1, 1954 Census of Business,* Tables 102, 102A, 103, and 103A.

The data analyzed in this paper were obtained from the 1954 Census of Business Retail Trade bulletins.[2] The two measures of retail trade activity used are the numbers of establishments and value of sales. The revised 1948 data on these two measures are used in this study because they are comparable with those of 1954. It was necessary to standardize the sales to a common price index base. This was accomplished by converting the 1954 sales into 1948 dollars.

The hypothesis of this study is that *the relative increase in retail trade has been greater in the suburbs than in the central cities of the S.M.A.'s during 1948-54.*

A corresponding shift in retail trade accompanied the tremendous movement of people, especially to the suburbs of the S.M.A.'s. In 1954, the 168 S.M.A.'s contained 55 per cent of all retail businesses in the United States. Between 1948-54, the number of retail stores in these S.M.A.'s of the United States increased three times as rapidly as in other areas of the country (Table 1).[3] Within the S.M.A.'s, the rate of growth was about one and one-half times as high in the outlying parts as in the 193 central cities. The greatest proportionate gain in retail outlets, 6.6 per cent, occurred in suburban areas with noncentral cities under 50,000 population. In the 53 noncentral cities of 50,000 or more population the increase in number of retail enterprises amounted to only 1.2 per cent.

As Table 1 shows, the suburbanization trend in the dollar volume of retail sales was much more pronounced than in numbers of stores during 1948-54. In terms of adjusted sales, the increase was greater in the 168 S.M.A.'s than in the nonmetropolitan areas and, while the gain in the central cities was only 15.8 per cent, that of the suburbs was 44.1 per cent, or three times as great.[4] Again, the greatest increase in sales in the S.M.A.'s occurred in the outlying parts having no noncentral cities with as many as 50,000 persons. This means that in the nation's major cities retail stores have followed their customers to the outlying subdivisions.

Suburbanization of Retail Trade by Size of Central City

Each of the eight size-groups of S.M.A.'s showed a gain in numbers of retail establishments during 1948-54 (Table 2). The smallest relative gains occurred in those S.M.A.'s containing central cities of

500,000 inhabitants and over, while the greatest proportional increases came in those with central cities of 400,000 to 500,000 and 200,000 to 300,000 population, in order. The only discernible growth pattern for all S. M.A.'s is a greater rate of increase for the small than for the large areas.

Table 2—Retail Trade Establishments in S.M.A.'s by Size of Central City, 1948-54 *

Size of Central City †	Total Establishments in the 168 S.M.A.'s			Total Establishments in the Central Cities			Total Establishments in Balance of the S.M.A.'s		
	Number (Thousands)		Per Cent Change,	Number (Thousands)		Per Cent Change,	Number (Thousands)		Per Cent Change,
	1948	1954	1948-54	1948	1954	1948-54	1948	1954	1948-54
Total	906.9	948.8	4.6	583.5	606.7	4.0	323.5	342.1	5.8
50,000-99,999	123.4	132.8	7.6	75.5	85.2	12.9	48.0	47.6	—.7
100,000-199,999 ‡	126.6	135.0	6.6	82.8	92.2	11.4	43.8	42.7	—2.5
200,000-299,999	49.7	55.0	10.7	32.9	37.3	13.3	16.8	17.7	5.6
300,000-399,999 ‡	46.0	50.1	9.0	32.9	36.8	12.0	13.1	13.3	1.4
400,000-499,999	36.8	41.2	11.9	28.0	31.9	13.8	8.8	9.3	5.9
500,000-749,999	79.5	82.0	3.1	48.6	51.1	5.2	30.9	30.9	—.1
750,000-1,000,000 ‡	105.8	111.5	5.3	65.5	63.8	—2.5	40.3	47.6	18.1
1,000,000 +	339.1	341.3	.6	217.4	208.4	—4.1	121.8	132.9	9.1

* The numbers of establishments do not necessarily add to totals because of rounding to the nearest thousand.

† Each S.M.A. is classified by size of the largest central city. Twenty-one S.M.A.'s contain either two or three central cities.

‡ The number of retail trade establishments reported in the 1954 *Census of Business* for the Cincinnati, Louisville, and Youngstown S.M.A.'s were changed from 5,452 to 5,450; and the 1948 Youngstown S.M.A. total was changed from 5,202 to 5,154. In Cincinnati, the S.M.A. totals were changed from 9,668 in 1948 and 9,930 in 1954 to 9,670 and 9,928, respectively; the 1948 Louisville S.M.A. total was changed from 5,452 to 5,450.

Source: *Retail Trade*, State Bulletins R-1, 1954 *Census of Business*, U. S. Dept. of Commerce, Bureau of the Census, Washington, 1956, Tables 102, 102A, 103, and 103A.

The five S.M.A.'s that had the greatest proportionate increases in number of retail outlets were, in order: Orlando, Florida, 47; San Jose, California, 46; Albuquerque, New Mexico, 39; Phoenix, Arizona, 35; and Lubbock, Texas, 34 per cent, all of which are in the South, Southwest, and West. The five experiencing the greatest losses were, in order: Terre Haute, Indiana, — 14; Savannah, Georgia, — 12; Wilkes-Barre-Hazleton, Pennsylvania, — 10; Laredo, Texas, — 10; and Buffalo, New York, — 8 per cent. They form no regional pattern.

Table 2 shows, *first,* that the suburban areas of the 168 S.M.A.'s had a relatively greater growth in numbers of retail units between

1948-54 than did the central cities. Most of the decentralization was limited to the 11 S.M.A.'s having central cities with 750,000 or more population. These accounted for 18,425, or 99 per cent, of the 18,624 increase in retail units outside central cities. *Second,* in the S.M.A.'s with central cities under 750,000 population, the increase in retail establishments was relatively greater in central cities than in adjacent suburbs. *Third,* retail stores multiplied relatively more rapidly in central cities below than in those above 500,000 in population.

Since retail enterprises vary considerably in size, the dollar value of sales is a more suitable measure of volume of retail trade activity than the number of businesses.[5] The dollar increase in retail business receipts in the S.M.A.'s was over twice as high in suburbs as in central cities. When the 1954 sales are expressed in terms of 1948 consumer dollars, the differential gain of retail receipts is 2.8 times as high in suburban areas as in central cities (Table 3).

Table 3—Retail Trade Sales in S.M.A.'s by Size of Central City, 1948-54 *

Sales, Adjusted for Change in Price Level

	Total Sales, All Establishments in the 168 S.M.A.'s			Total Sales, All Establishments in the Central Cities			Total Sales, All Establishments in the Balance of the S.M.A.'s		
Size of Largest Central City	Retail Sales (Billions of Dollars)		Per Cent Change,	Retail Sales (Billions of Dollars)		Per Cent Change,	Retail Sales (Billions of Dollars)		Per Cent Change,
	1948	1954	1948-54	1948	1954	1948-54	1948	1954	1948-54
Total	81.5	100.9	23.8	58.7	67.9	15.8	22.9	32.9	44.1
50,000-99,999 †	10.3	12.6	22.5	7.7	9.3	21.0	2.6	3.3	27.0
100,000-199,999 †	10.9	13.6	25.1	8.3	10.2	22.9	2.6	3.4	32.2
200,000-299,999	4.7	6.0	29.0	3.7	4.5	23.7	1.0	1.5	48.0
300,000-399,999 †	4.8	5.9	23.4	3.9	4.7	20.4	.9	1.2	37.0
400,000-499,999	4.0	5.2	29.7	3.4	4.3	24.1	.6	1.0	63.2
500,000-749,999 †	7.3	8.7	19.5	5.2	6.0	14.3	2.1	2.8	32.4
750,000-1,000,000	10.2	12.6	23.3	6.9	7.4	8.3	3.4	5.2	54.0
1,000,000 +	29.3	36.1	23.3	19.5	21.5	10.0	9.8	14.6	49.9

* Sales do not necessarily add to totals because of rounding to the nearest billion.

† The total sales of all retail establishments reported in the 1954 *Census of Business* for the Cincinnati, Columbus (Georgia), Louisville, and Youngstown S.M.A.'s were changed to agree with county totals for each area. In Cincinnati, the S.M.A. totals were changed from $862,622,000 in 1948 and $1,151,383,000 in 1954 to $862,626,000 and $1,153,340,000, respectively. The 1948 Columbus, Georgia S.M.A. total was changed from $106,389,000 to $106,377,000; the 1948 Louisville S.M.A. total was changed from $509,392,000 to $509,389,000; and the 1948 Youngstown S.M.A. total was changed from $461,644,000 to $461,580,000.

Source: *Retail Trade*, State Bulletins R-1, 1954 *Census of Business*, U. S. Dept, of Commerce, Bureau of the Census, Washington, 1956, Tables 102, 102A, 103, and 103A.

The proportionate increase in retail sales was higher in the suburban areas than in the central cities in all eight S.M.A.'s size-groups. This differential is especially marked in the two largest S.M.A. size-groups. Suburban growth rates of adjusted sales were 6.5 times as great as those of central cities of 750,000 to 1,000,000 population in the six S.M.A.'s of this class and were 5.0 times as great as in central cities of 1,000,000 and over in the five S.M.A.'s of that size (Table 3).

The greatest suburban increase in retail sales occurred in the S.M.A.'s with central cities between 400,000-500,000 population, followed, in order, by the S.M.A.'s having central cities with populations of 750,000-1,000,000, and of 1,000,000 and over. Retail trade grew relatively more rapidly in central cities below than in those above 500,000 inhabitants. With this one exception, change in retail sales bears no relationship to central city size whether in the total S.M.A. or in the suburban area.

The five S.M.A.'s having the greatest relative growth in retail sales during this period, in terms of adjusted dollar values, were, in order: Orlando, Florida, 87 per cent; Augusta, Georgia, 70; Albuquerque, New Mexico, 68; Flint, Michigan, 60; and Miami, Florida, 58 per cent. The five showing the lowest relative gains were, in order: Wilkes-Barre-Hazleton, Pennsylvania, − 4.5; Johnstown, Pennsylvania, − .5; Altoona, Pennsylvania, .4; Lawrence, Massachusetts, .4; and Galveston, Texas, .7 per cent.

Suburbanization of Retail Trade by Census Division

During 1948-1954, the number of retail businesses in the S.M.A.'s increased in eight of the nine census divisions (Table 4). The Mountain Division had the greatest relative growth, followed, in order, by the W.S. Central, Pacific, and South Atlantic Divisions. The Middle Atlantic Division was the only one to experience a decline. With the exception of the E.S. Central Division, the four highly industrial northern and northeastern divisions were the slowest-growing areas.

Table 4 shows three principal movements. *First,* the growth in numbers of retail stores was proportionately greater in the suburban areas than in the central cities of the New England, Middle Atlantic, E.N. Central, W.N. Central, and Pacific Divisions. In all four divisions of the North and Northeast, where most of the older metropolitan areas are located, suburban growth surpassed that of the central cities. *Second,* in the S. Atlantic, E.S. Central, W.S. Central, and Mountain Divisions, the percentage increase in retail businesses in the central cities exceeded that of the outlying areas.[6] *Third,* the most extensive suburbanization of retail units occurred in the Pacific, Mountain, and New England Divisions, while the E.S. Central and W.S. Central Divisions were the only two sustaining losses.

Table 4—Retail Trade Establishments in S.M.A.'s by Census Divisions, 1948-54 *

	Total Establishments in the 168 S.M.A.'s			Total Establishments in the Central Cities			Total Establishments in Balance of the S.M.A.'s		
	Number (Thousands)		Per Cent Change,	Number (Thousands)		Per Cent Change,	Number (Thousands)		Per Cent Change,
Census Division †	1948	1954	1948-54	1948	1954	1948-54	1948	1954	1948-54
Total	906.9	948.8	4.6	583.5	606.7	4.0	323.5	342.1	5.8
New England	67.7	70.3	3.8	38.7	38.1	—1.6	29.0	32.2	11.0
Middle Atlantic	302.4	298.4	—1.3	183.4	176.2	—3.9	119.1	122.2	2.6
E.N. Central	194.2	199.9	2.9	131.7	133.2	1.1	62.4	66.7	6.8
W.N. Central	53.4	56.5	5.9	39.3	41.4	5.3	14.1	15.1	7.6
S. Atlantic	80.6	89.8	11.5	55.5	63.4	14.2	25.1	26.4	5.4
E.S. Central	30.0	31.5	5.0	20.5	22.8	11.0	9.5	8.7	—8.1
W.S. Central	54.3	61.7	13.7	43.6	52.5	20.4	10.7	9.3	—13.5
Mountain	13.8	16.8	21.7	9.8	12.2	25.0	4.1	4.6	13.8
Pacific	110.5	123.9	12.1	61.0	67.1	10.0	49.6	56.8	14.6

* The numbers of establishments do not necessarily add to totals because of rounding to the nearest thousand.

† Eleven S.M.A.'s overlap into two or more census divisions. Each of the 11 S.M.A.'s has been divided and assigned to its respective census division.

The percentage increase in retail sales was greater in the suburbs than in the central cities in each of the nine divisions (Table 5). A differential suburban-central city growth especially marks the four northern and northeastern divisions. In the Middle Atlantic and W.N. Central Divisions, the increase in adjusted retail receipts was about five times as high in the suburban areas as in the central cities; and, in the New England and E.N. Central Divisions, the rate of gain in sales was three times as rapid in the suburbs as in the central cities. Only in the W.S. Central Division did the increase in retail sales in the central cities even approach that of the area surrounding them.

Table 5 also shows that the most diffused suburbanization of retail trade between 1948-54 occurred in the South Atlantic and Mountain Divisions, and the least in the W.S. Central and E.S. Central Divisions.

The foregoing findings partially sustain the hypothesis of the study and lay the ground for its extension through further research. While the findings on sales volume substantiate the hypothesis, those on numbers of establishments do not.

Table 5—Retail Trade Sales in S.M.A.'s by Census Divisions, 1948-54 *

Sales, Adjusted for Change in Price Level

Census Division	Total Sales, All Establishments in the 168 S.M.A.'s			Total Sales, All Establishments in the Central Cities			Total Sales, All Establishments in the Balance of the S.M.A.'s		
	Retail Sales (Billions of Dollars)		Per Cent Change,	Retail Sales (Billions of Dollars)		Per Cent Change,	Retail Sales (Billions of Dollars)		Per Cent Change,
	1948	1954	1948-54	1948	1954	1948-54	1948	1954	1948-54
Total	81.5	100.9	23.8	58.7	67.9	15.8	22.9	32.9	44.1
New England	5.7	7.0	23.0	3.6	4.0	12.7	2.1	3.0	40.6
Middle Atlantic	23.3	27.3	17.4	15.3	16.4	7.2	8.0	11.0	36.7
E.N. Central	19.1	23.4	22.2	14.3	16.3	14.1	4.8	7.1	45.9
W.N. Central	5.5	6.5	18.7	4.5	5.1	11.6	.9	1.4	53.1
S. Atlantic	7.7	10.1	31.4	6.2	7.6	23.2	1.5	2.5	64.2
E.S. Central	2.8	3.5	23.4	2.3	2.8	20.9	.5	.7	35.1
W.S. Central	5.2	6.9	32.8	4.6	6.2	32.5	.5	.7	35.0
Mountain	1.4	2.0	38.7	1.2	1.6	33.7	.3	.4	62.0
Pacific	10.8	14.2	31.5	6.6	8.0	20.3	4.2	6.2	49.5

* Sales do not necessarily add to totals because of rounding to the nearest billion.

Summary

This study has shown:

First, that the relative growth in retail trade activity, both numbers of stores and value of sales, has been greater in the S.M.A.'s than in the nonmetropolitan areas of the U. S. during 1948-54. Nevertheless, suburbanization proceeded beyond the S.M.A.'s showing an 18.7 per cent increase in retail sales during 1948-54 in spite of a population growth of only 0.5 per cent between 1950 and 1955.

Second, that within the 168 S.M.A.'s, the greatest increases in retail trade have occurred in the suburban areas rather than in central cities. Furthermore, the greatest increase in suburban areas has taken place outside the 53 noncentral cities with 50,000 or more population.

Third, practically all of the increase in the number of suburban retail stores occurred in the 11 S.M.A.'s having central cities of 750,000 or more population; the growth in retail businesses in the S.M.A.'s with central cities under 750,000 population was relatively greater in the central cities than in the outlying areas.

Fourth, the rate of gain in retail sales was greater in the suburban areas than in the central cities in each of the eight size-groups, and is especially pronounced in the S.M.A.'s with central cities of 750,000 or more population. However, there is no relationship between size of central city and change in suburban retail sales.

Fifth, retail trade increased relatively more rapidly in central cities below than in those above 500,000 inhabitants.

Sixth, the central cities in the New England, Middle Atlantic, E.N. Central, and W.N. Central Divisions had the smallest rates of growth in retail sales and stores of central cities in all nine divisions. Of the five divisions that had increased in central-city retail trade, those in the Mountain and the W.S. Central Divisions ranked considerably above the others.

Seventh, the increase in numbers of establishments was relatively greater in the suburban areas than in the central cities of the New England, Middle Atlantic, E.N. Central, W.N. Central, and Pacific Divisions. However, the proportionate increase in numbers of stores in the central cities exceeded that of the suburbs in the S. Atlantic, E.S. Central, W.S. Central, and Mountain Divisions. The greatest decentralization of retail outlets occurred in the Pacific, Mountain, and New England Divisions.

Eighth, in each of the nine divisions the percentage increase in retail receipts in suburban areas outstripped that of the central cities. The differential suburban-central city growth is most pronounced in the four highly industrialized northern and north-eastern divisions. The suburban areas in the South Atlantic and Mountain Divisions experienced the greatest proportionate growth in receipts, whereas the W.S. Central and E.S. Central Divisions had the lowest relative gains.

Inferences

In the light of present knowledge, the surging growth of satellite cities and small trade centers encircling large metropolitan centers will continue. Demographers forecast a sensational growth of the suburbs of S.M.A.'s between 1955 and 1975. According to the estimates, the suburbs will experience 80 per cent of the population increase in the S.M.A.'s occurring during this period.[7] The decentralization of retail trade probably will continue. Many department stores in large cities have already found that they must establish branches in the suburbs to maintain their sales volume.

However, this does not necessarily mean the extinction of downtown shopping areas, although it may portend revolutionary changes in their methods of operation. Central business districts may be able to retain highly specialized retailing services that tend to defy decentralization. Downtown merchants are attempting to revitalize the mid-town shopping areas and are conducting concerted campaigns to recover some of their losses to suburban centers. Their promotion efforts emphasize the advantages of central over suburban locations, such as the wider assortments and price range of merchandise and more comprehensive service. While this raises conjectures only incidental to this study, they seem to offer propitious advantages for future research directed at these and related questions.

This study finds that both population and retail sales volume are increasing more rapidly in the suburbs than in the central cities of S.M.A.'s, which is a simple quantitative relationship. For future research, as more adequate and refined statistics appear, a new, but closely related, problem emerges. One may state it thus: Do suburban retail sales grow in the same proportions as satellite populations cluster around central cities? Do suburbs offer as great a variety and specialization of consumer goods and services as the downtown shopping and service centers? Apparently "ten-cent stores," grocery stores, beauty parlors, taverns, motels, cafeterias, and drug stores, along with clothing stores, follow the population drift to suburbs, but there is still a question of whether or not exclusive and highly specialized trade and services can thrive as well in suburbs as in the downtown areas. In the case of medical service, does the specialist find suburbs inviting or must he still maintain his office in the medical arts center in the central shopping district? These are problems the present study can only broach but, it seems, they invite more extensive and intensive research as new data may permit.

FOOTNOTES

1. U. S. Department of Commerce, Bureau of the Census, "Civilian Population of the United States, by Type of Residence, April 1955 and 1950," *Current Population Reports, Population Characteristics,* Series P-20, No. 63, Nov. 1955.
2. *Retail Trade,* 1954 *Census of Business,* State Bulletins R-1, and *Retail Trade, United States Summary—Advance Report,* Bulletin R-1-1 Advance, U. S. Department of Commerce, Bureau of the Census, Washington, 1956.
3. Four of the S.M.A.'s reported in the 1954 Census of Business were omitted

from this study—Dubuque, Iowa; Hampton-Newport News-Warwick, Virginia; Fort Smith, Arkansas; and Tucson, Arizona. Two other standard metropolitan areas, Shreveport, Louisiana and San Bernardino, California, were adjusted to follow the 1950 Bureau of Census boundaries. Also, Long Beach, in Los Angeles, and Ontario and Riverside, in San Bernardino, California S.M.A.'s, were not considered as central cities in order to make the data comparable with the 1950 census standard metropolitan area classifications.

4. Actually, these figures understate the extent of suburbanization. Some of the 193 central cities in the S.M.A.'s have annexed suburban settlements during 1948-54. This tends, therefore, to reduce the growth of retail stores in suburban areas, while exaggerating the growth in the central cities.

5. One review of this paper suggested that relatively greater emphasis should be given the "sales" findings than to the "number" of establishments because sales appear to provide a much more exact measure of business activity than do counts of establishments. Both measures of retail trade are, however, desirable because the study proposes to ascertain relationships between central-city size, geographic location, and changes in numbers of stores as well as sales volume.

6. With few exceptions, the metropolitan cities in the South and Southwest had the greatest annexations of suburbs during 1948-54. The great expansion of the corporate limits in these areas accounts for much of the increase in retail trade in central cities and the relatively small increase in the suburbs.

7. *U. S. News and World Report,* March 2, 1956, pp. 37-40.

Part IV

Suburban Life Styles

The neighbors of the small-town man know much of what is to be known about him. The metropolitan man is a temporary focus of heterogeneous circles of casual acquaintances, rather than a fixed center of a few well-known groups. So personal snoopiness is replaced by formal indifference; one has contacts, rather than relations, and these contacts are shorter-lived and more superficial. "The more people one knows the easier it becomes to replace them."

C. Wright Mills

William H. Form

Michigan State College

STATUS STRATIFICATION IN A PLANNED COMMUNITY

Social scientists are displaying increasing interest in social stratification. Since the concept is very broad, much progress cannot be made in analyzing it unless the different factors upon which it is based are singled out and their interrelations then noted. Although this has been theoretically recognized,[1] further studies in specific areas of stratification are needed to refine stratification theory.

This paper describes the status or prestige structure [2] of a planned community and proposes an empirical method of finding the factors upon which status is built. These have been purported objects of several studies. Most of them focus, however, on small, old, stable, and integrated localities or groups.[3] Also, they confuse general stratification with other types of of stratification, or they concentrate on general "social" stratification without regarding the elements that make it up. Under these circumstances it is not surprising that many similarities are found not only in the outlines of status structures, but also in the factors underlying them, such as wealth, ancestry, length of residence, occupation, ethnic factors, style of living, and so forth.[4]

Such a practice is legitimate, but insufficiently refined. For one thing, the factors underlying status or general stratification are usually inferred from a "class" analysis.[5] Such a practice arises from a failure to distinguish conceptually and empirically the types of stratification. "Class" analysis of social settlements bury economic, status, power,

Reprinted from *American Sociological Review,* X, (October 1945) pp. 605-613, by permission of the author and *American Sociological Review.*

and other types of stratification under general labels of "social," "status" or "class" stratification.[6] As a result, it is impossible to discern the principles underlying each type of stratification, or the interrelationships of the individual stratification structures.[7]

We intend to overcome these difficulties in part in this study. One technique for doing this is to study settlements that obviously differ from the average in amount and type of stratification. One might compare a new and an old community, an economically homogeneous settlement with one having high economic differentiation, or a settled prestige-conscious group and a frontier community. Further questions could be asked, as: If a settlement has little economic variability may one also expect small status differentiation? Would a status pyramid appear in a settlement that had little or no concentration or political power?

Planned communities also make it possible to approach such questions, for planning means that some factors which are un-controlled in "crescive" settlements become subject to control. Greenbelt, Maryland, is a planned suburb built in 1937 by the federal government on the model of a "garden city."[8] Some of its unusual characteristics enable us to raise and partially answer such questions as were posed above.

One of these is the reputed minimum amount of stratification which the physical and social architects of Greenbelt envisioned.[9] Through the Farm Security Agency they tried to create conditions which would operate against the formation of "classes" and class antagonisms.[10] The main techniques they employed to insure this were: (a) the application of certain "rules" to guide the selection of Greenbelt residents, so that they would be socially and economically similar; (b) the establishment of a local economic and social life that would be popularly controlled and operated along cooperative principles; (c) the chartering of a city-manager form of self-government which (was supposed) to encourage active and responsible citizenship; and (d) the provision of a self-sufficient organizational program to satisfy most of the needs and interests of the townspeople.[11]

Other conditions operated against stratification. Since the town was inhabited almost overnight by people who were for the most part strangers to one another, the task of building its total social organization had to proceed afresh. No old families, no settled groups could erect social barriers against newcomers.

Status stratification could not be readily based on economic ground for at least three reasons: (a) only families of similar economic resources, roughly "lower middle class," were chosen as residents,[12] (b) all economic services in the town were organized along strict cooperative lines;[13] the cooperative principles proposed by the Government for the stores were encouraged to spread into non-economic organizations;[14] and (c) status or economic segregation could not occur on the basis of ecology because of the planned nature of the town.[15]

Other factors tended to reduce stratification. Most important of these was the rather homogeneous occupational composition of the heads of families. Three quarters of them were white collar workers employed largely by the federal government. The remaining were manual workers employed by the federal government and private enterprise.[16] All of the resident population was white and only 2.5 percent was foreign born. Thus the town of 880 families in 1942 was rather homogeneous in income, occupation, education, age,[17] nativity, quality of housing, and economic structure.

Determining the existence and shape of the status structure necessitated a rather involved method, the explanation of which cannot be given in detail here for lack of space. In general the method was largely concerned with the discovery of the existence, varieties, and directions of deference behavior. The author had an excellent opportunity to witness deference behavior, for he lived in Greenbelt as a participant observer for two and one-half years.[18] Other methods were employed that in general corroborated the results observed from participant observation.[19] First we attempted to outline the status structure and we sought to induct the principles along which it was based.[20]

When the town was opened for occupancy, a rash of social and organizational activity was evident. Participation in the numerous mushroom organizations that were arising was the main attention-getting device. Rivalry for leadership in these organizations was rather intense, and the circulation of their officers high.[21] At first, almost every adult belonged to a committee or was an officer. In four years, the process of social selection operated slowly until the town had developed a definite status structure. Some individuals dropped out of the status struggle entirely, some were concerned only with their status in a particular group, while others competed for status on a town-wide level. Often a person's rank in a group did not coincide with his status in the town as a whole. This study is limited to "generalized status."[22] A brief-psychological description of the eight main status groups that evolved in Greenbelt follows.

II.

(1) At the top of the status scale are the officials selected by the federal government to oversee the town. They include the Community Manager, his assistant, the Family Selection Agent, and several other officials. These people receive deference in all public and semi-public meetings. That they maintain distance is evidenced by the fact that they address others by their first names, although they are addressed by their surnames. Even though the officials live in the town, they retain a bureaucratic perspective by referring to the town as "the project."

The prestige of this group rests upon a number of factors. Due to a curious government arrangement, its members are local as well as federal officials. For example, the community manager, who is appointed by the federal agency, is also selected as town manager by the locally elected town council. As town manager, he appoints other local officials, who may be on the federal payroll.

The officials are at the top of the political-power pyramid. They frequently provide the initiative in local action. Their endorsement of pet local projects is usually necessary before these may be materialized. This does not mean, however, that local officials have no powers at all. Local power seems to be shared with and subservient to federal authority.

The officials keep in the public view constantly. Their names are published frequently and conspicuously in the local weekly, The Greenbelt Cooperator. Many of the organizations continually seek their sponsorship and approval. Despite this pressure, the officials and their families do not participate actively in many organizations or even in their neighborhoods.[23] However, when they do participate, their influence is weighty.

The officials constitute not only a political elite, but also an economic and educational elite. Their income and education is considerably higher than that of the townspeople.[24] Needless to say, the homes of the officials are more luxuriously furnished, and residents consider it an honor to enter them. The officials constitute a tightly-woven in-group. They know one another rather intimately. This is not the case for the next lower group to which the doctors, college professors, school principals, dentist, mayor, pastor, priest, and some school teachers belong. Since such people are highly esteemed in most communities, it is not surprising that they are accorded respect in Greenbelt.[25]

(2) The members of status group II are aware of their high status. They acknowledge deference with nonchalance but also with expectation. On the whole, they do not identify themselves psychologically or politically with the town's official family. They maintain a self-satisfied social and organizational independence. However, when they do evince the slightest interest in any organization, they are immediately selected as important committee heads or as officers.[26] For such participation they receive extra deference. Their advice is not ignored irrespective of their competency to give it. This accounts for part of the instability of some of the town's organizations.[27] This group is also an economic elite.

(3) About thirty of the town's "leaders" comprise status group three. They are members of the town-council, the head managers of the co-operatives, the editor of the local weekly, the board of directors of the cooperatives, and the presidents of the larger organizations such as the American Legion and the Athletic Association. This group is not as occupationally homogeneous as the others. Its members are, rather, specialists in participation; those who "have the interests of the community at heart," those who receive psychological gains from being consulted, those who think that they control the "destiny" of the town. They claim honor by virtue of the "service" they render, even though much of their efforts are directed toward entrenching themselves against slates of would-be officers.

The "leaders" constitutes a self-conscious group, that constantly tends to be atomized into cliques that show intense mutual antagonisms. To remain a "leader" one must maintain a democratic facade and, above all, continue participation on the neighborhood as well as on the organizational levels.

The "leaders" have some official contacts with the two upper status groups.[28] These relations with the "powerful" and the professionals are not only considered pleasant, but helpful in the quest for prestige.

The "leaders" continually try to personalize these contacts, while the upper two status groups try to maintain distance.

The wives of the three upper status groups are bound by intimate and sympathetic social ties. They have abandoned the democratic facade of their husbands and have created a "social" organization with closure rules. The Women's Club is the only organization in Greenbelt in which one becomes a member only by invitation.

(4) About sixty-five people make up status group four. Its members may be dubbed, "strainers and apprentices." They are the officers of the special-interest groups, the heads of important committees of the larger organizations, and the petty governmental officials. The latter receive recognition because of their association with the high federal officials; the former because of their services. Both groups often claim more recognition than they receive. They are ambitious for higher posts and the recognition accorded status group three. Although the latter does recruit most of its members from status group four, many others fail to achieve upward mobility. It is understandable that the personnel of the "strainer group" is changing continually.

The marginal characteristics of the group are displayed in various ways. Its members regard their roles with more seriousness than do others. At the public meetings they are visibly active, straining and intense. When given the floor they speak loud and long, displaying remarkably complete knowledge of the business, past and present. They become past masters at parliamentary tactics, using them to obtain attention as well as their ends. For this reason, they are often regarded as "obstructionists." [29]

The members of the four upper status groups are known to one another and to the townspeople at large. This is not the case for the lower status groups. In the lower strata the principles of status ranking operate along more categoric lines. If little is known about a person, his prestige tends to be determined by his occupation, which does not remain a secret long in this occupation-conscious settlement. [30] For example, non-participating professional people receive more recognition than manual workers who participate in one or two minor organizations, but not more recognition than officers of large organizations who are clerical workers.

(5) The fifth status group is the largest. It is composed of the "ordinary" clerical worker who is affiliated with one or two organizations. Although he receives no special recognition, neither is he the object of "negative prestige." He is the person who crowds the meeting rooms whenever a "crisis" occurs, but who stops participating when

the excitement dissolves. Some of these were "leaders" who lost in their struggle for status, or who redirected their energies along job-advancement channels.

(6) The status of "manual workers," unless they participate actively in town affairs, is lower than that of the "ordinary clerical worker." Since the average incomes of the groups are quite similar,[31] one may infer that the status differences are largely occupational. The manual workers, however, hesitate to admit their status inferiority.[32]

Greenbelt has had some difficulty in socially absorbing the newer "defense workers." Although the latter include men from the armed services and white-collar workers, the majority are manual workers. As the defense workers taxed the services of the town and caused some inconveniences, the "old Greenbelters" found them a suitable scapegoat. Consequently, it was easy to associate the ecological segregation of newcomers with their occupational "inferiority." Many of the defense workers are regarded as somewhat "crude," and not "belonging." [33]

(7) Status group seven consists of the town's maintenance laborers, those who cut the lawns, collect trash, drive trucks, keep the town clean, and make minor repairs. At first they consisted of about ninety people, who in general received lower incomes than the town's average. These laborers are known to many townspeople, for they are seen about the town doing their work. Curt salutations constitute practically the total contact of this stratum with the others. Most Greenbelters do not even bother to ascribe them "peculiar" characteristics. They are ignored not only on account of their low occupational status, but also because they do not even constitute a nuisance value in the competition for status. Local laborers attend meetings, but rarely participate actively. They do not have or seek to have any psychological or political affinity with other manual workers in the town. The laborers claim status superiority only over a small number of Negroes who provide janitorial services. This is a small status "gain," inasmuch as Negroes are not allowed to live in Greenbelt.

(8) The people of Hebraic faith occupy a peculiar position in the status structure.[34] The seven per cent of the population that claimed Judaism as a faith participated more actively than the general population from the very beginning. Their influence was most heavily felt

in those organizations that had ideological perspectives such as the cooperatives.

At first, prejudice against the Jews remained either latent or unorganized. They were appointed and elected to the highest offices. This happened because the town needed good organizers, and the Jews were willing to exert themselves in leadership positions. An organizational structure was not already existent to operate in a closure fashion against any group. Also, the Jews were not accused of pursuing uniform ideological paths.

As competition for officers become more acute, the factor of religious affiliation was increasingly interjected into campaign issues. The Jews were accused of "sticking together" and "monopolizing offices." [35] If the participation or occupational status of a Jewish person is unknown, he is usually assigned status somewhere below the fourth status group. If the two factors are known, he is accorded slightly lower status than a gentile with the same socio-economic characteristics. Thus, although Jewish physicians have high status, there is no doubt that they would receive even higher status were they gentiles.

III.

Despite the fact that a non-stratified society was envisioned for Greenbelt, we found that actually a rather complex status structure did appear within a few years. It was based primarily on organizational participation and secondarily on occupation. If we could, in turn, find what factors these rested on, we would arrive at a more exact picture of the principles of status stratification operating in Greenbelt. Since participation was more important than occupation, it was first necessary to measure it in some way, and then find the factors that made for high participation.

Membership or affiliation in organizations is admittedly a crude index of participation; but leadership and officerships are more valid criteria. We used both to measure participation. We found that the results as measured by affiliation supported those obtained by analyzing the leaders or officers. [36]

The examination of affiliational data is taken up first. Membership data for 1942 were gathered for all organizations, excluding the local churches and the Washington organizations. [37] The affiliation profiles of the heads of families were analyzed for such factors as age, duration of residence in Greenbelt, income and income changes, religion, education, occupation, occupational mobility, and occupation of father.[38]

Almost three-tenths of the heads of families in Greenbelt were affiliated with no organizations; i.e., they refused or were not permitted to enter the areas of status competition. Seven-tenths were affiliated in at least one organization, and forty-five per cent belonged to two or more organizations. The affiliation profiles of the wives almost exactly paralleled those of their husbands.

What socio-economic factors, if any, were related to affiliations? Affiliation and income were slightly and positively related at all times. Age and affiliation were also positively related, although age and income correlated only $+0.1$. A rank correlation of income and education, on the other hand, was significantly positive, $+618 \pm .145$. Those who remained in Greenbelt longer seemed to have higher incomes than the newer entrants. As late as March, 1942, occupational differences in regard to affiliation did not appear to be significant.[39] By late 1943 we found that the semi-professionals and the petty administrators and officials were participating more heavily than others. They had been the "higher clerks" (auditors, technical aids, etc.) before 1942. Thus, we may conclude that those who were members of more organizations, or roughly those who were selected for higher status, were slightly older, better educated, and longer residents of the town. Also, they had experienced more occupational and income ascent than the average earner. Any particular factor seemed insufficient to assure status, but when combined with length of residence, the probability of receiving status increased.

We suggested that the 115 officers of the town's organizations had high status. Apart from having status within certain groups, they participated in more organizations than the population as a whole.[40] An analysis of some of their socio-economic attributes might further clarify the factors that were important in the acquisition of social honor.

A statistical comparison of the officers for 1942 with the general adult population for the date when all entered Greenbelt indicated no statistically significant differences for such factors as age, income, occupation, and perhaps education.[41] Some differences between officers and general population did appear, although we were unable to detect their full significance. For example, no future officer on entering Greenbelt classified himself as having "no religion" or "no religious affiliation," whereas six per cent of the town's population fell into these categories. The officers were over-represented as Protestants and Jews and underrepresented as Catholics; [42] more of the former than of the latter.

Perhaps more important than the religious differences were the differences in occupational distribution of the fathers of both groups. The officers' fathers were represented in larger proportion in the semi-professional, proprietary, and managerial occupations, while the fathers of the non-officers were more concentrated in the manual and clerical occupations. This evidence suggests that the officers may have been reared in slightly higher socio-economic circumstances than the population as a whole.

Other differences appeared. Officers tended to be residents of the town for longer periods than the general population. They also had slightly larger families than average. The direct positive relation found between size of family and number of affiliations might have been expected, for parents join associations that were organized to acquaint them with the needs of their children.

Although no significant differences were noted between officers and non-officers for some factors at entry, this situation did not persist after four years residence in the town. This was especially the case for income and occupation. On the date of entry, no statistically significant difference between the groups was found for income. This situation was altered by June, 1943. The officers were then receiving a mean income of $2,755, as compared for $2,655 for the heads of all families including the officers.

This difference was reflected in part in the changed occupational profiles of the two groups. At date of entry no large differences were present. By 1943, the officers were represented in significantly larger proportions in managerial, sub-administrative, and administrative occupations. They also had larger proportions in professional, semi-professional, and "higher" clerical jobs. [43] The parent population had larger segments engaged in manual, technical, and "ordinary" clerical operations. The differential changes in income and occupation suggests that officers were those that showed on entry larger chances of income and occupational upward mobility.

IV.

The results of trying to locate factors underlying the status structure, although suggestive, were largely negative. This is important in itself, for it supports the contention that large status differences should not be expected in settlements whose populations are selected on the basis of their homogeneity. Nevertheless, despite efforts to limit stratification, some of it appears inevitable.

The Greenbelt experience suggests that the "strain toward stratification" in a particular place cannot be completely divorced from those factors which underpin the status structures in the larger society. Since most of the heads of families in Greenbelt worked in Washington, D.C., the factors which set status there partially operated also in Greenbelt. Washington's status structure tended to be categorically occupational for Greenbelters. At work their status-rank was assigned by their income, bureaucratic position, ethnic origin, and race. These factors set status in Greenbelt also, but usually in the framework of organizational affiliation and participation.

It is true that Greenbelters bestow prestige on the basis of their occupation alone—especially to independent professionals and technicians. This is probably in part due to the fact that the planned features of the town enforce an "achievement ideology." Participation and service are considered part of the achievement complex. This becomes clear when we note that the factors that underlie affiliation and participation, such as higher income and upward occupational mobility, approximate those factors associated with high status occupations. Even without high income and occupational mobility, however, status could be achieved by expending energy on projects of communal importance. This is what the town planners desired.

Apart from the deference to service, the planned nature of Greenbelt was responsible for a situation which gave particularly high status to the politically powerful. This is probably a departure from the case in crescive settlements, where the status of the governmentally powerful is often lower than that of the economically powerful.

It is interesting to note, however, a general tendency for the bases of the status structure to approach gradually some of those operating in crescive settlements. Length of residence, age of the breadwinner, size of family, membership in a dominant religion, and other such factors became increasingly important with time. There was also an added emphasis on income and occupation. These may follow inevitably from the formalization tendency seen in the social organizations of the town. Simultaneously, there appeared trends to monopolize recruitment channels of leadership, positions of authority, and "prestige-engineering" by pressure groups.[44]

These trends are, of course, disturbing to some town planners and social engineers. In the future they may desire to insure further a free and open status structure. In the light of the Greenbelt experience this may only be obtained by creating machinery from the beginning which aims at the rapid social absorption of neophytes in local organizations. Techniques such as limiting tenure of office and continually stimulating the desire for general participation may need implementation. Then the question should be faced squarely: Should trained leadership be cast aside for new leaders merely for the sake of insuring an open status structure, or is "traditional leadership" inevitable and desirable? The Greenbelt experience shows that some success is possible in planning a town which encourages free access to status. It may be still possible to get personal recognition in an impersonal social order by similar democratic planning.

FOOTNOTES

1. See especially Max Weber, *Wirtschaft und Gesellschaft,* Tubingen, 1922; Cecil North. *Social Differentiation,* Chapel Hill, 1926; P. Sorokin, *Social Mobility,* N.Y., 1927.
2. "Status" and "Prestige" are used synonymously in this paper.
3. See W. Lloyd Warner and Paul S. Lunt, *The Social Life of a Modern Community,* New Haven, 1942; Allison Davis, Burleigh B. Gardner, and Mary R. Gardner, *Deep South,* Chicago, 1941; J. Useem, P. Tangent, R. Useem, "Stratification in a Prairie Town," *American Sociological Review,* June, 1943; Earl H. Bell, "Social Stratification in a Small Community," *Scientific Monthly,* 1934; 38, 157-164; Harvey Zorbaugh, *The Gold Coast and the Slum,* Chicago, 1937; and the multitude of rural community studies.
4. Ibid.
5. In particular see Warner and Lunt, op. cit.
6. See Hans Speier, "Honor and the Social Structure," *Soc. Res.* 2:74-97, February, 1935, where a theoretical framework for the solution of this problem is discussed.
7. For a systematic analysis and criticism of typical stratification studies, see C. Wright Mills' criticism of Warner and Lunt, op. cit., *American Socio-*

logical Review, 7:263-271, April 1942. I am indebted to Professor Mills for an elaboration of the criticism.

8. For a classic description of the garden city see Ebenezer Howard, *Garden Cities of Tomorrow,* London, 1902.

9. Greenbelt, Maryland, is located thirteen miles northeast of Washington, D.C. The federal government built two other "greenbelt towns": Greendale, Wisconsin, and Greenhills, Ohio. Radburn, New Jersey is a similar example of a privately constructed garden city.

10. A non-stratification ideology permeated the early government literature about Greenbelt. See *Greenbelt Towns,* pamphlet of the Resettlement Administration, Washington, D. C., 1936.

11. Although Greenbelt is often referred to as a "community," its sociological characteristics are typical of a suburb.

12. The mean annual family income for families at the date of entry into Greenbelt was $1535; S.D., $240. The Administration at first ruled that anyone or any family making over $2200 per year had to move from Greenbelt. In 1939 almost ninety per cent of the family incomes were between $1200 and $2000. Since rentals were staggered according to size of the family, the differences in effective income were very small. Sixty-eight per cent of the families at entry had savings under fifty dollars, apart from insurance, while almost one-half had debts, under fifty dollars. Property ownership was negligible.

13. There are no production industries in Greenbelt. All of the gainfully employed, except employees of the local stores and local government, work outside of Greenbelt. Apart from the seven stores, the Credit Union, Health Association, and the nursery school are also cooperatively run.

14. A campaign for engendering the "cooperative spirit" and widespread participation was actively promoted from the beginning. Even a Community Church was sponsored to de-emphasize denominational differences.

15. All dwelling units from bachelor apartments to seven-room houses meet approximately the same housing standards. Determination of residence is not a matter of choice, for houses are assigned by a federal officer on the basis of size of family and the presence of unoccupied units. In 1942 one thousand "defense" homes were built around Greenbelt which did not come up to the housing and architectural standards of the original settlement. The newer areas houses a more heterogeneous group of servicemen and "defense-manual" workers.

16. Eighty per cent of all workers were employed by the federal government. Occupationally, 23.4% of all the workers were either manual or domestic workers; 8.1%, professional and semi-professional; 4.1% petty managers and officials; 0.9%, entrepreneurs; 63.5%, clerical and kindred workers. Almost three-quarters of the total were salaried employees. Except for a few professionals, the incomes of the occupations did not vary widely. See below.

17. In 1942 slightly over sixty-one per cent of all persons over twenty-five years old in Greenbelt had received a high school education or better. Only fifteen

per cent had no high school training. The median age of the heads of families in 1942 was only 35 years, with a P.E. of five years.

18. Two other resident professional sociologists, who were also interested in the community, confirmed the following description of the status structure.

19. The technique of asking people "who they look up to" is not completely satisfactory in a gesellschaft settlement. This method may be adequate for those people who have a large area of acquaintance. We used it for such cases in Greenbelt. For those people who had little or no contacts we had to utilize methods that involved more categoric definitions of status. Here we devised and used occupational status ranking scales, questions as to "what kind of people they looked up to," and other devices. The result of this intimate-categoric method of status ranking are presented below. The actual detailed description of the method will be presented elsewhere. See William H. Form, "Toward and Occupational Social Psychology," in a forthcoming issue of *The Journal of Social Psychology*.

20. In a settlement that is highly stratified, sometimes only the top and bottom strata are compared. See Useem *et al., op. cit.* For the methodological presentation see Howard Becker, "Constructive Typology in the Social Sciences," *American Sociological Review,* 5:40-56.

21. This appears to be a characteristic of planned settlements. See Robert B. Hudson, *Radburn, A Plan of Living,* Amer. Assoc. for Adult Educ., New York, 1939; Ruth Durant, *Watling: A Survey of Social Life on a New Housing Estate,* London, 1939.

22. For convenience, we may speak of "segmental status" as corresponding to segmental roles and "generalized status" for status in the community at large. Social structures wherein segmental and generalized status are coterminous may be called "uni-lateral"; where no coterminity, "multi-lateral."

23. The manager lamenting this, suggested to the members of his inner staff that they attend the local church. Simultaneously, he warned them not to become too intimate with the people, so that a charge of "favoritism" could be averted. Some were more successful than others in maintaining the precarious balance of "distance and democracy."

24. The officials are for the most part college graduates, while the median number of school years completed for the heads of families in 1942 was 12.5 years. The mean salary of the officials in February, 1942, was over $3,600 per annum, while that of the heads of families was $1,844.

25. See Mapheus Smith, "An Empirical Scale of Prestige Status of Occupations," *American Sociological Review,* 1943, 8:185-192; D. Anderson and P. E. Davidson, *Ballots and the American Class Struggle,* 96-97, Stanford, 1939. In systematically arranged interviews, 151 heads of Greenbelt families were asked to rank fourteen occupations according to prestige status. The professions were ranked higher than the government bureau head. This suggests that deference given to government officials in Greenbelt was based more on their power than on other factors.

26. There is no recorded instance of a member of this group being defeated in any organization when a candidate for a first term of office.

27. The Greenbelt Health Association, a medical co-operative, has had an especially stormy career. In no small measure this is due to the fact that doctors can get the support of their patients against the popularly elected board of directors. Most of the conflicts have been over matters of finance, policy, and publicity, over which the doctors showed no special competence.

28. For example, the councilmen must work with the federal officials; the board of directors of the Health Association with the doctors, the P.T.A. officers with the teachers and so forth.

29. Those who are successful in becoming leaders usually take a definite status quo or anti-status quo position. Those who try to straddle issues usually fail in the struggle for status.

30. When residents were asked to describe their occupations many were inclined to give the complete bureaucratic title provided by the Civil Service Commission or by the agency in which they worked. They relished giving a job title that indicated even the smallest amount of supervisory, administrative, or "technical" functions.

31. In fact, at date of entry into Greenbelt, even semi-skilled workers had higher median annual incomes than office clerks, $1528 and $1449 respectively.

32. A random sample of 151 heads of families were asked to rank thirteen occupations according to their prestige-value. The results, to be published elsewhere, showed that manual workers ranked manual occupations higher than did the white collar workers.

33. It is true that they are not as articulate as the "white collar boys." They do lack parliamentary knowledge and skill, and they do not regard Greenbelt as their permanent residence.

34. The religious distribution of the town was at first controlled. As of March, 1942, the religious composition was: Catholic, 24.9%; Jewish, 7.0%; and Protestant and others 68.1%.

35. Although the Hebrew Congregation was a slight cohesive force, the early cohesive force, the early "clannishness" arose primarily from their greater contact resulting from their heavy general participation.

36. No distinction between leader and officer was needed in Greenbelt. Leaders became officers. The latter did not tolerate "powers behind the throne." For the conception of leadership, see Paul Pigors, *Leadership or Domination,* Boston, 1935.

37. A statistical analysis of these data will be presented in detail elsewhere. Here they are abbreviated to indicate the directions to which they point.

38. These indices rather than others were selected because they were easily gatherable, measurable, convenient, and basic.

39. All such statements were statistically validated. The significance of the difference of two statistics (critical ratios) were computed for all numerical data. A critical ratio, D/OD of 2.7 or over was interpreted as a statistically significant difference. For formulas used see Henry E. Garrett, *Statistics in Psychology and Education,* New York, 1938, p. 211.

40. The mean number of organizations to which officers belonged was 3.7, as contrasted to the 1.6 for the heads of families and their wives.

41. The mean annual income for officers was $1,583, for general population, $1,535; for age, officers, 35.1 years, population, 34.8 years; median years of education, officers 12.8 years, population, 12.5 years. The P of the x^2 (chi-square) for the occupational distributions of both groups was .50, definitely an insignificant difference. For chi-square formula see Albert E. Waugh, *Elements of Statistical Methods,* pp. 222-230, New York, 1943.

42. Although no statistics were available, the writer sensed that the Catholics were to a greater extent native born of foreign or mixed parentage. This would indicate that the stratification may have been partially based on ethnic origin. It is interesting to note that although the Federal Agency claimed that Greenbelt was to represent a religious cross section of the Capital's population this never was the case. Catholics were underrepresented soon after the very opening of the town.

43. Treating the working population of Greenbelt as the universe, and the officers as a sample of it, we ran a chi-square test for goodness of fit for the occupational distributions for date of entry and for June, 1943. As of date of entry, the P of the X^2 was exactly 0.50, which showed an insignificant difference between future officers and parent population. However, the P of X^2 for the distributions in 1943 was 0.01 and obvious statistical differences. See Waugh, *Ibid.*

44. Pressure groups like the American Legion arose in the town. They tended to vote as a bloc in town-wide organizations, thus interfering with the natural rise of leaders.

Wendell Bell

University of California

SOCIAL CHOICE, LIFE STYLES, AND SUBURBAN RESIDENCE

Introduction

S*ocial choice and population types.* Within certain population types, the relationship between the food economy and population growth fairly well resembles the conditions described by Malthus (31). These societies, described by Notestein (35) as having high growth potential and described by Schultz (41) as having endogenous relationships between the agricultural sector of the economy and population changes, contain populations which tend to expand to the limits of the food supply. In these societies, the "positive checks" of Malthus operate to control population size; birth rates remain high and relatively stable, variations in population growth being tied to variations in the death rate. Adopting the fairly realistic assumption of a relatively uniform set of values making for as low a death rate as possible, one can observe that variations in population growth are the result of factors largely beyond the control of individuals in these societies. Famines and disease would be reduced greatly in these "backward" areas if the values of the people involved could be implemented.

In recent years the introduction of modern technology and medicine into many "underdeveloped" areas has resulted in such

This article is an elaborated version of a paper which first appeared in *Rural Sociology,* 21 (September-December, 1956) pp. 276-283, under the title, "Familism and Suburbanization: One Test of the Social Choice Hypothesis." The author wishes to express his appreciation to *Rural Sociology* for permission to use the original materials in this version.

value implementation, and the death rates in such areas have declined with the consequence of population increase. As Davis (12) has pointed out, this reduction in mortality has been accomplished by international disease control, not by economic development in the areas themselves. "It required no essential change in the customs and institutions of the people, no advance in general education, no growth in per capita income." (12:57) Consequently, little change in the relatively high fertility levels has occurred. Having little in the way of an industrial structure, no complex division of labor, and a subsistence level of living, these societies still offer little opportunity for the mass of their populations to maintain highly differentiated life styles or ways of living, the characteristic patterns of behavior being relatively homogeneous for all persons in the same age, sex and kinship categories. And in these societies there is still a tendency for the population to breed up to the limits of the food supply, poverty being widespread.

Although a large proportion of the world's people still live in areas of "High Growth Potential" or in agrarian societies which are growing because of disease control, it has been demonstrated that in large-scale industrial societies, population changes cannot be explained simply by changes in the agricultural sector of the economy or by the introduction of new medical practices.[1] These societies are freed from the Malthusian limits, and population variations within them will be an expression of a wide range of alternatives for individuals, death rates being characteristically low and stable and variations in population growth being tied to variations in the birth rate rather than to variations in the death rate. That is, in these societies the values regarding low death rates have been implemented effectively and the death rates are reduced about as much as they can be. At the same time the values regarding high and stable birth rates are subject to radical change as a consequence of the far-reaching economic transformations which have occurred with the transmutation of these societies from agrarian to urban-industrial types. Given modern methods of contraception and the general knowledge of their use within urban-industrial societies, variations in the birth rate are largely within the control of the individuals in these societies. The birth rate becomes a manifestation of the sum total of the many individual decisions made by the persons within the society as whether or not to have a certain number of children. These individual decisions are not randomly made nor are they solely a function of "personality" differences among various members of the society. On the contrary, they represent, for the most part, systematic preference patterns (which we will call "social choices") shaped by the character of the social structure and molded by the value system of that particular population. As Wrong has recently said, "The transition from a way of life in which few restrictions were imposed on fertility to a new era of birth control in which having children has become subject to voluntary choice is a momentous one. . . . There is some evidence that the upper classes of earlier civilizations deliberately restricted family size after marriage, but only in the urban-industrial societies of the modern world has planned parenthood been practiced by the mass of the population." (56:63)

Thus the pressure of the population on the food supply no longer explains population growth in urban-industrial societies, and other explanatory concepts are needed which refer to the social choices available within these societies. A range of preference patterns have been postulated which include *familism, upward vertical mobility* (or *career*), and *consumership*.

The three alternative choice patterns defined. The effect of changing technology, industrialization, and urbanization on the structure and function of the family is well known, and no quarrel with the many generalizations concerning lowered fertility, smaller families, loss of economic functions of the family, increase in working wives, etc. is intended here.[2] However, the emphasis on the decreasing functions of the family in industrial societies, or in populations of "Incipient Decline," has meant overlooking the possibility that the greater per capita wealth, leisure, and energy within these societies might be expended in a variety of ways—*on children and other traditional aspects of family living as well as on other alternatives.* Family living in industrial societies loses many of its utilitarian and instrumental aspects, but it can emerge as an end in itself. As Foote has recently pointed out regarding American society, ". . . the self-conscious recognition of family living as a distinctive and desired activity—quite different from operating a family business, 'raising a family,' or visiting relatives—is uniquely contemporary." (20:297)

By familism, is meant a high valuation on family living; marriage at young ages, a short childless time-span after marriage, child-centeredness, and other such characteristics being indicators of familism. *More than this, however, are the norms of consumption—the closely interwoven set of activities and possessions—that are correlated with and become symbolic of those who are representative of the familism preference pattern.* There is a "style of life" which is appropriate to and symbolic of familism.[3]

By the upward mobility pattern is meant the spending of time, money, and energy on one's career. Such an emphasis is often accompanied by actual movement into social positions of greater prestige, property, and power, but the important criterion, from the point of the social choice and style of life involved is that a person engages in career-relevant activities at least to the partial exclusion of alternative activities.

Familism and career preference patterns, and the "styles of life" which are typical of them, represent fairly common notions, and many writers have discussed the relationship between the family and economic systems, usually positing an inverse relationship between familism and upward mobility.[4] Recent writers have said, for example, that the spending of time and money in family life may have deleterious consequences for upward mobility; and, conversely, that the spending of time and money in one's career may limit one's family life by delaying marriage, postponing children, etc.

Those persons who eschew either career (beyond the day-to-day, 9 to 5 employment) or family life and prefer having as high a standard of living as possible in the present represent the consumership choice pattern, and exhibit the style of life characteristic of it.[5] These persons expend their efforts, time, and money on "having a good time," "living it up," or "enjoying life as much as possible," and they do this in ways which are unconnected with family or career goals. To say that the norms of consumption which comprise the consumership style of life are "unconnected" to family or career goals refers, of course, to the manifest function of these standards or the *intent* of the individual rather than to the possible latent function of these norms or standards. The consumership pattern, embraced wholeheartedly, has important consequences for the achievement of either the familism or career life style.

So far, we have discussed the three social choice patterns as if they were mutually exclusive alternatives for all persons in industrial, high-level-of-living societies; that is, as if everyone in these societies had to make an all-or-none choice between these three life styles.

Although there are some who do make such an all-or-none choice throughout most of their lives, others for one reason or another are able to combine in their life style some of the elements of each of these three preference patterns at some time during their life, now choosing one pattern, later another, and so on.[6] Still others may not *have* to "choose" between occupational achievement, familism, and consumership either because of their favorable economic placement when born, greater level of energy, or greater overall motivation.[7] Still others may not have the *opportunity* to "choose" between these three life styles in that their low income, lack of education, low state of information, etc. preclude their manifestation of any manner of living except that determined by rather narrow structural limitations.

However, for most of the population in urban-industrial societies the best and most complete elaboration of these three life styles cannot be achieved simultaneously, and for most of the population some choice is possible. Varying the emphasis of familism, career, and consumership in terms of the amount of time, money, and energy spent on them by an individual, I suggest the following hypothetical and general types of life styles:

1. Familism—great emphasis on familism, little emphasis on either career or consumership.
2. Career—great emphasis on career, little emphasis on either familism or consumership.
3. Consumership—great emphasis on consumership, little emphasis on either familism or career.
4. Familism-Career—emphasis on familism and career about equally divided, but little emphasis on consumership.
5. Familism-Consumership—emphasis on familism and consumership about equally divided, but little emphasis on career.
6. Career-Consumership—emphasis on career and consumership about equally divided, but little emphasis on familism.
7. Familism-Career-Consumership—emphasis on familism, career, and consumership about equally divided. An attempt to have "some of all" rather than "all of one."

Urban-industrial societies can support any of these life styles, and can be expected to vary in the degree to which particular life styles are dominant. Different societies or the same society at different times may have different distributions with respect to these life styles reflecting different value preferences on the part of their population.

Suburban residence related to life styles. It is clear that the total growth rate of a population will be affected by the relative numbers of persons in that population choosing these particular styles of life. Societies in which familism is an important part of the dominant life styles will have higher birth rates than will societies in which familism is less important; and in urban-industrial societies—where the death rate is relatively low and constant—growth rates will be higher for the societies with the higher birth rates. The sheer growth of an urban society means the growth of its cities, and this in turn, with our present day technology, will result in pressure on the peripheral area of metropolitan places. This peripheral area will continually be converted from agricultural uses to factory sites, office locations, commercialized recreational areas, and other uses—especially into residence areas. Thus the growth of suburban rings around central cities in metropolitan areas can be viewed simply as a part of the total growth of the society. The latter in turn depends on the level of the birth rate, and ultimately on the choices which individuals in the society are making.

It is not unreasonable to argue that the recent growth in the total population of the United States—thus the growth of the suburbs in this country—is the result of an increase in the emphasis on familism in recent years. Certainly declining ages at marriage, decreases in the number of persons remaining single, recent increases in the birth rates and fertility ratios, etc. are consistently with this notion.

Another way in which life styles can be related to suburbanization is through the internal rearrangements which are permitted as a metropolitan area extends its boundaries outward. A metropolitan population may be further differentiated as the suburban ring develops. Not every type of person becomes a resident in the suburbs, some selection of certain characteristics occurring in the process. Particular suburbs are not only symbolic of certain life styles, but their features offer differential opportunity for the achievement of these life styles at a certain cost. The fact that a residence area is expressive of its population's styles of life, and can be instrumental in its achievement, of course, is not restricted to suburban residences, but is true of any neighborhood in a metropolitan area.

Recent studies have shown that the differences between urban neighborhoods, as far as census variables are concerned, can be summarized conveniently by three sets of characteristics: economic, family, and ethnic.[8] Neighborhood types have been constructed using these three basic variables for the classification of the many sub-populations making up a metropolitan area. From this point of view suburban populations when compared to other neighborhood populations represent merely a type of neighborhood population characterized by a relatively high economic level, relatively much family life, and low ethnicity. Comparing suburban populations to central city populations, Duncan and Reiss say, "The suburban population is relatively homogeneous, ethnically; that is, a high proportion is native white. It enjoys a relatively high socio-economic status, as indicated by occupational composition, average educational attainment, or income. The suburban population shows evidences of a stronger familistic bent than the other urban population, in its comparatively high proportions married and levels of fertility, and its low rate of female labor force participation." (16:6)

Many other demographic studies as well as statistically analyzed surveys and impressionistic articles by popular writers support these findings of Duncan and Reiss.[9] These findings suggest that either the career life style (as indicated by the higher socio-economic level) or the familism life style (as indicated by larger family sizes, more married males, more intact families, fewer women at work, etc.) is reflected in the suburban move. That is, that the suburbs offer a residence area symbolic of and instrumental for one or both of these life styles. Thus, the selective or differentiating factors involved in the current move to the suburbs in American society result in filling the suburbs with either career-oriented or family-oriented persons.

The hypothesis of this paper is that *the move to the suburbs expresses an attempt to find a location in which to conduct family life which is more suitable than that offered by central cities, i.e., that persons moving to the suburbs are principally those who have chosen familism as an important element of their life styles as over against career or consumership.*

There is no need to enumerate here the advantages of the suburbs over many of the neighborhoods of the central city as a place to rear children. However, a few words should be included, in view of the generally higher socio-economic level of the suburban population when compared with the central city populations, to explain why the career style of life is not also regarded as an important reason why a person decides to move to the suburbs. (It should be clear that this discussion concerns the *average* differences between suburbs and central cities.) It is common knowledge that there are particular suburbs which contain mostly career-oriented, upwardly-mobile persons, as there are particular suburbs which contain mostly lower class persons, but in general most of the recent movers to the suburbs can be expected to epitomize the familism life style.

Some upward mobility is surely related to the recent suburban move, but only in that it has allowed a number of persons to reach a level of income below which a move to the suburbs was largely precluded. Much of this social mobility was undoubtedly not the result of individuals *qua* individuals moving up in the economic structure relative to others, but was a consequence of the general rise in level of living experienced by entire segments of the population. The fact that there are relatively few Negro suburbs in the United States probably reflects the converse of the above in that much of the Negro population living within metropolitan areas has not yet reached a level of living where much choice in life styles is possible, and urban Negroes consequently are concentrated in the deteriorated, low rent sections of central cities.[10] For example, comparing the occupational distributions of Negroes to the occupational distribution of whites in 59 Standard Metropolitan Areas as of 1950, Willis (54) concludes that Negroes are present in the higher socio-economic occupations only about 25 per cent as often as are whites.

The Sample

In order to subject the above hypothesis to empirical test, one hundred interviews were obtained in two adjacent suburbs in the Chicago metropolitan area. These were Park Ridge and Des Plaines, both of which have had relatively large population increases since the end of World War II. Park Ridge increased 37.6 per cent between 1940 and 1950 and about 44.6 per cent between 1950 and 1955. Des Plaines has had a somewhat larger relative growth, increasing its population 57.5 per cent between 1940 and 1950 and about 80 per cent between 1950 and 1955. Both have increased every decade since 1880; the largest relative increase over the years in each case occurred during the 1920's. Both suburbs are primarily residential in character, and are located along a Chicago and Northwestern Railway commuter line. Park Ridge has a somewhat higher average income, occupation, and education than does Des Plaines; and the sample, having been drawn from both places, contains a relatively wide range with respect to economic status characteristics. Thirty-two per cent of the sample are classified as blue-collar; 24 per cent, lower white-collar; and 44 per cent, upper white-collar.[11]

A sample of dwelling units was randomly drawn from those areas where about 30 per cent or more of the housing consisted of post-World War II building. Substitution of next-door neighbors was allowed in case the selected respondent refused or was not at home. Half of the field work was done on the weekends in order to obtain about an equal split between men and women respondents. The interviewing was done during the early summer of 1955. Most of the interview schedule was memorized by the interviewers, and the average interview was about 30 minutes long.

The Findings

Sixty-eight per cent of the respondents had been living in Chicago just prior to their present move to the suburbs; 24 per cent came from nearby areas, mostly other suburbs, outside of Chicago; and only 8 per cent came from other places. Persons of lower socio-economic status were more likely to have moved from Chicago than were those of higher socio-economic status—88 per cent of the blue-collar, 62 per cent of the lower white-collar, and 57 per cent of the upper white-collar persons reported their last residence within the city limits of Chicago.

Characteristically, the suburbanites interviewed had been apartment dwellers before moving to their present residence, 65 per cent so reporting. Thus the shift to these two suburbs typically involves not only a move from the central city, but also entails a move from an apartment to a house.

The bulk of each interview was devoted to probing the reasons the respondent gave for moving to the suburbs. The reasons given for the move were classified into five broad categories (Table 1). Four-fifths of the respondents gave reasons which had to do with bettering conditions for their children. Three-fourths of these re-

sponses concerned physical features of the suburbs in contrast to
those of the city (Table 2). More space outside the house with
less traffic and cleaner areas were cited as allowing the children
to play out of doors "like children should," with much less worry
and supervision on the part of the parents. Also, the fresh air,
sunshine, and other features of "the outdoors" were mentioned as
providing a "more healthy" life for the children. Living in a single-
family detached house—instead of next to, above, or below other
persons as in an apartment—was cited as giving the children more
freedom to run and play in the house without the constant repressive
demands of the parents. Also, the additional space inside the house,
according to the respondents, allows the children to have a place of
their own within the house, and permits them to "be children" without
constantly "being on top" of their parents. Naps are less interfered
with in the quiet of the suburbs.

Table 1—Broad Classes of Reasons Given for Moving to the Suburbs, and Percentage of Respondents Mentioning Each Type

Type of reason	Per cent*
Better for children	81
Enjoy life more	77
Husband's job	21
Near relatives	14
Other	3

* Since many respondents gave more than one reason, the sum of the percentages does
not equal 100.

Only a quarter of the responses having to do with moving for the
children's sake referred to social factors. The most frequent reason
was the belief that the schools would be better in that classes would
be smaller, more individual attention would be given by the teachers,
and the teachers in the suburbs would be more interested in the
children as well as generally more competent than those in Chicago.[12]
Other features concerning the social aspect of suburban living thought
to be better for children were the following: other children of about
the same age to serve as playmates for the respondent's children; more
organized activities available for children; owning one's own home,
which gives the children a sense of security they could never get in
an apartment; other adults in the same suburbs have children, and,

therefore, the adults treat all the children with understanding; and better churches in the suburbs to which the children can go.

Table 2—Percentage Distribution of Specific Reasons in the "Better for Children" Category

Specific reasons for moving to the suburbs	Per cent
Physical reasons (N = 172):	72.3
More space outside house	19.7
More space inside house	14.3
"The outdoors" (fresh air, sunshine, etc.)	12.6
Less traffic	11.8
Cleaner	6.3
No neighbors in same building	3.8
Quiet	2.1
No stairs	1.7
Social reasons (N = 66):	27.7
Better schools	10.2
"Nice" children to play with	9.2
Other children to play with	2.5
More organized activities	2.5
Home of own (security)	1.7
Adults "nice" to children	0.8
Better churches	0.8
Total reasons in this category (N = 238)	100.0

In 9 percent of these responses (a third of those classified as "social") there were words to the effect that there were "nicer" children in the suburbs to serve as playmates for one's children. When this reason was given, extensive probing was employed to determine whether or not an upward mobility motif was involved. In one case this seemed to be so. The mother said, "We moved here mainly because of my daughter. The environment and schools are better, and her companions are of higher caliber." (Interviewer probed "high caliber.") "I mean more highly educated families." (Interviewer asked what difference that made.) "If it's a girl I suppose you're thinking of who she's going to marry and grow up with." (Pause.) "When it comes down to it, it's a matter of income, isn't it? We want to give our child the best possible chance." (Interviewer asked what she meant by "chance.") "So she can enjoy life to the fullest and live graciously, I suppose."

This case was an exception, however, for probing indicated that other respondents giving this response seemed to be referring to their belief that there are fewer "juvenile delinquents" and "bad" influences among their children playmates in the suburbs. Thus, the response generally seems to indicate a maintenance of present social status rather than upward mobility aspirations for children.

Table 3—Percentage Distribution of Specific Reasons in the "Enjoy Life More" Category

Specific reasons for moving to the suburbs	Per cent
Physical reasons (N = 141):	44.1
"The outdoors" (fresh air, sunshine, etc.)	13.1
Gardening and "puttering around the house"	10.9
Quiet	7.2
Less crowded	6.6
Cleaner	4.1
More modern conveniences in house	2.2
Social reasons (N = 179):	55.9
Friendly neighbors	14.1
Feeling of belonging	8.8
Easier living, slower pace	8.1
Home of own (investment)	7.2
Privacy	4.1
Age, marital, and family status the same	4.1
Financial status the same	3.1
"Higher class" of people	2.8
Education the same	1.2
Racial stock the same	1.2
Friends moved here	0.9
Occupational level the same	0.3
Total reasons in this category (N = 320)	100.00

Three-fourths of the respondents (Table 1) gave reasons for their move to the suburbs which have been classified as "enjoying life more." These are shown in detail in Table 3. In these reasons, social features were mentioned more often than the physical features of the suburbs as being important influences in the decision to move. The respondents expected more friendly neighbors, greater participation in the community, and easier living at a slower pace than they had had in the city.

Another theme was the "people-like-ourselves" idea. Some respondents said they wanted to live in a neighborhood where people had the same age, marital, family, financial, educational, occupational, or ethnic status as themselves. Ten per cent of the responses fell into this category, and extensive probing seemed to indicate that the mobility motif was not involved, although a maintenance of the symbols of one's social class often were. It was a matter of feeling more comfortable and having more in common with persons of similar interests. For example, a white-collar man living in a predominantly blue-collar block indicated that he would move elsewhere in the suburbs because he didn't have much of a common interest with his neighbors. He went on to say that his chief concern, although by no means his only one was the fact that none of his neighbors played bridge.

Only 9 per cent of the respondents indicated that one of their reasons for moving to the suburbs was that they expected a "higher class" of person to be living there as compared with the central city. When probed on this point, the respondents referred to higher education and income, better occupations—especially engineering and sales occupations—good manners, quiet rather than loud and boisterous habits, a gracious manner of living, and intelligence. Certainly, a mobility motif must be admitted in most of these cases, but even here some persons seemed to be trying to find a group of persons "like themselves" with which to live, rather than trying to "better themselves" socially.

The physical features which attracted these suburbanites were the fresh air, sunshine, growing trees and other characteristics of the "open country" in contrast to the central city; also, the opportunity to garden and to "putter" around their "own home" was important. The quiet, lack of congestion, and cleanliness of the suburbs were also mentioned, as was the fact that a new house with modern conveniences was to be had in the suburbs for a lower price than its equivalent in the city.

As is also shown in Table 1, a fifth of the respondents said that the husband's job was a factor in their move to the suburbs. Of these, more than half were transferred without a promotion or increase in salary or were just moving closer to a job which they had held for some time. The others, 9 per cent of the respondents, indicated that their move was a consequence of upward mobility, although none felt that their move was consequential for future increases on the job.

In general these findings seem to agree with those reported by Rossi (40) in his excellent study of residential mobility in four neighborhoods in Philadelphia.[13] In discussing why families move Rossi says, "The findings of this study indicate the major function of mobility to be the process by which families adjust their housing to the housing needs that are generated by the shifts in family composition that accompany life cycle changes." (40:9) Shifts in family composition which accompany life cycle changes are highly correlated with the life style types constructed here. But the life cycle argument is only part of the explanation of residence moves and residence selection in that everyone does not experience such changes in family composition—the life-long bachelor for example; and in that of those who do, there are differential patterns and variations possible in the emphasis placed on familism, career, and consumership. What is needed is a study of more neighborhoods of many different types focused on (1) the limits of residential choice for different segments of the population, (2) the symbolic meaning of a residence area, and (3) the role of the social character of different neighborhoods in the achievement of the general life goals of individuals.

Social Choice Types

The following interpretation should be accepted with caution since these findings may not hold for the movement into suburbs of different types from those studied here. Even though a fairly wide range with respect to value of homes and occupations of respondents was included in the sample, different reasons for moving may be found in other types of suburbs, such as industrial suburbs or suburbs in which only families of the very top socio-economic stratum reside. For the two suburbs studied, however, the findings are quite convincing.

The respondents were classified with respect to the dominant theme underlying their reasons for moving to the suburbs. Upward vertical mobility, or career-orientation, does not seem to be greatly associated with choosing to live in the suburbs, despite the contention of some recent writers. In fact, only 10 per cent of the respondents could be classified as having upward mobility aspirations involved in their move to the suburbs, and even here most of these persons also had other reasons for moving.

On the other hand, 31 per cent of the respondents can be classified as exemplifying pure familism, no other reason being given for the suburban move. A familistic orientation, however, entered into the decision to move to the suburbs in a total of 83 per cent of the cases. That familism as it enters into the suburban move is largely "conjugal familism" is indicated by the fact that only a relatively small percentage of the respondents move in order to be closer to relatives not living with them while a much larger percentage indicated that they moved "because of the children." In fact, several who moved because of the children also noted that it was a little farther away from their relatives—a condition which they considered desirable.[14]

In many of the responses which were categorized as familistic, it was evident that the respondents tended to think of the move to the suburbs in terms of the move from an apartment to a house. Thus, some respondents pointed out that if they could have found the same house in the city they would have preferred to live in the city. Although they realized such sections did exist within the city, they also noted that homes in them cost more than in the suburbs. Also in these responses there was the definite notion that the move from apartment to house was mutually beneficial for parent and child. In fact, several of the wives, according to their own testimony, had been on the verge of nervous collapse living with small children in an apartment. Since moving to a house in the suburbs, they reported that they were no longer "nervous."

In general, the respondents reported moving because of the children, but they also reported that since they had lived in the suburbs they had learned to enjoy "suburban living" so much that they would never move back to the city. Seven per cent of the respondents, however, said that they would move back to an apartment in the city as soon as their children were married.

Ten per cent of the respondents were classified as pure examples of the consumership pattern, and an additional 43 per cent gave consumership reasons along with other reasons.

The three original life styles did not seem adequate to account for all of the responses given. A fourth theme, labeled the "quest-for-community," was apparent.[15] This was the idea of moving to the suburbs to get more friendly neighbors, greater community participation, and a sense of belonging to the community. About 73 per cent of the respondents included such reasons as important factors in their decision to move to the suburbs, and usually this was in conjunction with the familistic orientation.

A Further Test

The findings presented above support the notion that familism rather than career or consumership is the most important life style involved in the move to the suburbs. However, they are not conclusive since no comparative data were introduced. In order to obtain some comparative information small surveys were executed in four different census tracts varying with respect to suburban and city location and with respect to socio-economic status. Two tracts in the city of Chicago were selected, one of low economic status (Jackson Blvd.) and one of high economic status (Near North Side). Also, two tracts in the suburbs were selected: Bellwood, of low economic status, and Kenilworth, of high economic status.[16] All four tracts had relatively few members of subordinate racial and nationality groups. Random samples were obtained, although substitution was allowed, and in contrast to the Des Plaines and Park Ridge study discussed above all households in the tract were included, not just new movers. The field work was done in connection with a class project in the fall of 1956.

A scale of five questions was constructed, each one forcing a choice between familism, career, or consumership. The questions concerned the ways in which the respondent did or would spend his time and money.

Table 4 contains the percentage of first choices in familism, career, or consumership life styles for each of the neighborhoods. Comparing Jackson Blvd. to Bellwood and the Near North Side to Kenilworth, one notes that the larger percentage of first choices in the familism life style are given in the suburban areas rather than the city tracts, the percentages being 55 to 75 and 45 to 67 ($\Sigma\chi^2$, $p < .01$). Thus, these responses also support the notion of a linkage between familism and suburban residence.

Two other comments should be made about Table 4. First, that there is a tendency for the familism responses to vary by the economic status of the census tract as well as by its city or suburban location. the percentages being 55 to 45 and 75 to 61 when comparing Jackson Blvd. to the Near North Side and Bellwood to Kenilworth. And

Table 4—Percentage Distribution of First Choices in Each of the Life Styles by Suburban or City Residence and Neighborhood Economic Status

	Residence			
	City		Suburban	
	Jackson Blvd. (Low Econ.)	Near North Side (High Econ.)	Bellwood (Low Econ.)	Kenilworth (High Econ.)
Life Styles	Per Cent	Per Cent	Per Cent	Per Cent
Familism	55	45	75	61
Career	18	27	17	17
Consumership	27	28	8	22
Total	100	100	100	100
Number of Choices	74	113	80	100

second, that in spite of the variations in the selection of familism by location of residence and economic status, familism contains more first choices than either career or consumership in every tract. It should be kept in mind, of course, that these samples contain old residents as well as new in every tract, and that the samples are small.

Conclusion

In general, these two studies support the hypothesis that the new suburbanites are largely persons who have chosen familism as an important element in their life styles, and in addition the Des Plaines and Park Ridge study suggest a relationship between the desire for community participation or sense of belonging and the move to the suburbs.[17]

Dewey concluded from his study of suburbanization in Milwaukee County that ". . . movement into the rural-urban fringe is not a desire to escape anything that is inherent in urbanism as a way of life. . . ." [18] The data of the Des Plaines and Park Ridge study, only partially reported here,[19] confirm that suburbanites, in general, desire the advantages of modern technology and many of the facilities of urban "culture." However, if anonymity, impersonality, defilement of air and land by industry, apartment living, crowding, and constant nervous stimulations are inherent in "urbanism as a way of life," as some writers have said, then the findings of this study necessitate the conclusion that the suburbanite *is* seeking an escape from many traditional aspects of city living. The suburbanite seems to be seeking a way of life in which family, community, and immediate enjoyment through living the "good life" are dominant and interdependent ends.

However, whether the suburban trend is a "back-to-ruralism" movement, a search for bucolic pleasures, and a desire to live in a modern Arcadia remains to be determined. Some recent research seems to indicate that this is so,[20] but one might argue that the congested city was simply a form which large-scale society took at a given time at a particular level of technology, and that present day technology and that of tomorrow increasingly allow an even larger scale of society *but in a new decentralized form of population distribution.* If this is true, the suburban shift is not a "return" to anything, but merely a continuation of a long-time trend in industrial societies: *the increasing scale of organization and increasing bureaucratization.*[21]

FOOTNOTES

1. For an explanation of the relationship between the food economy and population changes, see Schultz (41). Since the discussion of population types must be brief in this paper, the case of the rapidly industrializing society has not been included.

2. For a recent discussion of the effects of technology on the family, see Ogburn and Nimkoff (36).

3. Discussions of "styles of life" in relation to social classes appear in Barber (3) and Kahl (27). The concept, however, need not be limited to differences between social classes. At least within certain occupational, educational, and income aggregates, we would expect some variation in life styles reflecting different degrees of emphasis on familism, career, and consumership.

4. For example, see Baltzell (2), Barent (6), Burgess and Wallin (10), Kaplow (11), Dumont (14), Heberle (24), Kantner and Kiser (28), Lemasters (29), Lysgaard (30), Myrdal (33), Riemer and Kiser (38), Westoff (51), and Winch (55).

5. Of course, there is a characteristic economic consumption pattern associated with each of these life cycles. Certain types of purchases should be most typical of those who have chosen familism, another type most typical of those who have chosen the career pattern, and still another type most typical of those classified in the consumership pattern. To the extent to which these choice patterns cut across class levels, it is expected that the associated life styles will vary in some specific items. For example, a summer tour of Europe may be a manifestation of a consumership orientation for an upper-middle class American, while the purchase of a new fishing

pole may manifest the same preference pattern for a working class American. However, the proportion of persons in the different choice patterns can be expected to vary for different social classes.

6. The scope of this paper does not permit a consideration of the decision-making process as it enters into the theory of social choice. Unfortunately, sociologists have devoted their efforts sparingly to this problem and most of our models, not always as relevant as they might be, come to us from economists or psychologists. Most relevant to the present discussion is Greer (22) who has elaborated the concept of preference patterns as specifically used in this paper. Lysgaard (30) has demonstrated the operation of mutually exclusive choices with regard to social mobility. Theories and models dealing with decision-making or its aggregate effect can be found in Arrow (1); Black (7); Buchanan (9); Edwards (17); Ginzberg *et al.* (21); Snyder, Bruck, and Sapin (46); Thrall, Coombs, and Davis (47); and Tiebout (48).

7. Sibley's recent discussion of higher education and earlier parenthood, for example, suggests the combination of familism and career. In discussing the returning veterans after World War II, he says that, "Rather than choose between going to school and establishing families of their own, they did both at once." (45:51) See Boggs (7a) for an example of the achievement of both familism and upward mobility in an upper-middle class California suburb.

8. See Bell (5), Shevky and Bell (43), Shevky and Williams (44), and Tryon (49).

9. For example, see Beegle (4), Bogue (8), Dewey (13), Duncan (15), Fava (18, 19), Hawley (23), Henderson (25), Jaco and Belknap (26), Rodehaver (39), Seeley, Sim, and Loosley (42), U.S. Bureau of Census (50), Whetten (52), and Whyte (53).

10. Restrictive covenants and "gentlemen's agreements," of course, operate to keep Negroes, except as servants, out of the many of the suburbs inhabited by whites. In the long run, however, one can speculate that more all-Negro suburbs would develop if the Negroes could pay for them.

11. Professionals, managers, officials, and proprietors were classified upper white-collar; clerical and sales workers were classified lower white-collar; and craftsmen, foremen, operatives, private household workers, service workers, and laborers were classified blue-collar. None of the sample dwelling units contained persons reporting the occupations of farm laborer, farm manager, or farm proprietor.

12. It is interesting to note that many of the respondents had found that since moving to the suburbs an acute shortage of classrooms and teachers had developed. In fact, at the time this survey was taken the "school problem" was a major one for the persons interviewed in some of the neighborhoods.

13. Also see Martin (32).

14. Cf. Jaco and Belknap (26).

15. See Nesbit (34) for an extended discussion of an aspect of this phenomenon.

16. The named places with their census tract designators and economic status scores according to the Shevky-Bell Typology as of 1950 are as follows:

Place Name	Tract Designator	Economic Status Score
City		
Jackson Blvd.	418	34
Near North Side	125	92
Suburban		
Bellwood	BW-1	48
Kenilworth	KW-1	97

17. Cf. Fava, *op. cit.*

18. Dewey, *op. cit.*, p. 125.

19. Data were also collected concerning the features of suburban life which the respondents liked or disliked "after having lived there for a while."

20. Especially see Fava (19).

21. For a discussion of the relationship between urbanization *per se* and scale of organization see Quinney (37).

REFERENCES

1. Arrow, Kenneth, *Social Choice and Individual Values.* New York: John Wiley and Sons, 1951.

2. Baltzell, E. Digby, "Social Mobility and Fertility Within an Elite Group," *Milbank Memorial Fund* Quarterly, 31 (October, 1953), pp. 411-420.

3. Barber, Bernard, *Social Stratification.* New York: Harcourt, Brace and Company, 1957.

4. Beegle, J. Allan, "Characteristics of Michigan's Fringe Population," *Rural Sociology,* 12 (September, 1947), pp. 254-63.

5. Bell, Wendell, "Economic, Family, and Ethnic Status: An Empirical Test," *American Sociological Review,* 20 (February, 1955), pp. 45-52.

6. Berent, Jerzy, "Fertility and Social Mobility," *Population Studies,* 5 (March, 1952), pp. 244-60.

7. Black, Duncan, "The Unity of Political and Economic Science," *The Economic Journal,* 60 (September, 1950), pp. 506-14.

7a. Boggs, Stephen T., "Family Size and Social Mobility in a California Suburb," *Eugenics Quarterly,* forthcoming.

8. Bogue, Donald J., "A Few Facts about Chicago's Suburbs," Chicago Community Inventory, 1954.

9. Buchanan, James M., "Social Choice, Democracy, and Free Markets," *The Journal of Political Economy,* 62 (April, 1954), pp. 114-123.

10. Burgess, Ernest W., and Paul Wallin, *Engagement and Marriage.* Chicago: Lippincott, 1953.

11. Caplow, Theodore, *Sociology of Work.* Minneapolis: University of Minnesota Press, 1954.

12. Davis, Kingsley, "The Unpredicted Pattern of Population Change," *The Annals of the American Academy of Political and Social Science,* 305 (May, 1956), pp. 53-59.

13. Dewey, Richard, "Peripheral Expansion in Milwaukee County," *American Journal of Sociology,* 53 (May, 1948), pp. 417-22.

14. Dumont, Arsene, *La Morale Base Sur la Demographie,* 1901.

15. Duncan, Beverly, "Demographic and Socio-economic Characteristics of the Population of the City of Chicago and the Suburbs and Urban Fringe: 1950," Chicago Community Inventory, 1954.

16. Duncan, Otis Dudley and Albert J. Reiss, Jr., *Social Characteristics of Urban and Rural Communities, 1950.* New York: John Wiley and Sons, 1956.

17. Edwards, Ward, "The Theory of Decision Making," *Psychological Bulletin,* 51 (July, 1954), pp. 380-417.

18. Fava, Sylvia Fleis, "Suburbanism as a Way of Life," *American Sociological Review,* 21 (February, 1956), pp. 34-37.

19. Fava, Sylvia Fleis, "Urban-Suburban Contrasts in Social Participation: A Study of Neighboring in New York City and Nassau County," unpublished Ph.D. dissertation, Northwestern University, 1956.

20. Foote, Nelson N., "Family Living as Play," *Marriage and Family Living,* 17 (November, 1955), pp. 296-301.

21. Ginzberg, E., S. W. Ginsburg, A. Axelrod, and J. L. Herma, *Occupational Choice, An Approach to a General Theory.* New York: Columbia University Press, 1951.

22. Greer, Scott A., "Working Papers Toward a Theory of Social Choice," mimeographed, Occidental College, 1955.

23. Hawley, Amos H., *The Changing Shape of Metropolitan America.* Glencoe, Illinois: The Free Press, 1956.

24. Heberle, Rudolf, "Social Factors in Birth Control," *American Sociological Review,* 6 (December, 1941), pp. 794-805.

25. Henderson, Harry, "The Mass Produced Suburbs," (in two parts), *Harpers,* 207 (November and December, 1953), *passim.*

26. Jaco, E. Gartly and Ivan Belknap, "Is a New Family Form Emerging in the Urban Fringe?" *American Sociological Review,* 18 (October, 1953), pp. 551-57.

27. Kahl, Joseph A., *The American Class Structure.* New York: Rinehart and Company, Inc., 1957.

28. Kantner, John F., and Clyde V. Kiser, "The Interrelation of Fertility, Fertility Planning, and Intergenerational Social Mobility," *Milbank Memorial Fund Quarterly,* 32 (January, 1954), pp. 69-103.

29. Lemasters, E. E., "Social Class Mobility and Family Integration," *Marriage and Family Living,* 16 (August, 1954), pp. 226-32.

30. Lysgaard, Sverre, "Social Stratification and the Deferred Gratification Pattern," unpublished Ph.D. dissertation, Purdue University, 1952.

31. Malthus, Thomas Robert, *An Essay on the Principle of Population as it Affects Future Improvement of Society,* 1798.

32. Martin, Walter T., *The Rural-Urban Fringe.* Eugene, Oregon: University of Oregon Press, 1953.
33. Myrdal, Alva, *Nation and Family.* New York: Harper, 1941.
34. Nisbet, Robert A., *The Quest for Community.* New York: Oxford University Press, 1953.
35. Notestein, Frank W., "Population—The Long View," in *Food for the World* (ed. by Theodore W. Schultz). Chicago: University of Chicago Press, 1945.
36. Ogburn, W. F. and M. F. Nimkoff, *Technology and The Changing Family.* Cambridge, Mass.: The Riverside Press, 1955.
37. Quinney, Earl, "Urbanization and the Scale of Society: A Conceptual Analysis," unpublished M.A. thesis, Northwestern University, 1957.
38. Riemer, Ruth, and Clyde V. Kiser, "Economic Tension and Social Mobility in Relation to Fertility Planning and Size of Planned Family," *Milbank Memorial Fund Quarterly,* 32 (April, 1954), pp. 167-231.
39. Rodehaver, Myles W., "Fringe Settlement as a Two-Directional Movement," *Rural Sociology,* 16 (March, 1947), pp. 49-57.
40. Rossi, Peter H., *Why Families Move.* Glencoe, Illinois: The Free Press, 1955.
41. Schultz, *The Economic Organization of Agriculture.* New York, 1953.
42. Seeley, John R., R. Alexander Sim, and Elizabeth W. Loosley, *Crestwood Heights.* New York: Basic Books, Inc., 1956.
43. Shevky, Eshref, and Wendell Bell, *Social Area Analysis.* Stanford: Stanford University Press, 1955.
44. Shevky, Ashref and Marilyn Williams, *The Social Areas of Los Angeles: Analysis and Typology.* Berkeley and Los Angeles: University of California Press, 1949.
45. Sibley, Elbridge, "Higher Education and Earlier Parenthood: A Changing Cycle of Family Life," *The Antioch Review,* Spring, 1957, pp. 45-59.
46. Snyder, Richard C., H. W. Bruck, and Burton Sapin, *Decision-making as an Approach to the Study of International Poiltics.* Foreign Policy Analysis Series No. 3, Organizational Behavior Section, Princeton University, 1954.
47. Thrall, Robert M., Clyde H. Coombs, and Robert L. Davis (eds.), *Decision Processes,* New York: John Wiley and Sons, 1954.
48. Tiebout, Charles M., "A Pure Theory of Local Expenditures," *The Journal of Political Economy,* 64 (October, 1956), pp. 416-24.
49. Tryon, Robert C., *Identification of Social Areas by Cluster Analysis.* Berkeley and Los Angeles: University of California Press, 1955.
50. U.S. Bureau of the Census, *Census of Population:* 1950, Vol. IV, *Special Reports,* Pt. V, chap. A, "Characteristics by Size of Place."
51. Westoff, Charles F., "The Changing Focus of Differential Fertility Research: The Social Mobility Hypothesis," *Milbank Memorial Fund Quarterly,* 31 (January, 1953), pp. 24-38.
52. Whetten, Nathan L., "Suburbanization as a Field for Sociological Research," *Rural Sociology,* 16 (December, 1951), pp. 319-30.

53. Whyte, William H. Jr., "The Transients," (in 4 parts), *Fortune,* 49 (May, June, July, and August, 1953), *passim.*
54. Willis, Ernest M., "A Comparative Study of Negro Segregation in American Cities," unpublished M.A. thesis, Northwestern University, 1956.
55. Winch, Robert F., *The Modern Family.* New York: Holt, 1952.
56. Wrong, Dennis H., *Population.* New York: Random House, 1956.

Philip H. Ennis

The University of Chicago

LEISURE IN THE SUBURBS:
RESEARCH PROLEGOMENON

To paraphrase Louis Wirth, who said it of urbanism in 1938, the degree to which the suburban way of life influences American culture is not fully measured by the proportion of the total population living in the suburbs. Its influence spreads in far wider circles beyond actual suburban residents to shape the living patterns of millions of people still living in cities. And a whole younger generation, not yet sure where and how it is going to settle down, sees in the suburban style a persuasive model of emulation.[1]

Not the least important part of this suburban style of life is its leisure; yet reports about the way suburbanites spend their free time are conflicting and contradictory. One set of images proclaims the informality, intimacy and relaxed pace of suburban leisure centered around home and family, but also close to nature and responsive to constructive community activities. Suburban leisure, this view contends, expresses the diverse, creative and individualized interests previously inhibited by the limitations of the city. The negative critics denounce the standardization of homes and the people in them, the imbalance in children's daily experience due to prolonged absence of the commuting male, the lack of cultural facilities, the trivialization of civic participation, the general privatization of leisure to the point of indifference to the larger scene, and finally the passive reliance upon the mass media to escape momentarily from work-engendered tensions.

This is an original article prepared for this volume.

248

It is vital to decide which of these images is most accurate, because the preparation necessary to meet the problems stemming from a continued explosive expansion of both leisure *and* the suburbs would take markedly different directions if the optimistic rather than the pessimistic overview were adopted. Yet, as is so often the case in important problems, the factual basis for such judgments is slight and fragmentary. This essay is designed, not to provide the answers, but to suggest a way of asking the relevant questions. In general, they can be compressed into three broad areas:

1) What do suburban residents do with their free time that the city dweller or those in small independent cities don't, or do more or less frequently? This simple matter of "social bookkeeping" is concerned with whether, for example, outdoor sports are more popular among suburbanites than among city dwellers, whether the mass media command more attention in the suburbs, whether there is more spectator or participant activity there, whether suburban residents in fact have more leisure than their city or country cousins and in general how they differ in allocating their free time.

2) Shading into this question is the difficult but more intriguing question of the quality of leisure in the suburbs, irrespective of the particular activities involved. Here our interest is in the meaning of leisure for the participant and in its value or quality for an observer. Compared to the city, is suburban leisure, for example, more creative; is it freer from the competitive tensions of everyday life; and does it more fully revive and fulfill people's deeper needs and interests? Another type of related question is the old chestnut of high culture vs. mass culture—does leisure in the suburbs enhance participation in the "finer things of life," music, art, the theatre, and is it freer from the narcotic dependence of the mass media and from reliance on commercial culture?

The difference between the first and second questions is that the former asks whether the suburbanite loafs on Saturdays as much as the city man; the second asks if loafing on the front stoop of an apartment building (or in the corner tavern) in Manhattan means the same thing as loafing on the patio of the ranch house in Manhasset.

3) Finally, does leisure as a mode of social behavior and personal experience have different implications for the *individual's* relations with the social structure of the metropolitan center than it does for the suburb? Correlatively, does the social structure of leisure—it too has

its organizational and institutional forms—differ in city and suburb, and with what consequences for other sectors of community life? This kind of question is broader in scope than the usual sociological inquiry about leisure which asks mainly about the relation between work and play.

Each of these questions explicitly compares the suburban residential community with its metropolitan center or with independent cities of similar size as the suburb. This is the only way the distinctive features of suburban leisure can be revealed. But the questions also cast an historical shadow as well: how are suburbanites now spending their leisure compared to a generation ago, or fifty years ago; have they changed their values more than others (has, for example, the puritanical centrality of work over play blurred more in the suburban than the urban populations); and, finally, how have leisure activities changed their functions in various kinds of communities?

Let us begin with the problem of what people do with their free time, then turn to the third, leaving the "quality" question for last since it is in many senses the toughest. The observations to be made are a peculiar mixture of direct observation of suburban life [2] and derivations from assumptions about suburban social structure. As such, therefore, the discussion invites correction from both empirical and theoretical positions.

Leisure Activities in the Suburb and City

The apparently simple question of how suburban families differ from their city and small town counterparts in the way they spend their free time is actually quite complex. Because the full span of a person's leisure ranges from activities that almost everyone engages in (reading the newspaper, relaxing with the family, watching TV, etc.) all the way down to those in which hardly anyone ever participates (hunting with bow and arrow, button collecting), it is difficult to characterize leisure patterns in a single statement. Here, for example, are five ways that suburban leisure patterns could be compared to city patterns.

1) The span of activities: do suburbanites engage in more or fewer things than people in the city.

2) The *distribution* of time, money and value investments within

the pattern. What are the central leisure interests in the city and the suburbs?

3) The commonness or rarity of leisure patterns. Any given activity can be rated according to its frequency within the population, and so too can particular configurations of activities.[3] Accordingly, how do suburbanites compare to city dwellers in this respect.

4) The heterogeneity or homogeneity of the leisure activities. To what extent do suburban families pour their leisure eggs in one basket or disperse them among a variety of activities? Boxing fans, for example, are more likely to be also interested in baseball than in opera, but do we find a greater diversity of interests in the suburbs than in the city?

5) The rigidity or fluidity of a leisure pattern. Because leisure is shaped to a large extent by life cycle and social class position, changes in either, or both, are points of potential change in leisure patterns. To what extent, therefore, are various types of persons responsive to expected alterations in leisure, and to what extent do certain activities persist? Since various leisure forms are differentially geared into life cycles or social class positions, this must be taken into account when comparing the stability of various patterns. The same question of relative fluidity of leisure can be asked, of course, about people within any given phase as well. Does their ordinary rhythm of spare time behavior show sporadic changes, sudden shifts of interests, or is it more placid? (Here, of course, is the location of the fad problem; what kinds of people take to new games; is an innovator in one leisure fad as likely to shift in others?)

Systematic data to answer any of these questions is hard to come by, in part because so few studies have directly addressed themselves to these problems, and in part because whatever data has been collected is seldom comparative of suburban and urban settings. What can be said about the patterning of suburban leisure in spite of these deficiencies? This is not the place to summarize the detailed descriptions of leisure activities presented in Lundberg, Komarovsky and McInerney's pioneer "Leisure, A Suburban Study," [4] nor the more recent "Crestwood Heights." [5]

These books must be read in bulk to appreciate the flavor of leisure in the communities described. They will be referred to subsequently when more analytical problems of leisure are referred to.

Here, instead, some empirical data of a strictly comparative character will be presented to illustrate the research perspectives outlined above.

One of the untapped reservoirs of information about leisure is to be found in studies of consumer expenditures. True, such material shifts the usual yardstick for comparing leisure from *time* (hours per week or occasions per month) to *dollars* with some inevitable loss thereby. But allocation of consumer income in its own way reflects in a standardized manner the value-guided results of leisure choices. An accessible and particularly useful study of this type is the Wharton School of Finance publication of materials collected and tabulated by the Bureau of Labor Statistics.[6]

The tables presented below are illustrative of a restricted empirical and explicitly comparative analysis of what people do with their leisure. They, of course, hardly scratch the surface of the Wharton material, and they lack the immediacy of real life that is found, for example, in the Lynds' "Middletown." [7]

First, as to leisure expenditures as a whole, the average family spends about 5 per cent of their income on leisure. This average does not change appreciably from metropolitan center to suburb to small city. In the northern region of the country, for example, families in large cities spend 5.4 per cent of their income on leisure, those in the suburbs also 5.4 per cent and those in smaller cities, 5.2 per cent.[8] Life in America apparently is so much of a piece that city or suburban residence fails to produce differences in leisure on such a gross level of total expenditure.

This surprisingly low figure of 5 per cent stems from the restricted definition of leisure expenses which included only these four categories:

1) Purchases of radio, television and phonograph equipment and purchases of musical instruments and related equipment.

2) Admissions to movies, plays, concerts, sporting and other spectator events.

3) Newspapers, magazines and books (plus book rentals and library fees).

4) "Other recreation" which includes toys, sporting goods and athletic equipment, phonograph records and sheet music, cameras and photographic supplies, pets and pet food, collection and craft hobbies, dues to social and recreation clubs, etc.

The first three categories are self-explanatory. The fourth, "other recreation," requires some interpretation. These activities, diverse in themselves, seem to be more active and more individualized than the other three types of leisure; individualized in the sense that they stem more from the interests and resources of the particular family; and more active in the sense that their content, pace and manner of expression is more directly controlled by the participants. This category thus becomes an important tracer in the search for differences between city and suburban leisure since it catches up to a great extent one of the major images of suburban life.

Three other major types of leisure expenditure not included are those for alcoholic beverages, vacations and travel, and household decoration and repair. This latter set of items, constituting the raw materials for the do-it-yourself movement, probably absorbs a greater share of leisure dollars (and time) in the suburbs than elsewhere.[9]

Even though these types of leisure expenditures are themselves heterogeneous, can we discern differences in the way suburban families allocate their leisure dollars among them, compared to city and small town dwellers? Not for all suburban families as a whole because the over-all expenditures are quite similar in large city, suburb and small city (Table 1).

Table 1—Allocation of Leisure Expenditures in Large and Small Cities and Suburban Communities

	Suburbs	Large Cities	Small Cities
Purchase of radio, television sets, etc.	32%	32%	17%
Admissions (movies, sports, events, etc.)	17%	20%	26%
Other recreation (hobbies, sports equipment, etc.)	36%	32%	37%
Reading (magazines, books, newspapers)	15%	16%	20%
Total	100%	100%	100%
Number of cases	(2181)	(6741)	(1879)

Source: Wharton School, *Study of Consumer Expenditure*, IX, Table 1, p. 3. Figures derived from last section (class of city) of table cited.

In suburbs and large cities the figures are strikingly similar to one another, with about a third of the leisure budget going for the purchase of radio, television and phonograph equipment, and another third expended on "other leisure" (the category containing the more personally controlled active leisure). The remainder is almost equally divided among admissions (largely motion pictures) and reading materials. In the suburb compared to the large city there is one difference which is suggestive: there is a slight tendency for suburban families to spend less on admissions (17 per cent) relative to the "other" category (36 per cent), compared to the city families (20 per cent compared to 32 per cent). This is the first and as yet slight evidence to support the notion that leisure in the suburbs is less dependent upon mass spectator forms of amusement characteristic of an highly urbanized society.

Admissions take such a large share in the smaller city (26 per cent), and television, radio, etc. expenses such a relatively small one (17 per cent compared to 32 per cent in suburb and large city), because at the time the data was collected (1950) television was only a few years new and had not yet reached the saturation point in smaller communities. Thus aside from this historical accident (now probably eradicated), allocation of leisure dollars in the three types of community as a whole do not diverge markedly.

But this homogeneity gives way when separate social strata are considered; various groups, that is, respond differentially to the suburban setting. For example, income and occupational positions, although not constituting social groups in the same sense that ethnic and religious ties do, nevertheless are important determinants of leisure, and as the following tables show, shape its use differently in the city and the suburb. The next two tables contrast leisure expenditures among three occupational strata in the large city and the suburb.[10] The occupational groups are a higher white collar group consisting of professionals and other self-employed persons and officials, a lower white collar group of sales and clerical personnel, and a blue collar group of skilled workers. In the first table (2A) are families from these three groups with incomes from $3,000 to $6,000; in the second (2B) the income for the same three groups averages $6,000 or more.

Ignoring, for the moment, city-suburb differences, it is interesting to see that even these crude categories of leisure activities reveal the familiar fact that lower income groups rely more heavily upon the pre-packaging programming of radio and television while upper strata express their leisure in more individualized and more active ways contained in the "other recreation." Thus skilled workers in the $3,000 to $6,000 income group spent about 40 per cent of their income on radio and television sets and only a quarter of their income on "other" activities, while the higher white collar families in the upper income group allocate their leisure for those two types in just the opposite way, about a quarter for television, etc., and about 40 per cent for the "other" things.

Among the lower income families (table 2A), city or suburban residence makes slight difference in the way leisure funds are spent, regardless of occupational class. If there is any trend, it is for the higher white collar group in the suburb to shift its expenses away

Table 2A—Income and Occupational Position and Leisure Expenses
For Families Between $3,000 and $6,000

	Radio, TV, etc.	Admis- sions	"Other"	Read- ing	Total	No. of Families
PROFESSIONALS, OFFICIALS AND SELF-EMPLOYED						
Living in: Large city	39%	19%	27%	17%	100%	(388)
Suburb	37%	14%	33%	16%	100%	(162)
SALES AND CLERICAL PERSONNEL						
Living in: Large city	36%	18%	31%	15%	100%	(299)
Suburb	39%	17%	28%	16%	100%	(103)
SKILLED WORKERS						
Living in: Large city	42%	17%	26%	15%	100%	(484)
Suburb	45%	15%	24%	16%	100%	(167)

Source: Wharton School, *Study of Consumer Expenditures*, IX, Table 16, 150-51. These figures derived from table cited, for northern region only.

from television and radio toward "other" leisure activities, compared to city families of the same occupational position. The lower white collar and skilled workers, on the other hand, shift the other way—more money for television and radio and less for other forms of leisure. While these changes are small, and hardly more than suggestive, they take on added significance when the higher income levels are considered (table 2B).

Once this income plateau is reached, it appears that the balance of spending *is* affected by the suburban community and dramatically so for the higher white collar group. Television expenses drop from 29 per cent in the city to 20 per cent in the suburb, and "other" leisure increases ten percentage points from 41 to 51 per cent. Proceeding down the occupational ladder, this shift is less pronounced (sales and clerical workers in the suburbs increase their other leisure only 5 per cent) until among the skilled workers there is practically no change.

Table 2B—Income and Occupational Position and Leisure Expenses

For Families with Incomes Over $6,000

	Radio, TV, etc.	Admissions	"Other"	Reading	Total	No. of Families
PROFESSIONALS, OFFICIALS AND SELF-EMPLOYED						
Living in: Large city	29%	17%	41%	14%	100%	(205)
Suburb	20%	15%	51%	14%	100%	(139)
SALES AND CLERICAL PERSONNEL						
Living in: Large city	30%	18%	37%	15%	100%	(54)
Suburb	28%	16%	43%	13%	100%	(29)
SKILLED WORKERS						
Living in: Large city	39%	21%	30%	10%	100%	(93)
Suburb	36%	22%	31%	11%	100%	(38)

Source: Wharton School, *Study of Consumer Expenditures*, IX, Table 16, 150-51. These figures derived from table cited, for northern region only.

These two tables reflect the two main directions leisure spending can take in the suburbs. The first is the familiar expression of bettered conditions—assuming the suburb is viewed as such by its residents—in more expensive material objects and in more of them. It is among the lower income groups, particularly the sales, clerical and skilled workers, that this pattern is seen. The second pattern is the emulation of an ideal of self-generating and self-controlling creativity and individuality, an ideal embodying fragments of life styles from a variety of American heroes, from the pioneer frontiersman to the playboy sportsman. The category of "other" leisure is its partial embodiment, and as such tells us that if the suburban community is more congenial to the modern amalgam of this leisure ideal, only those with the money to buy it and/or the cultural wherewithal to spend it seem to be stimulated by the suburban setting to do so.

The skilled workers, for example, show relatively little change in their leisure regardless of income and community location. Their style of life is crystallized around the conditions of their work, to be sure, but probably even more decisively, around ethnic and cultural lines, all generated and shaped by an urban tradition.

On the other hand, white collar workers, and those in higher positions in particular, being more detached from these encapsulating traditions, are more flexible in adapting their leisure styles to the ethos of their community. Being better educated, moreover, means that when the ethos points, as it does in the suburbs, to a more personalized and towards a "higher" cultural level, then the white collar group will show an even greater assimilation to the suburban model.[11]

An historical note in this connection is the comparison over a generation of leisure among various social strata in the New York suburbs. The previously mentioned leisure study of this area in 1955 repeated in foreshortened form the well known inquiry published in 1934 by Lundberg, Kamorovsky and McInerney. The most impressive comparison is that then and now middle class families had about the same amount of leisure and that it is used in roughly the same ways. The differences only underlined the basic similarity in the ways these families spend their free time. At both times, for example, a large segment of middle class women devote a considerable part of their leisure to some form of cultural expression; many of the same cultural organizations exist today that were active then.

An important difference, however, is that there has been a great proliferation of organizations and even more important their specialization into particular fields, art clubs, dance groups, choral societies, chamber music groups and so on. Formerly it appeared that cultural interests were often contained in multi-purpose organizations, the Women's Club being the best example. Today, however, cultural activities have broken through the relatively narrow class boundaries and involve lower social strata to a far greater extent. To be sure in the New York suburbs (and those around other major cities, as well) ethnic and cultural islands have assimilated into the middle class pattern more slowly and still retain to some extent the leisure patterns of a generation ago. This is especially true for the less educated semi and unskilled labor force staffing the industries in the larger satellite cities circling metropolitan centers.

The growth of musical, artistic and theatrical activities in the suburbs is perhaps one of the most striking changes that has taken place on the suburban leisure scene in the past twenty years. And this change is not due simply to an increased interest of old residents but is directly tied to the influx of new and younger people to the suburbs. A similar change here affecting the community structure more directly has been the channeling of free time into child-centered activities. The influence of children, particularly among the families with several children of school and pre-school age, ramifies throughout their leisure lives. On the simplest level is the redirection of activities away from evenings out, and a settling of the "pick up and go" pace of leisure into a more ordered and restricted one. More important, though, is the way problems of schools, playgrounds and "the right kind" of playmates channel the energies of the parents (mothers, for the main part) into the active organizational life of the suburban community. These more complicated features of suburban leisure—and discussions of what people do with their free time soon meet the problem of the connection of these activities with the larger social scene—and thus necessitate a more general look at leisure as a whole. We turn accordingly to our third question which was aimed precisely in this direction.

The Social Structuring of Leisure

The place of leisure in the social life of the suburb (or in any community, for that matter) is difficult to understand if only the common sense conception of the term is relied upon, for it holds at least two different meanings. One is the association of leisure with play, entertainment or recreation. This is a minimum definition implicitly bounded by the *subjective experience* of release and spontaneity wherein activities are ends in themselves. The other is a more inclusive idea; leisure is everything away from the world of work, and therefore, in addition to "play," can include more purposeful activities such as community or political participation and self-education.

While both minimum and maximum definitions have difficulties, the latter has the advantage of underlining the fact that free time activities are not a unitary kind of experience but vary widely among individuals and social groups (and for the same individual at various times). This is indeed the point of departure for a more systematic sociological conception of leisure. When viewed from this wider perspective, leisure occupies a peculiar place in our society, with three distinguishing characteristics that set it apart from other kinds of social behavior.

First, it is institutionally interstitial, a patterned gap in the social anatomy. To over-simplify somewhat, work is institutionalized into corporations, businesses, professional-client and buyer-seller relations; the family fairly well encompasses sexual relations, procreation and the early socialization of the young. Authority and its administration are organized into the political party and the agencies of government; religious needs and sentiment, especially those seeded in the ceremonies of birth, marriage and death, are located with the church. Of course there is "leakage" of these functions into other institutions and a multiplicity of functions for each institutional grouping; nevertheless, there is a dominant locus for these needs and activities. Leisure, on the other hand is not contained in any single institutional area but can be expressed in any of them. It invades them all in addition to creating its own institutions to a limited extent.

A second structural feature of leisure arises from its capacity to fulfill a variety of functions for the individual. At various times a person can find in his leisure tension release, creative expression, self-improvement, social integration, symbolic status defense or enhancement and other gratifications, some of which are less consciously apprehended. Other modes of experience, work, family relations, religion etc., are also multi-functional, but leisure differs from these in an interesting and strategic way. There is no hierarchical valuation among the possible uses of one's free time that has community (or national) consensus, since there is no agreed upon or clear conception of their relative importance to the individual or to society as a whole.

The functions of work, in contradistinction, are stamped with a fairly clear order of precedence, the maximization of economic return being the leading and almost unchallenged value. Religion and family life also are fairly unambiguous in their directives as to what is important to be desired. But the multiplicity of possible leisure goals and especially their lack of familiar ordering gives what amounts to an unpriced cafeteria selection quality to leisure and thus enhances its shifting and problematical character.

The final distinctive mark of leisure is that it is normatively indefinite, an individual matter. A typical expression of this fundamental prescription for leisure comes from one of the depression studies of leisure sponsored by the National Recovery Administration. This is a layman, not a sociologist, speaking:

> Leisure time by definition is free time. Any sense of obligation to do anything other than what one's tastes and interests invite is a denial of the very essence of leisure.[12]

Devolving on individual tastes and interests with an explicit denial of constraints from the stratification system, the power or economic or even family structures, leisure is cut adrift from any single source of normative regulation. This is not to say that there are no norms guiding leisure. The problem of identifying the norms is simply pushed back to their sources in a person's "tastes and interests" and the conditions under which they are expressed. Correlatively, the sanctions controlling leisure transgressions are equally unclear. The agencies stimulating or thwarting particular leisure choices seem to be somewhat different, more subtle, than those enforcing conformity to occupational civic or family norms. The pressures which keep a man going to the office every day, to select the simple case, are generally clear: no work no pay. But what are the consequences of withdrawing from the weekly bridge game, or switching from one TV channel to another (or of turning the set off altogether)?

These then are the three defining features of leisure: it is institutionally interstitial, unordered in its uses and values and normatively indefinite, with its sanctions at the extreme, minimal.[13] We might interject here, that it is this character of leisure, rather than its sheer increase that lies at the root of the much discussed "problem of leisure." People don't or won't know what to do with their expanded free times because the values and norms which might guide them are either too conflicting or too attenuated.[14]

What are the consequences of these structural features for leisure? First, from the institutional side, *since leisure is contained within no single institutional context it is competed for by all.* This is a competition not only for leisure dollars and hours but even more importantly for the public's value commitment. Churches and symphony orchestras, voluntary organizations and the television industry all want financial support or participation or attendance, to be sure; but even more they want their public to accept them fully and to become regular devotees. Each institutional structure seeks to convert the casual dabbler, the occasional participant into a full fledged member. These vested leisure interests, as we might call them, have guessed that the lability of leisure is bad for business. The casual movie or church goer, the occasional bowler or book reader is a greater risk than the fan since they can be more easily wooed away by the ubiquitous competition. In these attempts to enclose leisure, organization has proved to be a major weapon. It is easier to sell one man twelve books than it is to sell twelve men one book, as the publishing industry has discovered. Thus industry, religious institutions, civic groups, art galleries and symphony orchestras, not to mention commercial leisure interests ranging from bowling alley operators to the Mickey Mouse club, have elaborated endless ingenious organizational devices to contain the volatile leisure habits of the American public.

Not all leisure activities are susceptible to organization to the same extent, of course. It is estimated, for example, that only about 5 per cent of the nation's hunters and fishermen belong to regular clubs; on the other extreme, the bulk of bowling revenue comes from the vast architecture of leagues and tournaments which are clustered within the twenty million member American Bowling Congress. Among card games, bridge has a highly proliferated organization of tournaments; poker remains fiercely anarchistic. But even among those activities which are not *formally* organized there tends to develop an informal sub-culture which can absorb the major leisure energies of its adherents. Once, however, a particular leisure interest has been channelled into an organizational framework, the rest of the person's leisure needs and interests tend to be subsequently absorbed within the same framework, depending upon its flexibility in providing satisfactory activities. Thus, from both institutional pressures and individual tendencies, leisure moves toward coagulation into increasingly massive groupings.

Were these tendencies unchecked, all leisure would eventually be encapsulated into vast sealed compartments with little crossings over from one type of leisure context to another. The counter pressures which scatter leisure among a variety of activities stem in part from a person's rootedness in different institutions (he might want to spend all his free time with the boys in the company's bowling team but the demands of his wife force participation in other leisure contexts— the family and the community). Moreover, the sheer factor of satiation and desire for variety which, when coupled with the fact that some leisure interests are almost incapable of being contained within the same organizational structure, also place limits on the organizational drift.

A final potent, but unpredictable influence countering the organization of leisure, is the result of technological and cultural change which can alter or rescatter a stable leisure concentration by upsetting the balance of needs served by a particular activity. For example, recent and impending changes in the location of major baseball teams can be laid in part to the doorstep of the most eye-catching change in leisure technology of the past decade—television.

The strength of these pressures and counter pressures gives the leisure system as a whole a particular form at a given moment in time. Spatially, too (city compared to suburb, for example), the leisure scene can be characterized by the resultant vector of organizational and anti-organizational forces.

Leisure and the Suburban Community

Now we confront this view of leisure with some of the most familiar landmarks in the suburban scene. The first is the distinctive stratification and power system of the suburb. Suburban communities can be contrasted in this respect to the metropolitan center and to the smaller independent city, and it is in juxtaposition with this latter type of community (the Lynds' Middletown or Warner's Yankee City, for example) that the suburb's status system can be most readily understood.

In general, the character of relations between social strata is an antagonism of different styles of life competing for supremacy in defining the nature of the community.[15] Leisure accordingly is thrust into the front lines; compared to the city or the smaller town it is more pervasively enmeshed into the suburb's stratification-power system.

Leisure activities, therefore, become an important source of *self-identification*. In the status confused and highly transitory community —rapid population turnover is one of the subsidiary features of the suburb which intensifies the effect of the stratification system— leisure styles are often the basis of self image and subsequently of group membership criteria. Not infrequently, for example, neighborhood associations based on common interests (home ownership problems, children's playgrounds, exclusion from a local country club or simply propinquity) grow into stable and formal social organizations giving a definite framework for a social life.

Status defense is another major function of suburban leisure. This is more than the typical urban use of fad-tinted leisure to compete endlessly for momentary "fashionable" superiority; it is the more or less conscious use of some leisure activities to insulate a style of life against real or assumed encroachments from other groups. Exclusionary policies in social or recreational organizations illustrate the negative defensive use of leisure. The positive side appears to be more uniquely suburban and more extensive in scope. It is exemplified in the religious "community center" movement wherein churches and synagogues have developed a broad spectrum of secular activities to invest their parishioners' diverse interests with a sense of belonging to the particular denomination.

The same impulse—defense of cultural rather than religious boundaries—lies behind the innumerable groups dotting the suburban landscape which present concerts, art exhibits, dramatic productions, book reviews and the like. In the suburban soil, hard-won cultural attainment (as a mark of social distinction) must be nourished for adults and implanted into children. And again organization is the key tactic. In the city such cultural interests develop and are expressed in a situation of abundance (relatively speaking, of course, since cities distant from New York and other major centers feel deprived and therefore harbor their cultural energies more assiduously). But in the suburb where facilities of this type are sparse and scaled down to suburban size, people with little in common other than their cultural interests cluster together in common efforts to protect these interests and their status-defining attributes.

Yet, paradoxically, the status muddle of the suburb lends leisure quite an opposite function, that of integrating the community as a whole. Activities informed with this single end in view, however, are rare; it is more common that a few individuals marginally placed either between or above (although sometimes within) the competing status groups direct their leisure work toward overcoming the divisions within the community. Some activities, on the other hand, such as the Community Chest, or other community-wide service groups are braced with an explicit integrative goal. Aside from the community service activities, it is cultural efforts which attempt most often to

unite the various groups within a community. The following observation (made in a personal interview with the author) from one of
the leaders of an extensive cultural group in a New York suburb
expresses in compressed form the conscious use of leisure for status
defense and integrative purposes:

> Then you see another reason [for the founding of the organization]
> was that there were lots of people coming into the community, and we
> wanted to keep the quality of the community, so that our children
> would have good influences and opportunities for the cultural expres-
> sion, and it of course would benefit the others [the newcomers] so that
> the whole community would develop together and there wouldn't be
> any differences. And finally, we all have some creative instinct that
> we want to work at, both for ourselves and for the community as a
> whole.

Whichever way leisure is used in these status conflicts, and it is not
immediately apparent what kinds of people will use the different leisure
activities, it is likely that the more fragmented the community into
competing groups, the greater will be the proliferation of leisure
organization.[16]

One of the most frequent complaints, in fact, voiced by the respondents in a 1955 New York suburban study conducted by the author
was that their free time was not their own, that their communities
were over-organized and they were overworked. While such attitudes
create an undercurrent of resistance to the predominant mold of
suburban leisure—seeking, as it were, release not only from work,
but from leisure, the community's rough and ready volunteer way of
handling its problems, in addition to its structural impetus toward
civic participation, will continue to give leisure a normative thrust
toward diligent constructive activities in an organized form. And this
is intensified by the transitory nature of the suburb, where a highly
mobile (spatially and socially) population, moving too rapidly to form
stable primary group ties, invests in secondary organization with the
mission of introducing them to the community and of providing them
with friendships and sociability.[17]

We turn now to a final feature of the suburb which has important
but as yet not fully perceived consequences for leisure: the changing
lines of suburban dependence on the city. As people lead and then
follow the transplanting of urban facilities to the suburbs, the

character of the metropolitan center and the suburb itself will change. This decentralization, correlatively, will, in all likelihood, rework the ecology of leisure as well as its content. Here, for example, is a pattern observed in a New York field study which indicates what can be expected.

The audience for live concerts in New York City derives many more gratifications from coming to Carnegie Hall than the simple one of hearing fine music. Interviews with people who have moved to suburbs and decreased their attendance at such events in the city indicate that as they became involved in community affairs and found some cultural outlets there, the needs formerly clustered around attendance at live concerts were scattered among other more readily accessible leisure pursuits. For music, some found that hi-fidelity recordings were adequate substitutes; for the status-enhancing qualities of concerts, local cultural participation or even country club activities channeled the status-enhancing functions that concert attendance once gave, as well as satisfying to some extent their enjoyment of the ceremonial aspects of high cultural participation. This did not always, of course, occur. Some families maintain their contacts with the city, especially the wealthier and the older ones. Among the younger people, the familiar reasons of income limitation and the constraints of young children diminished their ability to return to the city for music. Even more significant: it was among younger people that there was a much higher acceptance of recorded music and a much livelier interest in local cultural activities. This presages a gradually diminishing reservoir of potential suburban audiences for the city's culture. So, too, does another aspect of the redistribution of population and facilities. As the density of the suburbs increases, there appear sub-regional centers often beginning as a retail hub for a group of surrounding suburbs. These, at least in the New York area, begin to show a reconsolidation of leisure facilities. Westchester County has, for example, three symphony orchestras which draw their membership and audiences from towns throughout the lower half of the county. Suburban communities on Long Island, too, are developing closer contacts with one another to exchange cultural information, organizational techniques and even audiences. This entire problem of the leisure consequences of the redistribution of urban facilities has been hardly touched and offers one of the most provocative research areas.

Beyond these features of suburban life discussed above there is

too much diversity among suburban communities to discuss *the* suburban shaping of leisure. At this point, detailed analyses of leisure in
different types of suburbs is called for.

The Quality of Leisure in the Suburbs

Granted then that suburban families do different things with their
free time and these are differently geared into their lives as members
of a community, is there another and an even more important difference in suburban leisure, a difference in its meaning and emotional
tone? It is very hard to generalize about the subjective quality of
leisure because when attempting to describe it we drop from the
abstractions of sociological categories to the immediacy of individuals
and come abruptly thereupon to a diversity of personality types as
wide as we would find in the city.

A particularly unfortunate error is the critical, sometimes denunci-
atory, evaluation of suburban leisure which often turns out to be in
reality an attack on middle class conventiality and conformity with
the ideals of middle brow culture. The "suburbs" seem merely to be
a shorthand expression for these other targets. Yet the corrective,
inherent in explicit comparisons between city and suburb, is difficult
to carry out on this level; we must rely on cultural anthropological
and impressionistic over-all judgments, winnowing out the per-
spectivistic distortions wherever possible.

For example, one of the most frequently reported qualities of
suburban leisure is its openness and indeterminancy, pessimistically
judged as creating confusion and anxiety and optimistically seen as
engendering a pioneering and unfettered use of leisure.[18] The basis of
both views lies, as we have seen, in the intensification of this general
leisure trait by the peculiar features of suburban social structure.
Thus without being committed to either value judgment it seems
probable that this amorphous quality of leisure is more strongly felt
in the suburb than elsewhere. And the response to it, of course, varies.
Some people choose the easy way out and fall into ruts of one sort or
another which satisfy or half satisfy their leisure needs, leaving
perhaps a residual restlessness. Others face the effortful and sometimes
painful pathfinding more directly, usually in groups, where in the
safety of numbers they can explore the leisure wilderness.

The general tone of this quality of leisure can be summed up in the words of a report carried out by a religious community organization designed to assist suburban parents in handling leisure problems of their children.

> Many parents would like to be more helpful in regard to their sons and daughters but need guidance. For one matter there seems to be no satisfactory norm of behavior which all of them accept, which they can use as a guide. . . . Parents have difficulty in knowing when to resist the demands of their children and when to give in. More often than not, they oscillate from one position to another.[19]

From some of the previously presented material, some other disputed qualities of suburban leisure can be reconciled or resolved one way or another. Is there more creative leisure in the suburbs? If the answer can be phrased in general terms, then we might say that since there appears to be a more widespread, active, self-initiated and self-controlled use of leisure, it is more creative than the city. If the answer is in cultural terms, then we must hedge; there appears to be more cultural activity in the suburb involving the general population as participants but there is not the high standard of performance, nor perhaps the sophistication that accrues with highly specialized audiences.

Is leisure freer from the tensions of work in the suburb? Here I think the answer is yes; suburban residents appear self-consciously to create a barrier between city and suburb, walling off the two worlds. But, given this imposed separation, new problems arise; does it work, what strains does it impose, and what difference does freedom from work tensions make if the suburbanite's leisure is invaded by the frictions of his local status contests? But these answers tend to be superficial if only inferences from actual behavior are used. For it is precisely toward the inchoate and unexpressed interests and needs that the questions are directed, and, therefore, more complete solutions must await studies which go directly and empirically to the inner significance of leisure. But perhaps at this early stage of suburban and leisure studies it is more important to be able to identify the right questions and to specify what constitutes adequate answers. It now does little good for example, to say only that ". . . leisure was becoming more passive, more formal, more organized, more mechanized and more commercialized," for this is the way Robert Lynd characterized Middletown in 1925.[20] And if we were to describe the suburbs today with these words, little besides affect is communicated.

FOOTNOTES

1. David Riesman in "The Found Generation," *The American Scholar.* Autumn 1956 (pp. 421-436) reports on a study of college seniors whose aspirations include the popular dreams of a secure and leisurely suburban life.

2. Drawn mainly from an exploratory field study made by the author of the New York Metropolitan suburbs in the spring and summer of 1955. In addition, previously reported descriptions of suburban life are included wherever relevant.

3. There are, therefore, two ways to "score" the commonness or rarity of a given pattern: either sum up the frequency scores for each *single* activity or assign frequency ranks to pairs or larger chains of activities. Thus, for example, if the rank for relaxing is 1 (most common leisure activity), sports car racing is 30 and bird watching 40, then a person doing these three things is scored 71 if we merely add the separate frequency scores. But if we took pairs of items—relaxing and bird watching or relaxing and sports car racing—the relative rank of these pairs would remain the same roughly, since almost everyone relaxed. But the relative rank of bird watching *and* sports car racing taken together would be extremely rare and produce a frequency score quite different than if the two activities had been treated separately.

4. Columbia University Press, New York, 1934.

5. John R. Seeley, R. Alexander Sim, Elizabeth W. Loosley (New York: Basic Books, 1956).

6. Wharton School of Finance and Commerce, *Study of Consumer Expenditure Incomes and Savings,* Vol. IX, Summary of Family Expenditures for Recreation, Reading and Education, University of Pennsylvania: 1956. Twelve thousand four hundred eighty-nine families were interviewed intensively in 1950-51 as to their expenditures for food, clothing, household expenses, recreation and a variety of other things. The Wharton School presented the data separately for families in suburbs of metropolitan areas, those living in large cities and those in smaller independent cities. Moreover, regional comparisons—Northern, Southern and Western states—are included as are numerous tables showing expenditures for families of different educational, occupational and income positions and for families in different stages of the life cycle.

 I am indebted to Rolf Meyersohn, Research Director of the Center for the Study of Leisure (University of Chicago) for suggesting this material and its possible use in analyzing suburban leisure.

7. See Chapter VII of *Middletown in Transition* in particular for penetrating use of expenditure data to reveal the impact of the depression on leisure.

8. In the southern and western states there is a slight tendency for people in suburbs to spend slightly more than those in the large or small city, but these differences rarely exceed 1 per cent.

9. By including expenditures for alcoholic beverages, vacation travel and housing and meals (not lunches bought by working members of the household) eaten out of home, the leisure budget expands to about 10 per cent of the family income. Based on figures from "Spending of Middle Income Families," Huntington, *op. cit.*

10. For the sake of clarity, data from the smaller city is omitted. The fact that television had not yet reached the popularity in these cities as it had in the large city and their suburbs would reduce the comparability of the material.

11. It should be clear here that the occupational categories used here by necessity are assumed to correlate with educational level and ethnicity.

12. *Report of the New York Committee on the Use of Leisure Time,* 1930, National Recovery Administration (p. 15).

13. In view of this apparent suspension above the social structure, it is not surprising that most interpretations of leisure tend to be psychological rather than sociological. See, for example, David Riesman and Ruel Denney's article, "Leisure in Urbanized America" in *Reader in Urban Sociology.* Hatt and Riess (eds.), Free Press, 1951. Here it is recognized that the familiar sociological categories are inadequate tools of leisure analysis. So, too, it is felt that purely psychological concepts lack the historical and social concreteness to do justice to the amorphous quality of leisure. Their own solution is the use of the social-psychological rubric of "character types," a conceptual level which lies midway between "social structure" and personality determinants. This is both its strength and its weakness.

14. This problem of leisure, therefore, is by no means a new one. Its roots have been traced to West European thought on the eve of the Enlightenment when the ancient questions about the meaning of life were informed with an awareness of the emerging fragmentation of life into work and "diversion." See Leo Lowenthal's germinal essay on the origins of criticism of popular culture. (Historical Perspectives of Popular Culture.) American Journal of Sociology, 1950, pp. 323-32.

15. I owe this formulation to Norman R. Roth (unpublished Ph.D. dissertation, Teachers College, Columbia University, New York, 1951).

16. See Komarovsky, M., "A Comparative Study of Voluntary Organizations in Two Suburban Communities," *The Annals,* Issue of the American Academy of Political and Social Science, May, 1932, where this point is empirically demonstrated. It is also confirmed in another comparative study of four Cleveland suburbs: Mary Schauffler, "The Suburbs of Cleveland," Ph.D. dissertation, University of Chicago, 1945.

17. Herbert Gans has illustrated this process among Jewish residents in Park Forest, Illinois, during the early days of its formation. Here religious ties formed the initial anchor for sociability, and soon resulted in more formal organizations. Herbert Gans, "Park Forest: Birth of a Jewish Community," *Commentary,* May, 1951, pp. 330-339.

18. David Riesman, whose method is one of "well tempered subjectivity," is one of the few writers who has seen the coexistence of both these possibilities.

19. "Study of the Characteristics and Leisure Time Needs of the Jewish Youth of the Five Towns," (Long Island) prepared by the South Shore Jewish Community Council (Study Committee). Mimeographed.

20. Robert and Helen Lynd, *Middletown in Transition*, Harcourt, Brace, 1937, p. 245.

Rolf Meyersohn
and Robin Jackson

The University of Chicago

GARDENING IN SUBURBIA

Introduction

Despite the open debate about the problems of suburban life, one is hard put to discover what these problems are.
Perhaps, as Irving Kristol has recently written about class, the suburbs
"play a far greater role in the sociological imagination than in
American society." [1] Much as people learn to drive at an early age,
sometimes even before they are old enough to get a license (sociologists have called this process "anticipatory socialization"), so they
learn how to live in the suburbs even before they are old enough to
get married and move to one.

This knowledge, like learning to drive, comes from the fact that
America is full of instructors, eager advocates of the suburban style.
At present perhaps the mass media are the best source of information,
not only in commercials but in the ever-recurring plots about
adventure and advantage on the fringe of city life.

We find out about commuting, about neighbors, about keeping the
grass cut and the drains unclogged. If we are more sophisticated, we
even know the perils of "other-directedness" and discussion groups.

The suburb, once a fad, or, earlier, the realm of the rich, is now a
realized statistical fact: The fad is a habit.[2] To the immigrants, suburbs
are visible and accessible.

But the sociologist knows that any rapid changes in distributions—

This is an original article prepared for this volume. It is a publication of The
University of Chicago Center for the Study of Leisure. The Center is supported
by a grant from the Behavioral Sciences Division of the Ford Foundation.

whether in income, suicide rates, birth rates, or, in this case, place of residence—are accompanied by dislocations in other respects. In the case of the suburban migration, what are they likely to be?

Only one small part of this question is considered here, and for that matter not even directly. We have set out to find out how commitment to a leisure activity differs in two suburbs—one, created as a result of the post war suburban migration, the other, while enlarged by it, is presumed to have kept its own identity.

Although leisure is held to be private, the spending of it is very much dependent on its setting. Leisure is highly susceptible to influence (since most leisure time is spent with other people), and while there are few formal rules about it, informal ones may apply rather strongly. Before moving to a suburb, people are prepared perhaps to play golf or garden or learn bridge, and the suburb may look like a perfect locale for all kinds of leisure. Certainly the kind of casualness that greets the newcomer gives that appearance. The pastel-colored houses, the informal dress, and the various outdoor temptations for spending time and the indoor gadgets for saving it—these all make the suburbanites' life look like one long vacation. Suburban life is indeed conducive to a great variety of leisure activities but is it conducive to a leisurely approach to them?

Norms for behavior in the suburbs (as well as some of the houses) seem jerry-built, by and for people who have been exposed to suburban styles but have had no practice in leading the good suburban life. Does this mean that in the realm of leisure and styles of life there is greater disparity between what people enjoy doing and what they actually do? Are people more likely to do things because they are in some way expected to? The work ethic for instance, demands that matters of taste take second place to other, instrumental considerations. But the nonwork ethic, if you will, particularly in the seemingly utopian leisure of the suburbs, how does *it* operate?

Such questions force a distinction between different kinds of suburbs, particularly between those with a tradition of wealthy commuters or a remnant of an indigenous population and those newly created by the current national flight from the city.

This is not to say that leisure activities themselves are necessarily different in different suburbs. Suburban living implies a number of leisure activities that are endemic, gardening, for instance; it facilitates others, like golf and the barbecue, and at present at least inhibits others, like walking (some modern suburbs seem to be built entirely without sidewalks). But commitment to leisure may be of a different sort.

A Comparison of Two Suburbs

With these questions in mind, the Center for the Study of Leisure undertook a small study of suburbanites' habits in one leisure activity: gardening. Interviews were made with a sample of 288 home-owners in two Chicago suburbs. The two suburbs were selected because of their differences. One of the suburbs, to be called "Fairlawn," is a postwar housing development, a community planned by a single builder and inhabited largely by young adults with young children. According to the 1950 Census, twenty-five per cent of its total population is under five years old and the median age is twenty-six. It consists of well-educated and well-off middle-class people; the median education is close to fifteen years of school, the median annual income over $5,000.

The other suburb, here called "Le Chateau," was, in the nineteenth century, a community on its own, and has been incorporated into the suburban realm only within the past thirty years. Le Chateau's inhabitants are older and with fewer small children (the median age is thirty-one plus and the percentage of children under five is twelve), they are not as well educated and somewhat less well-off (the median education is twelve years of school, the median annual income slightly less than $4,500). Only in population size does Le Chateau outdistance Fairlawn—or did in 1955, when special census was taken in both communities: it had 30,000 inhabitants as against 24,000 for Fairlawn.

These statistics are intended to point up similarities in size and class, differences in age range and homogeneity. But the more important differences were assumed without reliance on the Census Bureau: that Le Chateau can absorb without being altered, while Fairlawn may alter without absorbing or even becoming a settled community; that both are middle-class suburbs, but Le Chateau represents an older tradition, contains a body of elders, competing styles of life,— some in active contact, others insulated—a diversity of outlook as well as architecture.

In contrast to the newness of Fairlawn, a newness that extends from the actual physical setting to the fact that most of its population has only recently adopted a suburban way of life, Le Chateau is a much more settled and heterogeneous community. The age range is broader, and this in itself makes for greater differentiation of life styles.

These age and generational differences, coupled with the greater occupational diversity and the fact that Le Chateau evolved slowly as a community,—and was not entirely created more or less at once— all go into making it more heterogeneous.

Perhaps the broadest difference between the two communities is that the people of Le Chateau have much less in common with each other than the people in Fairlawn. It should not be taken that this is a community of isolated people, but rather one where many groups can find expression of their wants and ways of life; in Fairlawn the wants are more alike for everyone. The result is that people in Le Chateau are less concerned with their neighbors, less anxious to find ways and means of fitting into the group and its patterns.

Table I—"If a New Family Moved into this Neighborhood, How Much of a Garden Would People Expect Them to Have?"

	Le Chateau	Fairlawn
Whatever they feel like	23%	13%
Some gardening expected	76	84
(a well kept lawn sufficient)	(44)	(34)
(at least some flowers)	(32)	(50)
Don't know	1	3
TOTAL	100%	100%
N =	151	137

This difference in expectations was reflected in the answers we received to this question: "If a new family moved to this neighborhood, how much of a garden would people expect them to have?" In Le Chateau, perhaps because its respondents were readier to accept the view that a man's leisure is his own business, a number of respondents rejected the question and preferred to believe that such a choice was the newcomer's and his alone. Furthermore, of those who answered it, a larger proportion of Le Chateau residents, as compared to Fairlawn's, thought that a minimum garden was enough, while Fairlawn residents were more likely to feel that considerable gardening was expected.

One might have expected that in "settledness" comes rigidity and conformity, that infringement upon the individual's leisure comes out of the gradual acceptance of the give-and-take of community life, out of the shedding of tastes that might be thought eccentric, and the adopting of more common ones. If the estimation of high community expectations for gardening represents such restrictions, then the new suburb, Fairlawn, exhibited it to a greater degree.

To sum up the difference between the two communities, it might be said that in terms of the degree of "stability" exhibited, Fairlawn is the less stable: the people there have greater mobility, are younger and hence less settled in their life patterns, and perhaps most importantly, they lack the opportunity to meet the suburban culture-bearers of greater experience, the life-long residents.

Commitment in Gardening

Anyone who hates the outdoors would do well not to move to the suburbs; either that or he would *have to* do well enough to hire a gardener to keep the outdoors away from him. Apparently most people are aware of this; at least in our study an overwhelming majority found gardening a tolerable activity and only a small minority either could afford or even wanted to hire any outside help.

Table II—"Have You Ever Hired Anyone to Help You with Your Garden?"

	Le Chateau	Fairlawn
No	87%	80%
Yes		
Someone to mow lawn, do chores, etc.	8	15
Professional gardener	3	3
Landscape architect	2	2
TOTAL	100%	100%
N =	151	137

In other words, everybody gardens, or, more accurately, someone in every family gardens. In our study, usually the wife is the keeper of the culture, living and otherwise. But, in accordance with "togetherness," some division of labor is usually worked out, commonly one in which the husband is expected to do the heavy work.

Thus our discussion of the findings will treat the respondents as family units rather than individuals. Since most of the respondents were women, however, the viewpoint presented reflects predominantly the woman's rather than the man's.

If one were to rank leisure activities in terms of visibility, gardening would probably win out. There is nothing hidden (except possibly what grows behind the few large bushes) and what goes into the soil—in terms of labor as well as materials—can be easily seen. In the same way, what comes out is highly visible, and in this case to our interviewers. For in this study we obtained information not only from the respondents but also from the gardens themselves. Our knowledgeable interviewers could see what kinds of flowers were raised, and how well.

Gardening is an activity that permits considerable choice: there are perennial flowers and annuals, short-term investments and long-term ones, lavish arrangements and modest ones, room to show off and room to preserve privacy. To some extent the choice is of course a purely psychological one and a matter of taste; to some extent it depends on the kinds of patterns that are prevalent in the community or the neighborhood (roses seem to be the major flower, though the breeds are once again subject to all these distinctions). To some extent, too, the choice is one that reflects a kind of interest in permanence. The development of lilac hedges assumes a long-term view of life, the raising of petunias requires no such vision. Gardening, then, can be a measure of "rootedness," though it could as well be a measure of its illusion.

Here, then, are the means at our disposal for judging commitment to gardening. And while gardening is certainly a unique leisure activity, its patterns of determination are probably much like those of other leisure interests; perhaps the most important difference between gardening and any other leisure activity is that it is a compulsory extra-curricular activity among a larger number of people.

Several ways were used to find out how committed to gardening our respondents were. One way was to ask how much time is spent. At a time when there are increasing demands made on the suburbanite's time—and growing numbers of leisure industries as well as organizations competing for the somewhat less rapidly growing number of leisure consumers—this time-sheet measure of commitment seems highly relevant. Since our field work was done in July, it was possible to ask for the current number of hours worked. Slightly over half the respondents spent less than five hours per week on the garden.

Table III—"About How Many Hours a Week Do You Spend Working in the Garden?"

	Le Chateau	Fairlawn
Less than five hours	47%	63%
Five to ten hours	34	26
More than ten hours	19	10
No Answer	0	1
TOTAL	100%	100%
N =	151	137

A somewhat subtler way of measuring commitment is to find out whether the leisure activity is approached as a challenge or a routine. Is it treated as a sport, a struggle, or a chore? Is it approached in a way that presumes a fairly high degree of skill? Does the participant develop some special or advanced skills or is he satisfied with a fairly simple routine, mastering only the less complicated aspects of the activity? Just as in trout-fishing the "purist" uses dry flies, for example, and sneers at the idea of live bait, so in gardening, there are degrees in the challenge. Craftsmanship in gardening exists along several lines: the flowers raised may in themselves be difficult to care for; attempts can be made to grow from seed or cuttings certain kinds of flowers that are ordinarily bought as bulbs or young plants, or completely new varieties may be created by cross-pollinating plants. In measuring craftsmanship we found that a quarter of the gardeners could be considered skilled.

Table IV—Craftsmanship Involved in Raising Flowers

	Le Chateau	Fairlawn
Garden evaluated as containing predominantly flowers that are:		
Hard to raise	29%	22%
Easy to raise	71	78
TOTAL	100%	100%
N =	151	137

A third indication of commitment is the probable degree of antici-pated participation. Commitment to a leisure activity implies some permanence. But since there are always people who rush madly into an activity, and very soon thereafter rush out of it, it is important to find out whether the individual is likely to be involved briefly and superficially, or whether his present involvement gives us reason to believe he will continue to participate in the future. Without repeated interviews, such a measure can, of course, be only suggestive, but, as we said earlier, gardening lends itself well to such inferences about the future: by looking at what is planted, one can make some judgments about the degree of commitment, because flowers and plants divide along certain lines, some being annual and others perennial. With annual gardens, only one growing season is required for the whole thing to bloom and die; the garden can be completely different the next year—expanded or reduced to a thin grass covering. With perennial flowers the possible commitment is longer, depending on the life span of the plant itself—few people are prepared to dig up all the plants and start over again.

Perennial gardens can be further divided into those of greater and less possible life span. By a kind of "content analysis" of perennial gardens we were able to single out long-range gardens—those gardens that could be planned for a great number of years, possibly a lifetime. Here the botanical dimension of the activity implied a greater degree of permanence. Nineteen per cent of the perennial gardeners in our study were in this category of greatest possible commitment.

Table V—Extensiveness of Gardening Plans

	Le Chateau	Fairlawn
Gardening evaluated as containing predominantly:		
Long range perennials	22%	16%
Short range perennials or annuals	78	84
TOTAL	100%	100%
N =	151	137

These measures were combined into a dichotomy and respondents who showed any signs of serious interest in gardening—if they grew perennials, or flowers that were hard to raise, or if they spent a great deal of time gardening—were considered committed.

What does commitment depend on? We might expect that since in Fairlawn greater expectation for gardening seems to exist, there would also be more gardening done. But this was hardly the case: in Le Chateau there were more committed gardeners.

Table VI—Commitment Index

	Le Chateau	Fairlawn
Committed to gardening *	67%	55%
Not committed	33	45
TOTAL	100%	100%
N =	151	137

* A committed gardener was one who worked over 6 hours a week, and/or planted hard-to-raise flowers, and/or raised predominantly long-range perennials.

This difference in commitment seems to be very much related to the differences in age of Fairlawn and Le Chateau inhabitants', once the elder and younger are compared separately, it is less pronounced.

Table VII—Commitment to Gardening Among Young and Old

Per Cent Committed				Le Chateau		Fairlawn	
Age	%	N		%	N	%	N
Under 30	41	(22)					
30-34	51	(90)	Under 40....	54	(63)	51	(100)
35-39	59	(51)					
40-44	64	(50)					
45-49	71	(24)	40 and over..	76	(83)	64	(33)
50-54	80	(20)					
55 and older	86	(22)					
TOTAL	39	(279) *					

* The age was not determined in 9 cases.

Gardening, unlike most other leisure activities, can be pursued as easily by the old as by the young, and as the exigencies of life make it harder to play tennis, golf or other more rigorous leisure activities, it may naturally become more popular. Hence it is not surprising that in answer to the question "What are your favorite leisure activities?" Fairlawn respondents named more activities then Le Chateau respondents.

But gardening is vested with a special meaning which is perhaps more important for the young Fairlawn residents; as we mentioned, gardening has to do in part with enhancement of property values; it might also be taken as a sign of "rootedness."

Table VIII—The Number of Leisure Activities Mentioned as Favorite*

	Le Chateau	Fairlawn
None or one	0	0
Two	7	3
Three	15	4
Four	30	13
Five	28	25
Six	7	17
Seven	8	17
Eight	2	10
Nine	3	4
Ten or more	0	7
TOTAL	100%	100%
N =	151	137
$\bar{x}$ =	4.6	6.0

* Does not include gardening.

Such motives for gardening seem more likely to occur among the young and ambitious than among the older and more settled.

A closer look at the committed is necessary. One might assume that a relationship in gardening—as in all leisure activities—between commitment and enjoyment and success, indicates that it is more likely to be pursued for its own sake. If it were a "rational" activity, it would be most ardently pursued by people who enjoyed it and who had some talent for it.

Enjoyment was measured in two ways. When we asked for a simple yes or no to the question, "Do you really enjoy gardening?" almost everyone gave a simple "yes" answer. (Eighty per cent in Fairlawn, eighty-seven per cent in Le Chateau.) But when we asked in an open-ended question for a listing of favorite leisure-time activities, over half (seventy-five per cent in Fairlawn, sixty-five per cent in Le Chateau) neglected to mention gardening.

Talent was measured by results. Our interviewers graded the gardens in terms of their general appearance, taking into account differences in ambitiousness and effort. Here Fairlawn came in a poor second; its success "score" was thirty-five per cent as against Le Chateau's fifty-six per cent.

In other words, because they are younger and have more leisure activities to choose from, fewer Fairlawn residents were committed gardeners. But does this fact of youthfulness also indicate something else, a greater concern with the instrumental benefits of gardening? Among those who are committed gardeners, are there more in Fairlawn who don't enjoy it or show no talent? This group—we called them the "overcommitted"—was far larger in Fairlawn than in Le Chateau.

Table IX—Overcommitment in Le Chateau and Fairlawn

	Le Chateau	Fairlawn
Committed gardeners who		
Enjoy and/or show skill in gardening	77%	57%
Neither enjoy nor show skill	23	43
TOTAL	100%	100%
N =	101	76
(Uncommitted)	(50)	(61)

In the rest of this paper some attempt will be made to describe overcommitment, which may be one of the by-products of the current mood in leisure.

Overcommitment in Gardening

One feels about the overcommited that if it were up to them, they wouldn't garden, that gardening was not a leisure activity at all but a necessary chore. They were more ready to feel that considerable competitiveness centered around gardening. Certainly anyone involved in a popular leisure activity will be interested in the performance of others. Thus it is not surprising that among serious gardeners generally, a large proportion answered "yes" to the question, "Are people

Table X—"Are People Around Here Competitive about Gardening?"

	Le Chateau	Fairlawn
Per cent * believing that people are competitive		
Uncommitted	8	28
Committed	12	35
Overcommitted	17	45
Total	11	34

* The corresponding N's are as follows:	50	61
	78	43
	23	33
	151	137

around here competitive in their gardening?" But this was even more true of the overcommitted. Genuine self-expression was apparently less at play, and competitiveness, more so.

William H. Whyte has suggested that in newly developed, homogeneous communities like Fairlawn, recognition of shared problems and a desire to conform has tended to keep overt competition at a minimum.[3] But we discovered that Fairlawn respondents were generally more ready to declare the existence of competition than respondents in Le Chateau. Perhaps gardening is here an outlet for the competitive feelings that are held to be in poor taste if expressed around material goods and other more obvious status symbols. Because gardening often involves time more than money it might be more "acceptable"—inconspicuous consumption, in effect.

Table XI—Clothes Consciousness and Conservatism

	Le Chateau	Fairlawn
In matters of taste and dress, would you say you are more or less conservative than the average man (woman)?		
More	28%	38%
Less	11	24
Same as average	61	38
Total	100%	100%
Would you say you are more or less clothes-conscious than the average man (woman)?		
More	19%	34%
Less	23	38
Same as average	58	28
Total	100%	100%
N =	151	137

The desire or need to be different from others is greater in Fairlawn than in Le Chateau. When we asked whether they considered themselves more clothes conscious or less clothes conscious than the average, most Le Chateau residents answered "about the same," while in Fairlawn only about a third gave that answer. This was also true for the question "Do you consider yourself more conservative or less conservative than the average?"

And while Fairlawn residents want to be different, they may well prefer to stand out in their inconspicuousness; at least a larger proportion said they were more rather than less conservative, and less rather than more clothes conscious than the average.

In general, the overcommitted gardener showed little balance. He worked very hard, but he didn't enjoy it. He overestimated the community's expectations; he made elaborate plans, and was disappointed when they didn't work out. Yet the planning continued. After describing an ambitious plan for a rose garden and large beds of flowers all around her home, one hard-working but unsuccessful Fairlawn gardener burst out: "I really hate gardening; we both do. My husband never plays golf anymore and we do nothing all weekend but work in the garden. I mean work."

Raising flowers is a mysterious, unmanageable task, but it can be controlled; the weather may be bad, the weeds rampant, the "green thumb" missing, but the approach to gardening presumes on the part of those who are serious about it, some measure of control. In this respect, however, the overcommitted were very different from the other gardeners. While fewer Fairlawn residents than Le Chateau residents saw themselves in control, in both communities the overcommitted were noticeably more helpless.

Table XII—"Do You Feel that You are in Control of the Garden?"

	Le Chateau	Fairlawn
Per cent * saying they feel in control		
Uncommitted	54	43
Committed	82	60
Overcommitted	43	42
Total	67	48
* The corresponding N's are are follows:	50	61
	78	43
	23	33
	151	137

Who are the overcommitted? They are not merely the newcomers to the community. While the proportion of people who are not committed to gardening decreases with the length of residence in either community, the proportion of overcommitted among the old residents is about the same as among the new.

Table XIII—Overcommitment and Length of Residence *

| | Le Chateau | | Fairlawn | |
	Short	Long	Short	Long
Uncommitted	39%	29%	53%	35%
Committed ('c')	48	55	26	38
Overcommitted ('o')	13	16	21	27
TOTAL	100%	100%	100%	100%
N =	67	84	64	73
$\dfrac{'o'}{'o' + 'c'} =$	22	23	46	41

* Short residence includes those who have lived in the community less than four years.

The difference leads one to believe that overcommitment is an inherent part of Fairlawn's community life, something begun early and never given up.

It was most pronounced among the young in Fairlawn (see Table XIV) and among those who appeared to have greater aspirations for getting ahead. (This was measured crudely by asking respondents how much money they expected to earn three years from now, and separating those who thought they would earn at least $2,000 more then than now.)

Table XIV—Overcommitment and Age

| | Le Chateau | | Fairlawn | |
	—40	+40	—40	+40
Uncommitted	46%	24%	49%	32%
Committed ('c')	38	61	25	49
Overcommitted ('o')	16	15	26	19
TOTAL	100%	100%	100%	100%
N =	63	83	100	33
$\dfrac{'o'}{'o' + 'c'} =$	29	19	51	28

Here it can be seen that the enjoyment of leisure is something that is indeed not inevitable. The more mobile residents if they did not ignore gardening altogether, were likely to be involved with gardening without enjoying it or showing particular talent for it. It is perhaps this group that has found it useful to apply leisure activities such as gardening to altogether unleisureful purposes—to get ahead. Equally likely, they applied work ethics in the leisure realm.

In general, overcommitment can be expected in any community and among all groups; that it turned up more readily in Fairlawn than in Le Chateau, however, could be taken as a reflection of Fairlawn's lack of tradition and resilience. Overcommitment could in this respect be regarded as a product of the current migration to the suburbs, a mutation brought about by the rapid population shifts of recent years.

*Table XV—Overcommitment and Mobility *

	Le Chateau Mobile		Fairlawn Mobile	
	+	−	+	−
Uncommitted	33%	37%	43%	42%
Committed ('c')	57	45	25	34
Overcommitted ('o')	10	18	31	24
TOTAL	100%	100%	100%	100%
N =	21	91	60	50
$\dfrac{'o'}{'o' + 'c'} =$	14	28	56	41

* A person was considered mobile if he expected to earn at least $2,000 more three years from now than he does at present.

While overcommitment might stretch the conception of leisure that is commonly regarded as its ideal—namely, freedom from obligation—it does provide an important counterbalance to whatever passivity America is presumed to be afflicted with. Furthermore, the area in which this overcommitment was found is one which has a strong tradition and perhaps a stabilizing influence. Models for gardening, much as those for suburban life generally, have their roots in a leisure class which had been well equipped with an aesthetically sensitive way of life. Although there is a vast difference between a petunia patch in Fairlawn and a formal garden of an English estate, both are part of the same pattern. Only now the leisure class as well as its sensitivities have spread out, the latter perhaps too thinly. But because of its historical roots gardening is not the sort of leisure fad that temporarily involves masses of people who will drop it shortly for a new one. Rather, it is part of the environment which they are trying to adapt to and create. And perhaps overcommitment results in the long run in the best kind of creative adaptation. Those who are now over-committed are the experimenters in the changes in life styles that are occurring at an increasing rate. They, more than either the unconcerned or the deeply entrenched, will play the leading part in the eventual shaping not only of flower gardens but the ever-increasing forms of leisure that are likely to spring up in the future.

FOOTNOTES

1. *Commentary,* October 1957, p. 361.
2. See R. Meyersohn and E. Katz, "Notes on a Natural History of Fads," *American Journal of Sociology,* lxii, May 1957, pp. 599-600.
3. William H. Whyte, "The Consumer in the New Suburbia," in *Consumer Behavior,* Lincoln H. Clark, ed., New York University Press (New York, 1954), pp. 1-14.

Harold L. Wattel

Hofstra College

LEVITTOWN:
A SUBURBAN COMMUNITY

Instead of the objective social hierarchies of the economic, social, political, or ecclesiastical order which invariably sacrifice the living person to their utilitarian ends (for they are interested in the socially useful lie), Berdyaev proposes a charismatic *hierarchy of spiritual worth and character. . . . In other words, community cannot be created on mere sociological bases. There is no community without communion, without the relationship of a person with other persons on a spiritual level. Matthew Spinka,* Christianity and the Existentialists

Three strands intertwine to form the pattern of this study. The author maintains that suburban housing of the Levittown type represented a realistic housing alternative for the thousands upon thousands of families who wanted to raise children on something other than the streets of our major metropolitan population centers. Second, much of the negative criticism aimed at suburbia should have been directed instead at our national culture. Third, the final judgment of our contemporary suburbias will come from an analysis of the children produced in them, since these offspring are the only homogeneous element present in places like Levittown. The adult populations of the new large suburban developments reflect diversity to a greater extent than they do conformity.

The post-war American suburban development has become a whipping boy. Much of the criticism reflects an "intellectual" discontent with the general state of American living at mid-20th

This is an original article prepared for this volume.

century. Using a blunderbuss approach, critics have hit the speculative land operator, the profiteering builder, the sharping financier, the amoral real estate salesman, the jerry-built house, the bribe-taking officials at all government levels, and the limited physical and esthetic dimensions of suburban homes, their equipment, and their surroundings. The criticism extends to the family in the housing development for its "mass produced" aspirations, for physical goods and pseudo-culture, for being on an "acquisitions" treadmill fed by expanding consumer credit, and for its limited personal horizons. Community relationships which are forced and false and hence foster friction rather than "community" do not escape unscathed. The general restlessness of modern living is another target. All of this is meant to be an indictment of suburbia. Is suburbia guilty? Perhaps, but a closer examination of a modern suburbia nevertheless is necessary before a conviction may be handed down.

The Levittown Project

The construction firm of Levitt and Sons (Abraham Levitt and his two sons) conceived the Levitt community in terms of 2,000 sixty dollars-per-month rental units for veterans only. Plans were announced on May 7, 1947, but by the end of that month, additional land had been acquired for a total of 4,000 units. The total grew to 5,000 by the close of the year and to 6,000 by February 1948. Some three years later, on November 20, 1951, the *New York Times* announced the completion of the last home of the project, which by then had grown to 17,447 homes.

A change in the Federal Emergency Housing Act (Section 603) made the financing of rental homes difficult after 1948 so that after that date Levitt houses were built for sale only. Plans to keep 4,000 homes in the rental class were later modified when Levitt sold the rental units *en bloc*, and the units were later resold to individual owners. Today, one can find only a few rental units scattered through the community.

Whether for rent or for sale, Levitt had no problem marketing his homes. Fast talking real estate promoters were unnecessary. Newspaper reports of additional construction usually resulted in queues of veterans days before contracts could be negotiated.

The housing project is situated in the southeast quadrant of

Nassau County approximately 32 miles east of the Long Island Railroad's Manhattan terminal, Pennsylvania Station. Two branches of the railroad, two parkways for passenger cars only (Northern and Southern Parkways), and one major all-vehicle road (Hempstead Turnpike) tie Levittown to communities to the east and west. Most north-south traffic is handled by one parkway (Wantagh State Parkway) and one all-vehicle route (Wantagh Ave.).

Transportation facilities are of no small concern to Levittown families, since the majority of the breadwinners work outside of the county. Approximately 75 per cent of the present residents commuted when they first arrived in Levittown. Since their arrival, this percentage dropped to 60 per cent. Commuters to New York City accounted for 65 per cent of the earlier group and 52 per cent of the latter. Appreciation of the growth of the community as well as the magnitude of commuting can be had from the statistics of Long Island Railroad commuters which follow:

Table 1—Long Island Railroad Terminal Commuters [a]

Hicksville and Wantagh [b] to New York City or Brooklyn, 1926-1956

	Total	Hicksville	Wantagh
1956	79,829	44,322	35,507
1946	12,235	6,879	5,356
1936	8,398	4,706	3,692
1926	7,407	5,359	2,048

[a] Numbers of persons buying monthly commutation tickets or equivalent.
[b] Hicksville and Wantagh stations serve Levittown as well as contiguous areas.

Source: Long Island Railroad.

It is not strange that the average Levittowner commutes to "the City." For a large metropolitan center as New York City, it is taken for granted that the work force will not live close to the work shop. Trains, subways, trolleys, ferries, buses, and private vehicles have long carried a portion of Manhattan's work force from its sister boroughs of Bronx, Brooklyn, Richmond, and Queens. After World War II, population spilled north and east into Westchester County and Connecticut, west into New Jersey, and east into Nassau and Suffolk Counties. Whereas it has been estimated that only ten per cent of New York City's work force resides outside of the five

boroughs of the City, almost one-half of Nassau's work force commutes to the City.

But it is not commuting per se which is of special interest here.
Rather, it is the time element involved in such commuting. The
average Levittowner who works in Brooklyn or Manhattan must
allow almost 1½ hours per home-to-office trip, or about 15 hours
per week. More likely, his home-to-home day will begin at about
7:00 A.M. and end twelve hours later. This is a burdensome
schedule indeed in this age of the 40-hour work week. One might
well ask, "Is suburban living so attractive that the average man
is willing to subject himself to such day-in and day-out torture?"
Perhaps a wiser question is, "What are the alternatives?" These are
questions for which we hope to find answers.

The Levitt House and Its Setting

What drew thousands of families to Levittown? The attraction
can almost be inferred when it is known that 65 per cent of the
current residents "escaped" from apartment dwellings and 66 per
cent (not the same families necessarily) moved east from New York
City. There was a basic need for "lebensraum." Outside of the
factor of being able to afford the Levitt house, 48 per cent of the
present Levittown population indicated in response to a recent
survey that they sought a "good place to raise children," while an
additional 24 per cent were "interested in suburban living" itself.

In nostalgic moments, residents recall the "hardships" of the
"early days" when the promises of a carefree suburbia waited on
the completion of the project and its ancillary services. Roads were
finally ready, trucking and workmen emigrated from the community,
stores finally opened, the seas of mud were eventually covered with
grass, and in general the area emerged as anticipated. The dangers
associated with these new ventures into Suburbia were, on the
whole, civilized ones and required little more than patience and
perseverance to overcome.

Levittown was unique. The curvilinear street layouts were far
superior for safety and beauty to the typical gridiron pattern of
other neighborhoods, and four-way intersections were kept to a
minimum for safety. In addition to the varied housing facades,
homes were set back at different distances from the curbs in an

attractive staggered pattern. Each home was completely landscaped with grass, shrubs, and fruit and shade trees.

School sites were provided by the builder at strategic points throughout the area, as were 14 parks-playgrounds and nine swimming pools. (A $150,000 pool was provided for each 2,000 homes.) A $200,000 community center housing meeting rooms and a combination auditorium-dance hall was donated to the community by Levitt. Shopping-greens were located within the building area, and these have now been supplemented by other commercial properties in the center and on the periphery of Levittown.

These were arrangements prospective renters and buyers understood and appreciated. But Levitt was unable to plan for all circumstances. Other less tangible elements were to complicate life later, but were of little concern to the newcomers. What did it matter, at first, that the Levittown construction area did not coincide with certain preexisting boundaries? Levittown is not a single political entity, but is an unincorporated village or area falling within the two townships of Hempstead and Oyster Bay. Hence, it has no municipal government. Instead, the two townships are governed by elective boards which establish separate districts for fire fighting, garbage collection, water supply and so forth. That is only the beginning. The County provides police protection, property administration, and the court system. This leaves the school system as the only aspect of community living that is locally controlled. Levittown, therefore, is latticed by 4 school districts, 4 fire districts, 3 water districts, 2 Congressional districts, 4 postal districts, and 9 telephone exchanges.

Even the major school district (District Five) is a study in complexity since it encompasses homes built by contractors other than Levitt,[1] some of which use Wantagh and Seaford, as contrasted with Levittown, postal addresses. Clearly, "community" was not a built-in feature of Levittown.

The Levittown House

The original Levittown house was designed in the "Cape Cod" manner, with 720 square feet of space on the first floor. A concrete slab housed the radiant heating coils and served as the ground floor; there was no cellar. The heating unit (oil) was located in the kitchen. In addition to the kitchen, the first floor contained two bedrooms, a bath, a living room, numerous closets and a stairway which led to the unfinished (expansion) attic. Homes were situated on plots of 6,000 square feet or slightly larger. Although all interiors were exactly alike, four facades with assorted colors were used to vary the exteriors. The 1947-1948 "Capes" were followed in 1949, 1950, and 1951 by "Ranch type" houses of slightly larger dimensions (800 square feet). The concrete heating slab was retained to support a rearranged interior of four rooms. A brick fireplace opened into the kitchen on one side and the living room on the other. The living room featured a sixteen-foot thermopane (double glass with intervening air pocket) picture window opening on to the back yard. (Placing the kitchen in the front of the house and the living room in the rear is considered a Levitt innovation.) Slight modifications were made in 1950 when a television set was built into one living room wall and a carport was added to the exterior. The last model, built in 1951, eliminated the television set but contained a finished room in the attic.

All houses came equipped with refrigerator, electric stove, and automatic washing machine. National brands of equipment and hardware were used throughout.

The Cape Cod models were originally marketed at $6,990. and later at $7,990., while the "Ranches" started at $7,990. and rose to $9,000. ($9,500. for a corner plot). At original sale prices, the Levitt house represented the best "new housing" buy on Long Island. They are still excellent buys at current resale prices. (Levitt houses are advertised by "model year" with details of improvements.) Currently, the basic model resale price for the "Ranch" is about $11,500. (depending upon model) and about $10,000. for the "Cape." Improved models bring as much as $18,000., but there is an upper limit to the additional market value that improvements will bring. There is a feeling among consumers, abetted by real estate salesmen, that a family who can afford an $18,000 home can also afford a "better" address than Levittown. Some people prefer not to live in a "low" income community. In light of the original low prices and minute down payments, it is hardly surprising that Levittown became stigmatized.

Yet, this project constituted a departure from the accepted "trickle-down" approach to housing for the "low income" groups. It was a departure which represented a happy combination of private enterprise operating within the context of a government sponsored market. All such government nurtured projects, unfortunately, did not turn out as well as Levittown, and lurid tales of housing construction profiteering now pack volumes of Congressional reports. Although Levitt is reputed to have made $5,000,000 on the Levittown project, it was profit gained by providing 18,000 families with something better than "jerry-built" housing. An early forecast that Levittown would soon be a slum area was premature, to say the least.

What does it cost to live in a Levittown house? (The following analysis does not apply to the 3,800 more expensive non-Levitt-built homes in the area, some of which originally sold for as high as $19,000.)

We can start with a mortgage analysis of a 1949 "Ranch" which is assessed at about $3,650 (actually below the 44 per cent of market value provided by law). Monthly payments to the bank of about $75.-$80. cover the annual costs of the principal and interest ($524.), Fire Insurance ($18.), Insurance of mortgage payment ($32.), Local School tax ($200.), Town tax ($153.), and Water ($10.).[2] Outside of food and household supplies, the mortgage payment to the bank is the largest single budget item. A budget for a family of four might look as follows:

Table 2—Hypothetical Budget of Levittown Family, 1956

Mortgage	$ 900.
Electricity	120.
Oil and service	190.
Telephone	84.
Food and Household Supplies	1,800.
Transportation	500.
Clothing	250.
Medical	150.
Miscellaneous *	1,000.
	$4,994.

* Insurance, vacations, depreciation on auto, etc.

Judging from responses to a survey early in 1956, this budget is fairly representative. Seventy per cent of those interviewed indicated that $96. or more per week were required to make ends meet. If stated requirements actually reflected income (requirements probably understate income), then on the basis of responses, only 25 per cent of the families had annual incomes of $5,000 or less, while one-third had

more than $5,200. per year. A more detailed table of findings fol-
lows:

Table 3—Estimated Weekly Income Needed to Live in Levittown

Estimated Weekly Income	Per Cent of Responses
$ 60. or less	0.2%
61.-70.	1.1
71.-80.	7.5
81.-90.	14.1
91.-95.	1.4
96.-100.	42.5
101.-105.	.3
106.-110.	3.7
111.-120.	3.7
121.-140.	15.1
141. and over	5.1
No reply	4.8
	100.0%

Column does not add to 100.0 due to rounding.

Source: Levittown Self Survey.

While living costs rose about 15% in the period 1947-1956, only
about one per cent of the families reported a decrease of income
since arriving in Levittown. On the other hand, almost one-quarter
indicated that they had annual income increases of only one per cent
or less. At the other end of the scale, two-thirds reported increases of
three per cent per year or more.

In response to a different query, some 14 per cent of the population surveyed said that the expense of living in Levittown had
prompted them to consider leaving. Whether they will leave is another
matter. For those who would leave because of financial burdens, the
alternatives are few and relatively unattractive. It is true that there
are less expensive dwellings east of Levittown, but these are really
suitable only for those working on "The Island." Alternatives to the
west involve smaller rental quarters, sharing quarters with others,
and the like. Equivalent space in an inexpensive rent-controlled
apartment would be a rare find.

Most families find that their income is well suited to Levittown
living. This is especially true for the large group of professionals who
live in the community. These people tend to be unconcerned about
the address (about 22 per cent of the survey group entertained the

idea of leaving the community for a higher status neighborhood), and prefer to be the "Joneses" rather than try to live where they have to emulate them. It is this group which finds permanency in Levittown living as compared to those who have left or to those whose income has increased sufficiently to stimulate thoughts of leaving.

Whereas there are some relatively high incomes in the community (at least one as high as $25,000.), it is unusual for those with incomes above the range of $12,000.-$15,000 and with rising incomes, to stay. Those who do, remain for professional (doctors or lawyers) or political (elected officials) or business (insurance salesmen) reasons. Disregarding these more or less unique cases, the relative range of income is still fairly large, since the highest income may be as much as 200 per cent higher than the lowest income. But probably not more than $10,000. separates these extremes.

While on the subject of income and living costs, it should be noted that the Levittown family is favored by the presence of a highly competitive retail market. When shopping for groceries, the family has a choice between the following national and regional chain stores in addition to many more specialized independent groceries: A & P, Grand Union, Food Fair, Safeway, Acme, Bohack, First National, Penn Fruit, and Sunrise. For clothing, Levittown is served by J. C. Penney and Mays as well as by many national chain men's, women's and children's specialty shops. A large branch store of Sears, Roebuck is located in the community and a Montgomery Ward catalog store is in an adjacent community.

Added product variety and different price lines are found in such established shopping areas as Garden City, Hempstead, and Manhasset or in the newly developed "Shopping Centers" such as Roosevelt Field (Main store: R. H. Macy), Mid-Island Plaza (Main store: B. Gertz of Allied Purchasing Corp.), and Green Acres (Main Store: Gimbel Brothers). Many Levittown families shop at these stores regularly. These are within 30 minutes driving time from Levittown. For those who like to turn their shopping chores into day-long expeditions, there is always the Long Island Railroad and its westward terminal point, the shopping oasis of New York City.

Shopping within the local Levittown community cannot be compared to small town shopping; the greater portion of retail transactions is handled by professionally managed chain operations. This gives the market a highly impersonal character which is foreign to the small town resident, but not necessarily to the New Yorker. Despite the impersonal character of this market, many of these stores accommodate consumers with individual problems. In general, one might conclude that it is difficult to imagine a more fortunate arrangement of shops than that available to the Levittown family. The volume and variety of stores permits a tailoring of expenditures and shopping habits to individual incomes and desired living patterns.

The Family in the Levittown House

Young families populate Levittown. The average age of the Levittown adult in 1957 is only 35 years. And there are more children than adults in the community at present. The ratio is about 2.13 children per house. Children and parenthood have thrived where potatoes once grew, as the numbers below show:

Table 4—Number of Children in Families of Residents upon Arrival in Levittown and at Time of Survey, February 1956

Number of Children	Upon Arrival	Survey Period
0	17.6%	6.8%
1	33.3	18.8
2	35.0	41.3
3	10.3	22.7
4	2.2	6.8
5	.8	2.2
6 or more	.6	1.2
No reply	.2	.2
	100.0%	100.0%

Source: Levittown Self Survey.

It is hardly surprising that young families bore children after they arrived in Levittown. The community was sought for its surroundings, which were assumed to be congenial to child raising. Levittown has been conducive to child bearing, but it is questionable that husbands and wives have risen to parenthood as the result of the community environment as some charge.

But Suburbia has been charged for some time with fostering undesirable types of conformity in eating habits, dress, home furnishings, social activities, and thinking. How may one judge? Even ten years of community life could not have too great an impact on the adults who entered Levittown with 25 or more years of living and learning experiences. The children are the only true products of modern Suburbia, and they are still in formative stages.

Let us take a closer look at the parents and their children. The sixteen Levitt housing molds have not limited the community to sixteen family types. The individuality that each family brought to Levittown continues to show through in many ways; namely, the paint on the house exterior, the maintenance and arrangements of grounds, the design of house alterations, the home interiors, and, of course, in such personal aspects of living as clothing, cooking, selection of friends, hobbies, political and social thought, and the like.

For instance, Levittown home interiors for any particular model are identical until altered. But the physical location of walls and electrical outlets has not prevented families from furnishing homes in contemporary, Chinese modern, early American Colonial, overstuffed borax, and individual make-shift. Interiors run the gamut of the color wheel. Some floors are uncovered; others are covered with circular braided or other types of rugs, or carpeted from wall to wall in wool, cotton, nylon, or rayon. Brick fireplaces in some "Ranches" have remained untouched, while others are covered with mirrors, or have been painted green, red, white, black, etc., or have been extended with brick planters, mantels, and what not. In other words, individuality fed by market media and product-variety [3] transcends the physical setting of the project builder. The Park Avenue interior decorator might well turn up his nose at the poor taste with which some of the decorating has been handled. The point of the matter is, however, that it was individual taste that carried the day. Some work is in good taste and represents attempts to utilize mass produced house furnishings in imaginative ways. The more successful jobs have been given stamps of approval by being featured in such national periodicals as *Life, Better Homes and Gardens,* and *House Beautiful.*

Levittown families have held to individual tastes in other ways; they have not confused neighborhood acquaintanceships for friendships. Previously learned friendship patterns continue to dominate. The neighbor who unburdened her family woes to a neighbor out of a third-story window across an apartment court continues to unburden her soul in Levittown. The neighbor who sought and flourished in the anonymity of a Manhattan apartment may continue to enjoy a similar anonymity in Levittown.

It is not known whether internal family tensions have increased or decreased as families moved from urban to suburban living. It has been observed, however, that in addition to those with an honest interest in community, there are some whose community activity stems from a desire to escape the chore-dom, boredom, and tensions of family life.

And what about sex? Some sexual activity in Levittown must be normal insofar as heterosexual intercourse has produced thousands of children in wedlock. But within the community, the "big free and easy blonde" has not been unknown, and the taxi driver will tell of extra-marital excursions of commuters. But for wild cocktail-wife-swapping parties, there is neither the time nor the place if the inclination were to exist. How much different Levittown men and women are from the Kinsey-depicted sexes is not known, but the religious and income composition of the community would certainly suggest less extra-marital relationships than the average.

Friendship patterns on any street in Levittown are likely to be deliberate and depend more upon occupational and intellectual interests than on neighborhood arrangements. Family-visiting of neighbors is rare when compared to the volume of entertainment that exists on other bases. While some income homogeneity does exist, the variety of occupations which gives rise to these incomes is great. This may be illustrated by the occupations found on one street of 29 homes:

Table 5

Occupation	Number
Engineer	4
Teacher	2
Reporter	1
Accountant	2
Nurse	1
Purchasing Agent	1
Insurance Salesman	1
Diner Owner	1
Milkman	2
Retired	1
Insurance Administrator	1
Contractor	1
Personnel Manager	1
Industrial Wage Earner	5
Retail Sales	2
Architect	1
Industrial Sales	2

The absence of an independent suburban influence is evident in one highly sensitive aspect of the family's living pattern, its political orientation. In Nassau, a traditionally Republican County, it has been assumed that Democratic New York City families are transformed into Republican Nassau families as they move east across the political boundary between the two political entities. Even allowing for the neglect of the income factor (middle rather than low income families emigrated east from New York City), the thesis seems untenable in light of a soon-to-be issued analysis by Mr. Herbert Rosenbaum of Hofstra College. Irish Catholics in Levittown are switching allegiances from Democrats to Republicans, but this is happening to Irish Catholics throughout the nation. Jewish voters who have been traditionally Democratic in their voting habits continue to vote Democratic in Levittown.

In addition to the diversity of occupations, one finds religious heterogeneity. In the community, some 30 different "spiritual" organizations are found which represent the splintering of the three major faiths in the United States. Residents, when classified by church affiliation or religious heritage are estimated to be divided as follows: Catholic, 45 per cent; Protestant, 35 per cent; and Jewish, 20 per cent (these percentages have changed in the ten year period).

This heterogeneity does not mean that neighborhood relationships are less than warm and cordial. Common interests of home, car, and child care provide a strong basis for conversational "give-and-take" in which personality affinities come to the fore. Yardsticks used for the selection of the more binding sort of relationships are supplanted in these cases. In many senses, Levittown represents a horizontal version of vertical apartment living patterns of our urban centers.

Suburban living is permissive living. It permits rather than demands particular living patterns. As a result, heterogeneity rather than homogeneity is the key word. Families may entertain guests in their homes, but they may also entertain in their yards. That many families take the opportunity for outdoor living is no greater sign of conformity than that their metropolitan friends seek to be so entertained during the summer months.

The fact is there is greater informality in the suburbs. Many Levittown women, for example, wear shorts and slacks around the house and for shopping. But this informality is not a suburban development exclusively; this is a national development, if one may judge from the growth of motels (informal hotels) from one end of the United States to the other. As for the shorts and slacks, this attire is not inherently bad, despite the fact that all women do not look their best in such garments. Critics neglect to note that women other than suburban housewives are unable to select the proper dress style to flatter their figures (if this is important), and run instead with fashion.

By what standards is conformity determined to be good or bad? When Levitt built his homes, there were some 16 facades covering three or four types of interiors. Six years after Levitt completed his last home in the area, the community finds itself in the midst of a home improvement boom. The pressure of expanding families has forced many families staying in Levittown to finish the expansion attic or even to add an extra bedroom by expanding the house on the ground level. Improvements have not been limited, however, to bedrooms and attic dormers; construction of garages, dining rooms, dens, expanded living rooms, cellars, and porches have provided a basis for a growing home improvement industry in Levittown. Some work has been of the "do-it-yourself" variety under the tutelage of adult education courses which have featured attic finishing, landscaping, and so forth. Now that Levitt homes have begun to take on unique features, some people have begun to worry that competition will develop among homeowners to surpass each other in this way, and, further, that snobbishness will arise. The critic is a hard person to please.

To maintain the basic or expanded Levitt house and its 60' by 100' plot has necessitated a "pitch-in-and-help" attitude on the part of all family members. Conventional dividing lines between what was man's work and what was woman's work, consequently, have blurred, particularly in the white collar occupations. Father will do the family's weekly food shopping while mother may help paint the house; the male will help maintain the difficult-to-maintain black asphalt tile floors while the female will represent the family at a civic meeting; the husband will participate actively in the local Parent-Teachers Association, while the wife keeps the family's monthly accounts. At one time, the social scientist found this developing "equality" of the sexes healthy for the family; now, there is a growing tendency to deride the arrangement as detrimental to the male ego. The cry today is, "Don't submerge the male in a matriarchal society." Fashions apparently abound in social science, no less than in clothing, housing, and art.

So far, we have maintained that the Levitt house offered the only real housing alternative for the young middle-income ($5,000-$8,000 annually) family in the post-war period. The alternative turned out to be a good one, and in the course of ten years, more than 20,000 families have taken advantage of the opportunity. In the post-war inflation, the purchase of the Levitt house did not represent a millstone around the buyer's neck. Rapid resale of the Levitt house at higher dollar prices has been possible throughout the period. For most, the house and lot created greater responsibilities—as any home would after apartment living—so that within the family, some new relationships developed. The twenty or more years of living experience of the settlers have not been greatly disturbed by the move to Levittown, so that within the Levitt framework, a great deal of individual living is taking place. National developments such as television, consumer credit, informal living, frozen foods, foam rubber, plastic, freezers, aluminum storm windows and screens, outdoor grills, power mowers, hi-fi, book and record clubs, and the new automobile model, have penetrated Levittown. But this is not surprising, for the average Levittowner has sufficient income, credit, and education to be subject to and conditioned by national advertising which comes to him through periodicals, newspapers, radio, television, direct mail, and other media.

Space does not permit an examination of each and every facet of Levittown home life. Nor are there sufficient data to support all of the generalizations that are made about the Levittown community in particular and suburbia in general. But where there is some need to generalize, it is incumbent upon the investigator to do so with insight and caution. With this caveat, let us proceed to examine the "community" aspects of Levittown.

"Community" is an intangible something that a few worry about and work hard to promote in a housing development. Yet, when "community" is a reality, it has an *elan vital* which defies description. "You either have it or you don't."

Almost 16,000 young families now occupy Levittown homes. Are they being molded into "community" or are the counter pressures too great? What are the pressures for and against "community"? Certainly, the pressures against "community" in Levittown are manifold; namely,

1. There is no single political entity to which the residents can give allegiance; 2. Levittown as an area-concept covers more than Levitt built houses; 3. There is a diversity in occupations and education; 4. A portion of the population is transient; 5. There is a diversity of geographical backgrounds; 6. There is a diversity in ethnic backgrounds; 7. There is a diversity of religious backgrounds; 8. The community is new; and 9. There are a number of future problems which will be divisive forces. Points one and two have been dealt with above in this essay.

As has been noted earlier, there is a variety of occupations which provide income necessary for Levitt home ownership, and as a result, vocational interests are diverse. In the smaller more expensive suburban areas of Long Island, more homogeneity is found, since there is a limited number of occupations which make possible ownership of $30,000-$40,000 homes.

The industrial and wage structure of the Long Island economy are contributing factors to the large concentration of teachers and engineers in Levittown. The area is a center for electronics and aircraft production. In addition to the many public schools, there are three private and one public college close by. At the other extreme, there are few farmers or farm workers in Levittown, although some residents may work in the large horticultural industry that is spread throughout Nassau and Suffolk.

It is difficult not to overemphasize the diversity in geographical backgrounds of Levitt homeowners. For example, the unique character of the Levitt house has made resale simple. As a result, it has served well the housing needs of the somewhat transient work forces associated with the nearby Mitchel Field Airforce Base, the commercial air operations of Idlewild and La Guardia air terminals, and the major aircraft producing firms with their ever expanding and contracting production schedules. But, as noted above, this should not be underscored too heavily, for despite the relatively high home-turnover in the area (approximately 14 per cent per year), much of the population is apparently drawn from New York State. About 86 per cent of the current residents resided in New York State before arriving in Levittown, four per cent in other Middle Atlantic States, two per cent in New England, another two per cent in the Southwest, one per cent in the South, three per cent in other sections of the

United States and its territories, and less than one per cent in foreign countries.

Since 66 per cent of the families migrated to Levittown from New York City, it is possible that the area from which they came was far more homogeneous than that to which they moved. Religious and ethnic pockets of Irish or Italian or Jewish families are quite common in New York City. Although the aggregate composition of the Levittown population may not be too different from New York City, the distribution of the component elements is more equal.

One population factor that would make for heterogeneity is not present to any significant extent in Levittown; namely, the Negro. Levitt built for members of the "Caucasian" race; original contracts read, "No dwelling shall be used or occupied by members of other than the Caucasian race, but the employment and maintenance of other than Caucasian domestic servants shall be permitted." With some fuss and furor, the bar was broken as homes were resold, beyond the control of Levitt,[4] but there are only three known Negro families in Levitt homes at present. There are others, undoubtedly—some who have crossed the "line." And there is less than a handful of other non-Caucasians, such as Japanese and Chinese. These few families do not affect "community" beyond showing that co-existence is possible. Whether continued harmony would reign if the numbers increased is open to question.

Some might think that the youth of the community and the youthful families in it would be a sufficient welding influence, but the fact that "There were no precedents or customs, no status leaders, very few old people, and few established institutions"[5] compounded the problem. Not only were there no community leaders to prescribe decorum, no established institutions through which community could be fostered, but there were no communication lines through which diverse elements could exchange ideas.[6]

Since there were bound to be conflicts in the community, the establishment of a modus operandi for "problem solving" should have been a first order of business for the new residents. There was one abortive attempt by the major civic associations to form a civic council. The Levittown Self Survey represented a second attempt. Neither had a lasting influence on the residents.

Yet, in maturing, a certain amount of "community" has evolved.

Before moving on to a case study of conflict, a closer look at this "community" is necesssary.

When confronted with the survey question, "Do you consider yourself a resident of Levittown?", 76 per cent of the respondents answered affirmatively. The following factors were cited as reasons for negative answers: Post office address was not Levittown (14 per cent), Not in the Levittown school district (0.3 per cent), Do not have swimming pool privileges (0.3 per cent), House not built by Levitt (but within Levittown boundaries) (1.9 per cent), and other reasons (5.3 per cent). Less than two per cent did not reply or were uncertain. Certainly 22 per cent would seem to be a significant percentage of "nays," but against what standard should one measure? Is there any other established community so fractured by arbitrary boundaries?

Should one infer "community" from the "76 per cent" quoted above? Responses to a related question, "Regardless of your answer to the above question, do you consider yourself as having a community of interest with Levittown?" show that all "residents" are not "community" minded. To this question, the "yes" answers accounted for 70 per cent of the total answers and the "no's," 15 per cent. The drop of five per cent in the "community" category may have resulted from interpreting the second question to mean "interested in community affairs."

Some rapport with the community is suggested by the fact that the survey found that 94 per cent of the present residents would recommend the community to others. It was also discovered that 74 per cent of the families intended to stay in Levittown indefinitely (undefined) and only 10 per cent intended to remain less than three years. The most important reason for considering leaving the community turned out to be that the house was too small.

At the time of the Community Self Survey in February 1956, slightly more than one-half of the community had lived in Levittown five or more years. It was found, for example, that one-quarter of the original settlers (1947) has remained, as has one-fifth of the next wave (1948). The fact that a family has remained in Levittown does not imply complete satisfaction with the community.

Through the prompting medium of a survey questionnaire, Levittown residents were willing to imply that they faced many problems and that some vehicle for handling them was necessary. Almost 80 per cent (77.9) were willing to support a local nonpolitical community council, and slightly less than 70 per cent (68.9) indicated a willingness to work actively for community improvements.

It would be unfair to say that "community" and community improvement will have to wait for the establishment of a nonpolitical community council. Neighbors rub elbows in common cause in the more than 100 organizations currently operating in Levittown— a number sufficient to keep Levittown Hall and other meeting areas booked solidly throughout the year. The roots of these organizations tap interests in home ownership (witness the many civic associations), military service (the major veterans organizations have Levittown chapters), church affiliations (in addition to the numerous auxiliaries, some secular activities are church sponsored), political philosophy (major and minor political parties exist), and children (in addition to the exclusively adult activities, e.g., PTA's and Citizen Groups, there are many adult sponsored and managed children's activities, e.g., Little League Sports, Scouts, 4-H, and the like). The average Levittown family is involved in some organizational work in the community.

Despite the inroads made on the time of the average Levittown family by community organizations, house chores, commuting, and TV, it apparently has not given up the old-fashioned habit of reading. Three years after the first family moved into Levittown, the citizenry established the Levittown Public Library. From an initial stock of 3,000 volumes on opening day, June 30, 1951, the system has grown to 44,000 volumes and 3,000 phonograph records. (Circulation is now over 400,000.) In addition to the main location, there is a bookmobile which carries 3,000 books and covers 23 scheduled stops on a two-week schedule.

Apparently, the community appreciates the system, which costs them approximately $10. per home per year. Even in the period of international tension and book censoring, the Levittown Library was relatively free of controversy. Since the Library is financed through the school tax system, there have been isolated members of the community who would substitute the authority of the elected school board for the present authority of an elected independent library board. So far, the voters have preferred the independent board, which makes possible a more sophisticated and adult system.

One might draw the optimistic conclusion from the above that the core of the population (the 74 per cent that intends to remain in Levittown) is really imbued with "community." It is appropriate, therefore, to view the community in action; that is, look at one of its attempts at community problem solving. The case at hand is the Levittown school system.

The Levittown School Problem [7]

The problem may be stated simply and briefly. Levittown has had to create a school system which will have an estimated enrollment of approximately 23,000 by 1964-65. The problem is threefold. There was and still is an economic problem of financing the school expansion on the basis of an antiquated tax structure and inadequate base. There was and still is an educational problem of staffing the schools and building a curriculum for a new community which has not learned to live with itself. There was and still is the political problem of energizing the community to accept the responsibility of maintaining a public school system which will prepare young citizens for their future tasks. The data in Table 6 provide a basis for appreciating the magnitude of the financial problem.

Table 6—Selected School Statistics, Hempstead Union Free School District # 5, 1947-1963

School Year	Average Daily Attendance [a]	School Budget	Tax Rate Per $100. of Assessed Valuation
1947-8	35	$ 22,550	$0.73
1948-9	664	261,655	1.80
1949-50	1,549	570,202	1.80
1950-1	2,742	976,926	1.80
1951-2	5,076	2,051,715	2.40
1952-3	7,160	3,284,885	3.72
1953-4	9,085	3,822,015	2.91
1954-5	10,729	4,804,831	3.67
1955-6	12,201	5,904,720	4.65
1956-7	13,805	7,713,682	4.74
1957-8	14,839	9,249,665	6.06
1962-3 estimated	20,700	?	?

[a] Approximately 90 per cent of total enrollment.

Source: District Five School System.

It should be pointed out that the $6.06 tax rate for 1957-8 will not cover the full costs of schooling the 15,000 children. While public schooling in Nassau County is financed by local property taxation, grants-in-aid from New York State have become major sources of revenue for the fast-growing school districts. The State will contribute more than 40 per cent of the total District 5 School revenues in 1957-8. (Some districts receive federal government aid as the result of having children of U. S. military personnel enrolled in their schools.) But despite increases in State aid to growth districts such as Levittown, increasing sums have had to come from the local property tax.

The inadequacies of the local real property tax as a revenue source are well documented and will not be labored here. Levittown's reliance on the property tax, however, is complicated by the land-use pattern in the area. Since the community is almost exclusively residential, there is insufficient commercial and industrial property to share the burden. The land use pattern is shown in Table 7.

Table 7—Land Use in Hempstead Union Free School District #5, 1955

Use	Per Cent of Land
Apartments	0.1%
Other Residential	57.5
Business	2.8
Industrial	—
Recreational	3.2
Public	7.0
Vacant	5.6
Street	18.8
Parkway	4.9
Water	0.1
Total	100.0%

Source: Nassau County Planning Commission.

Since less than six per cent of the Levittown area remains vacant, the community must face the future with declining assessed valuations per child. In the face of a peak enrollment which is still some five years away, such a situation can only lead to frustration.

Neighboring communities have been more fortunate in this respect. Approximately 13 per cent of the total taxes paid in neighboring Hicksville are drawn from industrial properties, and in Carle Place, a short distance away, 23 per cent. Some communities have vacant land to which industry or commerce may still be attracted. It is clear that unless residential suburbs are high income communities, they cannot service their residents on the basis of a residential property tax alone.

The staffing problem is partly a financial problem, insofar as individual school districts vie with each other in the state and national personnel markets. The poorer districts do not compete well. But here, too, there are added problems. Without sound recruitment and promotional policies, there are bound to be problems which arise from promoting personnel too quickly, recruiting staff from relatively few sources, and so forth.

Curriculum problems are of particular importance, as citizens measure their children's school programs by their own experiences. Frustrations which emanate from financial matters tend to cause conflict in such areas as curriculum development. In Levittown, those favoring greater economy within the schools have also called for increased class size (currently averaging 30 pupils), limited curricula, limited school construction, limited school services, elimination of allegedly subversive curriculum materials, and the expansion of "spiritual" influences in the classroom. Those supporting school budgets and school building programs tended to line up on the opposite side of these issues, although they may have felt frustrated also by the financing problem.

Important decisions had to be made, and they were being made, although the bulk of the community was unprepared for the responsibility. The majority of the community came from New York City, where a board of education is appointed by the Mayor to administer the schools, and few citizens of New York City ever involve themselves in school policy matters. Consequently, citizen responsibility for schools was foreign to those coming from New York City.

Even at this late date, only a small fraction of the population attends public school board meetings and a hard-fought school board election or bond vote will induce only about 40 per cent of those eligible to vote. (This Levittown percentage, however, is much larger than that of other communities in the county.)

The local school board is an important and powerful body. In Levittown, the board currently makes educational policy within the framework of the New York State Education law, for 15,000 children at a cost of nine million dollars. Yet, the process by which one stands for election to this board is haphazard.

In the American tradition, the established political parties have stayed outside of this particular political arena. The Parent-Teachers organizations have remained more or less apolitical. The civic associations have been wont to split their memberships through partisan activity not directly related to property maintenance and improvements. Citizens' groups intimately concerned with educational practices have hesitated to involve themselves in the practical-political aspects of insuring the election of the candidates they favor.

As a result, would-be nominees with 25 or more signatures on a petition are able to run for this non-paying school board position. Any adult resident may seek the post. Organization and funds for campaigning continue to be handled in an *ad hoc* fashion.

Campaigns in the District appear to have been fought between those favoring a limited program of public education and those favoring a broad program. In the early days, some leadership for the former came from the active members of the pre-expansion residents. But growth of the new Levittown soon resulted in leadership drawn from the new community.

Although there are few persons in the community who would disagree overtly with the proposition that good schooling is a good investment for the family, community, and nation, Levittown has had to live with a school-centered controversy (Levittown claims to be a child-centered community) that tends to divide the community. Much worse is the tendency to view this cleavage, as much of the press does, as a religious cleavage, as Catholic versus Protestant and Jew. It is not difficult to view the problem in this way, since leadership and membership of the two camps may be superficially identified in this manner. Irresponsible spokesmen on both sides have done little to expunge this caricature, and individual churches of the major faiths have not been able to remain aloof.

Popular rationalizations of the "opposition's orientation" have compounded the problem. Partisan-non-Catholic-extremists tended to explain the Catholic's conservative position in terms of his interest in parochial schools and consequent disinterest in public schools; partisan-Catholic-extremists tend to view the opposition's position as irreligious, communist-oriented, and subversive. School board elections tended to be fought not in the free market place of ideas, but in the black market of rumors. Continued opposition to each other's position tended to polarize the two camps until each served as the other's "bete noir." The climax (but not the denouement) came in 1956-1957.

The School Board election in May 1956 resulted in a working majority for the "economy" camp. The new Board majority, unfortunately, took its election as a mandate to wage war on the School Administration. Much of what it did reflected a lack of familiarity with the fact that radical change cannot be legislated without arousing fear, confusion, and hate in a community.

In the autumn of 1956, responsible leadership throughout Levittown assembled as an interfaith group to explore the basis for relieving the tensions in the community and for devising an apparatus for handling the school's "religious" problems in the future. These people responded to the contention that religion was being used as a cloak by those who wished to exploit the school problem in order to prevent a rational approach to the real problems besetting the community. The interfaith group gradually pared itself to about 15 and met regularly, about every three weeks, from October to June. The final meetings were in sharp contrast to initial sessions when individuals came armed to the hilt with literature supporting their positions. Through a gradual process of an honest exchange of ideas and fears, suspicion was replaced by understanding and tolerance. A line of communications had been opened so that insecurities on both sides were out in the open.

This group was small and met without publicity. While the concrete proposals of the group, (1) the establishment of a religious advisory committee to the School Board, and (2) the establishment of an educational forum similar to the informal meetings held by the interfaith group, were never consummated, certain gains flowed from the meetings into the community.

For some, a record turnout for the School Board election and the budget vote, with the consequent election of a new school board majority and the passage of a record budget while communities around Levittown were moving in the opposite direction, was an important milestone. For a small group, and some of the group had supported losing candidates, the most important aspect of the election was that it was hard fought but on a "higher plane" than the preceding elections. Communications existed during the election campaign so that when "incidents" arose, an exchange of information was possible, and as a result, repetition of hasty actions was prevented and extremists were isolated on both sides.

On reflection, it is frightening to contemplate how close to chaos Levittown moved. If the school situation did in fact represent a religious war, then there would be little hope for Levittown. The truth of the matter is that the religious convictions turned out to be an important basis for understanding, once the more obvious trappings associated with the diverse backgrounds and training of the participants were cleared away. A similar concern for the individual, for the individual's right to pursue his own spiritual goals, for other's freedoms, lay beneath the surface. Once the insecurities were exposed, it was possible to forge a common bond in the interest of community.

Controversy has not been wiped out of Levittown; it is hoped, however, that the irrational and irresponsible elements which have intruded in the past will not be present in the future. It is too early to tell whether the latent discord based on diversity in Levittown will erupt in the future under the pressures of mounting school costs and general anxiety associated with international tensions. After ten years of rubbing some pretty sharp elbows, there is a sincere hope that some of the rough edges have been rubbed smooth.

Postscript

Levittown will be judged as a suburban development by the children it sends out into the world. The adults who emerge from Levittown childhoods will be more homogeneous in dress, speech, tastes, and education than the adults who now live in this ten-year-old community. Parents are aware of their responsibilities and may in their zealousness to do "the right thing" continue to clash with their neighbors. It will be easy to forget that one of the most enduring influences in their children's upbringing may be the examples of "peaceful problem solving" by a community. This lesson has not been learned fully as yet.

Is it really an apologia to maintain that if there are any cracks in the Levittown picture window, they cannot readily be laid at suburbia's doorstep? Are there not more powerful instruments at work? In rapping suburbia, aren't the critics really striking at the heart of the American culture? If there is a lack of planning in suburbia, is it not because we detest planning, especially governmental planning? If there is an overemphasis on the acquisition of goods, is it not because we take great pride in our productivity and like to exhibit its results? If we are restless and lack standards for much of what we do, is it not due to the mobility in our society, of which we are proud? If we place a low priority on education, isn't this a traditional pattern in American life? If we have antiquated political and economic structures for our public activities, isn't this the result of a national failure to reorient our lives in line with the harsh realities of a 21st century world?

The insecurities of suburban living are duplicated in both rural and urban living. Perhaps in this second half of the twentieth century, we will not be permitted the luxury of social introspection, the examination of the children of the post-World War II suburbias.

FOOTNOTES

1. Some 3,800 of these are found in the seven square mile Levittown area.
2. Those homes having a metered water supply have a significantly larger water bill.
3. The social scientist may be highly critical of contemporary communications media and industry product development, but these are national factors which affect rural, urban and suburban families.
4. William J. Levitt is quoted as saying, "The plain fact is that most whites prefer not to live in mixed communities. This attitude may be wrong morally, and some day it may change. I hope it will." Source: *Newsday* (a Long Island newspaper) October 2, 1957.
5. Citizens Committee for a Better Levittown, *Preliminary Report of Your Self Survey,* p. 1.
6. Only 19 per cent of the community relies on local papers (the most complete news) for news of the community, while 33 percent relies on the regional papers (less complete). Neither really serves as a forum.
7. This is a case study of the Union Free School District #5 of Hempstead Township, the district covering the bulk of the Levitt homes. Some Levitt homes have been incorporated into other long established school districts, and to some extent their problems are different.
8. The author wishes to acknowledge the following sources of information included in this paper: 1. District Five School System, *Miscellaneous Publications;* 2. Citizens Committee For a Better Levittown, *A Preliminary Report of Your Self Survey,* Levittown, New York, 1956; 3. Levittown Property Owners Association, *Our Levittown,* no date or publisher; 4. Nassau County Planning Commission, *Land Use, Levittown School District No. 5 Town of Hempstead,* Mineola, New York: February, 1957; 5. The New York State

Citizens Committee For The Public Schools, Inc., *The Case History of the District 5 Education Association, Levittown,* New York. Mimeograph Nov. 1954; and 6. The following newspapers: *New York World-Telegram and Sun, New York Times, Newsday, Long Island Daily Press, Levittown Tribune.*

Part V

Some Suburban Problems

But the question, to what end the wheels revolve, still remains; and on that question the naïve and uncritical worship of economic power, which is the mood of unreason too often engendered in those whom that new Leviathan has hypnotized by its spell, throws no light. Its result is not seldom a world in which men command a mechanism that they cannot fully use, and an organization which has every perfection except that of motion.

                                                    R. H. Tawney

Benjamin Fine

Yeshiva University

EDUCATIONAL PROBLEMS IN THE SUBURBS

Like a nagging child, school problems follow the parents. Part of the problems of urban regions—and a large part—developed from the natural urge of parents to give their children good educations. They sought out the suburban schools for their less crowded classes, more playground space, more flexibility in teaching, added personal attentions to the children and closer parent-teacher relationships. Now parents are discovering that they have traded old problems for new ones. The effects of mass housing have been felt most heavily by the suburban schools. The new families are being faced again with crowded buildings, teacher shortages and mounting school taxes.

Perhaps the city dwellers expected too much. Many had no alternative but to move to the suburbs, or else send their children to private schools. High tuition fees, however, make the private schools almost prohibitive for the average middle-class family with three or four children.

This is a problem for the individual family. For the nation there is a school problem, too, as evidenced by the program put forward by President Eisenhower.

He proposed that the Federal Government grant $1,300,000,000 during the next four years for school construction and provide $750,000,000 more to buy local school bonds. To receive the grants, the states or local communities would have to put up matching funds.

Reprinted from the Wednesday, January 30th, 1957, issue of *The New York Times,* by permission of *The New York Times.*

The proposal involving school bonds comes at a time when communities are encountering financial difficulties. The interest rates on bond issues have been rising, inflation has increased construction costs and the ability to tax in support of schools is reaching the saturation point.

Educators struggle against the financial squeeze knowing that the suburban schools will retain their attractiveness and that the mass movement from the city will not abate. The city schools are suffering from this exodus. They cannot afford to lose citizens whose financial support and leadership are important to public education.

Here are the deficiencies of urban schools:

¶ They are overcrowded. Many are on double or part-time sessions.

¶ Parents have little part in formulation of school policy. To give citizens a sense of greater participation, some cities have begun to decentralize their school administrations.

¶ The curriculum is geared to mass education rather than to the individual.

¶ The individual child is lost in the crowd. Larger communities find it difficult, if not impossible, to plan for the gifted or superior child.

¶ Teachers are unable, because of heavy working loads, to give proper guidance or assistance to children who need it most. In large cities teaching is frequently on a clock-like schedule. New York teachers, for example, have discontinued most extra-curricular activities. They insist they will continue this boycott until salary grievances are met. The children suffer as a result. In large cities the classes are usually larger than in suburban areas.

Suburban Advantages

Suburban schools have the following advantages:

¶ They are able to attract better teachers, since they pay higher salaries and give other teacher satisfactions.

¶ Buildings are newer, classrooms modern and up to date. Almost every suburb is engaged in a huge building program.

¶ More attention is paid to the individual child because of smaller classes.

¶ Standards are kept higher in the suburbs because as a rule there is a more homogeneous population. This is not discussed openly, but many parents leave the cities because of the growth of Negro, Puerto Rican or other "minority group" residents. The racial issue is strong in the minds of many New Yorkers.

¶ The economic level in the suburbs is usually higher. The suburbs spend more money on their public schools.

¶ Parents, through their Parent-Teachers Association and citizens' committees, take more active part in the day-to-day operation of the schools.

¶ New teaching practices and methods are introduced and evaluated. Suburban schools, being smaller, experiment more than do the city schools. Sometimes this proves to be a boomerang. On occasion the parents will kick up their heels at "progressive" methods, and force school programs to return to a more traditional pattern.

The advantages listed above unfortunately are leading to the suburban schools' own undoing. They have meant double sessions in many cases and strained the budgets to keep up with the need for facilities. Good teachers are hard to find. Suburban areas, to keep up their standards, must pay high for them. In some instances they have been forced to "pirate" them from neighboring towns.

To overcome these difficulties the following avenues are open to suburban school systems:

1. Consolidation. Two or more districts, sometimes as many as ten, unite to form one consolidated district. The independent systems disappear; their places are taken by one program, under one supervisory board.

Many suburban communities, however, resist any kind of coordinated program. Various reasons are advanced for this resistance. Local pride plays a part. Added to this is the fear of a community's losing control of its schools. If three or four districts vote to consolidate into one unit, one of them may have to pay higher taxes than might be necessary under the existing smaller district.

A consolidated program is not necessarily better than a small school district. However, there is a law of diminishing returns. If the district is not large enough to support a good high school, or if it spends an undue amount on supervision, consolidation might mean better and more efficient schools.

2. Centralization. A typical centralized school district combines two or more school districts to provide education from kindergarten through the twelfth grade. The centralized district is usually situated

in a community serving as a center for a surrounding trade area. New laws governing centralization of schools in New York State provide more favorable state financial aid to these districts.

In consolidation, the separate districts vote as independent units. A majority of each of the districts is required. But under centralization, a majority of the total votes in the combined districts is enough. Under centralization, the districts may retain their elementary schools through the first grade, if they existed prior to the amalgamation.

In a consolidated district, the new school district as a whole takes over the debt of the former constituent districts. On the other hand, in a newly formed central district, each of the old districts has to pay debts incurred previously. But the centralized district receives advantages in the form of additional state aid. It gets credit for up to 300 additional children a year to encourage centralization. This could amount, at $330 a child, to approximately $100,000 a year.

3. Going it alone. Most suburban areas, regardless of size, are willing to take a chance on school costs and on rising taxes. They believe they can do a better job by retaining personal control of their public schools.

Regardless of the size of the system, whether it is a coordinated or independent district, a rich or poor town, the major issue today is rising school costs.

Former city dwellers who never knew what it meant to pay direct school taxes now find themselves acutely tax conscious. They have seen the school tax, so earmarked, skyrocket on their modest home. They do not know how to avoid increasing school costs.

Another problem in many suburban areas involves controversy between old-time residents and newcomers. The "natives" object to higher school taxes and to the need for still heavier bond issues for schools. In some cases, the conflict hinges on the control of the school board, or the kind of school program to be taught.

School board elections sometimes are contests between the old and the new—with the new usually winning out. Unless the community puts up strict zoning laws and limits the number of new residents, the natives cannot stop the rush of city dwellers to their boundaries.

Suburban growth is found throughout the country, from Nassau County on Long Island, to the suburbs of Los Angeles. In large part, the problems are similar.

For example, the schools surrounding San Francisco have an edge

Table I—Examples of Growth in School Costs

The following table shows the comparative increases between 1945 and 1955 in population, school enrollment and school tax rates in typical suburban areas in the country:

	Population 1945	1955	Enrollment 1945	1955	School Tax Rates (Per $100) 1945	1955-56	Per Cent Increase
New York Suburbs:							
Carle Place, L. I.	1,220	10,400	174	2,600	$1.10	$4.16	278.2
Great Neck, L. I.	25,000	48,000	3,429	9,313	1.14	4.04	255.4
Rockville Center, L. I.	16,000	22,000	2,600	4,000	1.09	3.88	256.0
Levittown, L. I.	721	55,572	40	14,943	.73	4.24	480.8
White Plains	42,000	53,000	6,240	7,939	1.45	1.96	35.2
Tenafly, N. J.	8,000	13,000	1,789	2,820	1.86	4.56	145.2
Westport, Conn.	8,670	16,776	1,500	3,731	1.80	2.50	38.9
Boston Suburbs:							
Newton	77,257	86,535	11,194	14,679	.91	1.73	90.1
Dedham	16,659	21,450	2,626	3,540	1.31	2.02	54.2
Cleveland Suburbs:							
Parma Heights	1,330 *	22,000	3,153	10,078	.93	1.79	92.5
Garfield Heights	16,989 *	41,000	2,017	4,007	1.67	2.09	25.1
Michigan Suburban: School Districts							
Lakeview	13,053	38,500	767	2,208	.91	1.90	108.8
Inkster	9,474	30,600	1,308	3,925	1.10	1.80	63.6
Maryland-Virginia:							
Arlington Co., Va.	57,040 *	163,000	10,825	21,318	1.20	2.01	67.5
Prince George Co., Md. .	89,490 *	289,000	21,915	49,397	1.55	2.15	38.7
Denver Suburbs:							
Jefferson Co.	35,079	90,000	6,378	16,869	2.05	3.47	69.3
Aurora	4,200	30,000	750	6,133	2.59	2.19	—15.4 †
Los Angeles Suburbs:							
Beverly Hills	26,823 *	31,132	2,963	4,100	1.20	1.35	.12.5
Pasadena	81,864 *	117,564	21,465	29,157	2.04	2.70	32.4

* 1940 figures; 1945 not available.

† Decrease indicated is not actual tax reduction. All assessments were raised 100 per cent four years ago. Thus, present tax of $2.19 is actually $4.38 in terms of 1945 tax base, a 68 per cent increase.

on the city in quality of instruction, curriculum and teachers. The teacher shortage is severe in the entire state.

California will need 17,000 new teachers each year for the next ten years to meet current demands. Less than half that number will be graduated from the teacher training institutions in the state. Ten years from now California's schools will enroll 1,500,000 more than they do today.

To provide classrooms for such enrollment, California must build a twelve-room schoolhouse every day for the next decade.

In any metropolitan area taken at random, the city schools are deteriorating, the suburban areas improving. For example, while Cleveland is struggling to hold its school level high, the thirty-one suburban school districts of Cuyahoga County, of which Cleveland is the county seat, are flourishing. These suburban areas have the advantage of younger, more vigorous teachers who are willing to experiment.

Actually, though, it is not fair to throw all suburban school systems together under one general heading. They can be classified into different categories, depending upon their closeness to the city, the attitude toward large-scale housing developments, and their potential wealth.

Suburban School Systems

These three types of suburban school systems are found on the outskirts of New York and other large cities:

The mushroom developments, brought about by mass housing projects. A small village suddenly finds that it has grown from five to ten times in the space of five years. Hundreds of low cost houses appear overnight. Levittown, on Long Island, is a perfect example. Schools cannot keep up with the mass influx.

A second type is found in suburbs that try to limit new residents. These are the staid, settled communities. They will admit city-dwellers, but their zoning laws and other regulations keep control of the town in the hands of older residents.

Here the schools are usually of the traditional pattern. They are somewhat better than the overcrowded city schools, but not as good as the new residents would like them to be. In these communities, an ever-continuing struggle for school power usually is waged between the old and the new.

Third—the substantial middle class suburban communities, within commuting distance of metropolitan areas. In these communities, the new residents already have gained, or are about to gain, control of the school system. Usually the school program is superior to that found in the city. The teachers are well-paid and well-trained, the new buildings are of modern design and the classes are small.

L. I. Community Is Typical

A typical example of the well-planned suburban school system can be found at Carle Place, a small community on Long Island, twenty miles from New York City. Nestled between Garden City and Westbury, this town of 10,000 has shot up in almost no time. Ten years ago, not more than 1,000 residents lived in what was then known as "Frog's Hollow."

School enrollment has jumped from 174 to 2,600 in ten years. The tax rate has gone from $9.20 to $41.60 for each $1,000 of assessed valuation, a 278 per cent increase. But the residents do not complain. They say they are willing to pay for a good school system, and they are getting it.

The district principal, Clifford L. Rall, a cheerful, hard-working educator, is proud of the school program. He places great store on good teachers and has sought as far as the Midwest to get his faculty.

He has had to pay for them, however. Teachers now get from $4,000 to $8,000 a year—the salary range of New York City teachers. Ten years ago the top salary for a classroom teacher in Carle Place was $2,200.

The school buildings are modern, having been built within the last five years. One old structure remains, and is in part time use. The difference between the antiquated, pot-bellied stove room and the modern, ranch-type million-dollar school next door is startling.

The curriculum is modern, too. The emphasis is on basic reading, writing and arithmetic, plus all the extras that make for a sound education in an atomic age. The children, as well as their parents, seemingly are happy here.

The high school has a physics and chemistry laboratory that would be the pride of many a college. The results are evident— 25 per cent of the seniors take physics and 60 per cent of the students take chemistry. Pupils are permitted to work at their own pace. Small classes make that possible.

"I didn't care much for school before," explained Stanley Schechter, 16 years old. His family moved here two months ago from Manhattan. Stanley had attended Seward Park High School, in the lower East Side.

"For the first time, I really want to learn," he said. "I'm planning to go to college. I hadn't thought of it until we moved here."

In Rockville Centre, for example, 83 per cent of last June's graduates entered college. In Long Beach, the percentage ranged around 80. Scarsdale, in Westchester County, reports that 95 per cent of its graduates seek out colleges. Bronxville would go about that high, too.

What does this mean to the parents in the suburbs? The schools have become college-oriented. With this overwhelming number preparing for college, the school curriculum is lopsided. The schools are not prepared to give both a vocational and a college course. As a result, the 20 to 40 per cent who do not go to college are not adequately provided for.

A year ago a vocational survey was made in Nassau County to determine at first hand what suburban schools offered in vocational or technical training. Directed by Charles R. Wallendorf, the study included employers as well as high school youth. The two-volume report has been edited by Dr. Vivienne Anderson of the State Education Department.

Throughout Nassau County, only 777 high school students out of 25,052, are enrolled in vocational programs, even though more than 5,000 said they wanted such courses. Only at Sewanhaka, Lawrence, Lynbrook, Mineola and Roslyn high schools is there any attempt to offer vocational or technical work. Even here, it is on a limited scale.

Education, it would seem, is not geared to the demands of industry. Whether on a basis of providing a schooling for the 40 per cent who do not go to college, or on a basis of providing for a much-needed labor pool, the suburban schools are not doing the job many parents want them to do.

The Nassau survey, as Dr. Anderson notes, shows that employers in the rapidly expanding industries of that county are seeking young workers with specialized training. Employers believe that present shortcomings in employes' skills would be largely overcome if schools provided well-equipped shops and laboratories that simulated actual working conditions in industry.

The short supply of local youth with specialized training is forcing Nassau business and industry to recruit workers from outside areas. What is true at Nassau county is true elsewhere in the suburbs.

The reasons are apparent: when the suburbs began to be filled, the average newcomers were fairly well off economically. They sought out better schools, and hoped their children would enter good colleges. They did not want vocational or technical training. As a result, almost all school buildings that have gone up in the suburbs in the last few years are college-centered; little attention is paid to the vocational program.

But the movement to the suburbs has gone beyond the upper middle classes. Now many families in the medium and lower income brackets are coming to the suburbs. They are not convinced that their sons or daughters will go to college. The large cities, whence they came, did have vocational or technical high schools. But now they find their children will get a limited education as far as learning a trade or skill is concerned.

State to Add School

As in Nassau, other suburban areas are beginning to re-examine their schools. It will take time, but undoubtedly, as industry spreads toward the suburbs, the schools will help to fill the need for sub-professional and sub-technical employment.

The call for community colleges is one answer. New York State is planning to build these two-year institutions of higher learning. The Board of Regents has proposed $100,000,000 for ten such colleges. They would be spread throughout the state, but at least three would go to the suburban areas of Long Island. Others would be built in the suburbs of Westchester or upstate New York.

The community colleges would offer courses for high school graduates who do not want to go to a traditional college, but who need more education than the high school has offered them. The community colleges offer girls the choice of many secretarial jobs; the boys would receive training in scores of sub-professional areas.

By this time it is apparent that the full costs of the schools cannot be borne solely by the suburban communities. State and, if possible, Federal assistance will be essential if the tremendous demands on suburban school systems are to be met successfully.

Charles E. Stonier

Hofstra College

PROBLEMS OF SUBURBAN
TRANSPORT SERVICES

The suburban belts surrounding central cities have been the situs for the largest amount of economic expansion in the postwar era. This has been true of virtually every major city in the U. S. as it has in many other parts of the world. This development, which had been slowed during World War II, is not altogether new. The growth of cities generally followed a pattern of extending outward from a given nucleus, with tentacles along major transport arteries becoming more intensely suburbanized than the areas in between these arteries. In each instance this growth has been largely influenced by the state of technology and availability of different means of transport. Some of the major differences between the existing surburbanization and earlier forms of urban growth are discussed elsewhere in this book.

That the nature and rate of economic development is largely dependent on available transport resources is, of course, axiomatic. The suburbs of today again are most illustrative of this principle. Transport creates place utility—to the extent that goods are moved from locations where they would produce less want satisfaction, to others, where they gain in value; simultaneously, transport increases the value of land which is made more accessible. The structure of the suburb today and its problems are greatly influenced by the role and efficacy of existing transport facilities. Place utility, especially in connection with suburbia, represents an economic as well as a

This is an original article, prepared for this volume.

social function. Along with a change in the locale of economic activity, transport service improvements, particularly the greater use and dependence on automobiles, have facilitated changes in non-economic opportunities associated with suburban living conditions. For example, suburban dwellers have available a wider choice of outdoor recreational activities than do their urban counterparts.

Historic Role of Transportation

Prior to mechanized transportation, the choice of living quarters was limited to a few miles from one's place of work, a distance which could be traversed on foot or by horse and carriage. The modern concept of suburb as a place of residence goes back to the point when railroad made a journey between house and office practical. As a matter of fact, it was largely as a result of promotion by the railroads and later by interurban trolley car lines that impetus to suburban development was given. The railroads—now perhaps much to their regret, as their suburban passenger services are operated at a substantial loss—offered at first package tickets and later the more familiar types of commuter tickets which were sold at substantial reductions from regular one-way coach fares. Promotion of this type was especially prevalent in New England in the eighteen seventies and eighties. For example, the Old Colony Railroad offered a free pass from Boston to Williston for each house erected there. This promotion took place on the theory that it would create new passenger and freight traffic, and until competing transport agencies became more important, the suburban railroad business was fairly lucrative.

As suburban residential development took place at first along railroad lines, it was usually limited to a two-mile radius from the station. This radial pattern was in large measure predetermined by existing railroads whose primary purpose was to connect major cities. In other words, suburbs first grew along trunk lines. As building sites for such towns and villages as were adjacent to the trunk lines became exhausted, suburban branch lines were built to tap undeveloped sections. These branch lines generally did not alter the radial pattern, they merely intensified it by adding new spokes. Subsequently, the interurban railroad, really a suburban trolley car operation, was the chief instrument of such intensification. The building of interurban electric lines got under way primarily after the turn of the century and reached its peak in the mid-twenties. Today all but a few have been abandoned as the more practical forms of highway transport have taken their place.

Speed of service has, of course, a bearing upon suburban growth as well. As the downtown central business district could be brought closer to the suburbs (or vice versa), due to reduced transit time, the spread of suburbs further outward was made possible. It should be noted, however, that speeds of suburban railroad services have not changed substantially in virtually one-half of a century. Time tables of a 50 year vintage will reveal that trains at that time were capable of the same speeds as today's.

A third form of rail operation consists of municipal rapid transit lines some of which date back to 1888. They too were largely responsible for the growth of suburbs as their branches were extended from the central city core. Extension of subways today still plays a vital role in urbanization. As a mass transport agency it promotes vertical growth such as apartment house building, where horizontal development is no longer possible.

Thus railroads in the form of suburban trunk lines, interurban trolley services and rapid transit, were instrumental in determining the pattern of metropolitan growth. They played little or no part in inter-suburban services, an issue which is still of major importance today. This is contrary to experience with European subway systems where "ring" or "belt" lines fill the need for developing a community of interest among several areas, not just between the central city core and a suburb (e.g. London, Berlin, Hamburg).

The role of highways prior to the twenties was altogether secondary. It may be noted that inter-connection of major cities by post roads antedates railroad building. With the advent of the latter, which often followed existing routes because they already contained numerous trading posts and therefore potential traffic centers, the highway system went into an eclipse. As suburbs became more important in forming their own villages and towns, local cartage requirements had to be met by improving the roads for immediate village needs. The "bicycle era" of the latter decades of the nineteenth century cannot be overlooked as a factor in highway improvements. At this time attention was being paid to bettering roads leading out of the city, so that the suburbs in effect were among the first to benefit from the "Good Roads" movement prevailing at the time.

But it is not until World War I, when the automobile had become fully accepted as a mode of transportation, rather than just as a sport, and when the federal government became active in road construction on a major scale, that suburban growth became less dependent upon the radial transport lines. For the increasing mobility of auto, bus and truck made it possible to "urbanize" large tracts of land which were still essentially rural and which lay between the prevailing transport routes by rail. This progress was held in check only during depression years when there was little demand for new homes, while auto registrations also marked time. But with the large amount of savings accumulated after World War II, it took virtually ten years of expansion to bring supply of new homes in line with demand. These new homes together with commercial establishments occupied land located predominantly within a twenty or twenty-five mile radius from the center of a large metropolis. There were no longer any restrictions of access because of lack of transport.

The result has been that most of our major cities represent a spider web transport network wherein the major arteries have become the spokes, often dual spokes made up of both a rail and a highway artery, while the webbing consists of roads only. The core of the city remains, and so does an increasing demand for transport between the central city and suburban areas. There are few cities which do not conform to this pattern. Los Angeles is a notable exception. Its principal growth has come during the period when the automobile was the primary transport factor in urban expansion, with the result that this city does not have a single identifiable major core. The demand for transport services is therefore more diversified, i.e., it does not consist of a predominantly radial flow. It may be concluded that if cities had grown under conditions that would make for the degree of mobility now possible, their shape would have been much different and perhaps much more efficient in terms of movement of goods and people, than what is now possible in most of our major cities.

The role of aviation in suburban development has not properly begun. Commercial air service within the metropolitan locale is, in terms of numbers of passengers or freight tons, negligible. Where it does exist, helicopter services connect existing airfields and the central city. There is little reason to believe that helicopters will play more than an incidental role in the mass movement of freight and passengers in intra-metropolitan travel for another decade or two, although some increased participation may be anticipated shortly.

Private flying (helicopter or otherwise) makes it possible for persons to reside large distances away from their place of business. The earlier type of suburban estate—once reached by private limousine, but now too costly to maintain—may once again become popular and set the basis for a new suburban fringe. This may eventually parallel the impact of the automobile as private flying comes within the reach of a larger number of families.

Mobility Requirements

Today, suburban living is virtually impossible without the convenience of the automobile. The auto today is used for shopping, education, entertainment and other services, thereby supplementing public transport and pedestrian traffic. Places of business and recreational centers in the suburbs are and must be geared to the demands of auto traffic, or else they become useless. Correspondingly, numerous new institutions have become commonplace because of the shift in transport habits. These include shopping centers, drive-in banks, theatres, and lately churches. In some cases this has brought upheavals to the traditional village merchants whose shops sufficed when suburbs were essentially railroad-commuter oriented, and when most downtown areas were within walking distances. Today many of these merchants are hard-pressed in their old locales because traffic conditions make them inconvenient in comparison with newer, more accessible stores.

While some of the planning has adapted itself to the demands of suburban motordom, there is much that is left to be desired. For example, several suburban communities have been forced to look toward the attraction of non-residential land users, especially industry, in order to develop new and less costly sources of tax revenues so that growing municipal needs may be met. This makes it important for communities desiring such influx to stress their merits and improve disadvantages. Among the latter often are found inadequate transportation services. Frequently public passenger transport in the suburbs is generally not adequate in terms of seating capacity, routes and frequency of service. Access by private auto during rush-hours is becoming more and more difficult, while at the same time companies must lay out a substantial investment in parking lots for their employees. The typical cost per parking space in suburban sectors including surfacing and drainage is close to $1,000.* Light industry, the kind desired by suburban communities, typically must use truck transportation, especially for outbound shipments. In the absence of limited access highways, this often entails delays and adds to the cost of haulage. Unfortunately, the transport disadvantage is becoming progressively worse as new construction and other highway improvements cannot keep pace with road use demands. Thus transport may be becoming an increasingly more significant factor in limiting industrial development in suburban and rural-urban fringe areas.

Access by rail may be easier to obtain as it is common to "down zone" (an unfortunate misnomer) for industrial land use along existing railway right-of-way. However, railroad service is likely to be expensive. Typical suburban shippers require short haul delivery service within an area where real estate taxes are likely to be high, and with freight being brought to the plant with little promise of a return load—as products of light industry are hauled more economically by truck. Consequently, railroads have no choice but to establish high rates.

The influx of industry into the suburbs for the purpose of economic diversification and of increasing the local tax base requires careful scrutiny. Under certain conditions the desired results may not materialize, such as when the industry involved must bring in its own labor supply, adding to the population pressure and its consequences rather than balancing the economy. Furthermore, while it has been generally held that industry's contribution to the local tax burden is considerably larger than its cost, there is one category where this may not be true at all. This occurs when industry requires heavy trucking for in and outbound shipments of freight, and when these trucks in reaching the plant must traverse roads financed primarily by the local community, and which may not have been designed for heavy road use in the first place. This is quite often the case as suburban roads generally have not needed to be surfaced for anything more than light trucking. Under these conditions, local taxes have to meet the industry's transport requirements. To get maximum benefits,

* In some instances expansion is blocked because of the diseconomies of providing necessary additional parking space.

therefore, from this type of industry, it is best to locate it along state and federal government supported highways whose construction is more suitable for heavier road use.

Transportation Costs

The principal transport problem connected with suburban development can be summed up in one word: congestion. It is estimated, for example, that 40 per cent of the nation's highway traffic moves along one per cent of the available surfaced roads. Congestion includes not only the stagnation of traffic flow along streets and highways—caused primarily by a shortage of thoroughfare and parking facilities—but it is also common, especially during rush-hours, among railroads and subways. Lately too, it has become prevalent on auxiliary means of conveyance such as escalators and elevators.

It is paradoxical that the automobile has provided the flexibility of movement which made suburban growth possible along the patterns described above, while at the same time it has impaired mobility as suburbs mature. The rate of population growth in the urban fringe is outstripped by the rate of increase in vehicle registrations. An estimated 93 per cent of all suburban families drive at least one automobile, while 15 per cent drive two or more. The chief demand for auto traffic is for "rush-hour" transport between suburb and the central city of the metropolitan complex, which means that the problem is aggravated by the desire to use transport facilities all at one time. A similar congested period is found over weekends and holidays when Friday outbound and Sunday evening city-bound bumper-to-bumper traffic has become an American ubiquity.

The evanescence of transport services is its primary weakness. This results in a cost of metropolitan traffic which defies accurate estimation. It can be assumed to be a large one by considering merely some of the more obvious costs. These include: depreciation and automobile insurance, including liability and collision, high rate of property damage (death rate is lower than on "open" highways) and inefficient gasoline consumption; man hours wasted in transit, together with frequent delays and consequent tardiness in reporting for work; the cost of furnishing more highways and widening existing ones. This particular cost rises as less and less land becomes available for road use. To expand from a four to a six lane road in built-up regions is less expensive than to make a six lane road into an eight lane thoroughfare, as the latter may require the demolition of buildings. Approximating more land for road use often means taking it off the local tax rolls, a measure which few suburban communities can afford. Business may lose income during periods of construction or when traffic regulations (e.g. one-way streets, off street parking requirements, etc.) result in their locations being made less accessible. Along with expanded highways go the higher costs of administration and regulation of law enforcement. Some municipal highway departments cannot afford salaries to attract top civil engineering talent, for example, so that construction may actually not be the most efficient for each given situation.

Another cost of the metropolitan transport problem which defies measurement may be considered institutional. Lack of coordinated administrative planning, made difficult or impossible by the multitude of political jurisdictions, counties, villages, towns, boroughs, special districts, etc., may well add another sizable, although less obvious burden to the costs of traffic. Poor use of existing transport routes also contributes to this deficit as many rail links are idle while traffic over highways barely can move. All of this is without considering any direct human costs, such as wear and tear on drivers, damage caused by inhaling of auto exhaust fumes, etc.

The high cost of intrametropolitan rush-hour transportation is reflected in typical commuter railroad costs. There are many costs categories which are unique to this type of service, but applicable also to other urban and suburban transport agencies. First of all they include costs of excess capacity, for the transport plant must be large enough to handle peak loads. Since rush-hour periods covering literally 4 hours or 17 per cent of each twenty-four hour weekday period must accommodate from 40 to 50 per cent of the daily travel requirements, total capacity must be at least two to three times as large than what would be necessary if the traffic flow were spread evenly in both directions throughout day and night. If the latter case prevailed, the possible savings in fixed facilities, rolling stock and manpower,* become obvious. The poor utilization or load factor (e.g. revenue seats to available seats) is accentuated by the uneven traffic density over metropolitan routes. Traffic thins out as it

---

* Especially when train or bus crews are not permitted to work split shifts without overtime compensation.

progresses from the central city core toward the suburbs. Trains or buses, even during rush-hours, must operate much empty seat mileage in outlying portions of their routes. Private automobiles too, notwithstanding an increasing popularity of "car pools," provide much empty seat mileage as the *majority of cars* during rush-hours are occupied by only the driver. Another factor influencing utilization is the unidirectional flow of traffic during rush-hours. This, however, is beginning to show some change as the suburbs are becoming increasingly more important as centers of employment.* For the most part, there remains much necessary back-hauling which involves the production of unused transport service (i.e., seat-miles).

The railroads have additional problems because of an extra heavy tax load they must often bear as their lines traverse high valued lands within suburban and urban locations. The result had been the assumption of rapid transit operations by public agencies everywhere, except in Philadelphia, where the city owns the tunnels and leases them to the operator. The suburban railroad survives by virtue of subsidies from other railway operations and because of refusal to permit abandonment by regulatory agencies. For the railroads there remains every incentive to abandon or at least curtail communication services, as evidenced by many applications of this type in recent years.

In the meantime, the shift from rail to rubber can be construed to represent an expanding misallocation of resources. In the first place, rail rapid transit is much more adaptable to mass transport requirements in comparison with the private automobile or even the bus. For it is possible to move 40,000 seated passengers ** per track per hour under up-to-date conditions, while only $\frac{1}{10}$th or less can be expected to move by car per lane of highway. This means that to equal the passenger per hour capacity of railroads, ten lanes in one direction must be made available. This is, of course, generally impossible.

* For example, when the third tube of the Port of New York Authority's Lincoln tunnel was planned, it was intended to open it to eastbound (New York bound) traffic only during incoming rush-hours and operate it westbound only in the evenings. Already prior to its opening in 1957, such an arrangement would have been unwise, as traffic was equally heavy in both directions during the conventional rush-hour periods.

** Other estimates are as high as 55,000; see Norton, Henry K., "Is Monorail the Answer?", Mass Transportation, Jan. 1957. The New York Subway moves 132,000 per hour per track including standees.

Traffic densities for road travel follow the same patterns as rail within central city and suburban areas. This means that in order to assure a continuous flow of traffic, capacities must increase in the direction of the central city core, while they can afford to be decreased in the opposite direction. Unfortunately, the contrary is often true. For the feasibility of road construction is such that it is easier to furnish super-highways where there is relatively less built-up land. Consequently there is a tendency for road capacity to decrease at locations where it ought to be the largest. Where attempts have been made to correct this, by bringing freeways or other limited access roads directly into downtown, it was possible to do this only at extraordinary costs. It should be pointed out, however, that dispersal of traffic within downtown areas decreases the necessity of multiple lanes into the heart of the city. The greater the area of business, entertainment, shopping and other primary downtown functions, the smaller the need for a through highway to reach one central location. In this respect highway use has some advantage over railroad, where the latter is brought into one terminal point and which may no longer be located strategically for maximum convenience of passengers. This has happened where the core area has shifted (such as in mid-Manhattan) while railroad terminal areas have had to be maintained in their increasingly obsolescent locations. If patrons have to change to bus or subway after completing their journey by railroad, as is frequently the case, then there exists a major deterrent to railroad patronage. On the other hand, when suburban passengers can reach a variety of destinations in the central city core *directly,* much larger railroad use may be expected. This is not now the case, and it may account for the increasing popularity of a combination ride, automobile-and-rapid-transit or subway, or automobile-and-bus, where both of these types of public carriers offer a much greater variety of stop-off points within the city.

Pricing of Transport Service

Mention was made of misallocation of resources. Our economy relies upon market forces to bring about the greatest possible want satisfaction in relation to available resources and skills. While it is well-known that this principle operates in practice only imperfectly, perhaps there is no other circumstance where its performance is as subverted as in connection with metropolitan transportation. This is due in part to the difficulty in ascertaining to what extent pricing of transport services reflect the true cost of each. In the absence of this knowledge, existing prices cannot reflect true market conditions, and traffic therefore may be channelled from more to less efficient agencies. Examining the supply factor a little further we find that unit costs of public carrier services are highest during peak-rush-hour periods while rates tend to be lower. Per-mile commutation fares, or where tokens are offered at a discount for multiple trips, are lower than one-way fares, sometimes less than one-half of the latter. Such a pricing scheme is not conducive to efficient use of facilities and is contrary to accepted utility pricing principles. Electric power companies, telephone services, theatres, etc. normally charge higher rates for peak usage than for off-peak service, at which time incentive rates are offered in order to take advantage of available capacity. This system of discriminatory pricing results in larger utilization thereby reducing units costs and lowering the rate level as a whole. It is justified on this ground, and also because the peak user is held to be responsible for the investment necessary to accommodate peak loads.

It is true that transit companies, including suburban railroads, offer special off-peak, i.e. shopping or theatre fares at reduced rates; but this is still the exception, rather than the rule, and often the reduced fare may still be higher than the commutation fare. Urban rapid and surface transit lines usually offer a flat or zone fare which has the primary advantage of simple administration and collection which may outweigh that of a system involving separate rates for peak and off-peak travel. But it may well be that this anomalous price structure is one of the chief reasons for the financial failure of rapid transit lines which have been taken over by public bodies, and suburban railroad services which are subsidized by other railroad operations. This situation has been permitted to continue, partly for historical reasons, when commutation fares were set on the basis of encouraging suburban settlements, and partly because these lower fares were maintained on the principle of quantity discounts which normally reflect lower unit costs. This latter condition, however, was actually never true as long as regularity or persistence of ridership took place during peak periods at which time unit costs actually rise rather than fall. Meanwhile regulatory agencies have been reluctant to bring about major changes in the suburban rate structure for fear that it may have an upsetting influence, not only on the traffic pattern, but also on the process of land development. Furthermore, where the railroad's commutation business represented merely a small fraction of its total revenues, these regulatory agencies would tend to condone the principle that every service offered by a railroad need not be lucrative as long as out of pocket costs were being met.

This introduces another argument into the cost price relationship of railroad fares. What costs, other than those *directly* assignable to suburban service, should be included when facilities are being used jointly by several classes of service? While there are formulas in existence to facilitate the maintenance of accounting records, they are at best arbitrary and not helpful in estimating the true costs of suburban service. The most important element, however, of railroad costs at this point is the fact that the directly assignable unit costs vary with the time that the service is being offered. Yet rates have been established which ignore this variation. It may be surmised that the peak hour users of this service, who are responsible for the size of the suburban plant, do not pay fully for its cost while others overpay. Operating costs may be covered by virtue of the fact that service is performed with fully depreciated equipment, right-of-way, yards and stations. Railroad modernization of the latter is quite exceptional and comes about primarily when a carrier is ordered to improve its service by State Public Service Commissions tied to the granting of a rate increase.

At the present time, it is in the interest of the railroad to *discourage* commuter service, for every rate increase which drives passengers away, there is not only a rise in revenues, but also a savings in operating costs. By the same reasoning railroads by taking on more rush-hour patronage tend to increase their deficits, so that there is no incentive to make suburban service more attractive to passengers, unless a fare structure is adopted which reflects more fully the costs of each, peak and off-peak service.

When proceeding to an examination of highway costs, their determination in terms of how they are paid for and who are the beneficiaries is even more complex. First of all, each major metropolitan area contains highways which are financed in part by federal, by state and by local governments. The bulk of funds for highway construction at the federal and state level come from highway user taxes, while local revenue sources are made up essentially of the property tax. Furthermore, in several of the major cities in the U. S., special state or interstate authorities collect tolls from bridges, tunnels or otherwise. These funds may or may not be used for highway purposes. The Port of New York Authority, for example, derives revenues from several vehicular installations, and some of these may subsequently be applied to the development of aviation or marine facilities.

The metropolitan suburban automobilist generally uses all categories of highways with a large proportion of his driving taking place on city or otherwise locally financed streets. Under these circumstances, it is impossible to determine how much the motorist contributes to each and how much benefit he receives. It may be assumed that, to the extent that he uses primarily local roads and streets, he is overpaying for state and federal roads from which he gets little or no direct benefits, while at the same time he may not be contributing as a motorist, to the local thoroughfares.

The task of ascertaining costs and benefits becomes even more complicated when vehicular traffic is broken down into classes of users, i.e. private and commercial. Furthermore, highway user taxes in some states are entirely earmarked for highway purposes, while in other states they may be diverted to other uses. Conversely, there may be some phases of highway services which are financed from sources other than highway user taxes.

In order to get an accurate picture of the highway cost/service relationship, it is necessary to know: (1) the detailed driving habits of private automobile traffic, (2) the flow of commercial traffic, (3) the relative amount of wear and tear (a most controversial subject) due to each class of user and due to the weather, (4) the sources of funds which go into road improvements (sometimes difficult to determine when such improvements are combined with other projects) and (5) the amount of highway benefits allowable to the various classes of users, i.e., "thoroughfare use" and to those who benefit primarily from "access use" such as adjoining business and other properties. It is impossible, therefore, to measure those variables sufficiently to be able to conclude that the use of passenger vehicles in suburban areas is wholly supported by assessments against them or that motorists receive more or less in service than what is contributed by them. It is known, however, that user taxes collected by the state are generally not returned in toto to metropolitan areas where traffic deficiencies are greatest, and where there is the bulk of auto registrations. Thus the cost benefit relationship of highway transport is quantitatively indeterminate and lies wholly outside of the conventional market process.

Comparing highway and railroad transport reveals an important distinction which tends to encourage travel habits by motor vehicle at the expense of other means. The highway plant is publicly financed, with low interest rate (and often tax exempt) public bonds and with taxation. This reduces capital costs considerably in comparison with those of private enterprise. Furthermore, the railroads are subject to property, franchise and other special taxes which do not apply to highway transportation. This is of special significance in metropolitan sectors where property taxes are high and increasing in the direction of the central city core. Thus railroad right-of-way, terminals and other fixed properties (even though not all of these are devoted exclusively to suburban services) usually bear heavy tax burdens which give the service an entirely different cost base than highway users. This problem becomes especially significant when, for example, station improvements result in higher assessments, so that carriers are better off by making do with existing facilities. This has been a factor in the failure to modernize suburban stations.

The differing cost base between highway and railroad carriers, as well as the anomalous pricing structure, one sanctioned by the regulatory commission, leave traditional market forces inoperative. There appears to be no rational relationship between price and supply.

On the demand side the choice of transport service is, of course, not always guided by totally rational considerations. In this respect demand does not differ from that for other goods and services. There are, however, factors which make it more difficult for consumers to appraise their preference more realistically than if they were better acquainted with all the facts.

What do demand factors for transport services consist of? The element of convenience is, of course, largely subjective. Frequency of schedules, location of stations or bus stops at beginning and end of ride, transit time, all are instrumental in the choice of a carrier. The importance of each varies with each passenger. He may consider others, courtesy of drivers or traincrews, proximity to passengers, necessity to climb stairways, cleanliness of cars or stations, the social stigma involved in driving a car as against going by bus or train.*

The element of price, is perhaps less subjective. Yet, here too, there are certain connotations, which place the public carrier at a disadvantage. Automobile travel includes a number of expenses such as insurance, depreciation, parking, maintenance; some of these are not always taken fully into account. With charge accounts available for routine care and for fuel, actual cash outlays, such as are generally required in the purchase of commutation tickets, are not necessary. This tends to make the rider more "money conscious" when using public carriers and this is a competitive disadvantage to the latter.

Impact of Traffic Problems

It now remains to comment on the existing and possible consequences of a failure to correct present shortcomings. The total economic outlay attributable to metropolitan transportation *is without question very large*. How large is a matter of conjecture and would depend upon evaluation of productivity and utility of transport services rendered.** This, of course, varies from one type of city to another. But from the foregoing account of the inherent costs of rush-hour transportation and of the concentration/dispersal movements, there is a relatively large common denominator of low-productivity, i.e., high cost for little result.

The cost of transport in the suburbs to the individual is closely connected with his total housing costs. Transport as a function of

---

* There are of course certain standard characteristics pertaining to each mode of travel. The automobile gives the flexibility found in no other carrier. It can go anywhere, anytime. In these terms, its convenience is unsurpassed. Yet its mobility is being arrested because of traffic congestion and lack of parking space. The public carrier makes it possible for a passenger to be driven, making it possible for him to relax, read or otherwise entertain himself in a less strenuous fashion than what is now possible for a motorist. Dependence on schedules and transport to and from stations or bus stops are major disadvantages, as are crowded and unclean conditions; but these may be compensated for by faster transit time, no parking problem and generally less wear and tear on the nervous system.

** The N.Y.–N.J. Metropolitan Rapid Transit Commission estimates a $2 billion annual loss in the New Metropolitan area attributable to traffic congestion.

access tends to equate overall housing and transportation costs for each income level, i.e., housing and transport expenses tend to vary inversely as homes located on high access areas require less transport to and from the central business district. To assume the existence of a formula H (Housing) $+$ T (Transport) $=$ k (constant) is perhaps an over-generalization, for it assumes that convenience of access to and from the central business core is the only criterion for the degree of desirability or utility of residential location. There are of course others, but it remains one of the principal ones. Thus, the cost of rental of a home, similar in size, located closer to the central city core tends to be higher than that situated at a greater distance. Annual cost of housing for each, however, would tend to be the same, especially if the head of the household is a commuter. It is for this reason that it is frequently argued at commuter fare hearings, that a rise in rates would result in a lowering of property values.

Apart from the cost of the movement of passengers, the cost of the distribution of goods and services similarly tend to make suburban locations less valuable. To assemble goods in the central core and then to disperse them requires many elaborate terminal facilities in addition to rolling stock, branch warehouses and the like, and freight rates are necessarily high. They range from two to seven times the "line haul" rates applicable on comparable commodities. This is especially true of railroad service which must make a tax contribution on properties likely to be assessed at a high rate. Together with a lack of route flexibility this has resulted in making the truck the chief instrument of supplying commodities in the suburbs.

Another cost which is of particular interest to suburban dwellers is that of operating an automobile. Recent AAA data put these at 10 cents per mile allowing for average usage of 10,000 miles per year and assuming the operation of a major brand car in the lower price range. This is expensive transportation, but not surprising, considering that auto transportation requires a self-sufficient power plant for each vehicle as well as moving dead freight of about 2000 lbs. or more in areas where the supply of right-of-way is becoming increasingly more costly. The AAA data are said to represent a national average. If suburban driving were to be considered separately, even higher per mile costs are likely. The cost of automobile operation in central city areas alone has become almost prohibitive and in this sense the suburbs still have an advantage. The point is, however, that suburban existence necessitates wide usage of the family car, virtually for every economic and social function, so that a large segment of suburban living costs must be for expenditures for the private automobile. For suburban communities, the U. S. Department of Labor in 1950, estimated these expenditures to be about 12 per cent of total disposable individual or family income. (This is in addition to public transport use.) There is reason to believe that with greater dispersal, this percentage is on the increase.

Where suburban communities continue to preserve their residential characteristic and rely almost exclusively on the central city for employment and supplies, time and expenditure for transport will remain necessarily high. Where, on the other hand, decentralization in terms of economic diversification warranting its own, independent distribution system, is taking place, less transport costs may be involved. For example, if the head of a household can find employment nearer home, it can be assumed that transport costs will be less. This should be tempered however, for if fewer transport costs really are involved, his home becomes more valuable, and his rental or tax may be increased. Secondly, his transport costs may not be reduced for some time in the absence of a transport agency which is more economical than the private automobile. If he paid 2 cents per mile for commuting by railroad a distance of 20 miles one way, this is less than driving to work 5 miles at 10 cents a mile.* Only when more efficient common carrier services for intra-suburban travel and distribution of goods become available is there a chance for lower cost (time and money) of transportation in the suburbs.

Conclusion

The interacting relationship between land use patterns and available transport services is clearly demonstrated in the growth of metropolitan areas. The phenomenon of the modern suburbs has its roots in the first major uses of mechanical transportation, starting with developments along existing railroad trunk lines. This was supplemented with suburban lines, first built by railroads, and subsequently by interurban trolley and later by municipal rapid transit

---

* The economics of car pools become apparent—for two persons sharing one car who formerly commuted separately, there would be an actual saving.

systems. Since the demand for transport services consisted essentially, as they generally still do today, of a concentration/dispersal movement between suburb and central city, the residential pattern consisted of radial spokes extending from the metropolitan core. Large areas between these radii often remained rural as their access was limited. This was finally changed due to the flexibility of the automobile, so that today virtually all agricultural land uses have disappeared from the urban/suburban scene. The non-rural land uses extend roughly one and a quarter hours travel time from the city core. Progress in aviation is likely to extend this radius in the future.

Suburban growth today is a partial expression of the results of economic specialization which was formerly associated with urbanization. This new form of dispersal is making the problem of physical distribution and the flow of persons and commodities much more complex. The problem is vastly aggravated by the fact that conventional market forces are generally absent in the cost/price relationships among the various types of carriers. They are instead governed by institutional factors which have been responsible for encouraging less rather than more efficient modes of transport. Public policy for example, has favored rubber-borne transport over rail, with the result that major capital investments have been channelled into the former, while there has been little change in the physical status of the latter (other than deterioration). Furthermore there has often been too little advance planning which would promote the most efficient use of transport agencies.

The result has been that suburban existence requires unnecessarily large amounts of money and time to be devoted to the physical movement of persons and commodities. Because of the suburbs' dependence upon jobs, supplies and services outside of its own immediate area, the role of transport is of extreme importance. Furthermore, since suburbs are no longer accessible only to higher income groups, but to almost all levels of income, greater economic diversification—facilitated when adequate transport services are available—has become a necessity in order to finance municipal needs. For these reasons the transport problem in the suburbs is a crucial one, and one which requires urgent attention.

Unfortunately, political units as presently organized are inadequate to deal effectively with suburban needs. This is especially true of transport. Unless agencies are established which have the authority to deal with these problems on a regional basis, the economic health and well directed growth of today's metropolitan decentralized areas are being seriously impaired.

REFERENCES

Barger, Harold, *Transportation Industries, 1889-1946.* A Study of Output, Employment and Productivity, National Bureau of Economic Research, Inc., New York, 1951.

Baughman, M. Eugene, *An Answer to Multiple Jurisdiction.* In Traffic Quarterly, July 1955.

Davis, Harmer E., *Urban Transportation—Service or Chaos.* University of California, Inst. of Trans. and Traffic Engin., Berkeley, 1953.

Fitch, Lyle C., *Transportation Pricing in a Metropolitan Area.* Sacramento, 1955.

Gilmore, Harlan W., *Transportation and the Growth of Cities.* Free Press, Glencoe, Illinois, 1953.

Gross, Ralph F., *Urban Transportation Problems.* Traffic Engineering, December, 1953.

Kearns, E. E., *Coordinate Transportation for Metropolitan Communities.* In American City, April 1952.

Mitchell, Robert B. and Rapkin, Chester, *Urban Traffic, a Function of Land Use.* Columbia University Press, New York, 1954.

Mossman, Frank H., Editor, *Principles of Urban Transportation,* Western Reserve University Press, Cleveland, 1951, Chapters II-VIII.

Moving People in Metropolitan Areas, Proceedings of the Second Annual University of California Conference on City and Regional Planning, 1954.

Norton, C. McKim, *Metropolitan Transportation.* An Approach to Urban Planning, Gerald Breese and Dorothy E. Whitman, eds. Princeton University Press, Princeton, 1953.

Owen, Wilfred, *The Metropolitan Transportation Problem,* Brookings Institution, Washington, D.C., 1956. (This is the most comprehensive report to date.)

Stonier, Charles E., *Metropolitan Traffic Crisis,* Traffic Quarterly, April 1957.

A most complete bibliography may be found in: *Metropolitan Communities,* Government Affairs Foundation, Inc., Chicago, 1956, Chapter I, Section R.

Arnold M. Rose, Frank J. Atelsek, and Lawrence R. McDonald

University of Minnesota

NEIGHBORHOOD REACTIONS TO ISOLATED NEGRO RESIDENTS: AN ALTERNATIVE TO INVASION AND SUCCESSION

Introductory Note

This article reports on a study of the majority reactions to the introduction of a few Negro families into otherwise white neighborhoods. While the neighborhoods studied were in a city, the situation is more typical of suburbs, as it is into the latter that one or a few Negro families, rather than a wave of Negro families, typically move. Probably the majority of American suburbs are inhabited by middle, or upper income families. Half of the neighborhoods studied in this research were inhabited predominantly by middle-income families, and the findings apply to them just as they do to neighborhoods where the average income was low. It seems likely that just as the metropolitan area is developing new types of neighborhoods, such as the middle-income neighborhood, so the pattern of race mixture in the new neighborhoods is changing. Whereas, the rigidly segregated city used to be characterized by the pattern of race contact known as "invasion and succession," so the newer communities, no longer bound by restrictive covenants, are developing new patterns of racial accommodation and integration.

ARNOLD M. ROSE

The maintenance of residential segregation under a caste or semi-caste social system has resulted in a now familiar pattern of change when the minority group expands its numbers due to immigra-

Reprinted from *American Sociological Review*, Vol. 18 (October 1953), pp. 497-507, by permission of the authors and the *American Sociological Review*.

tion or to natural increase.¹ The process begins when the area of minority dwelling increases its population density much beyond that of adjacent areas of majority dwellings. Since relatively little new building goes on in the old areas where minority groups live, the process of increase in population density occurs by means of doubling up of families in existing dwellings and conversion of older large units into several smaller ones. The one-room kitchenette apartment is the characteristic end-point of this conversion process in the "Black Belt" of the large Northern cities where large scale immigration of Negroes from the South has been going on for several decades. Because of other aspects of the caste system, most members of the minority group have relatively low incomes and are not able to pay for new buildings or for complete and adequate conversion of old ones. The splitting up of large old apartments or large old houses in segregated minority areas provides small units at moderate prices for the largest possible number of people.

In this situation several economic factors combine to start the process of movement into adjacent areas then inhabited solely by whites. (1) Population density reaches a natural limit within the minority area; there are no more houses or apartments available for conversion and people with money to spend on rent have no place to live. (2) While the rent for the one-room kitchenette is relatively low per family, it provides an unusually high income for the owner of the apartment or building because of the small amount of space a unit requires. For example, a large apartment which originally rented for 50 dollars a month, when split into five apartments each renting for 20 dollars a month, nets a total rental twice as high after conversion as it did before. It therefore becomes highly profitable for potential landlords to seek other large units still available for conversion; these are to be found only in areas occupied by members of the majority group. (3) Because the minority group areas are old and heavily over-populated, they have a slum character. Some members of the minority group, not many but enough to have an economic influence, have sufficient incomes to afford much better housing in better areas if they were in free market competition.

The movement of minority persons into adjacent majority group areas usually begins when some member of the majority group, planning to move anyway, finds it highly profitable to sell a member of a minority group, or a third person, a real estate agent, usually, purchases in his own name a piece of property in the majority group area and turns it over at a very large profit to a member of the minority group. If all the members of the majority group are highly cohesive they are sometimes able to eject the sole minority group family, but generally there are some persons who either believe that a trend toward minority group movement invasion is inevitable and are willing to sell out to other members of minority groups in order to leave the area, or become panicky and think their property will become nearly worthless unless they sell quickly, or are willing to take advantage of the still-high prices for sales to minority persons. After two or three houses are sold to members of the minority group the property begins to change hands rapidly as the resistance of the majority group crumbles. For a brief period, ranging from a few weeks up to a year or so, the property of the area may be sold very cheaply. Quite often members of the minority group seeking housing do not have sufficient cash available to buy these cheap properties but they are sold to real estate agents or other people who intend to make money out of the real estate through conversion or resale. After the scare of selling period the prices of property in the area of transition go up sharply until they reach the high level prevalent in the old minority group area and are considerably higher than those in equivalent areas occupied by the majority group.[2] And so the solidly ethnic Black Belt, or the ghetto, or the Mexican district, expands.

In the last few years, however, new factors have entered the situation which are changing this pattern of "invasion and succession."[3] One factor is the change in attitude toward living near members of a minority group. Partly as a result of an organized effort to reduce prejudice and discrimination, and partly as a result of the housing shortage, more people are "willing" to live next door to members of minorities than was formerly the case. The second new factor is a Supreme Court decision of 1948 which removed the legally enforceable basis of the restrictive covenant, which has hitherto been the most powerful legal device used to prevent members of the minority groups from buying or renting in majority group areas. Since 1948, in most Northern cities and some Southern cities as well, Negroes have been moving into many white neighborhoods which under the old system would have taken them decades to penetrate, if ever they could have gotten in at all. There are now a large number of otherwise white neighborhoods into which one or two Negro families have moved. Mixed housing seems to be becoming the dominant pattern in at least the Northern cities.

What are the social consequences of this new pattern of Negro-white living in American cities? How do the whites react to Negro neighbors? One answer comes from studies of government-subsidized housing projects in which apartments are made available only on an unsegregated basis.[4] This type of study, however, was not designed to answer our questions. While suggestive, it has certain defects in indicating the social consequences of a general breakdown in residential segregation because: (1) the people involved are drawn mainly from the lower income classes; (2) the situation is one in which all of them are placed simultaneously in the neighborhood rather than one in which whites see a few Negro families entering "their" neighborhood; (3) there is a much more obvious source of pressure for unsegregated living in the projects, since there is government subsidy and government direction, whereas in an ordinary community the unsegregated living seems much more voluntary—being limited only by such impersonal factors as the housing shortage and inertia against moving.

Another type of research which would aid in determining how whites react to Negro neighbors in the newly developing pattern of mixed housing is a study of communities where one or two Negro families have been living for some time among a much larger population of whites. Such communities are found in Minneapolis, where our study was conducted. Minneapolis has otherwise a pattern of race relations not perceptibly different from that prevailing in other Northern cities. The one significant way in which Minneapolis differs from other Northern cities is in its proportion of Negroes: Only 1.3 per cent of the population of Minneapolis is Negro, as compared to 13.6 per cent in Chicago, 16.2 per cent in Detroit, 9.5 per cent in New York, and 18.1 per cent in Philadelphia. Other Northern cities have smaller proportions of Negroes. Whether this small proportion in Minneapolis makes it non-comparable with other cities is not known, but it needs to be stressed that in every other aspect of race relations Minneapolis does not differ from other Northern cities. There is a small "Black Belt" in Minneapolis, but a few Negro families have managed to obtain residences in most other parts of the city. Some moved into otherwise white neighborhoods many years ago, while others moved in fairly recently, and we shall compare these two types of neighborhood. In nearly every case there was some opposition to the Negro family moving in, and in one or two cases there was actual violence. But in all the cases we shall consider, the Negro family stayed and so did most of the whites (those whites who moved out were replaced by other whites). Other Negro families did not follow the first one into the neighborhood, since the pressure on Minneapolis Negroes to secure living space was not nearly as great as elsewhere, and consequently there was no process of "invasion and succession." This now seems to be becoming the new pattern for other large cities, at least in the North, as Negroes find it increasingly possible to move where they wish to, and not only into a Black Belt.

The data were collected by means of interviews, using a schedule with mainly check-list answers, conducted by volunteer students specially trained for the purpose. Interviews were conducted in the spring of 1951 in eight neighborhoods, chosen because they had only one Negro family (in one case, two Negro families) living in what was otherwise a white residential neighborhood. In four of the neighborhoods the same Negro family had been resident for at least ten years, while in the four others the Negro family had been resident less than two years. In each group of four neighborhoods, two were chosen as lower-income areas, and the two others as middle-income areas. The neighborhood was defined in terms of distance from the Negro's home and divided into a primary and a secondary zone: in the primary zone, consisting of the homes on both sides of the street within one block of the Negro's dwelling, one adult was to be interviewed within every home; in the secondary zone, containing all second blocks from the Negro's home on the same street, as well as one block on all adjacent streets, every other dwelling was included in the sample. Deviations were made from this plan because of odd block structures, the presence of factories and railroad tracks, and other neighborhood barriers. A total of 545 interviews were obtained; of the total original sample 9.6 per cent was lost because no person could be found at home after repeated visits or because of refusal to be interviewed. Information was obtained on the personal characteristics of the white and Negro families, but these data can only be used to explain apparent exceptions in the attitude and behavior patterns, since not enough neighborhoods were studied to make comparisons between types of neighborhoods in terms of the personal characteristics of the residents.

Before the study began, a number of hypotheses were set forth and used to formulate the questions in the schedule. They fell into the following subject-matter areas: (1) satisfaction with and participation within the neighborhood; (2) attitudes toward and knowledge about the Negro residents; (3) the extent and kinds of relationships with the Negro residents; (4) general endorsement of interracial housing and association. The specific hypotheses will now be presented with the relevant data.

1. The closer neighbors have more contact with the Negro family and are more willing to approve of the general idea of mixed racial housing and association than are those persons who live at a greater distance from the Negro family. For all neighborhoods where Negros had been living for at least ten years, 63 per cent of the white respondents in the primary zones speak with members of the Negro family, while in the secondary zones only 23 per cent had a speaking acquaintance with the resident Negroes. For neighborhoods where Negroes have been living for less than two years, 36 per cent of the whites living in primary zones speak with members of the Negro family as compared to 30 per cent in the secondary zones. This finding is consistent with that found in studies of areas that are racially homogeneous, that closer neighbors have more neighborly contacts than do relatively distant neighbors.[5] The measurement of approval of mixed racial associations was made by three questions whose answers were found to scale according to Guttman criteria.[6] These questions asked whether the respondent thought Negroes should be permitted to live in the same building,[7] to live in the same block, to go to the same school, as whites.[8] Table 1 shows that, for areas where Negroes have been living for at least ten years, respondents who live in the primary zones include a larger proportion in favor of interracial association than respondents who live in secondary blocks, but that for areas where Negroes have been living for less than two years there is no significant difference between those living in primary and secondary zones. When the question is raised concerning getting along with the Negro family the results are mixed. On the one hand, a significantly greater proportion of the primary zone population than of the secondary zone population said that their relationships with

the Negro families were very good (43 as compared to 10 per cent in areas where Negroes have been living at least ten years; 17 as compared to 11 per cent in areas where Negroes have been living less than two years); on the other hand the very few respondents who said they did not get along well were mostly also in the primary zone (3 per cent as compared to less than 1 per cent in both types of areas). The latter cannot be said to go against our hypothesis, since not getting along well with a specific family might reflect a reaction to a particular family rather than a reaction to Negroes in general.

Table 1—Attitude toward Interracial Association in Primary and Secondary Zones

Those Living in	Number Responding to All 3 Questions	Percentages Taking Each of Following Positions with Respect to Interracial Association:				Mean Score
		0 Sch., Blk., Bldg.—No	1 Sch.—Yes; Blk., Bldg.—No	2 Sch., Blk.—Yes; Bldg.—No	3 Sch., Blk., Bldg.—Yes	
Areas where Negroes have been living at least 10 years:						
Primary zones	(79)	4	35	30	30	1.85
Secondary zones	(174)	14	40	23	22	1.52
Areas where Negroes have been living less than 2 years:						
Primary zones	(90)	13	37	17	33	1.70
Secondary zones	(159)	18	30	20	32	1.66

2. Those who have more contacts with their Negro neighbors are also those who are more favorable to interracial association and who have a more favorable opinion of their Negro neighbors.[9] Some of the data already presented support this hypothesis. Whites who live in areas where a Negro family has been living for at least ten years, and live in primary zones close to the Negroes, both have more contact with their Negro neighbors and are somewhat more likely to be favorable to them specifically, and to interracial association generally, than are whites who live in areas where a Negro family has been living for less than two years. Whites who live in primary zones (i.e., closer to their Negro neighbors) are more acquainted with their Negro neighbors than are whites who live in secondary zones, and also tend to get along with them better. Primary zone whites are more favorable to interracial association generally, however, only if

the Negroes have been living in the neighborhood for a considerable length of time. Our direct correlational evidence also gives support to the hypothesis. While correlational evidence does not, by itself, indicate the direction of causation, in the light of the above mentioned considerations it seems reasonable to assume that the contact is the "cause" and the attitude toward interracial association the "effect." There is a more serious limitation of our data, however, due to the actually limited character of "neighborly" contact in a large city:

Table 2—Relationship of Contact with Evaluation of Negro Neighbors, and with Attitude toward Interracial Association

| | | Percentage Expressing Indicated Attitude Among Those Who,[1] in Areas Where Negroes Have Been Living | | | |
| | | At Least 10 Years | | Less Than 2 Years | |
Question	Answer	Speak with Negro Neighbor	Do Not Speak with Negro Neighbor	Speak with Negro Neighbor	Do Not Speak with Negro Neighbor
"Disregarding their race, how well do you think this family compares as neighbors with the other families in this area?"	Better	16	6	19	8
	About the same	81	85	72	79
	Not as well	3	9	9	13
Number of cases		(92)	(89)	(67)	(109)
Scale of attitude toward interracial association	0 Sch., blk., bldg.—no	4	14	7	21
	1 Sch.—yes; Blk., bldg.—no	32	44	23	35
	2 Sch., blk.—yes; bldg.—no	38	19	28	16
	3 Sch., blk., bldg.—yes	26	23	42	28
Number of cases		(92)	(154)	(72)	(153)

[1] Persons who indicate that they don't know their Negro neighbors are excluded from the top half of this table.

There were so few kinds of contact with Negro neighbors (with other white neighbors also, in most cases) that, among the various questions on contacts we asked, the only one eliciting enough positive answers to permit a significant cross tabulation was the contact of "speaking with" the Negro neighbor. Table 2 shows the relationship between this contact and evaluation of Negro neighbors and approval of interracial association. The differences showing the relationships are all consistent and all statistically significant at the five per cent level at least, but they are not very great.

3. The third hypothesis is that areas which are more integrated, and individuals within any area who are more integrated into it, will display a greater degree of unity in their response to the Negro family and to interracial association in general. To measure integration, a scale was formulated in the pattern of a social distance scale,[10] except that social distance was expressed toward a neighbor rather than toward minority groups. When comparisons were made between areas with highest and lowest average scale scores, and between individuals with high and low scale scores within all primary areas, on several indices of association with the Negro family and with attitude toward interracial association generally, no consistent or statistically significant differences in variation appeared. Thus the hypothesis is not supported by our data.

4. The fourth hypothesis is that those who are more integrated into the neighborhood, or who have a stronger "stake" in the neighborhood, are more inclined to accept the specific Negro family, where the Negro family has been living for a long time. The several relevant items of data in our study support this hypothesis. (a) A comparison was made of people with different scores on the general social distance scale, for people who live in the primary zones of areas where Negroes have been living for at least ten years. It shows that people who are less socially distant from their neighbors in general are slightly more likely to know their Negro neighbors, and this acquaintanceship is more likely that not to take the form of a friendly relationship. The difference is not great (52.5 per cent among the socially distant who get along with "very well" or "fairly well" with the Negro family, as compared to 61.6 per cent among the less socially distant) and the cases are so few (40 and 48, respectively) that the difference cannot be considered statistically reliable (at the 30 per cent level). (b) Ownership of property represents another index of integration into the neighborhood, and data relating ownership to acceptance of the Negro family are presented in Table 3. A larger proportion of owners than of renters are acquainted with the Negro families, and are as likely to evaluate them favorably as neighbors. In areas where Negroes have been living for at least ten years, there is no difference between the proportions of owners and renters believing that the presence of the Negro family lowers property values in the

neighborhood, although a differential appears in the areas where Negroes have been living less than two years. Owners are, of course, the ones directly affected by lower property values, and the fact that no more of them—in areas where Negroes have been living for ten or more years—believe that the presence of the Negro families decreases property values is undoubtedly a reason why they are as willing as renters to accept the Negro families.

Table 3—Comparison of Owners and Renters in Acceptance of Negro Neighbors and in Belief That Presence of Negroes Decreases Property Values

		Percentages Giving Indicated Response Among:			
		In Areas Where Negroes Have Been Living for at Least 10 Years		In Areas Where Negroes Have Been Living for Less Than 2 Years	
Questions	Answers	Owners	Renters	Owners	Renters
"Do members of this family ever talk to you or your family?"	Yes	34	23	30	27
"Disregarding their race, how well do you think this family compares as *neighbors* with the other families in this area?"	Better	8	3	8	10
	Same	55	51	52	45
	Not as well	4	3	10	3
	Don't know them	33	43	30	42
"Some time ago a Negro family moved into this neighborhood. Do you think this hurt property values in the neighborhood?"	Yes	34	34	51	30
	No	36	32	32	41
	Don't know	30	34	17	30
Number of cases		(213)	(35)	(190)	(62)

5. Complementary to the preceding hypothesis that the more integrated people in the neighborhood are more likely to accept the specific Negro family is another hypothesis that they are more likely to resist a more general interracial association. Using the respondents of the primary zones only, we find that the average score on the scale of interracial association for the more socially distant people is 1.92, whereas for the less socially distant people it is 1.88 (based on 40 and 48 cases, respectively). This is not a statistically significant difference but it is in the expected direction. Table 4 shows a more conclusive and more interesting comparison between owners and renters. On the mean score, in areas where Negroes have lived at least ten years,

owners are slightly less favorable to interracial association in general than are renters. The difference is in the direction which confirms our hypothesis but is not large enough to be statistically significant. In areas where Negroes have been living less than two years, the difference between owners and renters is sharply in the expected direction and is highly significant. The specific responses of those dwelling in areas where Negroes have been living at least ten years show that the owners are more likely than renters to be more favorable as well as less favorable to interracial association in general. This is possible

Table 4—Comparison of Owners and Renters in Attitude toward Interracial Association

Position on Scale of Attitude Toward Interracial Association	In Areas Where Negroes Have Been Living 10 or More Years, Percentage Expressing Indicated Attitude Among:		In Areas Where Negroes Have Been Living Less Than 2 Years, Percentage Expressing Indicated Attitude Among:	
	Owners	Renters	Owners	Renters
0 Sch., blk., bldg.—no	10	19	18	9
1 Sch.—yes; blk., bldg.—no	43	25	36	22
2 Sch., blk.—yes; bldg.—no	24	28	18	19
3 Sch., blk., bldg.—yes	23	28	28	50
Mean score	1.59	1.65	1.56	2.10
Number of cases	(213)	(35)	(190)	(62)

because owners are more likely to take the position that Negro children should be allowed to go to the same school as white children go to, but that Negro families should not be allowed to live in the same block or building that white families live in. Thus owners express both their friendliness to Negroes—which we suggest arises from their satisfactory relations with their Negro neighbors—as well as their concern about the value of their property.

6. Children in a family create for their parents both a stronger relationship to the neighborhood—including Negro neighbors—and at the same time an anxiety about the effect of Negro neighbors on the children. Therefore we hypothesize that respondents with young children—who would create anxiety but are too young to create relationships—will be more distant from the Negro neighbors than are respondents without children, but that respondents with older children have counteracted their anxiety because of the increased relationship with the Negro neighbors for which the children were responsible. Table 5 provides striking confirmation of this hypothesis for areas in

which Negroes have been living for at least ten years. Respondents with children of pre-school age are least likely to have relationships with the Negro neighbors and most likely to be hostile to interracial association in general, whereas respondents with older children are much more likely to have contact with the Negro family and less hos-

Table 5—Relationship Between Presence of Children in the Family and Contact with Negro Neighbors, and Attitudes toward Interracial Association

In Areas Where Negroes Have Been Living at Least 10 Years:	Percentage of Respondents Giving Indicated Answers Among Those with:			
	No Children	Pre-School Children	School-Age Children	Children 19 and Over
Percentage speaking with members of Negro family	31	12	39	43
Position on scale of attitude toward interracial association				
0 Sch., blk., bldg.—no	8	23	13	16
1 Sch.—yes; blk., bldg.—no	41	53	31	40
2 Sch., blk.—yes; bldg.—no	27	13	22	20
3 Sch., blk., bldg.—yes	24	10	33	24
Mean score	1.66	1.10	1.76	1.52
Number of cases	(118)	(34)	(56)	(28)
In Areas Where Negroes Have Been Living Less Than 2 Years:				
Percentage speaking with members of Negro family	24	28	27	22
Position on scale of attitude toward interracial association				
0 Sch., blk., bldg.—no	15	7	24	28
1 Sch.—yes; blk., bldg.—no	42	33	34	24
2 Sch., blk.—yes; bldg.—no	16	24	13	20
3 Sch., blk., bldg.—yes	27	35	29	28
Mean score	1.55	1.86	1.47	1.48
Number of cases	(86)	(57)	(40)	(27)

tility toward interracial association. Respondents with school age children, as compared to respondents without children, include a slightly larger proportion hostile to all three types of interracial association as well as a larger proportion not hostile to any of the three types. In areas where Negroes have been living for less than two years, the hypothesis does not hold up at all. There are no significant differences in percentage of families speaking with members of the Negro family, and the major difference in attitude toward interracial association generally is that whites with pre-school age children are more favorable than any other group. We might hazard the guess that the state of attitudes predicted in our hypothesis has not yet had a chance to take form in the short time Negroes have been living in the neighborhood.

7. Our seventh hypothesis is one that has several times been confirmed in earlier studies.[11] It is that the more educated the person the more likely he is to be favorable to interracial association but the less likely he is to have had contact with his Negro neighbor. Table 6

Table 6—Relationship Between Education and Contact with Negro Neighbors and Attitudes toward Interracial Association

In Areas Where Negro Family Has Been Living for at Least Ten Years:	Indicated Responses Among Persons with Educational Attainment at Level of:			
	Grade School Only	High School Only	Some College	College Graduation
Mean score on scale of attitude toward interracial association	1.40	1.74	1.97	2.04
Percentage who speak with Negro neighbor	36	36	29	29
Number of cases	(64)	(125)	(36)	(23)
In Areas Where Negro Family Has Been Living Less Than Two Years:				
Mean score on scale of attitude toward interracial association	1.43	1.59	1.83	2.31
Percentage who speak with Negro neighbor	30	35	24	40
Number of cases	(57)	(113)	(46)	(22)

gives direct confirmation of this. Especially in attitudes toward interracial association there are striking differences between respondents of different educational levels.

8. We had no hypothesis about the relationship between religious affiliation and attitudes toward interracial association, but a comparison of scores of different religious groups on the scale of attitude toward interracial association shows that the religious groups are not very apart. For areas in which Negroes have been living at least ten years, the score of Catholics (52 cases) was 1.59, of Lutherans (106 cases)—1.55, of members of the other large Protestant denominations (51 cases)—1.55, of the fundamentalist Protestants (16 cases)—1.50, and of those who said they had no religious affiliation (29 cases)—1.73. For areas in which Negroes have been living for less than two years, the score of Catholics (62 cases) was 1.46, of

Lutherans (97 cases)—1.72, of members of the other large Protestant denominations (38 cases)—1.92, of the fundamental Protestants (12 cases)—1.84, and of those who said they had no religious affiliation (26 cases)—1.63.

Conclusion

The evidence of this survey of eight neighborhoods of Minneapolis where a single Negro family lives in an otherwise white neighborhood indicates that there is a tendency to accept or to accommodate to the Negro as a neighbor.[12] Those who live close to the Negro neighbors have more contact with them and are more favorable to them and to interracial association generally than those who live farther away. This is especially true in neighborhoods where Negroes have been living for a long time. Those who have more contacts with their Negro neighbors are more favorable to them specifically and to interracial association generally. Those who live in neighborhoods where Negroes have been living for at least ten years, and live close to the Negroes, are somewhat more likely to have contact with their Negro neighbor and to be more favorable to them and to interracial association generally than whites who live in neighborhoods where Negroes have been living less than two years. Those who are more integrated into the neighborhood and who have a stronger "stake" in it are more inclined to accept the Negro family, although not to be more favorable to interracial association generally. We used home ownership—as opposed to renting—as an index of "stake in neighborhood" and it is significant that the owners—in areas where Negroes have been living ten or more years—were as favorable toward, probably because they were more acquainted with, the Negro family, and no more inclined to believe that the presence of the Negro family hurt property values. Renters are slightly more likely to be favorable toward interracial association in a neighborhood, however, while owners are slightly more likely to be favorable toward interracial association in the schools, in areas where Negroes have been living at least ten years. In areas where Negroes have been living less than two years, owners are less likely than renters to be favorable to interracial association and more likely to believe that Negroes hurt property values. Well-educated whites are much more likely to be in favor of interracial association, but not more likely to have actually had contact with their Negro neighbors, than are poorly educated whites. In areas where Negroes have been living for a long while, families with school age children are more favorable to interracial association than are families with pre-school age children. This pattern has not developed, however, in areas where Negroes have been living less than two years. The dominant religion of the whites in a neighborhood does not seem to affect any of the above patterns, although data not presented suggest that the more heterogeneous the population, in terms of religion and national origin, the more favorable is the area toward Negroes.

In so far as the limited data of this survey of Minneapolis can be generalized, if the residential pattern of Northern cities takes the form of a scattering of Negro families living in predominantly white areas, the prognosis is that this would tend to increase the acceptance and accommodation of Negroes by whites.

FOOTNOTES

1. The process has been documented by several researches. See, for example: Herman H. Long and Charles S. Johnson, *People vs. Property*, Nashville: Fisk University Press, 1947; Robert C. Weaver, *The Negro Ghetto*, New York: Harcourt, Brace, and Company, 1948.

2. Studies on the racial factors in property value movements include: Elsie Parker, "Both Sides of the Color Line," *The Appraisal Journal*, January 1943, pp. 27-34; July 1943, pp. 231-49. George W. Beehler, Jr., "Colored Occupancy Raises Values," *The Review of the Society of Residential Appraisers*, September 1945, pp. 3-6, 12. Paul F. Cressey, *The Succession of Cultural Groups in the City of Chicago* (unpublished Ph.D. thesis, University of Chicago, 1930). Oscar I. Stern, "The Long Range Effects of Colored Occupancy," *The Review of the Society of Residential Appraisers*, January 1946, pp. 4-6. Homer Hoyt, *One Hundred Years of Land Values in Chicago*, Chicago: University of Chicago Press, 1933. Richard Marks, "The Impact of Negro Population Movement on Property Values in a Selected Area in Detroit," unpublished study made for the Mayor's Interracial Committee of the City of Detroit, 1950. Egbert F. Schietinger, *Real Estate Transfers During Negro Invasion: A Case Study* (unpublished M.A. thesis, University of Chicago, 1948), 118 pp. Belden Morgan, "Values in Transition Areas: Some New Concepts," *The Review of the Society of Residential Appraisers*, March, 1952, pp. 5-10. Luigi M. Laurenti, "Effects of Nonwhite Purchasers on Market Prices of Residences," *The Appraisal Journal*, XX (July, 1952), pp. 314-329.

3. These are terms borrowed by Robert E. Park from plant ecology to de-

scribe the analogous human process we are considering. Robert E. Park, "Human Ecology," *American Journal of Sociology,* XLII (July, 1936), pp. 1-15; "Succession, An Ecological Concept," *American Sociological Review,* I (April, 1936), pp. 171-179. Also see: Bessie McClenahan, *The Changing Urban Neighborhood,* Los Angeles: University of Southern California, 1929, pp. 5, 26-29, 83-89. While Park used the term "invasion" in an ecological context of competitive relationships, the term is an unfortunate one since its popular meaning has a strong connotation of conflict. In its use by realtors, newspaper writers, and other nonsociologists—although they have learned the term from sociologists—"invasion" has a moral connotation of unrighteous seizure of property from unwilling sellers. The term has probably helped transform a competitive process into a conflict process.

4. A carefully designed research of this type, involving comparison of housing projects that are completely unsegregated with projects that have Negroes living in segregated sections, is that of Morton Deutsch and Mary Evans Collins, *Interracial Housing,* Minneapolis: University of Minnesota Press, 1951. This study has been followed up and its results are confirmed in a study by D. M. Wilner, R. P. Walkley, and S. W. Cook, "Residential Proximity and Intergroup Relations in Public Housing Projects," *Journal of Social Issues,* 8 (1st issue, 1952), pp. 45-59.

5. L. Festinger, S. Schachter, and K. Back, *Social Pressure in Informal Groups,* New York: Harper, 1950; T. Caplow and R. Forman, "Neighborhood Interaction," *American Sociological Review,* 15 (June, 1950), pp. 357-366.

6. Louis Guttman, in S. A. Stouffer *et al., Measurement and Prediction,* Princeton: Princeton University Press, 1950, pp. 46-90.

7. Living in the "same building" is an ambiguous matter, since some respondents live in duplexes and apartment buildings, while most live in single-family homes.

8. The exact wordings were: "Do you think that Negroes should be permitted to live in the same building with white persons?" "Do you think Negroes should be permitted to live in the same block with white persons?" "Would you object to Negro and white children going to the same school?" The answers permitted were simply "yes" and "no."

9. This hypothesis gets support from many other studies, with certain qualifications. See Stuart W. Cook, "Contact and Intergroup Attitudes: Some Theoretical Considerations," Presidential address to Society for the Psychological Study of Social Issues, September, 1952.

10. The principles underlying social distance scales have been formulated by Emory J. Bogardus. See his "Measuring Social Distance," *Journal of Applied Sociology,* 9 (1925), pp. 299-308; and "A Social Distance Scale," *Sociology and Social Research,* 17 (1933), pp. 265-271.

11. See the summary contained in: Arnold M. Rose, *Studies in Reduction of Prejudice,* Chicago: American Council on Race Relations, 2nd edition, 1948, pp. 19-24.

12. In Duluth, virtually all Negroes live in neighborhoods that are predominantly white, and a survey by Turbeville reports that "over 82 per cent of the heads of households stated that they had not been victims of neighborhood discrimination because of their race." Gus Turbeville, "The Negro Population in Duluth, Minnesota, 1950," *Sociology and Social Research,* 36 (March-April, 1952), pp. 231-238.

Henry Fagin

Regional Plan Association

PROBLEMS OF PLANNING
IN THE SUBURBS

Someone has observed that mankind solves only a small part of his problems. Most of them never are worked out: rather, they fade away. The circumstances that give rise to particular problems are transitory. The new situations which replace the old substitute their own array of new problems for the old ones. This generalization may help to clarify the subject of suburban planning problems in three distinct metropolitan eras: city and suburb, urban region, and regional city.

Era of City and Suburb

The recent era of city and suburb reached its peak in the New York metropolitan region around the time of the first World War. There were two major physical planning problems in the suburbs in this era: how to construct a satisfactory residential environment and how to get back and forth to the central city. Neither problem had been solved completely when the present era of the urban region arrived, bringing a relative stability of employment levels in central areas and great increases in the suburbs.

In the earlier period the suburbs were simply communities near cities where some who worked in the cities lived with their families. These suburban communities, of course, also contained people who provided goods and services for the commuter families.

This is an original article, prepared for this volume.

362

The suburbs were superimposed over earlier settlement patterns. There had been rural farms and villages serving the farm folk. And there had been small and medium size manufacturing centers, many of them located at fall lines on the rivers, where water power was abundant and goods could be floated down-stream to the ports. During the latter part of the nineteenth century when the suburbs of New York City were growing, some nearby manufacturing centers like Paterson, N. J., and Danbury, Conn., also were growing. The largest centers, like Newark, N. J., were important enough to have their own dependent residential suburbs beyond their municipal borders. But many of the small manufacturing centers were declining and since have virtually gone out of existence. Old mill ponds with no mills are their chief trace.

Horace Greeley, editor of the New York Tribune, was typical of the early commuters. He lived 30 miles north of New York City in Chappaqua and made a daily round-trip journey on a branch of the New York Central Railroad opened just before 1850. In time Chappaqua became a "Sub-urb," a predominantly residential settlement related to the nearby city and directly dependent on daily commutation to it. This pattern of dependence was clearly visible. The daily movement of persons between suburb and central city was there for all to behold. It went on six days a week. Indeed, Saturdays the commuter was likely to be joined by his wife and children and the maiden aunt in a shopping and amusement jaunt to the central city.

The major problems of physical planning in this railway-based suburban era, then, had to do with the extension and improvement of commuting services and with the provision of community facilities in the new suburban settlements—sanitary facilities, local streets, libraries and the other urban amenities for which the suburban settlers had a taste.

For many years the first of these needs—expanding commuter services—proved a profitable subject for the investment of venture capital. Existing railroad companies established commuter service on their trunk lines and added many miles of commuter trackage. New railroads came into being to furnish additional commutation service. The six-day work week and the virtual monopoly of retail trade and services (except for daily convenience items) enjoyed by the central business district of the major city meant a maximum use of rail service by all members of the suburban family.

By the nineteen-twenties, the trend toward a maximum concentration of the region's economic activity on the lower half of Manhattan Island had reached its zenith. Facilities for railroad commutation from the outer suburbs and rapid transit commutation from the suburbs within the central city were being improved. These appeared on the verge of providing thoroughly satisfactory service to meet the suburban needs. But three key developments intervened to throw the system out of joint.

One was the northward shift of commercial expansion on Manhattan Island. The second was the development of the automobile and bus as flexible means for serving commuters. The third was the reduction of the work week to five days.

These factors and their ramifications reduced the annual usage of some existing rail commuter lines below the limits of profitable operation despite still-crowded rush hour loads. Reduced service and fiscal trouble tended to follow, particularly for commuter lines focused mainly toward lower Manhattan. Other lines, like the Long Island Railroad system, have been unable to cope adequately with enormous increases in rush hour commuter demand accompanied by so many hours of slack operations and revenues.

Moreover, the shifts in Manhattan employment patterns have caused new origin-destination demand patterns for which no convenient rail pathways exist: for example, between New Brunswick and Madison Avenue. In some suburban places, such as Bergen County, N. J., bus systems have been developed to provide the new service required. But many suburban areas to this day remain connected to important central employment districts only by makeshift and circuitous links. The commuter railroad problem has changed perhaps from that of providing *more* service to that of providing *more convenient* service.

As to the second major physical planning problem of the city-suburb era, a few communities were able to meet it with distinction, but most were overwhelmed by the pace and size of their growth. Then as now the uncoordinated efforts of the many components of the private building industry—subdividers, builders, realtors—proved insufficient to produce fully livable suburban neighborhoods. Community planning emerged as a consciously-felt need.

A number of suburban commuter-settlements planned just before and after 1900 are among the earliest modern applications of the idea of coordinating the diverse elements of urban growth according to a plan. Katonah, ten miles farther out than Chappaqua, is an early planned suburb. It was laid out by the Olmsteads, a firm which previously had designed Central Park in New York City. Forest Hills Gardens and Garden City on Long Island are of this period. So is Llewellyn Park in New Jersey.

Era of Metropolitan Anarchy

But, before these two major problems—adequate commuter service and orderly residential neighborhood development—were fully solved, several important new developmental factors appeared. Chief among them were electricity and the automobile, truck and bus. These have been at work transforming the simple city-and-suburb pattern into a new and far more complex form of human settlement. In it, urban elements are scattered almost at random throughout the metropolitan environs—hence, the descriptive phrase, metropolitan anarchy. In this new kind of urban region, the very word "suburb" takes on significant new meanings. The old-style suburbs and their old style problems remain as dominant factors, but entirely new kinds of suburbs, are emerging too, and with them new kinds of suburban problems.

In the case of many varieties of commercial and industrial activity, the new inventions in the transmission of energy, goods and persons have broken the former monopoly of central city districts. It has become possible to assemble the required factors of production in many locations throughout what previously had been only the *residential* hinterland—the classical "suburb."

The physical character of today's urbanizing region is being shaped by an interplay of the older city-suburb relationships and a number of newer trends such as:

(1) *Increasing specialization by area.* In contrast with the typical heterogeneous urban street of the nineteenth century which might contain a mixture of houses, flats, stores and workshops, the present trend toward specialized districts has led to the emergence of the regional shopping center, the industrial park, the estate-type subdivision, the garden-apartment community, and a narrowing of the functions of central business districts toward economic activities which assemble people rather than things.

(2) *Increasing size of areas of homogeneity.* For example, in terms of economic homogeneity, whole suburban towns are becoming composed almost exclusively of families with quite a narrow income range. In ethnic terms, we find more Negro persons living today within the enormous and relatively homogeneous area of Harlem than perhaps in any single residential district in the South similarly uninterrupted by white neighborhoods. The same trend is exemplified by the large regional shopping center with its rows of retail establishments unbroken by funeral parlors, warehouses, churches, hotels or homes. It can be seen also in terms of huge industrial plants, some on single sites larger than whole cities. Idlewild Airport, is nearly as extensive as Manhattan south of Central Park.

(3) *Spread of urban-type activities and establishments to locations throughout suburban areas.* For example, this trend has sent administrative offices of national companies to Westchester, Bergen and other inner ring counties, has placed multi-story apartment buildings 10 miles and more away from Manhattan, and has distributed nearly 100 branches of central stores to suburban places.

(4) *Increasing variety in types of travel between home and work.* In the city-suburb era, other than for persons employed in their immediate home neighborhood, almost the only kind of work trip was radial—toward the central business district in the morning and back again in the evening. The term "commuter" had a fairly simple meaning. In general, the commuter came to work from a separate suburban municipality and took a railroad train rather than a trolley car, "el", or subway. Today, it is true, the tremendous daily radial tides of travel between the rings of residential neighborhoods and the central business districts still predominate in the transportation pattern. The volumes of persons moving inward in the morning and outward each evening continue to reach levels which can be accommodated only by high-capacity mass transportation systems. But significant numbers of persons now travel to and from work along nontraditional pathways. *Reverse commuting* is an example of this. It is reported for example that as many as 75,000 persons go to work daily from New York City to New Jersey, a reverse movement which crosses the 150,000 traveling in the conventional direction. But large numbers also make their work trip from one suburban location to another, moving at right angles to the direction of the central city. Some, for example, go from residential districts of suburban cities to

widely dispersed employment places: others from homes in open areas to scattered plants or office headquarters. The pattern of work trips has become a complex interweaving of thousands of shuttling movements in every direction, intermeshed with the basic radial webbing.

(5) *Move to one-family homes.* Austin J. Tobin of the Port Authority has referred to the Americans' permanent love affair with his auto. It is accompanied for many citizens of the metropolitan area by a similar attraction to the one-family house on the largest lot the owner can afford to own—and to reach from his daily work place.

(6) *Rapid geographic spread of the metropolitan region.* Vigorous population growth, the spread of work places, the decline in average persons per household, the predominance of one-family homes, and the trend to larger lot sizes—all these have combined to roll great carpets of suburban development into the rural environs, with runners stretching as much as 50 miles out in several directions.

(7) *Polarization.* Municipalities favored in their tax base tend to attract home and other establishments which contribute well in relation to the costs of the services they require. Conversely, municipalities with poor tax bases tend to receive predominantly unfavorable residential or commercial additions from a fiscal viewpoint.

In basic form, the new-style urban region might be described as having a core area, an inner ring and an outer ring. The core area contains the central business, commercial, industrial, governmental, cultural, amusement and dense residential districts of the central city, which remains an indispensable part of the region. The inner ring contains extensive industrial belts, numerous "regional shopping centers," low-density apartment districts, and a great many one-family homes of central-city-employed commuters. It also contains some cities which in an earlier period were relatively independent of the major central city. (In most cases the population and employment levels of these cities are stable or declining.) The outer ring has a scattering of large industrial establishments; many old shopping and service centers, villages or small cities; and a burgeoning number of new residential "developments," some for the families of the new local industrial workers, some for those of the higher-paid employees of the inner and outer rings.

The foregoing brief developmental history of the metropolitan region provides the setting necessary for a discussion of today's

suburban planning problems. It should be clear by now that the term
"suburban" has come to mean much more than it formerly did. It
covers perhaps all parts of the metropolitan region except three: the
core areas of the central city, the areas still farmed as part of a rural
economy, and lands in park, recreation or watershed reservations.
Consequently, the physical planning problems of the suburbs run the
gamut from the replacement of obsolete districts in large and small
old urban centers to the creation of new urban environments out of
raw land.

Almost none of the problems encountered in the new-style suburbs
is at all peculiar to the suburbs. The problems embrace such general
urban planning challenges as how to: (1) provide transportation
systems which insulate pedestrians from moving vehicles, and separate
different streams of traffic from each other; (2) how to design
residential neighborhoods which afford a desired measure of social
homogeneity in living patterns but also bring diverse groups into
civic contact with each other; (3) how to achieve greater beauty in
the appearance both of home communities and work places; (4) how
to bring compatible land uses together and protect incompatible ones
from each other; (5) how to assure an adequate provision of needed
facilities and services in old and new areas; (6) how to provide for
a changing environment to meet new needs, new standards and new
conditions; (7) how to provide well-designed districts for all the
activities needed for modern metropolitan living and earning a living;
(8) how to secure and preserve adequate open space for active and
passive recreation in the places where people live and work.

Every one of the suburban physical planning problems is encountered in essence throughout all parts of the metropolitan region—
the central city, suburban city, village, town, and fringe countryside.
But though the problems are similar, *the conditions under which they
must be solved* are significantly different in several respects as we move
from populated older cities to the newly developed suburbs.

First, the increment in property value as land is converted from
rural to urban uses is so great as to cause sudden special-interest
pressures of an extreme intensity in the outlying localities. In this
setting, it becomes relatively more difficult for local officials to represent the broad interests of the public.

Second, the "public" which will occupy the new communities in
the suburbs is simply not present when the key decisions are made.

The nature of new community development, therefore, is based on the outlook of a very narrow segment of the metropolitan community.

Third, the pace of expansion when it takes place tends to outrun the ability of the new suburban community to accommodate and assimilate the growth. This is true not only in the sense of providing the standard of facilities and services essential for individual and community life but also in terms of receiving large numbers of newcomers into the community while maintaining its basic sense of community. For example, for an exceptionally fine school system, it may be harder to expand the faculty with teachers indoctrinated in the spirit of the place than merely to build the needed additional classroom space.

Fourth, the sheer cost of starting a community from scratch and attempting to build and finance all the necessary accoutrements simultaneously in a single generation is wellnigh overwhelming. This puts special pressure on every community to try constantly to "upgrade" the economic level of its potential newcomers, whether residential or industrial. A destructive type of competition among municipalities tends to ensue which may be harmful to the metropolitan area as a whole. It tends to bring about a land use pattern warped by the accident of tax-district boundaries rather than being shaped in response to broader ecoonmic forces. It is this undisciplined struggle among tax districts that suggests the description of the contemporary period as "the era of metropolitan anarchy."

Fifth, the typical previous experience of the persons likely to be in control of the local government structure when the time of urbanization arrives tends to find them ill-prepared for the kinds of decisions that must be made.

And sixth, as compared with the core city any single suburban community is less likely to be of a size and shape that enables an independent solution to many planning problems. For such needs as water supply, waste disposal, library services, transport facilities and public health facilities to be met efficiently often requires districts or units of considerable magnitude, much larger than typical suburban municipalities.

This list of special conditions attending suburban development is not exhaustive. But it should be sufficient to suggest wherein present approaches to the planning of the metropolitan suburbs must be supplemented by additional measures and devices, some of them not yet invented.

The traditional means available to suburban municipalities for influencing and regulating their land development include: (1) master plans, which provide a framework for the coordination of public facilities and of the spacial relationships among the various land-using elements of the community; (2) zoning ordinances, which regulate aspects of the use of private property; (3) subdivision requirements, which govern the cutting up of raw land into streets and building lots; and (4) official map controls, which protect lands needed for future streets and drainage courses from encroachment by buildings.

This array of planning devices and controls has been used in suburban communities with great effectiveness. Yet despite the high quality which marks the physical environment of many of the newer suburban neighborhoods, unsolved problems do loom up beyond the individual neighborhood and beyond this year's fiscal balance.

Era of the Regional City

Existing local planning powers are not designed nor intended to cope with the kinds of forces which underlie the metropolitan trends enumerated above nor to cope with many unfavorable conditions which are resulting from such trends. Yet there is a growing consensus among people throughout this and other metropolitan regions that some of the trends and conditions are undesirable. There is a widespread search for means to affect what might be called the larger figures in the pattern of metropolitan development. A great search is under way for new political inventions to put an end to metropolitan anarchy while at the same time guaranteeing strong elements of local political responsibility.

Just what governmental innovations this search for better direction, coordination and control will discover we cannot yet foresee. Is it not likely, however, that when they are found and applied, their very existence and operations will usher in a third great metropolitan phase, beyond both the old city-suburb era and the present age of metropolitan anarchy? And in this new phase will not many of the problems that today perplex the suburbs vanish from the community agenda not because we have solved them but because they no longer exist?

There once was a town containing three independent school districts, each receiving taxes from its own part of town. The residents spent a great deal of time at the town hall trying to amend the zoning ordinance. Each district wanted a large quantity of "clean" industry to bring in taxes. Each resisted having any lots zoned in a way suitable for industrial employees. Then one day the three school districts were combined into a single fiscal unit, though the three still retained local control over many matters of curriculum and other local concerns. Overnight, the district pressures on the town government for zoning changes vanished. It became possible to lay out the industrial districts for the best economic use of the land and the transport facilities, unhampered by extraneous considerations. Thus, the change in school district organization enabled an important improvement in physical pattern.

Is there not a possible metropolitan analogy? Would not the governmental advances marking the onset of the era of the regional city enable new metropolitan physical patterns—patterns taking fullest advantage of the great technological advances of this twentieth century?

Part VI

Suburban Perspectives

*Among democratic nations new families are constantly spring-
ing up, others are constantly falling away, and all that remain
change their condition; the woof of time is every instant
broken and the track of generations effaced . . . the interest of
man is confined to those in close propinquity to himself.*

Alexis de Tocqueville

David Riesman

The University of Chicago

THE SUBURBAN SADNESS

I speak in this paper from the perspective of one who loves city and country, but not the suburbs; one who feels that the suburban styles of life tend increasingly to become *the* American styles, with ensuing loss of certain kinds of diversity, complexity, and texture—and my emphasis here is on what has been lost rather than gained by the move to the suburbs. This is a value-loaded paper, not a fact-filled one: it draws on fact where possible (including some of the studies reported elsewhere in this volume), and on impression and judgment where necessary. Above all, it is an effort to link questions concerning the quality of suburban living to more general questions about work and leisure in America; that is, to understand the relation between a consumption-oriented society and the decentralization of consumption and leisure to the suburbs. Thus, I see the suburbs today as signifying, in their familism and search for community, a tacit revolt against the industrial order—a revolt signs of which also appear in attitudes towards work itself. I am, of course, not implying that all suburbs are alike, or mean the same things to their residents, or suffer from the same sorts of meaninglessness. I am talking primarily

An earlier version of this article, written especially for this volume, appears under the title, "The Suburban Dislocation," in *The Annals,* Fall 1957, pp. 123-146.

This is a publication of the Center for the Study of Leisure at the University of Chicago, established under a grant from the Behavioral Sciences Division of the Ford Foundation. I have drawn for the article on research conducted by Rolf Meyersohn, Research Director of the Center, and Robin Jackson, Research Assistant; and I am indebted for helpful suggestions to my colleague, Robert S. Weiss, and to Nathan Glazer.

of an ideal-typical suburb, more nearly approximated by the newer post-War developments and tract housing than by older suburbs, and more typically inhabited by middle- and lower-middle-class people than by the upper class or by unskilled workers.

The very fact that the suburbs have become in the last dozen years so characteristic a feature of the American landscape creates problems in separating what is due to suburban life and what to American developments in general.[1] The suburbs, for example, make more visible the theme of conformity with which this paper begins. It is likely that many students of the suburbs have observed phenomena there which could, in principle, be seen anywhere. The fact that World War II delayed housing starts and family starts, moreover, brought about a concentration of young married people in the new suburbs; and we may overgeneralize about their total life-careers from their situation at this particular point in their life-cycle, when they are simultaneously being socialized into "organization men" and family men. In general, the differences which divide Americans today depend less and less on where one lives, what one does, or who one is (in terms of lineage), and more and more on style, on social character. But at the same time, the concentration of people of a single age-grade and a single class in a suburb, without the presence of old people, servants, and teen-age children, has itself been a factor in homogenizing modes of thought and feeling. Only a beginning can be made here in sorting out the web of consequences.

Is Conformity the Problem?

In the days of Lincoln Steffens and later, people emphasized the "shame of the cities," and in the Twenties major novelists emphasized the constraints of small-town and occasionally of small-suburban life. Today, the comparable worry, in the books dealing with the suburbs, is conformity: writers point to the uniformity of the ranch style, the everpresent television antennae, the lamp in the picture-window (which usually provides a view of the nearly treeless street, the cars, and someone else's picture-window). Observers have been struck by a kind of massification of men in Levittown and other housing developments such as was once postulated for the endless residential blocks of the cities created by the industrial revolution.[2] Even in a Canadian suburb, where one might expect slightly more hierarchial traces, a team of social scientists has found similar tendencies.[3] In the light of these commentaries, the emphasis on status in "Middletown" or "Yankee City," "Elmtown" or the New York suburb which marks the point of no return for Charlie Gray in Marquand's novel—this emphasis on graded ranks seems almost archaic; in contrast, the new suburbanite appears to suffer, less from exclusions, than from a surfeit of inclusions.[4] John Keats, in his angry and incisive *The Crack in the Picture Window*, discusses the observations of the sociologist Harold Mendelsohn concerning the excessive dependency of development dwellers on each other and on experts, coupled with monotony both in exterior trim and internalized affects.[5]

Actually, uniformity and conformity are quite different matters (as Georg Simmel observed in his essay on fashion): [6] the former may dictate to men only in inessentials, whereas the latter involves some psychological mechanism. And the conformity of the new suburbs is, in some important ways, far less stringent than that of the old; if it is not quite the case that "anything goes," lots of things do go which once would, if known, have brought ostracism. If one does not seek to force the new suburbanite back across the ethnic tracks he has just crossed, he is quite tolerant, even bland: if he is political at all—rather than parochially civic-minded, tending to a "garden" which includes the local schools and waterworks—he is apt to be an Eisenhower Republican, seldom informed, rarely angry, and only spasmodically partisan.

Indeed, what is missing in much of ~suburbia, even where the quality of life has not overtly deteriorated, is not the result of claustrophobic conformity to others' severe sanctions. Rather, there would seem to be an aimlessness, a pervasive low-keyed unpleasure which cannot be described in terms of traditional sorrows, but on which many observers of the American scene and the American visage have commented, notably Erich Fromm [7] and Percival and Paul Goodman [8]. For millions of people, work no longer provides a central focus for life; and the breadwinner is no longer the chief protagonist in the family saga—just as Saturday night no longer provides a central focus for festivity: in fact, the decentralization of leisure in the suburbs is not only spatial but temporal, as evenings from Thursday through Sunday are oriented to play rather than work and are not individually accented or collectively celebrated.[9]

Affectless Work and the Burden of Leisure

At the same time, leisure has not picked up the slack (as, in earlier writings, I was too sanguine that it might): whatever balances of work and play might have been possible for pre-industrial man, post-industrial man is keyed to greater expectations, has learned more "needs," and cannot in any case reconstitute the institutions industrialism destroyed. It is almost inconceivable, for example, to imagine a reconstitution of the folk arts which everywhere—in Nigeria as in New Orleans, in Damascus as in Tennessee—prove fragile in the face of mass-produced music and imagery. In *Communitas*, the Goodmans devoted much ingenuity to suggesting how, in their New Commune, work could be made more varied and interesting: by job-rotation on a grand scale, by alternating supervision and apprenticeship, by scrutiny of all work in terms of means as well as ends. But automation as presently interpreted moves us yet further away from such a re-examination of work routines, even though, were our values different, it could provide an opportunity for eliminating monotonous work and bringing far more variety and spark into it. We can see in the bored teen-agers who don't like school, and are already sated with sex unmitigated by love, what leisure is like for most people when life lacks the accent and structure given it by work—at least where it is not simply stand-by "work" but some effortful and periodically challenging activity.

In the studies of unemployed men made during the Great Depression, the observation of the demoralizing nature of being without work was often made, but it was sometimes assumed that this was mostly a matter of status, and of poverty forcing the unemployed man to hang uselessly about the house. And in the studies of men who have retired the same theme recurs: they are demoralized because the job gave status and income, and also because they grew up in a work-minded era and were not prepared for the Age of Leisure. I myself had thought that when a whole generation had been reared which was not driven to work by the agreed-upon motives of hunger and gain—often unconsciously driven because work-mindedness was instilled, so to speak, with mother's bottlefeeding on schedule—such people could retire more comfortably than the elderly now do because they had been preparing for it all life long. Presently, however, I am inclined to believe that work is still necessary because our inventiveness has not found ways of relating masses of men to creative activity or to each other outside of work—though the artist of whatever sort, for whom there is no real division between work and play, indicates what may someday be possible; but even the artist, whatever his ideology of *l'art pour l'art*, needs usually to feel he is being of some use (if only in acting out a counterpoint to Philistine utilitarianism).

The Revolt against the Urban-Industrial World

It is in this context that the loss of older forms of work-mindedness (including Veblen's "instinct of workmanship") and the growth of hedonism in the middle class (now permeable to the values both of the upper and the lower classes) combine to give the mass movement to the suburbs a new quality as well as quantity. Suburban dwellers are, I suggest, in the vanguard of an immense but tacit revolt against industrialism. It is a very different sort of revolt from either that of the machine-smashers of the early 19th century or of the various anti-industrial sects—socialist, anarchist, agrarian, and so on—of a later day. Large manufacturing industry is increasingly moving toward a luxurious "conspicuous production," and backbreaking toil and harsh physical conditions are vanishing (except in industrialized farming and the service trades) with the coming of electricity, inflation, full employment, unions, and personnel men. But the luxury, which is often used to make the work more gregarious and less effortful, is seldom used to make it less monotonous; [10] naturally, men treat their work as delinquents treat school (though schools are less likely than plants to pioneer the partial truancy of the four-day week!), escaping and sabotaging when they can. Managers and foremen try in vain to restore the "old school spirit" among their employees and, failing, seek through automation and quality control to make up for the deliquescence of the "instinct of workmanship" once so painfully built into the labor force. Observers of factory life have repeatedly pointed out that status within the plant is no longer gained by hard work and craftsmanship, but rather by one's consumer skills outside; and men dream, not of rising in the factory, but of starting a small business, such as a motel or gas station or TV repair shop, in the shabby and open-shop underside of our economy. [11] For youngsters from subsistence farms, for hillbillies and Southern

Negroes, a Detroit or Gary factory is still glamorous, or at least a liberation from drastic poverty and insecurity; but for second- and third-generation factory workers, it no longer holds much meaning; other than as a (hopefully temporary) source of funds and fringe benefits.[12]

To be sure, there is a new industrialism of electronics, plastics, aviation, etc., which retains a certain appeal that the older industries have so largely lost, but the new firms, increasingly located where people want to live, that is in the suburbs, or that great semi-sub-urban fringe of California, the Southwest, and Florida, speed the movement out of heavy industry and merge factory and suburban life in a blend Patrick Geddes would probably disown. But we see in these industries precisely the form that the revolt against indus-trialism has taken today, namely to partially incorporate the "enemy" so that industrialism is not compartmentalized but rather, in muted form, spreads into all parts of the culture. This is, of course, what happens in so many social struggles: one defeats the enemy by becoming more like him.

Suburban Pastoral

Let me pursue this further by looking at what is happening to the older form of industrial and commercial metropolis. When, a few years ago, I studied interviews done with several hundred college seniors at twenty representative universities, asking them what they would like or expect to be doing in fifteen years, I was struck by the fact that the great majority planned to live in the suburbs. They expected to be married, and in describing their prospective spouses they hoped for what we might call station-wagon types: educated, companionable, civic-minded, and profoundly domestic. There were few who recognized some incompatibility between focus on suburban life and focus on big-city ambitions (for instance, a senior who wanted to go into advertising, yet not live in or near New York), and they were (with some exceptions especially among the South-erners) willing to sacrifice the heights of achievement, though not the plateaus of the luxury economy, in favor of their goals of sub-urban domesticity and peace. Those who hailed originally from the suburbs suffered from no disenchantment, and wanted to return to them—often to the same one—while both city-bred and small-town boys also preferred the suburbs (I assume that some of the latter in an earlier day would have wanted to leave Main Street behind and make their mark in the city, whatever lingering agrarian fears and suspicions of it they still harbored).[13] The city today, for many, spells crime, dirt, and race tensions, more than it does culture and opportunity. While some people still escape from the small town to the city, still more are escaping from the city to the suburbs.

The successful book and movie, *The Man in the Grey Flannel Suit*, dramatizes these values quite explicitly. The hero chooses unromantic suburban cosiness, with (in the movie version) a not altogether inspiring wife and progeny, in preference to a high-pressure but potentially exciting business opportunity.[14] The head of the business is portrayed as having destroyed his family life and as virtually alienated from all human contact. Very likely, some of his junior executives would describe the company as a "mink-lined rat-trap," thus explaining and justifying their withdrawal of affect from the work itself, while recognizing that they are still competitive. A recent survey presents fragmentary evidence that managers are less satisfied with their work even than unskilled workers, and it is conceivable that the middle-class occupations in general will soon be regarded as sources of funds and of periodic contacts and activity, much as the working-class occupations are now largely regarded.[15] If work loses its centrality, then the place where it is done also comes to matter less, and the access to variety in work that the central city provides may also come to matter less. Indeed, so much is this the case already that advertising for engineers in *Scientific American* and in trade journals looks more and more like the vacation advertising in *Holiday,* and Minneapolis-Honeywell offers "seasons" and skiing as a counter-lure to the aircraft and electronic suburbs of the Far West.[16] In this regimen, white-collar and blue-collar move towards one another, as each group now emphasizes the consumer side of life, and sees the suburbs as its locale.

The Withdrawal of the Elite

Obviously enough, I have not stressed here the vicious circle of urban decay and Negro and poor-white in-migration which, for many middle-income families, contribute an additional push from the city quite apart from the direct appeal of suburban domesticity. Whereas the European immigrants at the turn of the century appalled many middle-class people, it led them in countless ways to counter-attack: recall the fights against Tammany and other immigrant-based bossisms, the drive to "Americanize" and simonize the newcomers, the sanguine belief in the melting pot—and the shutting off of immigration. This last measure is unavailable against our own colonials, whether in the South or in Puerto Rico or, for all practical purposes, in Mexico; and the energy, arrogance, and hope that sustained the good-government counter-attack seems to be missing now in all but those few cities where the upper-income elites have retained faith in redevelopment and in moderate racial integration.

Although upper-class and upper-middle-class people have lived in the suburbs of our great cities since the 1880's or earlier, the cities before World War II still retained their hegemony: they engrossed commercial, industrial, and cultural power. The city represented the division and specialization not only of labor but of attitude and opinion: by discovering like-minded people in the city, one developed a new style, a new little magazine, a new architecture. The city, that is, provided a "critical mass" which made possible new combinations—criminal and fantastic ones as well as stimulating and productive ones. Today, however, with the continual loss to the suburbs of the elite and the enterprising, the cities remain huge enough for juveniles to form delinquent subcultures; but will our cities be able to continue to support cultural and educational activities at a level appropriate to our abundant economy?

This is a serious, not a rhetorical question. For the fact is that we understand very little about the role of numbers as such in cultural advance. The effective population of Athens at the height of its glory was far smaller than that of Newark today. We know that the encounters of people with each other are psychological as well as ecological and that, of course, creative contact is not simply a matter of numbers and chance encounters. We know, too, that some academic communities in small towns have been quite stimulating, while some huge city universities have been barren. And we have the example of Denmark where, under the leadership of the metropolis, rural life in the last century has become highly literate. Conceivably the cultural consequences of suburban scatteration can be surmounted.

But the problem of political consequences remains. In one of the suburbs we have been studying outside of Chicago, we have found a number of extremely capable men, active in their businesses or law firms downtown, who seem to enjoy involving themselves in suburban issues that, at least to the onlooker, seem excessively trivial and small-scale. They will spend time on whether dogs should be on leash or not, on whether parking meters should be installed on the main shopping street, and on minuscule questions of zoning—as well as on the board of the school whose reputation was one reason for coming to the suburb in the first place. And while one might contend that even small issues symbolize the suburban way of life and its defense against "unsocialized" newcomers from the city, it remains true that these men have retreated from the great problems of the metropolis, and perhaps of the nation, to the more readily manageable ones of the periphery. Indeed, as American business and professional men get nicer, better educated, and more cultivated, they neither go into politics directly nor turn politics over to kept officials, but seek to put all their bets on administration (which appears clean and uncontentious), and the suburban life encourages this form of housebroken activity.[17] The elite, however, tend to associate with like-income neighbors rather than with like-minded civic leaders, thus dispersing their potential for leadership that looks beyond township boundaries.

Undoubtedly for some migrants to the suburbs civic activity on a manageable scale has taken the place of feelings of impotence in the face of urban blight and consequent political apathy. But for others suburban civics would seem to be child's play, enjoyable as recreation but hardly a challenge or a source of significant political experience.

Yet there is an irony lurking in this development, for it may soon turn out that the suburbs themselves are no longer manageable precisely because millions of other people are also choosing to live there.[18] And, as already indicated, I am speaking here of suburbs which are no longer viewed as bedroom communities, from which men commute to an industrial and commercial world which absorbs their main energies; rather, men today as well as women seek the good life in the suburbs and are not satisfied to be merely good providers.

In this perspective, early marriage and the rise in the birth-rate are so many rivulets of individual, only barely self-conscious, protest against the values inherited from industrialism and the low-birth-rate middle-class metropolis—so many decisions to prefer companionship in the present to some distant goal, and so many mortgages of the future in the benevolent shadow of the luxury economy and its escalator of slow inflation, promotion, and protection. Whereas men once identified themselves with commerce and industry—with its power, its abstractions, its achievements—and forced women to remain identified with domesticity (save for those women who broke through the barrier and became man-imitating career girls), now, as many observers have pointed out, a growing homogenization of roles is occurring: women take jobs to support the suburban menage periodically, while men take part in its work (do-it-yourself), its civic activities (PTA, etc.), and its spirit.[19] Rather than delegating religion to their womenfolk, they go to church in increasing numbers, occasionally as in an earlier day to be respectable or to climb socially, and occasionally out of a genuine religious call, but more typically because the church, like the high school and the country club, has become a center for the family as a social and civic unit.

The Decentralization of Leisure

All this brings with it an increasing decentralization of leisure. Just as the suburban churches tend, within the boundaries of the "three faiths," to an amiable syncretism, ignoring doctrinal or liturgical differences, so too the other leisure activities of the suburbs tend to reduce the specialized differentiations possible in a metropolis. What I mean here can be illustrated with reference to music. A metropolis has enough music-lovers to organize highly differentiated groups: Mozart lovers may split off from Bach lovers and would never encounter lovers of Wagner, while in the suburbs the music-lovers, if they are to support communal activities at all, must in some measure homogenize their tastes and hence create a local market for "classical": indeed, they will be exposed to a good deal of community pressure to support the musical activities of their friends, in return for having their own enterprises supported. The same holds, *parri passu,* for the other arts—just as it does for the differentiation of specialty stores, churches, and museums found in a large city; by the same token, the suburban activist can feel his own contribution matters, as he is likely to feel in the big city only when he is very rich, very active, or very influential. People brought up in the suburbs may not realize what they are missing, and they may relate their emotional ties entirely to their locality, not going downtown to shop or to visit friends or (as Philip Ennis observes, *supra*) to go to the theatre.

Suburbs differ, of course, in what they make available, and so do central cities; thus, Morris Janowitz showed that many people who, to the visitor's eye, live in Chicago actually live in a small neighborhood that might as well be a suburb.[20] Moreover, central cities are increasingly influenced by suburban styles of life: people trained to a suburban attachment to their cars drive downtown even when good and commodious public transportation is available, and they wear the casual dress of the suburbs when they do.

The suburban dweller believes, in fact, that he has the best of both worlds. In the interviews with college seniors I referred to earlier, in which such stress was placed on suburban domesticity, many students also emphasized their wish not to lose the cultural amenities they had enjoyed in college.[21] Some of these amenities will certainly be distributed in the suburb, though frequently in diluted doses, piped in through TV and radio and hi-fi sets; the suburb may even support a theatre group and, in a few cases, amateur chamber music; the local high school will provide entertainment of a sort, as well as facilities for adult education.

However, as the radii lengthen on which people move away from the city—as they must with the crowding of the suburbs leading to the jump to the exurbs—people either learn as in California to drive great distances for dinner or confine themselves to their immediate environs: the central city as a meeting place disappears—a process which has gone further in Los Angeles and Chicago than in Boston or New York: the neighbors make up little circles based (as William H. Whyte, Jr., showed for Park Forest [22]) largely on propinquity.

The decentralization of leisure in the suburbs goes further than this, however, as the home itself, rather than the neighborhood, becomes the chief gathering place for the family—either in the "family room" with its games, its TV, its informality, or outdoors around the barbecue. And while there are values in this of family closeness and "togetherness," there is also a loss of differentiation as the parents play pals to their children and the latter, while gaining a superficial precocity, lose the possibility of wider contacts; at worst, there is a tendency for family talk and activity to seek the lowest common denominator in terms of age and interest.

Some of these matters are illustrated by an interview with a housewife who had recently bought a house in one of the wealthier suburbs north of Chicago. Her husband had been transferred to Chicago from a southern city and had been encouraged by his company to buy a large house for entertaining customers. Customers, however, seldom came, as the husband was on the road much of the time. The wife and three children hardly ever went downtown (they had no Chicago contacts anyway), and after making sporadic efforts to make the rounds of theatre and musical activities in the suburbs, and to make friends there, they found themselves more and more often staying home, eating outdoors in good weather and looking at TV in bad. Observing that "there is not much formal entertaining back and forth," the wife feared she was almost losing her conversational skills; yet she felt that her family had been pulled closer together by the shared activities (in which the husband joined on weekends) around the home. After listening to her list and discuss the friends made at church and golf, it became evident that her immediate environment just missed providing her with people close enough to her in taste and interest for intimate ties to develop.

One interview, of course, proves little, and many factors are obviously involved in choice of friends; suburban location in an older, non-homogeneous suburb is only one of them (I recall obtaining such interviews in Kansas City, too, among people who had lived there all their lives, and had potential access to wide strata in the metropolitan area). Nevertheless, there seems to me to be a tendency, though not a pronounced one, to lose in the suburbs the human differentiations which have made great cities in the past the centers of rapid intellectual and cultural advance. The suburb is like a fraternity house at a small college, in which like-mindedness reverberates upon itself as the potentially various selves within each of us do not get evoked or recognized. For people who move to the suburb when adult, of course, matters are different than among those who never knew another milieu. And, to be sure, creative human contact need not be face-to-face but can often be vicarious, through print or other mediated channel: certainly, highly differentiated human beings have grown up in locales which gave them minimal support (moreover, though the non-neighborly seldom seek the suburbs,[23] a few doubtless manage to survive there). Ease of movement, in any case, permits periodic access to others, although as these others themselves scatter to the suburbs, this process becomes more difficult.

The Social Psychology of the Auto

Indeed, at least until each of us has his own helicopter or rocket, this pattern of life requires us to spend a great deal of time in automobiles, overcoming decentralization—but driving is itself a terribly "decentralized" activity, allowing at best for car-pool sociability, and at worst mitigated by the quiz-bits, frequent commercials, and flatulent music of AM radio. As compared with the older suburbanites who commuted by train and read the paper or did homework or even read a book (whatever tensions there might be in catching the train), the present and increasing tendency to travel to work by car seems aggressively vacuous and solipsistic.[24] Whereas in pre-industrial cultures, and in the lower classes in industrial society, people sometimes just hang on a corner or sit vacantly, it is striking that in a society which offers many alternatives people will consent to drive vacantly but not refreshingly—woe betide the careless or unspry pedestrian or bicyclist who gets in the way of industrial workers pouring out of the factory parking lots or white-collar workers coming home on a thruway. The human waste here is most important, but the waste of resources and land, the roadside *dreck*,[25] the highways which eat space as railroad yards even in St. Louis or Chicago never did, are not negligible even in a huge rich country.

Where the husband goes off with the car to work (and often, in the vicious circle created by the car, there is no other way for him to travel), the wife is frequently either privatized at home or must herself, to escape isolation, take a job which will help support her own car, as well as the baby-sitter.

The children themselves, in fact, before they get access to a car, are captives of their suburb, save for those families where the housewives surrender continuity in their own lives to chauffeur their children to lessons, doctors, and other services which could be reached via public transport in the city. In the suburban public schools, the young are captives, too, dependent on whatever art and science and general liveliness their particular school happens to have —again contrast the metropolis, with its occasional choice of high schools, as most notably in New York.[26]

The Suburban Pueblos

The captivity of the housewives, tied down in the suburbs by their young children, the lack of a car, and the lack of servants (or of grand-parents to act as part-time homemakers and baby-sitters), has struck many observers. I know that on the few occasions when I have inter-viewed in the morning in new suburbs south of Chicago, I have been struck by the eagerness of the housewives to talk to somebody (and not only to a man!) who is not a salesman (occasionally, they must be weaned away from the TV). It is not only the visiting intellectual who finds the lives of these women empty, their associations fragmentary (my colleagues, Donald Horton and R. Richard Wohl, speak of the "para-social intimacy" they attain with the celebrities of the TV variety shows [27]); they themselves, if at all sensitive or well-educated, complain of having their contacts limited to their young children and to a few other housewives in the same boat. And, as a result of efforts to understand the extraordinary philoprogenitiveness of the suburban middle classes, I have come to entertain the suspicion that, once started on having children, these women continue in some part out of a fear of the emptiness of life without children, and of the problems they would face of relating themselves to their menfolk without the static, the noise, the pleasures, the "problems," that the presence of children provides.

Indeed, the suburban kaffee-klatsch is proverbial in which the women sit around and discuss their children—the main "surrogates" they have in common. Their husbands, working downtown or in a nearby plant, have some opportunity to meet people on an occupa-tional basis who are of different backgrounds, different ages, and different life-chances than they themselves; but the wives, falling into or forced into a neighborly gregariousness, tend to see others of similar age, setting, and TV exposure.[28] Whyte has described the pressures in the new suburbs favoring a pueblo-type extended-family sociability of the rental court or cul-de-sac street. Selectivity of friends on grounds that might be suspected as snobbish would cause trouble with the neighbors (in whose yards the children play); cross-sex friendships are ruled out by lack of sophistication in such rela-tions and by the lack of privacy. And the husbands, if not the tired businessmen of legend, are less eager than some of their wives to drive long distances at night for out-of-suburb contacts, because as just indicated the men have had a chance at work (and perhaps in a drink after work, or on "business" trips) to meet a greater variety of people. In this situation, many women of college education feel trapped, aware of falling behind their own ideals and their husbands' in breadth of view and nourishing experience. The various leisure-time activities they undertake do not seem to fill this void.

Our Center for the Study of Leisure has been conducting studies of limited scope in several Chicago suburbs in an effort, *inter alia,* to see what happens to people who leave the city for the suburbs in terms of new commitments and new demands; we have also done a very inconclusive study of how people in the city spend their weekends. We have the impression that the suburbanite, tied to his house as the doctor is to his practice, may actually be less likely to take off for a weekend in the country than the urban dweller whose janitor can look after his apartment and even the cat (and who can also, of course, descend with no other responsibility than a gift of liquor on his suburban relatives and friends). Indeed, it is the city people freed by industrialism from long hours of grinding work who (along, of course, with an ample supply of untied suburbanites) make up a large proportion of the outboard population of our lakes and rivers and of the thirty-five million fishermen (more than twice the number of those urban sportsmen, the bowlers). Although air-conditioning makes even the most humid and dirty city potentially habitable, people can't wait to leave town on weekends and during the summer, even though in many parts of the country it means fighting for space on roads, on lakes, and at motels with like-minded crowds.[29]

Snobbery and imitation of the rich play a declining part in this exodus, and in the movement to the suburbs. I would argue that there is often less "front" in the new suburbs than in equivalent sections of a metropolis, and less pressure for a lace-curtain life concealing back-stage scrimping and meanness than there once was. People don't usually learn the idea of a garden suburb either from British models or Mumford or Clarence Stein: the idea, in its uncomplicated forms, it is an omnipresent dream, carrying overtones of the Bible, of peasant life and folk imagery. The widespread wish for contact with nature has for many Americans been crystallized around the habits of the British gentry and their middle-class imitators—but,

more modest than the aspidistra-lovers of the London suburbs, we
prefer not to give fancy names to our own "villas" but to let this
dumb show be done for us by the realtors: in the Chicago area,
for instance, a number of suburbs have either "Park" or "Forest"
in their names (two of them have both!). Furthermore, social mobility
means that many, perhaps most urban dwellers will have suburban
relatives or friends: the mass-production of suburbs, especially in the
post-war years, has made them accessible to almost everyone (only
in the rural and impoverished parts of the South and Great Plains
farming regions are we likely to find many people who don't know
anybody who lives in a suburb, and have never had occasion to visit
one). Beyond that, the vicarious socialization of Americans into the
experiences of consumption they are about to have is the continuous
task of the mass media, many of which, at a variety of income levels,
are devoted to expounding the suburban way of life directly in ads
and features; other media are indirect vehicles for suburban styles
in the homes pictured in stories, the sport-shirts worn, the idols of
consumption portrayed.[30] The American ethos, which in the populist
era revolved about the dialectic of pure country versus wicked (but
exciting) city, seems to me now aerated by the suburban outlook,
which homogenizes, without fully integrating, both city and country.

The Garden Suburb

While on the whole the lower-middle and middle-income suburbs
sponsor the relaxed life, there is one area where they impose an
imperative which many city-dwellers have not met, namely that of
having some sort of garden—less as a cultural amenity (as the culture
of flowers has traditionally been in Japan) than as a minimum contribution to civic decency: a kind of compulsory outdoor housekeep-
ing. Indeed, in the study of gardening in two Chicago suburbs conducted by our Center for the Study of Leisure [31] we gained the
impression that garden clubs were not extremely active in either one
(though we have found very active and prestigeful clubs on the North
Shore); garden clubs are much more characteristic of small older
communities, where they represent a familiar activity of some of the
established families, than of the new suburbs, where gardening must
compete with many other hobbies and activities, outdoor and indoor.
We found in Fairlawn, a new developer's suburb, for example, that

to many housewives the garden was simply one more chore: it represented not a contrast with the asphalt jungle of the city or a pleasure in growing things, or a rage for order, but a tax imposed by neighborhood consciousness. And we realized that many people who have moved newly to the suburbs to escape the city come without awareness of the constraints they will find, or mistakenly interpret, in the suburb: like the appointment in Samara, they meet pressures they had thought to leave behind, though altered in form and impact.

The Meyersohn-Jackson study reported elsewhere in this volume makes certain suggestions as to how this comes about in a suburb where everyone is new—often new to family life and suburban life, too—and is looking to neighbors for cues as to how to spend leisure time. But the misinterpretation of these cues still needs to be understood; for there is a tendency for families in this new suburb of Fairlawn to assume that their neighbors, who were in fact quite tolerant, were putting pressure on them to have not merely a passable but a good garden. Actually, the neighbor's visual sense was not that highly developed, nor their emulative sense either: they were tolerant of each other's gardens as of each other's life in general. Yet the Fairlawn housewife (quoted in the Meyersohn-Jackson article above) was not taking advantage of her community's casualness when, after describing to the interviewer an ambitious plan for a rose garden and large beds of flowers all around the house, she blurted out:

> "I really hate gardening; we both do. My husband never plays golf anymore and we do nothing all weekend but work in the garden. I mean work."

In reflecting on this, I recall analogous comments made by students who were working allegedly to prepare for an exam, which their intelligence told them they could not easily fail; I recall other such comments by business and professional men who created anxieties in their work in order to give it drama and bite. I realize that, since we are not really attached to anything we are doing, we look for spurs when life no longer automatically provides them. Perhaps the housewife just quoted cannot make herself (or her spouse) work at all without picturing dire consequences for failure (or perhaps she has in this case simply projected her own moralism or malice into her neighbors—possibly also as a part of an internal family argument with an indifferent or indolent husband). Games, the arts, conversation are all activities which have institutionalized short bursts of effort as the price both of pleasure and performance. The suburbs, however, in seeking to take the place of the city, provide insufficient comparable agendas, and housewives such as those we saw who gardened with neither pleasure nor skill still clung to the demand that neighbors and nature seemed to make.

One factor here, as John R. Seeley and his colleagues have emphasized in *Crestwood Heights,* is the need to locate in external demands some rationale for the inner discomforts that suburban living with its seeming amenity have not removed. Having put industrialism and many of its drives behind them, people are still unhappy, and sometimes seek the comfort of finding in their new situation "justifications" for this paradox. At a more sophisticated level, existentialist philosophy—popular in one suburb we have been studying—may take the place of a garden.

Putting ultimates aside for the moment, it is striking how few of the gardens examined showed much sense for overall plan in time and space; items were often unrelated to each other by any visual aesthetic we could reconstruct. Perhaps, in time, the gardeners will learn better, though I am not too sanguine about this. Their pleasure in flowers, or in the more casual arrangements of nature, do not strike me as very intense. I am not speaking of "taste" in the sense of high taste, but rather of the quality with which visual experience is assimilated. And I am certainly not speaking of the uniformity of the gardens: the row houses in Baltimore or Philadelphia are often handsome in ways which our most effortfully varied suburbs fail to achieve. In the course of the industrial revolution and the rise of the middle classes, both elite taste and traditional taste decline. Today, despite frequent improvement in advertising and magazine layout, in interior decoration, and in corporate and public building, the sense of visual imagery of Americans remains stunted, and the children of the suburbs grow up accepting the neat, the new, the shiny, but with minimal awareness of vista, proportion, or independent critical judgment of the look of life around them.[32]

Dilemmas and Opportunities of the Planner

I went back the other day to reread that remarkable and neglected book, *Communitas: Means of Livelihood and Ways of Life,* by

Percival and Paul Goodman.[33] This book includes a commentary on utopian community planning in the past and some suggestions as to potential utopias within the American scene of our day. On at least two grounds, it makes strange and disturbing reading now. In the first place, it is easy to forget how much enthusiasm there was, during and immediately after World War II, for creative planning and re-organization of communal life, both here and in Europe; ten years later, the air is sodden—as if a fall-out over intellectual life had already occurred—the Cold War absorbs much of our political energy, and we struggle, not to plan, but even to register what is happening to our fantastically expanding economy, population, and metropolitan malaise.[34] In the second place, it is curious how many of the Goodmans' then-utopian suggestions have been incorporated into our lives, ten years later, without planning and with fundamental change coming about interstitially only. Their first, and ironical, plan—for a city of efficient consumption—we have come much closer to approximating, though our shopping centers are suburban rather than urban: certainly our advertising is more "efficient" than pre-War, and our waste more exuberant.[35] Their second plan, for the decentralization of work and life, has come about in some measure: through turning the home into a do-it-yourself workshop, through some degree of suburbaniza-tion of industry, and through greater labor mobility; but the quality of this plan, aimed at minimizing central political and economic con-trol and at making work and leisure more meaningful, seems further away than ever. Their third plan, which aimed at a subsistence economy for security on top of which a luxury economy would be reared, has come about in an utterly paradoxical form: we have now a dual economy, one part of which is luxurious, pays high wages, lives in handsome plants, and generally engages in "conspicuous produc-tion," while the other part of the economy lives as if on another continent, paying low wages, not practicing Harvard Business School techniques, and seldom financing itself out of retained profits and quick depreciation accounts. The Goodmans' third plan was intended to minimize government regulation, and private price-administered regulation also, but our dual economy depends on continued war preparation, suitable tax and credit policies, and agreement between labor and management in the high-wage economy to let the consumer, and sometimes the stockholder, pay the costs of private socialism and creeping inflation.[36] Yet the consumer also benefits from the dual economy if he works for the high-wage, managerial side of it, or if, while working for the underprivileged economy, he can somehow use the former as leverage or "host" for raising his own income, without the corresponding inplant efficiencies and extra-plant responsibilities of the managerial side. Moreover, as W. H. Whyte argues in *The Organization Man,* the new neatly-assembled suburbs, with their handsome school plants and their neighborly fraternalism, are the consumption side of the managerial economy, valuing a similar "social ethic" and suffering from a similar lack of ultimate goals. Likewise, the residual but still immense slums to be found in both country and city are the domestic or consumer side of the low-wage, non-expense-account economy.[37]

This latter economy lacks the subsistence security at which the Goodmans aimed—rather, it remains the principal arena in which one is allowed to fail, or to make a very fast buck. And the luxury economy exercises a ceaseless pull, both in its styles of production and in the spread of these, via the expense account, into so-called private life.[38] Thus, private life gets further and further from even the possibilities of a subsistence minimum. At least it does so apart from the possibility, conceivable but unlikely, of a Savonarola-type revolt against high standards of living, and the economic and social structure that accompanies these.

Perhaps the most significant difference between the Goodmans' books and the present state of the American experience and imagination is that the latter are encased in an additive or extrapolative mode of perception. When we have a problem, we have a standard remedy: more.[39] We add a road, a wing to a school, a new department or government agency. Seldom do we rearrange the givens so that they become "takens," into a new configuration (as was done, for notable examples, in the TVA and the Marshall Plan). This is not the old American formula of "bigger and better" merely, or the old American optimism, now in any case considerably attenuated. Rather, it is something which goes deeper into the way Americans structure their very image of physical and social reality. In his perceptive essay, "What is American about America?" John Kouwenhoven gives many illustrations of the additive principle, from the land-grant section to the reiterative beat of jazz, the roll of film, the highway grid of our cities, the added stories of the skyscraper or high-rise apartment, our soap-opera serials, our assembly-lines.[40] Dorothy Lee, on the basis of linguistic studies, has shown the lilt and drive of analogous tendencies in the changing patterns of American English.[41]

One could argue that these are no more than minor American variants of Western dualism and the decimal system and other similar categories which govern our perception and communication. But America is today, as in Tocqueville's time, freer for better and worse of alternative perceptions rooted in feudal or ecclesiastical history— even the South is being rapidly colonized. Moreover, for a variety of reasons, planning has become almost a specialty of the large corporations which are committed to the additive principle by the very nature of their annual balance sheets, tax returns, and inventories—just as government agencies can seldom plan for more than one or two years by the nature of our budget and electoral systems. While Federal expenditures and hence capital investment are held on a plateau by past wars and the present strife of the services, and while states and local governmental units seek to keep up with yesterday, big business has at least some opportunity to look ahead in terms of capital spending and, where financially-backed foresight has monopolistic support as with Bell Telephone and General Electric, even to look further than the next annual report.

Forecasting, however, is almost always wrong, in part because it is confined to certain parts of the society; it assumes that other things will stay the same—they never do. In earlier generations, when America was an underdeveloped country, the limits of prophecy could always be set by reference to England or some other fully industrialized and urbanized place, but now we have become an overdeveloped country and have outrun our models. (We use the USSR in this capacity whenever they will oblige.) Thus, we turn to our own past for a model, and go on extrapolating. For instance, it seems generally to be assumed by business planners (some government officials are less sanguine) that a larger population will produce and consume proportionately more than a smaller one, despite the friction its very size may create and the possible loss of much of its potential productivity through inadequate schooling and low morale. (The inadequate schooling will reflect *inter alia,* the much smaller energy for foresight that civic and educational institutions typically have, in comparison with the huge self-financing corporations, which often would as soon set staff men to work on forecasting and a thousand other things as raise dividends and pay more taxes.)

At any rate, with these few exceptions, there would seem to be in this country, considering the increased ability to plan given by more subtle techniques in the social sciences,[42] a recklessness on the part of the whole society not much different in temper from the way millions of individual families have decided to live now, pay later: to finance on credit a shaky structure of personal plans and possessions which no insurance can protect against the mischances of illness, separation, untimely death—quite apart from socially-induced disaster.[43] This absence of personal planning, this foreshortening of individual time perspectives, is sometimes attributed to the fear of war and the bomb, but in my opinion such a fear (which for purposes of international sanity one could wish were more widespread) can only be a very small part of the explanation. Likewise, the rational fear that inflation will dissipate savings is also only a limited factor in the present-orientation of people—indeed, this fear often serves to rationalize extravagance. Rather, we have lost some traditional fears—anxieties about living on credit, about spending as such, about enjoyment. Having had the cornucopia upturned over our heads, we feel it, if not a duty to consume, at least a kind of civil liberty to do so. The democ-ratization of consumer values has made people refuse to put up any longer with what they regard as arbitrary deprivations, whether in old-model cars or homes or styles of life in general—this is behavior familiar enough in all the newly rising "democratic nations."

A parallelism of individual and social behavior—in which the recklessness of families is reduplicated in state and nation—is not essential: there can be a prodigal society based on thrifty citizens, and vice versa, for institutions and elites mediate between the largest whole and the motives of individuals. But democracy means that in-dividuals influence institutions and, in time, may reshape them ac-cording to heart's desire. And as already stated radically alternative ways of life which might evoke different desires are strikingly absent from the visual and psychological landscape of America, which is why we see parodies of the Goodmans' and other utopias rather than serious attempts, on a scale comparable in our time to Radbourne in the 1920's, to experiment with new forms.[44]

There are, fortunately, counter-tendencies. Victor Gruen's plan for Fort Worth, Mies van der Rohe's plan for the Gratiot Area in Detroit, are examples.[45] But I found a recent summary of such plans by Catherine Bauer in the *Architectural Forum* depressing, when I realized that most of the work described originated in the 1920's at the Bauhaus or was the achievement of a few aging visionaries like Frank Lloyd Wright.[46] Not that I object to the Bauhaus: I think that the Weimar period was one of the great creative bursts of Western history: rather, its emissaries, though they have some disciples, are not self-renewing, and the problems of scale and quality of life are much greater now. We expect more of life than did our parents and grand-parents—more, even, than freedom from want and the standard package of consumer durables: our very abundance has increased the scope of our expectations about what life could be like and therefore has made our situation potentially revolutionary.

The Freeway Cult

Meanwhile, of course, subtopia marches on, and people who have fled the metropolis to escape its traffic, its tax-rates, and above all the threats to status and schooling from ethnic minorities, find these catching up with them. The waves of succession within the city proper do not halt at its boundaries (though they may be temporarily blocked by working-class violence, as in Cicero, Illinois). Indeed, as my colleague, Morton Grodzins, has noted, some cities may reincorporate suburban enclaves to prevent being overwhelmed by the Negro vote.[47]

In this situation, some suburbanites will be tempted to become exurbanites, putting the ever-approaching city another few miles away, and hoping to solve the problem of being distant from some people and intimate with others by a super-highway.

However, in this quandary the emphasis on super-highways—and on super-cars which require them—takes on much of the lunatic quality of an arms race: as highways get bigger and better, they invite more cars, destroy what undeveloped and unschematized country (or central city) remains, and require still more highways in an unending spiral.[48] People have been drilled by industrialism in the values of efficiency—as narrowly defined in terms of speed, perform-ance, and a kind of streamlined look (what Jacques Barzun has re-ferred to as "America's Romance with Practicality")—so that even when they flee from the cities and the style of life industrialism has brought about, they cannot change the style of thought which sees the solution to ribbon developments in stretching them still further until our East and West Coasts threaten to become continuous roadside slums.

House Beautiful

What is true of the planning, or lack of it, of our road-centered culture as a whole, is also true of domestic architecture. Efficiency here is less stark—and consequently often less attractive—since it must compete with traditional definitions of a suburban free-standing home; but, as many architects have pointed out, the interiors are highly "modern" in terms of mechanization. Indeed, one reason why husbands have been willing to become domesticated is that they have been promoted from dishwashers to dishwasher-operators—just as they use power mowers to give crew-cuts to handkerchief-sized lawns (and pierce their wives' and neighbors' ears with the screams of hi-fi). The open plan of the very newest ranch-style homes puts the TV set on a swivel in the center, where it can be seen from all parts of the house, so that urban news, fashions, gossip, and jokes can circulate in the home throughout the daily cycle of the members of the family. But all these improvements are bought at the expense of space for the individual, whose bedroom in the suburban development is often smaller than in city tenements—this is especially true, as Albert Roland of *Household* Magazine has pointed out to me, of the newest suburban homes which have both a family room and a living room (the latter, like the old parlor, used only for state occasions), with the family room big enough for games, the TV, an inside bar-becue, and general clutter.

Nor does the lawn or backyard provide a bounteous free space in most of the new developments. In comparison with the size and cost of the house, plots are small (much as they have traditionally been in Midwestern cities where people wanted to avoid the row house but not to be too far from their next-door neighbors). Moreover, the fact that there is both a front and a backyard (the latter being, in many developments, the "family room" and the former the "parlor") means that what space there is becomes divided. And just as the homes have no interstitial spaces, no nooks and crannies, so the lots have no texture taken individually or together.[49] I keep asking myself what the lots will look like when the explosion of our population doubles the numbers in the suburban hegira without, in all probability, increasing proportionately the services that our new expectations crave. Will houses and lots get smaller, when people can no longer spread further afield? People have been moving to the suburbs in many cases in pursuit of an inchoate dream of spaciousness; they have looked for a release from urban tensions, from crowded and ugly schools, from indoors. And ordinarily this release has more than compensated for losses in urban qualities which are difficult to sense or describe— qualities of possibility, often, rather than of actual use.

The Future

Indeed, for millions of suburbanites, their post-War experience has been prosperous and open far beyond their Depression-born expectations. For them, the suburbs have been one vast supermarket, abundantly and conveniently stocked with approved yet often variegated choices. The children are less of a worry than on city streets; the neighbors often more friendly than those city folk who "keep themselves to themselves"; life in general is more relaxed. The confidence such people often have that things will continue to go well for them is revealed in the story told one journalist in a Southern California suburb where employment depends on nearby defense plants, when he asked people what would happen to them in case of a depression or cancellation of defense contracts: "Why then the government will stockpile cars." [50] Life on credit has worked out well for many such home-owners, allowing them to have their children young, and in circumstances far better than those in which they themselves grew up. Whatever the outsider might say about the risks blithely taken, with no allowance made for personal or social setbacks, or about the anemic quality of the relaxed life or its complacency, he would have to admit that such first-generation suburbanites had found the taste of abundance pleasant and, for the younger ones with wages rising faster than prices, not notably problematic. But what will occur when the urban qualities have been dissipated, while the suburban ones elude all but the rich?

Such questions assume, as I have here been doing, that Americans have ceased being socially inventive, outside of the corporate or military spheres; they assume that we will not discover the governmental or voluntary channels either to give many people alternative satisfactions to large families or to create forms of life and livelihood appropriate to another age of population expansion—this time, with no frontier left. Certainly, there is now a kind of private inventiveness in the suburbs among people who, having lost "the track of generations" and traditional standards of judgment and taste, are somehow managing, with ambivalent aid from the media, to create new forms and styles. The leaders of Park Forest and several other new communities, surrounded by others as green as they, often managed to develop some communal decencies and controls; in that sense, the town-meeting spirit is far from moribund. It is easy to see the negative and ironical features of the suburbs—harder to see emergent crystallizations.[51]

As things stand now, however, the suburbs, like the families within them, can scarcely control their own immediate environs, let alone the larger metropolitan and national orbits that impinge on them and decide their eventual atmosphere. And here is where the suburbanites' immense liking for Ike is portentous: it expresses the wish of so many of the college seniors mentioned above that civics and the Community Chest replace politics; it expresses the hope, built into the very structure of credit and the additive-extrapolative style of thought, that nothing serious will occur, that everything will go on as before. And it expresses this hope, of course, at the very moment when private decisions, irresponsibility influenced, to buy or not to buy, to propagate or not to propagate, store up our destinies (quite apart from the similar activities of the rest of our small planet). In interviews done in Chicago suburbs by Louis Harris before the 1956 elections, he asked potential voters how they felt about a part-time, golf-playing president; many were indignant, saying they'd play golf too, if they had such problems—though when asked to name serious problems facing the country, they could often get no further than high taxes. Plainly, Ike's complacencies mirrored and supported their own (Eisenhower, of course, like almost anyone in Washington, is far less complacent than these constituencies), and their defenses against untoward apprehension were too great to allow thought for the morrow.

City planners are, of course, well aware of these matters, try as some of them do to act like highway engineers or administrative efficiency experts. Some of them know that the motives which once gave structure to both work and leisure, and the interchanges and journeys between them, have also been disappearing, even though millions of people, shorn of other rationales for activity, still go after money: not in the form of capital but in the form of consumer goods. Our new middle-class large families are, in part, the result of an effort to fill this gap, as our suburbs are an effort to build a life not based on work, but instead on the family and on voluntary associations. It is surely an advance to prefer children to capital gains, and suburban *Gemütlichkeit* to urban pavements (though, as British planners discovered in building the New Towns and as writers for the *Architectural Review* have insisted, there were values concealed in the most seemingly depressed urban conglomerations which were lost in the move to the more hygienic and aseptic planned communities— much as farmers for a long time failed to realize that worms and other "varmint" were essential to a well-nourished soil). But the advances cannot be consolidated unless they are made on a broader front; otherwise, people may quickly oscillate again towards such apparent security as industrialism gave them.[52] Faced with the mounting depreciations of the crowded suburbs and aware of their own powerlessness, they may turn to strong authority which promises to clean up the already foreseeable mess. Even now, drivers in a traffic jam, frustrated by each other's presence, are not the most amiable of men, despite the fact that, once on the move again, it is largely the sense of moving, rather than anything they actively do or enjoy, which gives them pleasure and release.

Writing ten years ago about the Goodmans' book, I was up against the planners' perennial problem: how to get from here to there, when "here" is the omnipresent educator, the agent of socialization. Yet, as makers of goods and ideas know, Americans are almost too ready to abandon one thing for another, provided they are persuaded by the media or friends that the other is somehow "better" or, preferably, "the best," along a dimension which is already given. To be sure, the range of such persuasion is not terribly wide, and is wider of course in inessentials or externals, though the last ten years have seen radical changes in food habits, men's clothes, child-rearing, and other (one might suppose) tenacious things. More problematic is the persuasion itself, which when mobilized for the planners' good ends is frequently self-defeating because it almost inevitably uses the given means, such as appeals to snobbery or to a fake efficiency. Yet the fear of this problem, with its practical and ethical dilemmas, seems to me at present to have intimidated thinking about what the good ends are, so that even if people could be persuaded, there is nothing to persuade them of. Plans, as history occasionally shows, have their own persuasive power, particularly in unexpected historical junctures. Many Americans will soon discover the loss of urban and suburban texture, and might then be ready to do something, were a model available. The social processes I have touched upon in this paper are moving people into the service trades and professions and out of industry and farming, and we need to find meaningful work for the displaced ones, rather than locating still more of them in selling, public relations, and looking after each other. The country can "use" poets, painters, planners, and prophets in virtually unlimited amounts. With poets in recent years the country has not done too badly; with painters (despite all I have said about visual blight and the country of the blind) not too badly, either. But planners and prophets?

FOOTNOTES

1. The city is not necessarily the seat of urbanism, and the suburban way differs from the city way only at the polarities of each, based on variables not entirely dependent on ecology or visible from a helicopter. See, for observant commentary, Gregory P. Stone, "City Shoppers and Urban Identification: Observations on the Social Psychology of City Life," *American Journal of Sociology,* LX (1954), pp. 36-45; also Wendell Bell and Marion D. Boat, "Urban Neighborhoods and Informal Social Relations," *Ibid.,* LXII (1957), pp. 391-398, and references there cited; Sylvia Fleis Fava, "Suburbanism as a Way of Life," *American Sociological Review,* vol. 21, 1956, pp. 34-37.
2. Compare William H. Whyte, Jr., *The Organization Man* (New York: Simon & Schuster, 1956), part VII; also, an unpublished thesis on Park Forest by Herbert Gans, Social Science Divisional Masters Program, University of Chicago. And see Frederick Lewis Allen, "The Big Change in Suburbia," *Harper's* (June 1954), pp. 21-28, and (July 1954), pp. 47-53; and H. Henderson, "The Mass-Produced Suburbs," *Ibid.* (November 1953), pp. 25-32, and (December 1953), pp. 80-86.
3. See John R. Seeley, R. Alexander Sim, and E. W. Loosley, *Crestwood Heights: The Culture of Suburban Life* (New York: Basic Books, 1956); and cf. the perceptive discussion by William S. Newman, "Americans in Subtopia," *Dissent,* vol. 4 (1957), pp. 255-266.
4. As in the witty but unrevealing novel of exurbia, Max Shulman's *Rally Round the Flag, Boys!* (New York: Doubleday, 1957); see also the slight topographical variations in exurbanite status dissected by A. C. Spectorsky, *The Exurbanites* (New York and Philadelphia: Lippincott, 1955).
5. Boston: Houghton Mifflin Co., 1956.

6. The essay, which originally appeared in *International Quarterly*, vol. 10 (1904), pp. 130-155, is reprinted in *American Journal of Sociology*, vol. 62 (1957), pp. 541-558; see especially pp. 553 *et seq.*

7. See Fromm, *The Sane Society* (New York: Rinehart, 1955).

8. *Communitas: Means of Livelihood and Ways of Life* (Chicago: University of Chicago Press, 1947) (now out of print). Cf. my discussion in "Some Observations on Community Plans and Utopia," *Yale Law Review*, 57: 173-200, 1947; reprinted in *Individualism Reconsidered* (Glencoe, Ill.: The Free Press, 1954). See also Ernest van den Haag's brilliant essay, "Of Happiness and of Despair We Have No Measure," in Bernard Rosenberg and David White, eds., *Mass Culture* (Glencoe, Ill.: The Free Press, 1956).

9. I sometimes consider the drive-in movie the archtypical symbol of decentralization, where people go to the theatre not in stalls which permit circulation of elites but in cars which keep the family or the dating couple together, with no sense of any shared experience outside the sedan.

10. Cf. Peter Drucker's discussion of job enlargement and related measures in *Concept of the Corporation* (New York: Harper & Bros., 1946). Union leaders who once were in the forefront of the drive to make work less exhausting—often an extrapolative matter of lowering hours, slowing the assembly line, lessening dirt and noise—have seldom moved into the more difficult area of making it less uncreative. (According to Nelson Foote, they have eliminated the grim silence that suited a Puritanical management.)

11. Cf. e.g., Ely Chinoy, *Automobile Workers and the American Dream* (Garden City, N. Y.: Doubleday, 1955); and, on older patterns of work-morality, Eugene A. Friedmann and Robert J. Havighurst, *The Meaning of Work and Retirement* (Chicago: University of Chicago Press, 1954).

12. My colleague, Anselm Strauss, has been engaged in a study of the informal tone or aura of cities, their images of themselves; I have profited from conversations with him about city life. Cf. David Riesman, "The Study of Kansas City: An Informal Overture," *City Lights*, No. 4 (1953), pp. 3-9.

13. Cf. "The Found Generation," *The American Scholar*, vol. 25, 1956, pp. 421-436; see also Eric Larrabee and David Riesman, "Company Town Pastoral: The Role of Business in 'Executive Suite'," reprinted in Bernard Rosenberg and David Manning White, *Mass Culture* (Glencoe, Ill.: The Free Press, 1956), pp. 325-337.

For an interesting study showing the relation between urbanization and upward social mobility, see Seymour Martin Lipset, "Social Mobility and Urbanization," *Rural Sociology*, vol. 20 (1955), pp. 220-228.

14. There is an equivalent rejection of a wartime love affair with an Italian girl. The business in question is broadcasting—typical for the luxury economy and far removed from traditional industrialism.

15. See Nancy C. Morse and Robert S. Weiss, "The Function and Meaning of Work and the Job," *American Sociological Review*, vol. 20, 1955, pp. 191-198. It should be noted that many men in the professions (the study included only men) and many in sales express satisfaction with their work.

16. An occasional ad is more work-minded and will feature opportunities for responsibility and creativity along with the suburban fringe benefits.

17. This is so only on one level; on another, as James S. Coleman points out, the small community, once conflict arises, is more likely to become split by fierce personal feuds than is the large, more impersonal city. See his monograph, *Community Conflict* (The Free Press, 1957).

    And the point I have made in the text must also be qualified by reference to the well-known principle that the busier people get more done, and that those who belong to some voluntary associations are likely to be candidates for others. In the suburb just referred to, live some distinguished and enormously energetic men who do their "housekeeping" chores in the suburb without stinting on their duties to city, state, and nation.

18. Just as, after a certain point is reached, a society begins to regard itself as urban, so, too, suburban living becomes, not an isolated (though frequent) personal decision, but a recognized fad. Cf. Rolf Meyersohn and Elihu Katz, "Notes on a Natural History of Fads," *American Journal of Sociology,* vol. 62 (1957), pp. 599 *et seq.*

19. In view of the many unfounded assertions flying about concerning the dangers of women being defeminized by holding jobs (they seldom, even in the middle class, have careers, and they and society are the poorer for it), and the corresponding dangers of men being domesticated by doing the dishes, I want to make clear that I regard these softenings of sex-role as desirable. (Cf., for fuller treatment, "Permissiveness and Sex Role," *Human Development Bulletin,* vol. 9, 1958, pp. 48-57. Traditional sex-role allocations have a large element of superstition in them, and a large element of patriarchal prerogative (with women as frequently indulged captives). The difficulty is that this, on the whole valuable, liberation from ascriptive distinction is occurring simultaneously with the decline of some achieved differences in the texture of metropolitan life, that is, with a rejection of the gamut of variety, for both good and ill, which the cities of the now-diminishing industrial and commercial age supplied. So, too, it is a good thing that men as well as women take part in the PTA, but it is a loss to many men and women, as well as to society, that work has lost its savor and that energies must spill over into voluntary associations, having no place to go.

20. *The Community Press in an Urban Setting* (Glencoe, Ill.: The Free Press, 1952).

21. Colleges themselves make the same claim that the suburbs do. I recently had occasion to go through a large number of college catalogues, as well as the descriptions colleges give in brief compass in the *College Board Handbook;* all but the huge urban universities did their best to present themselves as near the advantages of a large city, but far enough away for suburban safety and charm. (Correspondingly, some teen-agers, raised in safe suburbs, find glamour in going downtown, at least for a time.)

22. *Fortune,* May, June, July, August 1953; also in *The Organization Man, op. cit.,* Part VII.

23. Cf. Sylvia Fleis Fava, "Contrasts in Neighboring: New York City and a Suburban County," *supra*.

24. To be sure, driving may offer some commuters a change of pace and a chance to be alone. Cf., for general discussion of the elements of irrationality hiding under slogans of convenience in driving to work in the metropolis, David Riesman and Eric Larrabee, "Autos in America: History Catches up with Ford," *Encounter,* vol. 8, 1957, pp. 26-36.

25. A few super-highways have been designed to refresh the traveler and increase his sense of visual possibility, as well as to speed him on his way; the Taconic State Parkway in New York is a fine example.

26. I doubt if even the very superior schools of Scarsdale or Winnetka are as good in the arts as the High School of Music and Art, or in science as the Bronx High School of Science—or at least this was so before New York City became so largely a point of entry for Southern and Carribean migrants. The suburban schools, of course, can hardly cope with the crowding their very advantages have brought about—just as the suburbs, to which people go to escape the city's dirt, suffer from a water shortage and may shortly not be able to wash away their own dirt.

27. See Horton and Wohl, "Mass Communication and Para-Social Interaction: Observations on Intimacy at a Distance," *Psychiatry,* vol. 19, 1956, pp. 215-229.

28. When families schooled in development styles of sociability move to older suburbs and more heterogeneous ones, they are frequently wounded by what they interpret as snubs from neighbors not interested in knowing them better. The neighbors in turn, if at all sensitive, are troubled to discover the expectations their very presence creates and may reluctantly succumb to the pueblo pattern—or head again, like the traditional frontiersman, for open country.

29. It is, however, striking how much of this movement, though largely "private" and unorganized and unideological, is determined by fashion—in this respect, resembling residential location itself. On warm winter days Central Park and its rowboats are often nearly deserted, as is Jackson Park in Chicago; likewise, the Atlantic beaches such as Coney Island, in their off-season magnificence, are as unpopulated as the Labrador coast. People feel it is arbitrary to be cooped up in the city on a summer weekend, in some measure because they accept the definitions of "living it up" provided by the media and conversation.

30. Cf. Leo Lowenthal, "Biographies in Popular Magazines," in Paul F. Lazarsfeld and Frank Stanton, eds., *Radio Research, 1942-43* (New York: Duell, Sloane and Pearce, 1943).

31. For a report on this study, see Rolf Meyersohn and Robin Jackson "Gardening in Suburbia," *supra*.

32. Let me stress again that the themes I am discussing are peculiar neither to the U.S.A. nor to the twentieth century. Just as cities are older than industry, so are suburbs and their splendors and miseries. It is the democratization and extension of the phenomena I am describing, and the re-

sultant constriction of alternatives, which gives them a new and cumulative quality.

33. *Op. cit. supra,* note 8.

34. The countries of Western Europe do not appear to be greatly in advance of America in these respects, but instead to be trying to enjoy with prosperity our new problems as well as their traditional ones—a far cry from, for example, the radically reconstitutive hopes expressed in the French Resistance press during the German Occupation. *Cf., e.g.,* the interesting book by Karl Bednarik, *The Young Worker of To-day: A New Type,* Renée Tupholme, tr. (Glencoe, Ill.: The Free Press, 1956); and see also recent articles in *Encounter* on "This New England" and "The Younger Generation" of the Welfare State. For a comparison of French working class leisure with American, see Joffre Dumazedier, "Ambiguité du Loisir et Dynamique Socio-Culturelle," in *Cahiers Internationaux de Sociologie,* Nouvelle Série, vol. 12 (June 1957), pp. 75-96.

35. We buy more services than the Goodmans allowed for, which lowers our efficiency in production and distribution—and absorbs what would otherwise be a labor surplus.

36. I am indebted to Eric Larrabee for stimulating discussions of the "dual economy." The concept is analogous to that of the dual state described by Ernest Frankel for Nazi Germany, and resembles the contrast of controlled (i.e., abundant) and free (i.e., pinched) sectors in a totalitarian economy.

37. To be sure, there live in the slums Negroes and other migrant groups who have jobs in the high-wage economy but have not yet had a chance to adopt, at least in the residential pattern and usually also in family style of life, the suburban concomitants. And the slums also contain many elderly people, only rarely at work in the high-wage economy, whose skills and tastes antedate the spread of the dual economy, both on the production and the consumption side.

38. The low-wage economy has its expense accounts, too, and being mostly small business and small government, these have often more gravy if less finesse than those in the luxury economy; but they are confined to the boss and his nephews and friends: they are not institutionalized.

39. Cf. the discussion by Paul T. Homan, "The Social Goals of Economic Growth in the United States," *American Economic Review,* vol. 46, 1956, pp. 24-34.

40. *Colorado Quarterly* (Spring, 1954); reprinted in *Harper's,* vol. 213 (1956), pp. 25-33.

41. "Freedom, Spontaneity and Limit in American Linguistic Usage," *Explorations,* VI (1956), pp. 6-14.

42. Such a phrase, in a paper of this length, must do duty for an elaborate dialectic. While I am not one of those sanguine social scientists who believes that, if only our "industry" had atomic amounts of money, we could solve the planners' problems, I do feel that "survival through design" can be carried much further with the aid of our somewhat better understanding of how to discover what people "need" and can learn to want. Thus, social

science has helped us to realize the hidden values even in slums and hence
to temper rashness in erasing them; it has also tempered the ethnocentrism
of planners and other officials—sometimes, to the point of reducing them to
weathervanes. For an interesting example of the use of social science
thinking by an architect, cf. Robert Woods Kennedy, *The House and the
Art of Its Design* (New York: Reinhold, 1954).

43. The surveys of consumer finances and purchases by George Katona and
his colleagues of the Survey Research Center document the relation between purchases and private optimism. See the discussions in the several
volumes of *Consumer Behavior,* edited by Lincoln Clark and published by
New York University Press.

In comparison with willingness to spend on consumer goods, people are
today less willing to spend on their children's education, let alone to save
for it: They expect the state or other scholarship aid to do that. This is one
reason why college tuition has not risen in proportion to the ability of
some families to pay and many to borrow (nor are many students willing
to give up having a car in order to pay more tuition). In this case, too,
families look to the society or its agencies to take care of the future, while
they live up to and beyond their incomes now.

44. Most fictional utopias have themselves become, either anti-utopias like *1984,*
or parodies in the form of science-fiction—the latter genre appears to
harbor much of what little creatively satirical thinking about the future
now goes on (as in the work of Ray Bradbury or Frederik Pohl).

45. *Cf.* Gruen, "How to Handle this Chaos of Congestion, this Anarchy of
Scatteration," *Architectural Forum,* September, 1956, pp. 130-135; also
"The Miesian Superblock," *Ibid.,* March, 1957, pp. 129-133.

46. Catherine Bauer, "First Job: Control New-City Sprawl," *Ibid.,* September,
1956, pp. 105-112.

47. "Metropolitan Segregation," *Scientific American,* vol. 197 (October 1957),
pp. 33-41.

Readers of an earlier version of this article suggested that I might be
guilty of ethnocentrism in failing to see what contributions to urban variety
Negroes and Puerto Ricans could and did make. I have, of course, been
discussing prevailing stereotypes and their consequences for suburbanization, and not in this connection my own opinions and prejudices. Gunnar
Myrdal could conceive of an urban culture to which Negroes and whites
would contribute from their several traditions, but the difficulty here would
appear to be that the Negro middle class is the prisoner of white middle-
class values, thus bringing no true heterogeneity to the multi-racial city.
Cf. the forceful argument of Franklin Frazier in *Black Bourgeoisie* (Glencoe, Illinois. The Free Press, 1957).

48. Highway engineers resemble guided missile engineers in an understandable
irritation with the tiresome "human factor," which is bound to produce
accidents—and every effort has typically been made to reduce the functions
of individual drivers or soldiers, thus making them more bored and more
accident-prone.

Lewis Mumford has been pointing these things out for so long that he resembles the hero in Wells' story, "The Country of the Blind," who comes close to wishing he could share the visual defects of his fellow-men, for it would be more comfortable that way for everybody.

49. It would seem as if Americans, gaining some of the feelings towards the city and its works and ways that Thoreau had, have succeeded in blending his values with those of Carnegie. However, as indicated earlier, they are far from having Andrew Carnegie's concern for hard work, wealth, and thrift—let alone his self-taught passion for literacy—but they do have his interest in serving an image of efficiency, modified by Dale Carnegie's concern for gregarious friendliness.

50. *Cf.* Bruce Bliven, Jr., "The Golden Age of Buy Now, Pay Later," *The Reporter,* May 3, 1956, pp. 19-21, who presents an analogous account.

51. Cf. my discussion in "Some Observations on Changes in Leisure Attitudes." *Antioch Review,* vol. 12, 1952, pp. 417-436; reprinted in *Individualism Reconsidered.* See also the thoughtful hopefulness concerning changed forms of inventiveness in Conrad M. Arensberg, "Work and the Changing American Scene," in Arensberg, *et al.,* eds., *Research in Industrial Human Relations* (New York: Harper & Bros., 1957).

52. For a more hopeful view, critical of the position here taken, see Herbert J. Gans, "Some Notes on the Definition of Mental Health: An Attempt from the Perspective of a City Planner," unpublished address at Massachusetts General Hospital, February 27, 1957.

Index

409